The Johannine Community in Contemporary Debate

INTERPRETING JOHANNINE LITERATURE

The Interpreting Johannine Literature series is born from the desire of a group of Johannine scholars to bring rigorous study and explicit methodology into the teaching of these New Testament texts and their contexts. This series explores critical and perspectival approaches to the Gospel and Epistles of John. Historical- and literary-critical concerns are often augmented by current interpretive questions. Therefore, both a variety of approaches and critical self-awareness characterize titles in the series. Hermeneutical diversity and precision will continue to shed new light on the multi-faceted content and discourse of the Johannine Literature.

Titles in the Series

The Johannine Community in Contemporary Debate (2024)
Christopher Seglenieks and Christopher W. Skinner

That the Scripture May Be Perfected: The Use of the Jewish Scriptures in the Johannine Passion Narrative (2024)
David M. Allen

Reading John through Johannine Lenses (2021)
Stan Harstine

Follow Me: The Benefits of Discipleship in the Gospel of John (2020)
Mark Zhakevich

What John Knew and What John Wrote: A Study in John and the Synoptics (2020)
Wendy E. S. North

Come and Read: Interpretive Approaches to the Gospel of John (2019)
Alicia D. Myers and Lindsey S. Jodrey, eds.

The Johannine Community in Contemporary Debate

Edited by
Christopher Seglenieks
Christopher W. Skinner

LEXINGTON BOOKS/FORTRESS ACADEMIC
Lanham • Boulder • New York • London

Published by Lexington Books/Fortress Academic
Lexington Books is an imprint of The Rowman & Littlefield Publishing Group, Inc.
4501 Forbes Boulevard, Suite 200, Lanham, Maryland 20706
www.rowman.com

86-90 Paul Street, London EC2A 4NE, United Kingdom

Copyright © 2024 by The Rowman & Littlefield Publishing Group, Inc.

All rights reserved. No part of this book may be reproduced in any form or by any electronic or mechanical means, including information storage and retrieval systems, without written permission from the publisher, except by a reviewer who may quote passages in a review.

British Library Cataloguing in Publication Information Available

Library of Congress Cataloging-in-Publication Data

Names: Skinner, Christopher W., editor. | Seglenieks, Chris, 1983- editor.
Title: The Johannine community in contemporary debate / edited by Christopher W. Skinner, Christopher Seglenieks.
Description: Lanham : Lexington Books/Fortress Academic, [2024] | Series: Interpreting Johannine literature | Includes bibliographical references and index. | Summary: "This volume offers new proposals for understanding the emergence of the Johannine Literature, building upon existing perspectives on the Johannine community. Featuring a lineup of international experts, the book consists of constructive essays on the question of the Johannine Community, followed by responses from three senior scholars"— Provided by publisher.
Identifiers: LCCN 2024015002 (print) | LCCN 2024015003 (ebook) | ISBN 9781978717312 (cloth) | ISBN 978-1-9787-1733-6 (pbk) | ISBN 9781978717329 (epub)
Subjects: LCSH: Bible. John—Criticism, interpretation, etc.—History—21st century. | Bible. Epistles of John—Criticism, interpretation, etc.—History—21st century. | Communities—Biblical teaching.
Classification: LCC BS2601 .J63 2024 (print) | LCC BS2601 (ebook) | DDC 226.5/06—dc23/eng/20240613
LC record available at https://lccn.loc.gov/2024015002
LC ebook record available at https://lccn.loc.gov/2024015003

♾️™ The paper used in this publication meets the minimum requirements of American National Standard for Information Sciences—Permanence of Paper for Printed Library Materials, ANSI/NISO Z39.48-1992.

To the memory of Chris Spinks:
friend, colleague, and editor extraordinaire

Contents

Acknowledgments	ix
Abbreviations	xi
Introduction *Christopher Seglenieks and Christopher W. Skinner*	1
Chapter 1: The Rise, Demise, and Afterlives of the Johannine Community *Christopher W. Skinner*	3
PART I: NEW APPROACHES TO THE JOHANNINE COMMUNITY	21
Chapter 2: Reading the Johannine Community in the Letters: A Method *Christopher Seglenieks*	23
Chapter 3: The Language of John: Idiolect, Sociolect, Antilanguage, and Textual Community *David A. Lamb*	45
Chapter 4: Disentangling "Mom's Spaghetti": A Socio-Cognitive Approach to the Complexity of the Johannine Community *Christopher Porter*	67
Chapter 5: Triangulating a Johannine Community from John 18:28–19:22 *Laura J. Hunt*	89

viii *Contents*

Chapter 6: The Johannine Community and the Johannine
Community Vision: Historical Reflection, Rhetorical
Construction, and Narrative Ecclesiology   115
Andrew J. Byers

Chapter 7: Renewing Johannine Historical Criticism: A Proposal   139
Hugo Méndez

Chapter 8: The Legacy of the Beloved Disciple: The Johannine
Letters as Epistolary Fiction   157
Elizabeth J. B. Corsar

**PART II: THE WAY FORWARD?: RESPONSES TO THE
PROPOSALS**   173

Chapter 9: Who Are the Children of God?: Rhetoric, Memory, and
Creating Communities with the Johannine Writings   175
Alicia D. Myers

Chapter 10: The Johannine Situation: An Advance over Imagined
Communities   197
Paul N. Anderson

Chapter 11: Seeing with the Eyes and Hearing with the Ears:
Community Hypotheses in Johannine Scholarship   223
Adele Reinhartz

Bibliography   237

Index   267

About the Contributors   275

Acknowledgments

I would like to begin by acknowledging the contribution of my co-editor, Chris Skinner. This project began with a conversation in early 2020 and has slowly come to fruition amidst the challenges of Covid as well as of our respective family commitments. I appreciate the chance taken on a relatively unproven junior scholar, and the opportunity to learn just what is involved in bringing an edited collection to publication. I would also like to thank our great group of contributors, who have brought some fresh ideas to an issue with some entrenched views, and I hope this will be a launching point for further work in the area. My colleagues here at Bible College SA have been positive voices as they have heard both my own ideas and the progress of the project overall. Above all, I would like to thank my wife, Steph, and my children, Joshua and Hannah, for their support and encouragement, as well as for their understanding in the (fortunately few) occasions where this project has impinged on our life together.

—Christopher Seglenieks

I would also like to begin by acknowledging my co-editor, Chris Seglenieks, whose diligent work and keen mind have contributed to this being an enjoyable project with an exceptional end-product. I also want to acknowledge the great work of our stellar cast of contributors. This book is poised to make an impact on a decades-old discussion in Johannine studies largely because of their excellent work. I am grateful for each of their contributions. At Loyola Chicago, I am surrounded by colleagues and students who make me better as a scholar, teacher, and human being. Chief among them are my colleagues in the NT-EC section, Dr. Olivia Stewart Lester, Dr. Brian Lee, Dr. Edmondo Lupieri, Dr. Bob DiVito, and Dr. Tom Wetzel. Being able to teach and direct doctoral students for the past eight years has been the singular joy of my academic life, and it is probably true that their presence in my life has benefitted me more than I have benefitted them. I am grateful to Dr. Zach

Eberhart, Dr. Scott Harris, Dr. Jonathan Bryant, Dr. Joseph Mukuna, Dr. Scott Brevard, and (soon to be Dr.) Eric Zito for many conversations about life in Chicago, teaching, writing, family, the job market, the Johannine community, the NFL, the MLB, the NBA, stupid internet memes, and a host of other subjects. Whether they are aware of it or not, these students have given me life and have kept me going amid some of the more difficult moments since the inception of this project in 2020. As always, my greatest joy and source of inspiration is my family: my wife Tara alongside whom I have lived these past twenty-seven years, and my three (now mostly grown) kids, Christopher, Abby, and Drew. Holding this book in my hands is a fulfilling thing, but it all pales in comparison to the fulfillment these four bring into my daily existence.

—Christopher W. Skinner

Abbreviations

PRIMARY SOURCES

Aphthonius, *Prog.*		*Progymnasmata*
Aristotle, *Rhet.*		*Rhetorica*
Cicero, *Top.*		*Topica*
Demetrius, *Eloc.*		*De elocutione*
Dio Cassius, *Hist. rom.*		*Historia Romana*
Eusebius, *Hist. ecc.*		*Historia ecclesiastica*
Hermogenes, *Prog.*		*Progymnasmata*
Irenaeus, *Haer.*		*Adversus Haereses*
John of Sardis, *Comm. Aph.*		*Commentary on Aphthonius' Progymnasmata*
Josephus,	*A.J.*	*Antiquitates judaicae*
	B.J.	*Bellum judaicum*
	C.Ap.	*Contra Apionem*
Nicolaus, *Prog.*		*Progymnasmata*
O. Bodl.		Greek Ostraca in the Bodleian Library at Oxford
P. Oxy.		The Oxyrhynchus Papyri
P. Wisc.		The Wisconsin Papyri
Philo,	*Abr.*	*De abrahamo*
	Ebr.	*De ebrietate*
	Legat.	*Legatio ad Gaium*
	Migr.	*De migration Abrahami*
	Mos.	*De vita Mosis*
	Somn.	*De somniis*

xii *Abbreviations*

Plutarch,	*Cat. Maj.*	*Cato Major*
	Mor.	*Moralia*
Ps.-Cicero, *Rhet. Her.*		*Rhetorica ad Herennium*
Quintilian, *Inst.*		*Institutio oratoria*
Suetonius, *Dom.*		*Domitianus*
Theon, *Prog.*		*Progymnasmata*

SECONDARY SOURCES

AB	Anchor Bible
AJEC	Ancient Judaism and Early Christianity
AYBRL	The Anchor Yale Bible Reference Library
BBB	Bonner biblische Beiträge
BBR	Bulletin for Biblical Research
Bib	*Biblica*
BibInt	*Biblical Interpretation*
BInS	Biblical Interpretation Series
BMSEC	Baylor-Mohr Siebeck Studies in Early Christianity
BNTC	Black's New Testament Commentaries
BR	*Biblical Research*
BTB	*Biblical Theology Bulletin*
BVB	Beiträge zum Verstehen der Bibel
BZNW	Beihefte zur Zeitschrift für die neutestamentliche Wissenschaft
CBQ	*Catholic Biblical Quarterly*
CBQMS	Catholic Biblical Quarterly Monograph Series
CBR	*Currents in Biblical Research*
ConBNT	Coniectanea Biblica: New Testament Series
CQ	*The Classical Quarterly*
CRINT	Compendia Rerum Iudicarum ad Novum Testamentum
CurTM	*Currents in Theology and Mission*

ECC	Eerdmans Critical Commentary
ECL	Early Christianity and its Literature
HTR	*Harvard Theological Review*
HUCA	*Hebrew Union College Annual*
Int	*Interpretation*
JBL	*Journal of Biblical Literature*
JECS	*Journal of Early Christian Studies*
JIBS	*Journal for Interdisciplinary Biblical Studies*
JRS	*The Journal of Roman Studies*
JSJ	*Journal for the Study of Judaism in the Persian, Hellenistic, and Roman Periods*
JSNT	*Journal for the Study of the New Testament*
JSNTSup	Journal for the Study of the New Testament Supplement Series
JQR	*Jewish Quarterly Review*
LBS	Linguistic Biblical Studies
LCL	Loeb Classical Library
LNTS	The Library of New Testament Studies
MTSR	*Method and Theory in the Study of Religion*
NCBC	New Century Bible Commentary
NICNT	New International Commentary on the New Testament
NovTSup	Supplements to Novum Testamentum
Neot	*Neotestamentica*
NTL	New Testament Library
NTS	*New Testament Studies*
NTM	New Testament Message
PBM	Paternoster Biblical Monographs
PNTC	Pillar New Testament Commentaries
PRSt	*Perspectives in Religious Studies*
RBL	*Review of Biblical Literature*
RBS	Resources for Biblical Study
RelSRev	*Religious Studies Review*
RevExp	*Review & Expositor*

xiv *Abbreviations*

RHR	*Revue de l'histoire des religions*
RSR	*Recherches de science religieuse*
R&T	*Religion & Theology*
Sal	*Salesianum*
SAN	Studia Aarhusiana Neotestamentica
SBLDS	Society for Biblical Literature Dissertation Series
SJT	*Scottish Journal of Theology*
SNTS	Society for New Testament Studies
SNTSMS	Society for New Testament Studies Monograph Series
SP	Sacra Pagina
SR	*Studies in Religion/Sciences Religieuses*
TBN	Themes in Biblical Narrative
TENTS	Texts and Editions for New Testament Study
TNTC	Tyndale New Testament Commentary
TynBul	*Tyndale Bulletin*
WMANT	Wissenschaftliche Monographien zum Alten und Neuen Testament
WUNT	Wissenschaftliche Untersuchungen zum Neuen Testament
WW	*Word and World*
ZECNT	Zondervan Exegetical Commentary on the New Testament

Introduction

Christopher Seglenieks and Christopher W. Skinner

The Johannine Community has been a canon of critical orthodoxy for nearly six decades. Despite more recent questions among scholars about its viability, it remains an important topic of conversation, even looming in the background of those scholarly proposals that want to dispense with it altogether. This book, which arose out of a series of conversations between the two editors following the 2019 meeting of the Society of Biblical Literature, aims to explore the ongoing significance of the Johannine Community construct in New Testament scholarship. We are now more than fifty-five years removed from J. Louis Martyn's foundational work on the subject and we felt it was time to survey the landscape of contemporary scholarship to see how the idea of a Johannine community was being employed, altered, or even dispensed with altogether.

This book does not purport to be a comprehensive portrait of all the views currently operative in scholarship on this question. That said, we have tried as diligently as possible to include voices of junior scholars and senior scholars working in various parts of the world. What emerges is a representative sample of the ways in which the Johannine Community construct is presently understood by specialists in the Johannine literature. The title of this book is *The Johannine Community in Contemporary Debate*, and we hope that readers feel the title is reflective of the book's content. We also hope that this book proves to be generative for students, professors, and other scholars working with and deliberating on the emergence of the Gospel and Epistles of John.

As we were in the process of completing this book, one of our friends and professional colleagues, Dr. Christopher Spinks, succumbed after a hard fought battle with glioblastoma. Chris was a bright light, a generous spirit, a wise and judicious editor, a family man, and a good friend. We dedicate this book to his memory with both gratitude for his time on earth and a grief that persists in the proleptic hope of future life.

Chapter 1

The Rise, Demise, and Afterlives of the Johannine Community

Christopher W. Skinner

Few scholarly constructs have proven as influential or as durable as the Johannine community. A product of the era in New Testament studies dominated by redaction criticism,[1] the Johannine community construct as articulated first by J. Louis Martyn[2] and later by Raymond E. Brown[3] emerged with an explanatory power that proved persuasive to many scholars deliberating on the provenance and emergence of the Johannine literature for the next fifty years. However, recent years have seen this once dominant paradigm questioned by many of those working with the Gospel and Letters of John.[4] An examination of the current state of the question shows that there is little consensus among scholars. Some reject outright the notion of a Johannine community. Others continue to employ the construct while jettisoning some of the particular details associated with its articulation by Martyn, Brown, and others. The idea of a Johannine community—either as something upon which to build or as something to which scholars respond and abandon altogether—does not appear to be going anywhere anytime soon. In short: the Johannine community remains an essential topic of conversation for those engaged in Johannine studies.[5]

The conception and production of this book has been motivated by the desire to explore the current state of the question while shining a light on new and constructive proposals for understanding the emergence of the Johannine literature. Some of the chapters that follow proceed under the assumption that a Johannine community ostensibly existed in some form, even if not in a one-to-one correspondence with the reconstructions that dominated Johannine studies for the latter part of the twentieth century. Other chapters take as their starting point a complete rejection of the idea that the Johannine writings arose from within a community context. In this way, our book represents a robust portrait of the current state of the question among scholars working in various parts of the English-speaking world, including Australia (Porter, Seglenieks), Canada (Reinhartz), the United Kingdom (Byers, Corsar, Lamb), and the United States (Anderson, Hunt, Méndez, Myers).

Against that backdrop, this chapter will briefly survey (1) the rise of the Johannine community hypothesis and its reception within scholarship, (2) its demise among some scholars, and (3) the various positions some Johannine scholars presently take on the question, most notably those authors represented in the remainder of this book. The brief sketch that follows is representative rather than comprehensive as the goal of this chapter is to prepare the reader to interact meaningfully with the essays that follow. This means that, for pragmatic purposes, my treatment of the rise and demise of the Johannine community may appear tidier than we know such complex discussions to be. Below I attempt to plot major developments rather than trace the history of the discussion comprehensively. Numerous treatments of the reception of the Johannine community among scholars have appeared in recent years. For those readers interested in a more complete treatment of the question, I recommend accessing one of those.[6]

THE RISE OF THE JOHANNINE COMMUNITY MODEL

In order to recount the emergence of the community model in Johannine studies, it will prove helpful to look back briefly at the emergence of that model in gospel studies as a whole. As far back as the early twentieth century, gospel scholarship had operated under the nearly unquestioned assumption that the gospels were written by/for individual communities, churches, or social networks of churches. This assumption—which emerged during the eras dominated by form criticism and redaction criticism—reigned as one of the assured results of modern gospel scholarship until the late twentieth century. One foundational assumption for both form and redaction critics was that the gospels reflected a fractured portrait in which the reader could see both the original historical context of Jesus in the late twenties CE, as well as elements of the historical situation(s) of those responsible for producing the gospels in the seventies to nineties CE. These two settings were known as the *Sitz im Leben Jesu* and the *Sitz im Leben der Kirche*, respectively. In other words, the gospels were vehicles for the life of Jesus set in the context of some major concerns of early Christian communities. For these critics, the gospels were, at least partially, windows into the communities that produced them. It follows, then, that at least some of the dialogue in the gospels consisted of material intentionally put into the mouth of Jesus and his interlocuters and framed

The Rise, Demise, and Afterlives of the Johannine Community

to reflect concerns of the communities to which those gospels were written. The end product was a text that interpreters could read at two levels. All of this methodological framework ultimately provided J. Louis Martyn with the raw materials for his brilliant "two-story reading" of the Fourth Gospel. His was a reconstruction of a first-century CE Jewish community in crisis over internecine debates about Jesus which led one group of Jews to expel another group of Jesus-believing-Jews from the local synagogue.

Another major assumption was foundational for Martyn's proposal. He questioned the at-the-time dominant paradigm that the Fourth Gospel should be understood primarily against Hellenistic and/or Gnostic backgrounds.[7] Instead, Martyn set his proposal against a Jewish background with emphasis upon a proposed intra-Jewish conflict. He further regarded the literary tension between Jesus and "the Jews" (οἱ Ἰουδαῖοι)[8] throughout the Fourth Gospel as one of the key elements to unlocking the *Sitz im Leben* of the author(s).

With these assumptions in place, Martyn's argument proceeded along the following lines: The emergence of the Fourth Gospel can be accounted for by tracing the backstory of the conflict between "the Jews" (οἱ Ἰουδαῖοι) and Jesus across the gospel. Since this conflict is likely not rooted in the experience of the historical Jesus, but rather the "community" to which John is writing, we must search for the origins of this conflict in the author's *Sitz im Leben*. A key to this interpretive agenda is found in the gospel's three uses of the term ἀποσυνάγωγος ("out of the synagogue"; 9:22; 12:42; 16:2)—a term otherwise unattested in Hellenistic Greek prior to its appearance in the Fourth Gospel. John envisions a scenario in which some "Jews" (οἱ Ἰουδαῖοι) are expelling other Jesus-believing Jews (viz., "Christians") from the synagogue. There is no evidence for exclusion on a wide scale taking place during the lifetime of Jesus.[9] Here, Martyn introduces a point critical to his overall thesis (and one which will later be a site of controversy)—the so-called *Birkat Ha-Minim*, or "curse against the heretics."

The 1898 publication of "Genizah Specimens" by Solomon Schechter contained a version of the "Eighteen Benedictions," a daily programmatic prayer ritual for pious Jews.[10] The Genizah text of the Twelfth Benediction, the *Birkat Ha-Minim*, contained a curse upon the heretical "Nazarenes," which scholars of early Christianity took to be a euphemism for Christians. Martyn overlooked that fact that this extant version of the curse dated to a period between the ninth and tenth centuries CE and argued that late-first-century rabbis introduced this liturgical curse against Christians into their prayer cycle. This, he argues, provides the background for passages in the Fourth Gospel about Christians being excluded from and/or cursed within synagogues. These Jesus-believing Jews are thus the ἀποσυνάγωγοι, those who have been cast out (or to use Martyn's phrase, "smoked out") from synagogue fellowship. For Martyn, the three Johannine ἀποσυνάγωγος passages (9:22; 12:42; 16:2) reflect the Fourth Evangelist's historical setting near the end of the first century CE. This was a period after the first Jewish revolt (66–74 CE) when the proto-rabbis at Jamnia declared that Jewish followers of Jesus were not to be considered part of Israel's religious community. Thus, the conflict with "the Jews" (οἱ Ἰουδαῖοι) resulting in synagogue expulsion that is pictured in the Fourth Gospel was taking place *during the author's time* and *not during the historical ministry of Jesus* in the late twenties CE.

Against the backdrop of the methodological assumptions of his time, Martyn's thesis was a revelation for Johannine scholars. In the early days after its publication, the monograph was received enthusiastically. In his review of the first edition, Raymond E. Brown writes that "Martyn makes the most thoroughgoing synthesis of these ideas yet achieved," and further that he (Brown) stands "in substantial agreement with the essential points of this ably-argued presentation."[11] In his 1968 *JBL* review, T. A. Burkill refers to the monograph as "an unusually important work which will surely affect the course of scholarly research."[12] In a review of the second edition, which appeared in 1979, R. Alan Culpepper refers to the book as the "the most important monograph of the 1960s for Johannine studies as measured by its influence on Johannine scholarship in the 1970s."[13] These reviews communicate succinctly what fifty years of subsequent research would demonstrate, namely that Martyn's thesis represented a sea change in Johannine scholarship and it was nearly impossible to pursue a course of study on the Fourth Gospel without at least referencing his foundational work.

Other important developments on the way to cementing the Johannine community as a scholarly dogma include Wayne Meeks's 1972 article, "The Man from Heaven in Johannine Sectarianism."[14] Meeks also questioned the dominant Bultmannian position that the Fourth Gospel arose from within a Gnostic milieu and, like Martyn, situated the Johannine literature in the context of Jewish wisdom. Motivated by the desire to understand John's Christology in light of the gospel's dualisms, particularly the ascent/descent motif, Meeks explores the conflicts narrated in the gospel and epistles and concludes: "Thus we have in the Johannine literature a thoroughly dualistic picture: a small group of believers isolated over against 'the world' that belongs intrinsically to 'the things below,' i.e., to darkness and the devil."[15] In other words, the gospel conflict is not simply between one group of Jewish Christians and another group of Jews, but rather the forces of good "from above" and evil "from below." If Martyn's work laid the foundation for our understanding of a community in crisis, Meeks's article furthered this by emphasizing the parochial, sectarian nature of the Johannine community.

In 1979, Raymond E. Brown—a longtime colleague of Martyn at Union Theological Seminary in New York—published *The Community of the*

Beloved Disciple: The Life, Loves and Hates of an Individual Church in New Testament Times.[16] Brown had already articulated portions of his understanding of the Johannine situation in other publications, most notably his two-volume commentary in the Anchor Bible series.[17] In *The Community of the Beloved Disciple*, Brown provides considerably more substance to his previous theories by tracing a community situation that unfolds in four phases.

Following Martyn, Brown accepts as a foundation, the idea that the community situation begins with a controversy between Jesus-believing Jews and other Jewish members of the local synagogue. However, Brown differed a bit from Martyn in the details of his proposal. The original group of Christ-confessing Jews also consisted of followers of John the Baptist, and these were later joined by a second group, consisting of some Samaritans. For Brown, the introduction of this second group can help explain Jesus's brief Samaritan ministry in John 4. Further, in the early chapters of the gospel we witness a distinct attempt to establish the superiority of Jesus vis-à-vis both John the Baptist (cf. 1:6–8; 19–28; 29, 34, 36; 3:30–35) and Moses (cf. 1:17–18). Brown argues that the Jesus–Baptist tension can be traced to the original group while the Jesus–Moses tension is traceable to the second, in which Samaritans were present. Understanding Jesus in terms of traditional Davidic messiahship would have been essentially correct but insufficient. Jesus was more than just a Davidic messiah, a recognition which led to the introduction of a higher Christology embraced by the Christ-confessing Jews in the synagogue. This high Christology would have led some synagogue Jews to feel that their traditional monotheistic understanding was being threatened, and it was this perceived threat that led to the synagogue expulsions. Brown's tightly structured hypothetical scenario represented his understanding of phase one in the Johannine community's development and evolution, which took place between the fifties and eighties CE.

Phase two of the community situation (ca. 90 CE) is the period during which the Fourth Gospel was composed and presupposes the community situation envisaged in phase one of Brown's reconstruction. Brown argues that the Beloved Disciple was an actual historical figure with a place of prominence in the community. His role spans the period between the historical ministry of Jesus and the second phase of the community. Phase three (ca. 100 CE) is the period during which the three Johannine Epistles were composed, and this phase includes another controversy between Johannine Christians and a group Brown labels, "the secessionists" (cf. e.g., 1 John 2:15–29). The epistles are all written by the same individual, but that person is not the Beloved Disciple. The fourth and most speculative phase is fraught with questions of ecclesiastical authority. While those in the Johannine community could appeal to things they believed to carry real authority, such as the role of the Spirit/Paraclete in their midst and their knowledge of the new confession (e.g., 1 John 2:8–11), there was not an authority structure in place to sustain their community. Eventually, Brown speculates, the secessionists outnumber the "orthodox" members of the community (cf. 1 John 4:5) and commandeer the gospel for their own theological ends, while the "orthodox" move toward (or are absorbed by) later heterodox movements such as Gnosticism, Docetism, and Montanism.

Brown's proposal, with its four hypothetical phases, was both more speculative and arguably more tendentious than the theory originally offered by Martyn, something Brown appears to acknowledge.[18] Nevertheless, Brown's multi-phase model proved to be paradigmatic for future scholars working on the emergence of the Johannine literature.[19] Throughout the 1980s and into the early 1990s, one can detect a distinct emphasis on stages of gospel development and phases of community evolution in scholarship on the Johannine literature.

Given more space, we could detail further the reception of the Johannine community theory in major scholarly works throughout the 1970s, 1980s, and 1990s.[20] There is little doubt that the contributions of Martyn, Meeks, Brown, and eventually others cemented the scholarly orthodoxy of a Johannine community. This was a sectarian group consisting of Jewish-Christians at odds with other "Jews" (οἱ Ἰουδαῖοι) over a loyalty to Jesus which served as the impetus for their isolation and expulsion from the synagogue. The community also evolved in various stages over time as a result of internal conflict and theological debates. This basic understanding of the Johannine community was a *default assumption* for those working with the Gospel and Letters of John in the last three decades of the twentieth century. With few detractors, the Johannine community construct held firmly among scholars until the 1990s.

THE DEMISE OF THE COMMUNITY MODEL

At least three scholarly trends that were taking place in the 1990s ultimately contributed to the dissolution of the consensus view that there was a Johannine community. Two of these trends operated at the broader level of gospel scholarship, while the third was more directly focused on the Johannine Literature.

First, the literary turn in New Testament studies that began in the early 1980s with the emergence of narrative criticism, had become a full-blown enterprise among gospel scholars in the 1990s.[21] An overarching emphasis on the coherence and autonomy of each gospel text led scholars to produce works that more carefully considered how a text moved from start to finish and what its overarching message(s) might be. One consequence of employing literary methods was that scholars were not as concerned with speculating about the genesis of the gospels, but were rather more focused on tracing their internal narrative rhetoric. This methodological shift did not have the net effect of casting doubt on the idea of gospel communities as much as it often failed simply to take such a construct into consideration.

For a period in the 1980s and into the 1990s, narrative criticism and its concomitant assumptions struggled to arrive at an uneasy truce with historical criticism. In his 1992 article, "Narrative Criticism, Historical Criticism, and the Gospel of John," Martinus deBoer describes the narrative critic's assumption that a given work possesses internal unity, then wonders, "Can any avowedly *critical* method, however, really presuppose coherence, whether thematic or literary, as an unquestionable principle?"[22] While numerous scholars have ably demonstrated that it is possible to deal responsibly with historical and literary questions at the same time, some historical critics continue to express concerns over the use of literary methods in gospel research.[23] For many narrative critics, historical and literary concerns simply go hand in hand.[24] It cannot be denied, however, that some streams of narrative criticism throughout the 1990s and into the 2000s chose to jettison concerns about the origins of the New Testament narratives in favor of a sole emphasis on the "world of the text."[25] At the very least, the literary turn in New Testament studies caused some to turn away from highly speculative proposals about the contexts in which our early Christian literature emerged.

A second important trend was inaugurated in 1998 with the publication of Richard Bauckham's influential book, *Gospels for All Christians.* This work represented the first substantial challenge to the "gospel communities" hypothesis.[26] As discussed above, a key observation arising from this strain of scholarship is that those who engaged in reconstructing gospel communities tended to be skeptical about the historical quality of the material narrated in the gospels while being more optimistic about arguments regarding the community settings in which the gospels emerged. Thus, a consequence of this approach was to reject the historicity of much of the content of the gospels, while creating and defending—often with conviction—a historical reconstruction of the community's evolution, religious convictions, and inner conflicts. A further byproduct of this approach was the habit of reading the gospels not as narratives about Jesus, but rather as narratives about reconstructed hypothetical communities standing behind the texts themselves.

Critiquing this approach, Bauckham began with the assertion that all four gospels were intended for Christian audiences, as opposed to being written for the purpose of evangelizing non-Christian audiences. He goes on to argue that: (1) unlike the letters of Paul which are clearly addressed to individual communities, the gospels are examples of Greco-Roman biographies, and so presumed a much wider readership, (2) the early Christian movement is not just a group of isolated and independent churches but a cohesive network of churches that kept in fairly close contact with one another, (3) the earliest churches saw themselves as part of a worldwide movement, and (4) even if they existed, the gospel communities ultimately have no real hermeneutical bearing on our interpretation of the gospels. For many, Bauckham's criticism of this trend was valid and demonstrated a need for a nuanced corrective. Responses to Bauckham's thesis were mixed but equally effusive in both directions, and the ripple effects of his argument are still felt today.[27] It is safe to say that, at least for some scholars, Bauckham's thesis led to a lack of confidence in the ability to reconstruct hypothetical communities behind the gospel texts.[28] Thus, serious questions arose among some scholars regarding the validity of the community construct across gospel research.[29]

A third trend that led to the demise of the Johannine community consensus was directly related to an analysis of flaws in the theories set forth by Martyn and Brown. In particular, some scholars questioned whether the *Birkat Ha-Minim* represented a first century development. Since the Genizah text of the Eighteen Benedictions that served as the basis for Martyn's proposal dated to a period between the ninth and tenth centuries CE, scholars began to express considerable doubt as to whether or not the curse could reasonably be traced back to a first century CE tradition.[30] Questions were also raised concerning the Hebrew term נוצרים/נצרים ("Nazarenes") and whether or not it should be understood as a reference to Christians.[31] To cast doubt on these two critical portions of Martyn's original thesis is to do serious damage to the rest of his argument.[32]

Others took aim at the legitimacy of the two-level reading of the Fourth Gospel, especially its emphasis on the ἀποσυνάγωγος passages,[33] a strategy that was in some cases influenced by the work of Bauckham on the larger gospel tradition. One clear example of applying Bauckham's skepticism to the Fourth Gospel in light of other questions about the theses of Martyn/ Brown is Edward Klink's monograph, *The Sheep of the Fold: The Audience and Origin of the Gospel of* John (2007).[34] Klink, a student of Bauckham, takes a thoroughgoing approach to the question and concludes that the Fourth Gospel was intended for a general audience. Klink is one among an ever-growing number of exegetes to reject the legitimacy of the Johannine community construct.[35]

All three developments traced above did considerable damage to the prior consensus of a Johannine community and helped usher in new ways of thinking about the genesis of the Johannine literature. As it currently stands, scholars are divided over the question and a new consensus among scholars appears unlikely in the near future. In many cases, decisions about whether the Johannine community existed are drawn clearly along methodological lines. In other cases, it seems clear that the prior theological commitments of a given scholar determine, to a large degree, the trajectories of their conclusions. As with our discussion above, much more could be written about the rise of skepticism over the legitimacy of the community construct as a whole, and the demise of the Johannine community consensus in particular. However, this brief outline of major works and assumptions is sufficient to bring us to the present day and the contributions of the present volume.

THE AFTERLIVES OF THE JOHANNINE COMMUNITY (OR THE JOHANNINE COMMUNITY IN CONTEMPORARY DEBATE)

The foregoing summary and analysis is meant to serve as a foundation for engaging with the various chapters in this volume. The remainder of this book is divided into two unequal sections. The first section consists of seven constructive chapters that provide various approaches to the question of the Johannine community. The first five of these seven chapters all proceed under the assumption that the idea of a Johannine community should be retained or that a Johannine community can be recovered in some form, albeit with different foci than have traditionally been offered in various reconstructions of the community situation.

The first in this grouping of five is Chris Seglenieks's chapter, "Reading the Johannine Community in the Letters: A Method." He argues that, while there are good reasons to see the Fourth Gospel as having a wide intended audience, such a position does not preclude knowledge of the setting in which the Gospel was written. Rather, this view excludes the social and economic realities of ancient writing. Against that backdrop, he begins by establishing the methodological validity of reconstructing various features of a supposed community context based primarily upon the Johannine Letters. Genre conventions dictate that those letters are forms of communication aimed at *particular locations and contexts.* This observation is the basis for his exploration of various features of the Johannine context which are evident in the letters, particularly the contested nature of the community, along with the role of Christology and ethics as boundary markers. He concludes with an exploration of how reading the Gospel within such a context might shape our interpretation.

The next three chapters in this grouping of five introduce various theoretical models, including social, sociological, cognitive, and linguistic factors to articulate an understanding of the Johannine community.

First, building upon his previous work on using sociolinguistics to investigate the Johannine community,[36] David Lamb's chapter, "The Language of John: Idiolect, Sociolect, Antilanguage, and Textual Community," (1) offers a clarification of his model of "register" and its relation to "context of situation"; (2) provides a defense of the application of contemporary linguistic theory, particularly register theory; (3) reaffirms his stance that "antilanguage" is an inappropriate description for the language of the Gospel; and (4) considers the relevance of Brian Stock's concept of "textual community" for the community debate.[37] He concludes that we must read the Johannine writings primarily as documents intended to communicate an interpersonal message and not treat them simply as sites for historical excavation. Additionally, an analysis of the language of the Gospel and Letters suggests one, distinctive voice behind the Gospel, but an "embryonic community" behind the Epistles, whose associates wish to promote the Gospel's status as "scripture," while aware that the true Gospel is more than a written text.

Second, and also building upon his previous work,[38] Christopher A. Porter's chapter, "Disentangling 'Mom's Spaghetti': A Socio-Cognitive Approach to the Complexity of the Johannine Community," shines a light on some of the sociological assumptions underlying previous work on the question of the Johannine community. He pursues this avenue of inquiry as a way of arriving at some clarity about the possibility of retaining the community model going forward. Porter notes that the notional Johannine community has been informed and constructed by a plethora of implicit and explicit sociological models along with the exercise of a given exegete's sociological imagination. He seeks to disentangle some of the foundations, both named and unnamed, upon which the Johannine community edifice is built, examining them through the lens of Social Identity Theory to gain some methodological objectivity. Ultimately, he concludes that while the Fourth Gospel pushes toward a possible future social identity for the audience—along with an implicit post-hoc community formation—the more likely location for a putative Johannine community is to be found with the Johannine Epistles.

The third theoretically oriented chapter is Laura Hunt's "Triangulating a Johannine Community from John 18:28–19:22." Hunt seeks to alleviate the problem of inferring a community almost entirely from a text. She suggests setting boundaries on interpretation by using three theoretical tools, thereby triangulating a proposed audience: Semiotics, Probability, and Social Identity Theory. After some preliminary introductions to these theories, she applies them to John 18:28–19:22 by first hypothesizing a distinct setting for the gospel (Ephesus at the turn of the second century CE) and then conducting a semiotic analysis of νόμος within Roman and Jewish encyclopedias. Finally, a Social Identity Theory analysis of the passage concludes that it presents Jesus as an exemplar for both identities. However, she argues, triangulation also reveals shortcomings in drawing further unwarranted conclusions. The probability analysis using Bayes' Theorem requires further comparisons with other analyses starting from different hypothesized settings. She notes further that Umberto Eco's *Semiotics* helped reveal a missing element in Social Identity Theory studies of biblical texts: they uncovered a rhetorical movement, but not the starting point of the auditors. The Social Identity Theory study, in turn, takes a determined direction because of the specific key words chosen. Hunt closes by suggesting that the insights arising from her study represent one contribution that needs to remain in conversation with other scholarly triangulations.

The last chapter in this grouping of five is Andrew Byers's "The Johannine Community and the Johannine Community Vision: Historical Reflection, Rhetorical Construction, and Narrative Ecclesiology." Here Byers explores the imaginative work of "Johannine world-building," a term he applies both to the scholarly exercise of reconstructing John's context as well as to John's rhetorical work of shaping his audience with a future-oriented vision of community. Byers identifies two key challenges to historical reconstruction (John's fusions of temporal horizons and his integration of theology with history), then discusses three points of access to John's historical context using the language of "windows," "mirrors," and "vistas." A "window to the past" arises from the recollection of Jesus's historical ministry, while "mirrors of the present" provide a reflection of the evangelist's present. Byers uses "narrative ecclesiology" to commend more urgent attention to "vistas to the future" in which John casts a vision as an act of prescription or construction that relates to the historical context, yet in a less direct way because of its aspirational nature.

The final two chapters in this section start from the assumption that the Johannine community construct should be abandoned. In his chapter, "Renewing Johannine Historical Criticism: A Proposal," Hugo Méndez insists that any attempt to reinvigorate the historical criticism of John must begin by thinking outside three "undertheorized" and "unproductive" models: (1) the Johannine community hypothesis; (2) the idea of social links between the supposed Johannine community and Gnostic communities; and (3) the concept of a Johannine "sociolect." Against that backdrop, he proposes an alternative way of understanding the same data these models are meant to explore, suggesting that the Gospel and Epistles of John likely represent a lineage of falsely authored works, written by authors in different social matrices, whose works influenced readers across the spectrum of second-century Christianity.[39]

In that same vein, Elizabeth Corsar's chapter, "The Legacy of the Beloved Disciple: The Johannine Letters as Epistolary Fiction," follows a recently growing trend to consider our biblical materials in the context of ancient literary practice, and offers an alternative proposal regarding the production of the Johannine Letters that does not rely on a Johannine community hypothesis. To this end, she suggests that 1–3 John are epistolary fictions—pseudo-historical letters that are composed in the name of the Beloved Disciple as a means of continuing the legacy of this legendary figure. Her argument challenges the hypothesis of the Johannine community by reading the Johannine Gospel and Epistles in light of ancient literary practice.[40] After outlining the theory of imitation—the practice of borrowing and reworking predecessor texts and composing a new text—she presents examples from 1–3 John where the author/s have consciously imitated the Fourth Gospel and composed new pieces of writing. She concludes by providing illustrative examples of ancient texts where authors imitate narrative material and compose their new piece of writing in the epistolary genre.

The final section of the book consists of detailed responses from three important senior scholars—Paul Anderson,[41] Alicia Myers,[42] and Adele Reinhartz[43]—each of whom has articulated their own take on the Johannine community in the context of related historical, theological, and ethical discussions of the Johannine literature. All three authors respond to the seven previous chapters in this volume from their own perspective on the Johannine community. Since Anderson, Myers, and Reinhartz all have differing methodological approaches to the question of a Johannine community, readers are treated to a substantive discussion which offers a wealth of insights to help advance the conversation. It is our hope that this book will enter into the current space in which the Johannine community remains an important discussion, and inspire ongoing constructive work on the provenance and emergence of the Johannine literature.

NOTES

1. Redaction criticism was more immediately concerned with the Synoptic tradition. Some in Johannine studies working with the same assumptions as redaction criticism have referred to their methodological approach as "composition criticism."

2. Cf. J. Louis Martyn, *History and Theology in the Fourth Gospel* (San Francisco: Harper & Row, 1968). The second edition of this work appeared in 1979 and the third in 2004.

3. Raymond E. Brown, *The Community of the Beloved Disciple: The Life, Loves and Hates of an Individual Church in New Testament Times* (New York: Paulist, 1979).

4. For our purposes in this book, we define the Johannine writings as the Gospel and Letters traditionally attributed to John. Though there has been a move among some scholars in recent years to consider Revelation as part of the Johannine literature (cf. e.g., Rodney Reeves, *Spirituality According to John: Abiding in Christ in the Johannine Writings* [Downers Grove, IL: IVP Academic, 2021]), we will not include it here.

5. An ATLA Serials search conducted on January 9, 2024, using the terms "Johannine" and "community" immediately returned 273 results consisting of monographs, peer-reviewed articles, book chapters, and book reviews, spanning the period from 1973 to 2023. More and potentially more variegated results are likely to have appeared with the introduction of more and/or different search terms.

6. See especially Wally V. Cirafesi, "The 'Johannine Community' in (More) Current Research: A Critical Appraisal of Recent Methods and Models," *Neot* 48.2 (2014): 341–64; idem. "The Johannine Community Hypothesis (1968–Present): Past and Present Approaches and a New Way Forward," *CBR* 12.2 (2014): 173–93. Other helpful treatments can be found in Edward W. Klink III, "The Gospel Community Debate: State of the Question," *CBR* 3.1 (2004): 60–85; Robert Kysar, "The Whence and Whither of the Johannine Community," in *Life in Abundance: Studies of John's Gospel in Tribute to Raymond E. Brown, S.S.*, ed. John R. Donahue, S.J. (Collegeville, MN: Liturgical, 2005), 65–81; and Martinus C. de Boer, "The Story of the Johannine Community and Its Literature," in *The Oxford Handbook of Johannine Studies*, ed. Judith M. Lieu and Martinus C. de Boer (Oxford: Oxford University Press, 2018), 63–82.

7. Two major figures in Johannine studies working in the period before the appearance of Martyn's monograph were Rudolf Bultmann and C. H. Dodd. Bultmann's epoch-making commentary on John situated the Fourth Gospel against a Gnostic background (see Rudolf Bultmann, *The Gospel of John: A Commentary*, trans. by George R. Beasley Murray, R. W. N. Hoare, and J. K. Riches [Philadelphia: Fortress, 1971], original German, 1941), while C. H. Dodd's two important volumes situated the Fourth Gospel within a Hellenistic milieu (see C. H. Dodd, *The Interpretation of the Fourth Gospel* [Cambridge: Cambridge University Press, 1953], idem. *Historical Tradition in the Fourth Gospel* [Cambridge: Cambridge University Press, 1963]). An early outlier in this period is Peder Borgen's important monograph, *Bread from Heaven: An Exegetical Study of the Concept of Manna in the Gospel of John and the Writings of Philo*, NovTSup 10 (Leiden: E.J. Brill, 1965). Borgen represents a mediating position between an overly simplistic separation of the "Hellenistic" on one side and the "Jewish" on the other by situating the Gospel in the context of Hellenistic Judaism. By this period, scholars had slowly come to realize that Hellenism and Judaism were inextricably intertwined in the first century CE.

8. The question of how to define the term οἱ Ἰουδαῖοι in the Fourth Gospel is fraught with difficulty. For recent, helpful treatments of this question, see Adele Reinhartz, "The Jews of the Fourth Gospel," in *The Oxford Handbook of Johannine Studies*, ed. Judith M. Lieu and Martinus C. DeBoer (Oxford: Oxford University Press, 2018), 121–37; idem. "'Jews' and Jews in the Fourth Gospel," in *Anti-Judaism and the Fourth Gospel: Papers of the Leuven Colloquium, 2000*, Jewish and Christian Heritage Series 1, ed. Reimund Bieringer, Frederique Vandecasteele-Vanneuville, and Didier Pollefeyt (Leiden: Brill, 2001), 341–56; Steve Mason, "Jews, Judaeans, Judaizing, Judaism: Problems of Categorization in Ancient History," *JSJ* 38 (2007): 457–512; Wally V. Cirafesi, *John within Judaism: Religion, Ethnicity, and the Shaping of Jesus-Oriented Jewishness in the Fourth Gospel*, AJEC 112 (Leiden: Brill, 2021).

16 *Christopher W. Skinner*

9. Jonathan Bernier (*Aposynagōgos and the Historical Jesus in John: Rethinking the Historicity of the Johannine Expulsion Passages*, BInS 122 [Leiden: Brill, 2013]) is unique among Johannine exegetes in arguing that the ἀποσυνάγωγος passages plausibly reflect a situation facing the followers of Jesus during his lifetime.

10. Solomon Schechter, "Genizah Specimens," *JQR* 10 (1898): 197–206.

11. Raymond E. Brown, review of J. Louis Martyn, *History and Theology in the Fourth Gospel* in *USQR* 23 (1968): 392–94.

12. T. Alec Burkill, review of J. Louis Martyn, *History and Theology in the Fourth Gospel* in *JBL* 87.4 (1968): 439–42.

13. R. Alan Culpepper, review of J. Louis Martyn, *History and Theology in the Fourth Gospel* in *RevExp* 76.4 (1979): 573–75.

14. Wayne A. Meeks, "The Man from Heaven in Johannine Sectarianism," *JBL* 91 (1972): 44–72.

15. Meeks, "The Man from Heaven in Johannine Sectarianism," 68.

16. For the full bibliographic reference, see n. 3, above.

17. Raymond E. Brown, *The Gospel According to John I-XII*, AB 29 (New York: Doubleday, 1966); idem. *The Gospel According to John XIII-XXI*, AB 29a (New York: Doubleday, 1970).

18. In the preface, Brown writes, "I must warn the reader that my reconstruction claims at most probability; and if sixty percent of my detective work is accepted, I shall be happy indeed" (Brown, *Community of the Beloved Disciple*, 7).

19. The most thoroughgoing example of this approach in English is Urban C. von Wahlde, *The Gospel and Letters of John*, 3 vols., ECC (Grand Rapids: Eerdmans, 2010). Von Wahlde's three volumes (published in 2010 but written over the three previous decades) trace a community situation with multiple phases and three distinct versions of the gospel reflecting those phases. For von Wahlde's further reflections on the Johannine situation, see idem. *The Earliest Version of John's Gospel: Recovering the Gospel of Signs*, Good News Studies (Collegeville, MN: Michael Glazier, 1989); idem. *The Johannine Commandments: 1 John and the Struggle for the Johannine Tradition*, Theological Inquiries (Mahwah, NJ: Paulist, 1990); idem. *Gnosticism, Docetism, and the Judaisms of the First Century: The Search for the Wider Context of the Johannine Literature and Why It Matters*, LNTS 517 (London: Bloomsbury/T&T Clark, 2015).

20. Among other works, see, in chronological order, Birger Olsson, *Structure and Meaning in the Fourth Gospel: A Text Linguistic Analysis of John 2:1–11 and 4:1–42*, ConBNT 6 (Stockholm: Almqvist, 1974); R. Alan Culpepper, *The Johannine School: An Evaluation of the Johannine School Hypothesis Based on an Investigation of the Nature of Ancient Schools* (Missoula, MT: Scholars Press); Severino Pancaro, *The Law in the Fourth Gospel: The Torah and the Gospel, Moses and Jesus, Judaism and Christianity according to John*, NovTSup 42 (Leiden: Brill, 1975); Oscar Cullmann, *The Johannine Circle: Its Place in Judaism, among the Disciples of Jesus and in Early Christianity*, trans. John Bowden (London: SCM Press, 1976); David Woll, *Johannine Christianity in Conflict: Authority, Rank, and Succession in the First Farewell Discourse*, SBLDS 60 (Chico, CA: Scholars Press, 1981); Peter F. Ellis, *The Genius of John: A Composition-Critical Commentary on the Fourth Gospel*

The Rise, Demise, and Afterlives of the Johannine Community   17

(Collegeville, MN: Liturgical, 1984); Jerome Neyrey, *An Ideology of Revolt: John's Christology in Social-Science Perspective* (Philadelphia: Fortress, 1988); David Rensberger, *Johannine Faith and Liberating Community* (Philadelphia: Westminster Press, 1988). The most recent monograph employing this earlier approach is Kari Syreeni, *Becoming John: The Making of a Passion Gospel*, LNTS 590 (London: Bloomsbury/T&T Clark, 2020).

21. Narrative criticism was introduced into New Testament studies via two important works that appeared in consecutive years in the early 1980s. First, David Rhoads, a New Testament scholar, and his colleague, Donald Michie, a scholar of English literature, published *Mark as Story: An Introduction to the Narrative of a Gospel* (Minneapolis: Fortress, 1982). This was the first work to apply principles of the so-called New Criticism within English literary studies in a systematic way to a New Testament text. The following year, R. Alan Culpepper published *Anatomy of the Fourth Gospel: A Study in Literary Design* (Minneapolis: Fortress, 1983). These two works inaugurated the broader enterprise of applying narrative and literary-oriented methods to the New Testament narratives. By the 1990s, narrative criticism was no longer in its nascent stages and was proving to be a formidable methodological competitor for historical criticism.

22. Martinus C. deBoer, "Narrative Criticism, Historical Criticism, and the Gospel of John," *JSNT* 47 (1992): 35–48 (here, 43), emphasis in original. On this tension, see the insights in Adele Reinhartz, "Building Skyscrapers on Toothpicks: The Literary-Critical Challenge to Historical Criticism," in *Anatomies of Narrative Criticism: The Past, Present, and Futures of the Fourth Gospel as Literature*, RBS 55, ed. Tom Thatcher and Stephen D. Moore (Atlanta: Society of Biblical Literature, 2008), 55–76.

23. On this, see Urban C. von Wahlde, "Narrative Criticism of the Religious Authorities as a Group Character in the Gospel of John: Some Problems," *NTS* 63 (2017): 222–45. See also my response to von Wahlde: "Narrative Readings of the Religious Authorities in John: A Response to Urban C. von Wahlde," *CBQ* 82 (2020): 424–36.

24. See especially Francis J. Moloney, *Belief in the Word: Reading John 1–4* (Minneapolis: Fortress, 1993); idem. *Signs and Shadows: Reading John 5–12* (Minneapolis: Fortress, 1996); idem. *Glory Not Dishonor: Reading John 13–21* (Minneapolis: Fortress, 1998); and Andrew T. Lincoln, *The Gospel according to St. John*, BNTC (London: Continuum, 2006), among others.

25. Mark Allan Powell traces three iterations of narrative criticism that operated in New Testament scholarship over its first three decades: (1) author-oriented narrative criticism, (2) reader-oriented narrative criticism, and (3) text-oriented narrative criticism. Cf. Powell, "Narrative Criticism: The Emergence of a Prominent Reading Strategy," in *Mark as Story: Retrospect and Prospect*, ed. Kelly R. Iverson and Christopher W. Skinner, RBS 65 (Atlanta: Society of Biblical Literature, 2011), 19–43.

26. Richard Bauckham, ed., *The Gospels for All Christians: Rethinking the Gospel Audiences* (Grand Rapids: Eerdmans, 1998). This book is an edited collection, but Bauckham's opening chapter, "For Whom Were the Gospels Written?" proved to be the most influential for contributing to the demise of the community model.

27. For critical engagement with Bauckham's thesis, see David C. Sim, "The Gospels for All Christians? A Response to Richard Bauckham," *JSNT* 24.2 (2001): 3–27; Philip F. Esler, "Community and Gospel in Early Christianity: A Response to Richard Bauckham's *Gospels for All Christians*," *SJT* 51 (1998): 235–48; and Margaret M. Mitchell, "Patristic Counter-Evidence to the Claim that 'The Gospels Were Written for All Christians,'" *NTS* 51 (2005): 36–79. Edward W. Klink's edited volume, *The Audience of the Gospels: The Origin and Function of the Gospels in Early Christianity*, LNTS 353 (London: T&T Clark, 2010) also contains several helpful responses to Bauckham's thesis.

28. Some of the community reconstructions of the mid-to-late twentieth century were too speculative, but there is little doubt that those responsible for writing the gospels were members of social networks. Those networks shaped and informed their understanding of Jesus, his ministry, and its significance for their immediate circumstances. Bauckham is correct that the gospels were widely disseminated early after their composition, but it does not naturally follow that therefore they were intended for "all Christians." It is possible for the gospels to have been written for and within a specific social network *and* for them to have been widely distributed to Christian communities. For an approach that takes these complementary claims as its starting point, see Craig Blomberg, "The Gospels for Specific Communities and All Christians," in Klink, ed., *The Audience of the Gospels*, 111–33.

29. Portions of this section were adapted from several paragraphs in chapter 1 of my forthcoming book, *The Gospel of Mark*, New Word Biblical Themes (Grand Rapids: Zondervan Academic, 2025).

30. Cf. e.g., Uri Ehrlich and Ruth Langer, "The Earliest Texts of the *Birkat Haminim*," *HUCA* 76 (2005): 63–112; Edward W. Klink III, "Expulsion from the Synagogue? Rethinking a Johannine Anachronism," *TynBul* 59.1 (2008): 99–118.

31. On the use of the נוצרים/נצרים as a reference to Christians, see Reuven Kimelman, "*Birkat Ha-Minim* and the Lack of Evidence for an Anti-Christian Jewish Prayer in Late Antiquity," in *Jewish and Christian Self-Definition*, Vol. 2. Aspects of Judaism in the Greco-Roman Period, ed. E. P. Sanders (Philadelphia: Fortress, 1981), 232–44; and Martinus C. de Boer, "The Nazoreans: Living at the Boundary of Judaism and Christianity," in *Tolerance and Intolerance in Early Judaism and Christianity*, ed. Graham N. Stanton and Guy G. Stroumsa (Cambridge: Cambridge University, 1998) 239–62.

32. Other challenges to Martyn's theory include Udo Schnelle, *Antidocetic Christology in the Gospel of John: An Investigation of the Place of the Fourth Gospel in the Johannine School*, trans. Linda M. Maloney (Minneapolis: Fortress, 1992); and Stephen Motyer, "The Fourth Gospel and the Salvation of Israel: An Appeal for a New Start," in Bieringer, Pollefeyt, and Vandecasteele-Vanneuville, *Anti-Judaism and the Fourth Gospel*, 84–87.

33. Cf. Tobias Hägerland, "John's Gospel: A Two-Level Drama?," *JSNT* 25 (2003): 309–22. Adele Reinhartz has devoted a great deal of time discussing the various elements of this supposed two-level drama. See Adele Reinhartz, *The Word in the World: The Cosmological Tale in the Fourth Gospel*, SBLMS 45 (Atlanta: Society of Biblical Literature, 1992); idem. "The Johannine Community and its Jewish

Neighbors: A Reappraisal," in *"What is John?" Literary and Social Readings of the Fourth Gospel*, ed. Fernando F. Segovia, SymS 7 (Atlanta: Scholars Press): 111–38; idem. "Forging a New Identity: Johannine Rhetoric and the Audience of the Fourth Gospel," in *Paul, John, and Apocalyptic Eschatology: Festschrift Martinus de Boer*, ed. Jan Krans, L. J. Lietaert Peerbolte, Peter-Ben Smit and Arie W. Zwiep, NovTSup 149 (Leiden: Brill, 2013), 123–34.

34. Edward W. Klink III, *The Sheep of the Fold: The Audience and Origin of the Gospel of John*, SNTMS 141 (Cambridge: Cambridge University Press, 2007).

35. See, for instance, Bennema's curious claim that such a reading "defies the Gospel's genre" (Cornelis Bennema, "The Historical Reliability of the Gospel of John," *Foundations* 67 [2014]: 4–25 [here, 5]).

36. David A. Lamb, *Text, Context and the Johannine Community: A Sociolinguistic Analysis of the Johannine Writings*, LNTS 477 (London: Bloomsbury T & T Clark, 2014).

37. Cf. e.g., Brian Stock, *The Implications of Literacy: Written Language and Models of Interpretation in the Eleventh and Twelfth Centuries* (Princeton: Princeton University Press, 1983); idem. *Listening for the Text: On the Uses of the Past* (Philadelphia, PA: University of Pennsylvania Press, 1990).

38. Christopher A. Porter, *Johannine Social Identity Formation after the Fall of the Jerusalem Temple: Negotiating Identity in Crisis*, BInS 194 (Leiden: Brill, 2022).

39. This chapter assumes as its starting point doubt over the existence of the Johannine Community as it has been classically articulated. For more on Méndez's approach to this question, see Hugo Méndez, "Did the Johannine Community Exist?," *JSNT* 42 (2020): 350–74.

40. On this trend and its potential implications for the wider field of New Testament studies, see Robyn Faith Walsh, *The Origins of Early Christian Literature: Contextualizing the New Testament within Greco-Roman Literary Culture* (Cambridge: Cambridge University Press, 2021).

41. Cf. e.g., Paul N. Anderson, *The Christology of the Fourth Gospel: Its Unity and Disunity in the Light of John 6*, third ed. (Eugene: Cascade Books, 2010), 195–265; idem. "The Sitz im Leben of the Johannine Bread of Life Discourse and its Evolving Context," in *Critical Readings of John 6*, ed. R. Alan Culpepper, BInS 22 (Leiden: E.J. Brill, 1997), 1–59; idem. "The Having-Sent-Me Father—Aspects of Agency, Encounter, and Irony in the Johannine Father-Son Relationship," *Semeia* 85, ed. Adele Reinhartz (1999): 33–57; idem. "'You Have the Words of Eternal Life!' Is Peter Presented as Returning the Keys of the Kingdom to Jesus in John 6:68?" *Neot* 41:1 (2007): 6–41. idem. "Bakhtin's Dialogism and the Corrective Rhetoric of the Johannine Misunderstanding Dialogue: Exposing Seven Crises in the Johannine Situation," in *Bakhtin and Genre Theory in Biblical Studies*; Semeia Studies 63, ed. Roland Boer (Atlanta: Society of Biblical Literature, 2007), 133–59.

42. Cf. e.g., Alicia D. Myers, "Just Opponents?: Ambiguity, Empathy, and the Jews in the Gospel of John," in *Johannine Ethics: The Moral World of the Gospel and Epistles of John,* ed. Sherri Brown and Christopher W. Skinner (Minneapolis: Fortress, 2017), 159–76; idem. *Reading John and 1, 2, 3 John: A Literary and Theological Commentary*, Reading the New Testament: Second Series (Macon, GA: Smyth

& Helwys, 2019); idem. "Us and Them: Lessons from 1 John's Antichrist Polemic," *WW* 41.1 (2021): 42–50; idem. "Jesus's Ongoing Ministry in 1 John: Priestly Purification and Intercession in 1 John 1:5–2:2," *PRSt* 48 (2021): 243–55;

43. In addition to the bibliography in n. 33 above, cf. e.g., Adele Reinhartz, "Judaism in the Gospel of John," *Int* 63 (2009): 382–93; idem. "'Common Judaism,' 'The Parting of the Ways,' and 'The Johannine Community,'" in *Orthodoxy, Liberalism, and Adaptation: Essays on Ways of Worldmaking in Times of Change from Biblical, Historical and Systematic Perspectives*, Studies in Religion and Theology 15, ed. Bob E. J. H. Becking (Leiden: Brill, 2011), 69–87; idem. "Incarnation and Covenant: The Fourth Gospel through the Lens of Trauma Theory," *Int* 69 (2015): 35–48; idem. "Story and History: John, Jesus, and the Historical Imagination," in *John and Judaism: A Contested Relationship in Context*, ed. Tom Thatcher and Paul N. Anderson (Atlanta: SBL Press, 2017) 113–26; idem. *Cast Out of the Covenant: Jews and Anti-Judaism in the Gospel of John* (Minneapolis: Fortress Academic, 2018).

PART I

New Approaches to the Johannine Community

Chapter 2

Reading the Johannine Community in the Letters

A Method

Christopher Seglenieks

The problem of the Johannine Community is primarily a methodological one. How one approaches the Johannine texts, and the tools one uses, will shape not only the sort of community one might reconstruct, but also the confidence in any such reconstruction. Raymond Brown reflected the question of confidence in the introduction to his *Community of the Beloved Disciple*, where he acknowledged that his work was to some extent speculative, a creative and learned extension of the evidence rather than a necessary conclusion drawn from the data.[1] Yet subsequent work confidently asserts the existence and nature of the community, as well as its accessibility through the text of the Gospel of John.[2] With the rise in popularity of the argument for a broader audience, others have equally confidently dismissed the existence of any such Johannine community. Yet both approaches share the fact that key methodological assumptions go unquestioned.

In what follows, I will address this methodological challenge for recovering the context of the Gospel.[3] The key issue is the use of the Gospel itself as a window into the context in which or to which it was written. The dominant paradigm of the later twentieth century, the two-level reading championed by J. Louis Martyn and Brown, assumes that reading the Gospel as a window into its context is possible.[4] Their model offered resolution for some challenging interpretative issues, notably giving a convenient explanation for the Gospel's hostility toward "the Jews" by reading the Gospel in the context of a split between church and synagogue, and enabling a later context to frame the understanding of the expression ἀποσυνάγωγος.[5] While at a broad level

24 *Christopher Seglenieks*

this account seems plausible, as Adele Reinhartz has argued, it is not applicable across the Gospel in a methodologically sustained way.[6] If the Gospel contains these two levels, then as Jörg Frey argues they are inextricably linked.[7] This points to the methodological challenge of seeking to uncover the context of the Gospel through the Gospel itself. If the Gospel both relates past events and speaks into a contemporary situation, the crucial question is how to distinguish the two without bringing presuppositions regarding the context, thereby determining the results before coming to the evidence.

To approach a method for recovering the context of the Gospel, we need to establish the relationship between the text and the context. In order to do so, I will examine the critiques that have been made regarding the possibility of reading a community out of the text of the Gospel of John. First, I will consider Richard Bauckham's model of a wide audience for the Gospel to ask whether it would preclude the existence of a context that lies behind the Gospel. Second, I will address the critiques of Stan Stowers and Sarah Rollens regarding the nature of New Testament texts and the ways they may or may not reflect their context. Their work has rarely been brought into the discussion of the Johannine Community, but their critiques must be acknowledged if we are to develop a more robust method. The combination of these critiques leads to the position that the Gospel alone cannot viably be used to reconstruct a community behind the text. Thus, the proposed method here will use the letters as a starting point for considering the Johannine context, before returning to the gospel in light of what the letters reveal.

BAUCKHAM AND THE NON-PARTICULARITY OF THE GOSPEL

One of the primary objections to a Martyn-style reading of a community reflected in the Gospel comes in the argument for a broad audience for the gospel. Bauckham in *The Gospels for all Christians* sets out an argument that all the gospels were written for a broad audience.[8] The implication for a Johannine community is that a broad intended audience is incompatible with the idea that the Gospel reflects specific incidents within one group of Jesus-followers. Such specific events would not represent the universal experience of other Christians, nor would those beyond the local context know the events that are rewritten in the form of stories about Jesus. While Bauckham's proposal has received criticism, evidence for some sort of broader audience continues to grow. This includes the work of some contributors to this volume, including David Lamb's challenge to a sociolinguistic assertion that the language of the Gospel is that of a close-knit or sectarian group.[9] More recently, Christopher Porter's work from a social identity framework has demonstrated that the audience of the gospel has a broader social identity when compared to either the Johannine letters or Qumran texts such as 1QS or CD.[10] Meanwhile growing evidence that John knew one or more of the Synoptic Gospels further supports the idea of a broader audience, for if the gospel author is familiar with other gospels that circulated widely, there would be grounds to expect a similar narrative account of Jesus's life to circulate through early Christian networks.[11] These arguments do not define the scope of a broader intended audience, whether it entails "all Christians," regional networks, or a subset of the wider Christian networks that was aligned on personal or theological grounds.[12] However, the evidence makes it difficult to maintain that the Gospel of John was only written for a narrow audience.

A broader audience would imply that the Gospel is not deliberately or primarily encoded with reference to a specific local context. This presents a serious problem for any attempt to read the situation of a community off the surface of the text. However, the likelihood of a broad audience does not therefore exclude the existence of a Johannine community. Some proponents of a broad audience depict the Gospel as essentially unmoored from any context, such that it could have been written in any local context without that having any bearing upon the Gospel.[13] Yet the concerns and issues of any local Christian group that the author of the Gospel was part of or interacted closely with are likely to have shaped what was included in the Gospel and how that material was presented.[14] This would be true even if the primary intent was to write for a broader audience. Thus, accepting that there is evidence that the Gospel was written for a broader audience than a single local community does not mean it will bear no traces of its context.

However, if the Gospel is written for a broader audience, then identifying features of the context of the Gospel becomes more challenging. The context that likely influenced the Gospel is more the context of its writing than that of the intended audience. As such, a more sophisticated methodology is required, as this context is less likely to be reflected in simple surface features, as it is with a text addressed to a specific audience. Fortunately, in the case of John's Gospel, we also have the Johannine letters which are written to a specific audience in the way that the Gospel is not. The distinction in audience means that we have more access to the context of those letters, although that access is still not direct and requires careful consideration of the available evidence.

STOWERS, ROLLENS, AND THE ASPIRATIONAL
NATURE OF BIBLICAL TEXTS

A second key consideration in the pursuit of a sound methodology for exploring the context of the Gospel is the function of the text, particularly in terms of its rhetorical agenda. All the New Testament texts are rhetorical, in that they reflect attempts to evoke responses in their audiences. As a result, we must consider the extent to which a text reflects what is desired in the audience rather than the reality. The challenge that NT texts may be causative of social formations rather than representative can be traced back at least to Abraham Malherbe.[15] However, key recent voices of methodological challenge are those of Stowers and Rollens.[16] Their critiques around the rhetorical nature of the NT texts have implications for how we approach these texts for evidence of their audience.

While recognizing that NT texts have a rhetorical agenda is not novel, Stowers highlights the way that this rhetorical agenda can shape references to the audience. Talking particularly in the context of the Pauline epistles, he identifies that these texts seek to evoke a certain kind of community, at times through the assertion that they already are what they should be in practice.[17] This is not a rhetorical tactic evident in the Gospel, which presents its ethical agenda through exhortations toward what the audience ought to do. The Gospel's rhetorical agenda is explicit in John 20:31, "that you might believe that Jesus is the Christ, the Son of God." Also central to the rhetorical agenda are the repeated calls to love one another (13:34; 15:12,17) and to keep Jesus' commands (14:21, 23; 15:10). These exhortations are presented in general terms, as even the Christological confession uses titles that are commonly used across a range of NT texts. Thus the rhetorical agenda aligns with the Gospel addressing a broader audience, rather than primarily focusing on issues that may be specific local concerns. By contrast, the letters address specific local situations, giving both critiques of some actions and events, while offering encouragement and exhortation for others. While the Johannine Letters can speak in idealized terms (1 John 3:1–2; 4:4), these describe a relationship to God rather than the nature of the community. Thus, the challenge posed by the rhetoric of the Johannine letters is not the same as with the Pauline epistles. Yet their rhetorical character still requires careful attention to the rhetoric of the text to differentiate between those elements that might reflect what *is* and those that reflect what *ought to be*.

To investigate how the rhetoric of a text relates to its context, we need clarity regarding the sort of audience that we envision for the text. One of Stowers's critiques is that the idea of a community often assumes or imposes a unity to a group that is not justified.[18] Stowers applies his critique to

Bauckham's implicit idea of a broadly uniform Christian community across the Roman empire. Such an assumption is neither integral nor explicit in Bauckham's argument, but the use of his model can imply it. However, envisioning a wider audience for the Gospel does not require the church to be a "socially and ideologically uniform and cohesive social formation/institution," for some degree of unity is possible without uniformity.[19] We do not have to embrace uncritically Bauer's model of diversity in the early church to recognize that various groups would have been shaped by local conditions, challenges, and possibilities.[20] Given a broader audience for the Gospel is likely, the more local groups that comprise the audience, the greater the diversity. Thus, seeking to identify detailed features of the audience from the Gospel becomes more implausible, for a broader, more diverse audience may share few defining features beyond the most general commitments, such as a concern for the person of Jesus and his words and deeds. This further necessitates the use of the letters, as their narrower audiences are more likely to share common features. However, even with the letters we must not project an image of a uniform group onto the text.

A further critical issue is the extent to which a text can represent a complex social group. With arguments that are generalizable to other gospel-like texts, Rollens critiques the idea that Q represents a community's project "to articulate its totalizing religious ideology."[21] The relationship between the text and any community is more complex. Rather than representing a total ideology, Q represents the activity of Q people as authors.[22] Thus rather than the symbolic meaning of the text, it is more productive to ask how ideas are deployed by the authors. This is a means to gain insights into the Q people without reading the text symbolically.[23] As with Stowers, this centers attention on the rhetorical agenda of a text. Rollens sees the Johannine texts as offering more of a basis for investigation of the community than does Q, as they provide more data along with some sense of an awareness of a community identity, although the same theoretical issues still apply.[24] Indeed, this critique may apply all the more to the letters, for as shorter occasional texts, they are even less likely to convey something like a totalizing religious ideology. As such, we need to accept that our picture of the audience of the letters will only be partial, reflecting the issues that the letters bring to the surface, rather than a complete picture of a complex group.

As much as Rollens points to a community identity reflected in the Johannine texts, we must not overplay the role of a "community" in the production of these texts. Returning to Stowers, he observes how other ancient texts are considered products of individuals in their social and historical context, rather than as products of communities.[25] Some reconstructions of a Johannine community give the community rather than an individual a prominent role in composing the Gospel at least, if not the letters as well.[26] As

Stowers argues, this would be quite different to how other ancient texts were produced. While there are some ancient texts that might plausibly be described as community texts, such as the Homeric epics or some OT texts, they are texts that have a long development, including potentially long oral pre-histories. What we do not have are any contemporary examples of community developed texts from the Imperial period. While the Gospel may have some later editorial additions, narrative critical approaches have stressed the literary unity of the text, which combined with the relative lack of time for the text to develop, suggests that as with other ancient literature it should be understood as primarily the product of a single author.

However, Stowers points to the fact that ancient texts are studied in their social and historical contexts, and thus rejecting community authorship is far from grounds for severing the text from its context. However, the examples noted by Stowers as comparanda are texts from the literary elite. While such literary elites may have written particularly for other elites, even at a distance, the Johannine texts do not exhibit the sophistication of such elite texts.[27] As such the audience, and the nature of the relationship between text and audience, may not be entirely analogous. The audience, especially for the Johannine letters, appears to be one that primarily shares a perspective with the author.[28] That suggests that we can speak of a community as the audience of these texts, in the sense of a group whose identity is primarily one of adherence to Jesus, and with the letter genre implying a geographically defined recipient. This does not imply homogeneity within the group, but it does allow the possibility of using the letters to describe the nature of this community, within the limits of the evidence.

These critiques from Stowers and Rollens point to several weak points in previous attempts to describe a Johannine Community, critiques that have yet to be well integrated into methodological approaches. When combined with the critiques outlined previously, whether from Reinhartz or Bauckham and others who advocate a wide audience model, it points to the attempt to discover a community behind the Gospel from the text of the Gospel alone as an ultimately doomed enterprise. Indeed, even the use of the Johannine letters to gain an understanding of the context of the Johannine writings is not immune from some of these critiques. However, while we cannot use the letters as a simple window into a community, we can use them in a methodologically responsible way to understand at least some features of their context.

THE CONTEXT IN THE LETTERS

The letters, as texts written to specific local audiences, reflect something of the characteristics of those audiences.[29] However, we cannot read this context out of the letters naively, as the preceding discussion highlights. Indeed, the problems of seeking to read the context out of NT letters are well known, highlighted by John Barclay's work on mirror reading.[30] An analysis of the context of the letters must take into account the rhetorical shaping of the text.[31] Questions need to be asked regarding the rhetorical aims of the text and the response they seek to evoke, but also how arguments are presented and what that might reveal about the situation into which the letter speaks. By also attending to what is assumed we can find clues to where the audience might be expected to agree, and where they are already acting in accordance with the ideals that the author advocates. In the analysis I assume that the audience has unifying features, but they are not homogenous.

In what follows, the letters will be treated together under thematic headings. This is not to deny the complexity of considering the specific author(s) and audience(s) of the three letters. Common authorship of the letters is plausible although not essential for the following analysis.[32] Similarities in language and themes indicate a close connection between the letters, pointing to commonality in origin.[33] There may be some distinction in the audiences, with one suggestion being that the more homiletical 1 John is written to an assembly which the author is part of, while 2 and 3 John are written to nearby assemblies.[34] These groups are geographically distinct but not distant, with close connections to each other, as reflected in the references to people moving between the groups, as well as the author's own intent to visit in person (2 John 12; 3 John 3,14).[35] As such they can be described as a network of assemblies within which the author(s) has an influential role. The chronological sequence for the three letters is indeterminate, however, this does not substantially affect the interpretation of the kinds of evidence for the audience that can be derived from the letters.[36] The following analysis will focus first on the social context and then on the theological and ethical context of the letters in order to determine what we are able to know of the context of the Johannine writings.

Social Context

We begin exploring what the Johannine letters reflect of their context by focusing on the social context. Initially we can clear some ground by setting out what the letters do not tell us. There are no significant indications of the economic situation of the audience, such as members who are notable for their wealth or poverty.[37] There is an assumption that the audience will be able to support others, either in the context of sending on those who are travelling ministers (3 John 8) or meeting the needs of those within the group (1 John 3:17). The latter equally expects that there might be those within the group unable to meet their basic needs. However, the majority of the economic world of the Roman Empire was at or slightly above subsistence, which would account for both those who might fall short of what is needed, as well as those who might have enough to give to others.[38] Along with the lack of economic indicators, there are no references to particular trades or occupations among the audience.

The ethnic identity of the audience is similarly undetermined. There are no geographic indicators to locate the audience in a particular cultural context, with the connection to Ephesus/Asia Minor commonly advocated in scholarship being a matter of tradition more than direct textual evidence.[39] There are no references to Jews, nor to practices often considered central to Jewish identity such as Sabbath, circumcision, or dietary laws. This is surprising given the focus on "the Jews" in the Gospel and is a significant factor in proposals that reconstruct a community history with two distinct conflicts, one with the local synagogue and one more theological. One feature that might point to a Jewish audience is the use of Scripture in 1 John 3:11–12. However, this is the only explicit appeal to Scripture, it is used as an example rather than a rule (illustrating a point already made) and does not require knowledge of the story to be understood. What is more, there is no reason to presume that a non-Jewish but Jesus-following audience would be unaware of Scriptural stories, especially key details of an important story.

Equally, there are no explicit references to pagan practices aside from the warning against idolatry in 1 John 5:21. The brevity of the reference means that it is slim evidence upon which to try to argue that idolatry was a particular issue for the audience. On the one hand, this might support reading a Jewish audience, as similar warnings against idolatry appear in Second Temple Jewish texts (Wis Sol 13–14; Sir 30:19; Ep Jer 6:44).[40] However, it could simply reflect a context where ongoing participation in idol worship and associated practices is not a pressing issue. We can note that while there is extensive attention to issues around idolatry in letters such as Romans and 1 Corinthians, such prominence is absent from Ephesians which also has an explicitly Gentile component to its audience. The only mention of Gentiles comes in 3 John 7, where the audience are exhorted to support traveling gospel workers so they do not need support from gentiles (ἀπὸ τῶν ἐθνικῶν). While this could indicate the audience is Jewish rather than gentile, it may function simply as an outsider designation rather than emphasizing ethnic identity.[41] Thus, the text itself does not give any significant support for identifying the audience as either Jewish or gentile. From a wider knowledge of early Christianity, we might posit that a Christian group in the first century is likely to be at least partially, and potentially majority Jewish, the letters do not require such an interpretation.[42] As such, the ethnic makeup of the audience remains undetermined, although the lack of ethno-cultural concerns

Reading the Johannine Community in the Letters 31

would exclude the possibility that the audience is defined by an ethnically characterized division.

While the letters do not identify an economic or ethnic setting, there are indicators of the social context of the audience. The audience is not an isolated group, as there are several references to outsiders coming into the group (2 John 10; 3 John 5). The encouragement to support traveling gospel workers indicates involvement in mission beyond the local group (3 John 5–8). Not only are outsiders able to enter the group, but they are welcomed and supported. The label of "co-workers" (συνεργοί) is positive, indicating approval for such movement beyond local groups. This appears to rule out a narrowly sectarian context.

Additionally, the letters reflect a context of multiple groups in different locations. The author is not present with his audience in 2 John 12 and 3 John 13–14.[43] It may be that the reference to "the elect lady" and "the elect sister" symbolize different communities, either directly or through reference to leading figures within those groups.[44] The greetings delivered in 2 John 13 and 3 John 15 suggest that the groups of the audience and those from where the author is writing are known to each other. 3 John 3 depicts movement between the audience group and the local group of the author, indicating the connections between the groups involve more than just the author.

The conflict with Diotrephes presents further evidence for the social setting. There is a group over which Diotrephes appears to exert significant influence, being able to affect whether letters and visitors are received, even being able to expel group members. There appears to be a contest of authority between the author and Diotrephes, with their differences presented in personal and power terms rather than a matter of theological or ethical differences.[45] While Diotrephes is cast in wholly negative terms, it could be expected that Diotrephes would see the events in quite a different light and may well have seen his exercise of authority as legitimate; however, the context of contested leadership remains. The way the contest is depicted reflects a situation of two interconnected groups, where the author feels they should have some authority over the other group. However, there are no appeals to titles or official authority over the other group, suggesting an informal relationship between the groups, operating on personal authority rather than a hierarchical structure.[46] The author makes no threat of return exclusion for Diotrephes or those who support him, nor are they described in a way that presents them as an outgroup. Rather, the situation with Diotrephes reflects a division within the ingroup.

A key part of the description of the conflict with Diotrephes is the reference to "the assembly" (3 John 9, 10). It is used absolutely, rather than qualified as being Diotrephes' group. This suggests that the assembly is the gathering of Christians in that geographic location. The fact that 3 John is addressed

32   *Christopher Seglenieks*

to the individual Gaius rather than the assembly, coupled with the statement of 3 John 9, indicates that while Diotrephes may have effective control over the gathered assembly, there are others in that geographic location who have not acceded to Diotrephes's control. The use of second person singular in the letter implies that the letter is written to Gaius as an individual rather than as a leader of another group of Christians. However, the greetings (3 John 15) imply that there are others who respect the author. The evidence is not sufficient to cast these as a formal group, however the existence of a Christian gathering beyond that of Diotrephes in this location cannot be excluded.[47] They may well be part of a single local assembly, recognizing that groups and boundaries can be fluid. Thus, the audience of the Johannine letters can be described as a group with subgroups, between which there can be both positive interactions and social conflict, with some degree of openness to those beyond the local group.

While the group to which Diotrephes belongs is not presented as an outgroup, there are indicators of an outgroup elsewhere in the Johannine writings. Both 1 and 2 John refer to deceivers, antichrists, and those who have gone out (1 John 2:19, 22, 26; 3:7; 2 John 7).[48] In both cases these refer to a group distinct from the audience who comprise the ingroup, and they are construed in hostile and exclusionary terms. This outgroup also largely lacks definition. That is, they are not presented in ethnic or geographic terms, nor are they linked to named individuals. Rather, the central point of distinction is on theological grounds, with theological questions as the primary boundary marker between the ingroup and outgroup. The outgroup is not presented as a clearly defined group with an ongoing cohesive group identity.[49] While 1 John indicates a group that departed, 2 John 7 implies that there are others with a similar theological position moving within the wider networks that connect to the audience of these letters. Thus, the Johannine audience sits within a wider network, distinguishing itself theologically from some others within that wider network.

Theological Context

Turning to the theological context, a key point is the nature of division between the audience and their outgroup. This division is christological in nature, as the outgroup are described as "not confessing the coming of Jesus Christ in the flesh" (2 John 7). The meaning of the statement is debated, with the traditional view that it refers to a docetic-like view of Jesus. While others suggest it is a rejection of Jesus as Messiah, a Jewish rejection of Jesus as Messiah does not adequately account for the qualifier "in the flesh."[50] However, it is equally going beyond the evidence to identify this group with a later more defined theological position, seeing them as Gnostics or Cerinthians.[51] While precision on the details of the debated theological issue might be impossible, there are other ways we can consider the evidence.

We can ask whether the letters assume that the audience knows and understands the theological issues. Neither 2 nor 3 John make an attempt to teach doctrine. Nor do either of them devote significant space to persuading the audience to adopt the author's perspective. That suggests that the audience not only understands the view championed by the author, but also that the author assumes that they agree. This is supported by the brevity of the description of the opposing view as well. What makes for a cryptic statement for modern scholars was presumably understood by the original audience, indicating the author assumes they have the contextual information to comprehend readily what was at issue. Aside from the reference to "Christ coming in the flesh" (2 John 7), theological statements are in general terms rather than addressing particular doctrinal issues.

The way that 2 and 3 John speak of the truth also suggests that the audience is perceived by the author as holding to the "correct" view. Thus 2 John refers to those who know the truth (2 John 1), the truth remains in us (2 John 2) and the children "walking in the truth" (2 John 4). Third John is more explicit in its references to Gaius' fidelity to the truth (3 John 3), as well as walking in the truth (3 John 3–4). Aside from these references to the truth, 3 John does not champion particular doctrines, nor does it critique or reject other views. Thus, it appears that both 2 and 3 John assume that the audience holds to the same theological views as the author. As a result, the context of the letters is not one of theological dispute but rather primarily one of theological unity.[52]

The lack of theological issues may be a feature of the brevity of 2 and 3 John, for 1 John devotes more attention to theological topics and argumentation. There is more attention to an outgroup that is theologically divergent from the audience. However, the presentation of the christological issue is in the form of statements rather than arguing for a particular position, which is part of the reason why it is difficult to pin down the nature of the disagreement. The argument functions to encourage a potentially wavering audience that they are correct rather than to teach or convince the audience of the right view. The closest the author comes to christological teaching only comes in 5:5–13, and this is not linked to the earlier references to the outgroup. The author states his purpose as writing in response to those trying to deceive the audience (2:26). This presents a picture of an audience who accepts the view championed by the author, but that their view may be challenged. The author writes to reassure the audience within a broader context of contested Christology. However, the divergent views are located outside the audience, as the author affirms that they are those who believe (5:13).

Christology is not the sole theological concern within the letter, however other theological topics are often not developed at length or serve primarily as support for ethical arguments. Thus there is attention to theology proper in the declaration, "God is love" (4:8). However, the theological statement is used as support for the ethical arguments that run throughout the letter, as God's love is to be an example for the conduct of the audience (4:11). Similarly, theological anthropology is present, such as in the identification of the author and audience as God's children (3:1–2), but this is again asserted and set in service of ethical concerns as this identity provides motivation for purification (3:3). Pneumatology also features, although here the connection is less to ethics and more to Christology, as the Spirit is linked with truth and testimony, especially regarding the coming of Jesus (4:2,13–14; 5:6–8). Sin is as theological topic that is developed to a greater extent, through talk of confession and forgiveness (1:8–10), the need to avoid sin (3:4–6), and the idea of sin that does not lead to death (5:16–17). However, the connection to ethics is perhaps most evident at this point, given sin has to do with wrong actions. The pattern across a range of theological topics is for brief statements rather than extended arguments, set primarily in ethical contexts. Therefore, the letters indicate that the only significant contested theological issue is Christology, and the locus of that contest is between the ingroup of the audience and those outside the ingroup.

Ethical Context

As the preceding section identified an ethical concern as central to 1 John, we can turn now to consider the ethical context of the letters. Here we need to be attentive not only to the ethical issues raised, but also the rhetorical framework within which they are set, and how that might reflect the context. In particular, this means asking the question whether ethical exhortations are presented in a way that implies an existing problem, that the audience are currently transgressing this ethical imperative, or whether it is an encouragement to go on doing the right thing, or to do more of the right thing.

The ethical outlook of 2 and 3 John is broadly positive. Both describe the audience as "walking in truth" (2 John 4; 3 John 3–4). This general statement may indicate holding right theology or doing the right things, or in view of the concerns in these letters for both theology and ethics, it may indicate both. In 2 John 5, the affirmation is followed by the command to love one another. If the affirmation is ethical as well as theological, then the love command is an encouragement to go on doing what they are already doing. The clear indications that the audience already know this command (2 John 5–6) support the idea that this is encouragement rather than either new teaching or correction of current wrong actions. Indeed 2 John contains no direct ethical condemnation, with negative statements reserved for those with divergent Christology. In 3 John the positive situation is more prominent, for the affirmation is

Reading the Johannine Community in the Letters

followed by asserting that the audience are acting faithfully (πιστὸν ποιεῖς, 3 John 5). In this case the author singles out their support for fellow believers who come to the assembly. Here too an ethical exhortation is given, that they send on such visitors with adequate support (3 John 6–8). The positive framework suggests that this is an encouragement to go on acting faithfully, and perhaps to do more so that these itinerant gospel workers can be fully supported. Additionally, 3 John 11 instructs the audience to imitate what is good. The general nature of this exhortation suggests that it forms encouragement rather than correction.[53] Thus, 2 and 3 John convey concern for right ethical action, but the audience is only in need of encouragement to continue doing good rather than being in error and needing correcting.

When we come to 1 John the ethical focus of the letter is more complex. Some have read all the ethical injunctions as referring to the outgroup.[54] However, the majority of these ethical exhortations and injunctions are general in scope. Thus, the negative statements are hypothetical statements that form part of an argument, rather than direct exhortations for the audience to stop doing something that they currently are doing.[55] This is reinforced by positive comments, notably those in 2:12–14 which assure the audience that their sins are forgiven, that they have overcome evil/the evil one. The positive exhortations are also primarily general in character, focused on the command to love one another. This echoes not only the Gospel of John (13:34; 15:12,17), but it is also analogous to the summary of the law in the gospels (Matt 22:39; Mark 12:31; Luke 10:27) as well as in the OT (Lev 19:18; Deut 6:5). The general nature of the commands makes it difficult to draw conclusions about the ethical character of the audience.

However, the extent to which the letter focuses on ethical matters, which are prominent through every chapter, strongly suggests that the audience is not fully acting as the author sees that they should. They fall short of demonstrating love to each other, perhaps particularly in the area of providing for physical needs (3:17). Yet the framing of the argument is as an exhortation toward better alignment with what is right (2:3,10; 3:3,7). They are to admit their imperfections (1:9) and strive to do what is right (2:6; 3:3). Thus, unlike what we might see in letters like Romans or 1 Corinthians, there do not appear to be differing understandings within the audience as to what right action entails. While some might take this as evidence for a Jewish audience who would know and understand the Law, it is also compatible with a community that has established ethical norms.[56] Even the specific command to "keep yourselves from idols" (5:21) does not imply that the audience are currently engaged in idolatry, but rather warns against the possibility, while its brevity implies that the instruction would not be contentious. The audience knows what is right, they are simply in need of exhortation to do it, and to do it even more.[57]

36   *Christopher Seglenieks*

At first glance, ethics can appear as a boundary issue in 1 John, as it uses outsider language of those who act wrongly. But in the Johannine epistles such harsh outgroup language is not applied to specific individuals, rather only to those who might hypothetically transgress the expected norms. Even Diotrephes, who receives condemnation for his works, including slander (3 John 10), is not labeled as an outsider. The implication is that their Christology is not deviant, thus they still belong to the ingroup, and the division is an intra-group issue. Thus the overall function of the ethical exhortations is as an encouragement to do better for those who are insiders, in contrast to the function of Christology as the boundary marker. As a result, the audience can be characterized as broadly agreeing to the ethical norms reflected in the letters, albeit with varying degrees of compliance, and without any ethical issues being notably contentious.

The Johannine Community in the Letters

The picture of the audience of the letters, the Johannine community, is only a shadowy one. We have no clear defining economic, geographic, or ethnic features. Socially, we see a network of connected groups within which power is contested, although without formal structures of authority. Theologically, the central concern is for Christology, which is the key issue that defines who is in and who is out. A group that holds a divergent view has departed from the Johannine network, although there may be others in the wider regional Christian networks who hold similar views to those who departed. The ingroup appears to be broadly in agreement theologically with the author, as there is little attempt to explain and argue for theological views. Ethics is the other prominent issue, although this is primarily presented in general terms, and in a way that indicates that the audience agree with the ethical norms but need encouragement for ongoing or increased compliance. This picture of the Johannine community is admittedly less exciting than some that have been proposed, with less dramatic events in the life of the community. Yet while a vision of action and controversy might better engage our imaginations, as scholars we must allow our imaginations to be constrained by the text in our attempts at reconstruction.

THE GOSPEL READ IN CONTEXT

We can now return to the Gospel with what we have identified of the context. This enables us to read the Gospel in a different light, along different contextual contours than are identified in traditional community readings. Space precludes a detailed investigation, but I will highlight three key areas

Reading the Johannine Community in the Letters

where reading the gospel in light of the proposed context may shape our interpretation.

The first is that the context proposed here requires a reassessment of the role of conflict with "the Jews" in the Gospel. In contrast to a traditional community reading, the context depicted in the letters does not center conflict with a Jewish group. Existing approaches tend to situate explanations of that conflict in the narrative within a similar conflict between a group of Johannine Jesus followers and a synagogue. If the context of the gospel is not primarily shaped by conflict with a synagogue, that necessitates revisiting the question of why such conflict appears prominently in the narrative if it does not directly relate to the situation of the audience.[58] Yet while much Johannine scholarship has assumed the conflict reflects the context of writing, other solutions include understanding it as having a role in persuading the audience towards unity, or to encourage them to publicly practice their faith despite hostility.[59]

On a more positive note, the proposed context encourages reading christological concerns as central. Additionally, the implication is that the development of Christology is not necessarily a response to external factors, shaped by conflicts with a synagogue or Jewish rejection of Jesus as messiah. It may be a more positive development in reflection upon the words and deeds of Jesus remembered, as suggested by the motif of memory within the Gospel (2:22; 12:16). Alternatively, the letters suggest that Christology is contested within the wider Christian networks within which the Johannine communities are situated. This may have contributed to the development and exposition of Christology as reflected in the Gospel. However, it is unclear whether the Gospel was written to address such contested Christology given the complicated reception history of the Gospel in its use both against and in support of what would later become orthodoxy.[60] Whatever paradigm is adopted, the context for the Gospel outlined here undermines any reconstruction that presents the Christology of the gospel as shaped through conflict with Judaism.[61]

Similarly, the proposed context centers ethical concerns, which also has several implications for interpreting the Gospel. It draws attention to one dimension of the role of "the Jews," which is as the object of ethical critique. This is most evident in John 8, where Stephen Motyer has argued that the rhetoric used draws attention to ethical failures in a similar way to some other second temple texts.[62] Beyond this, a context where ethical concerns are prominent gives added justification for reading implicit ethics in John. Recent work on Johannine ethics has emphasized this dimension of how John conveys ethics.[63] If the audience is concerned with ethics, then they would have been alert to ethical shaping through the narrative of the Gospel.

Johannine studies needs a more methodologically sound approach to investigating the context of the Gospel. I have presented such an approach, which takes into account questions of genre, purpose, rhetoric, and audience. Building on the evidence from the three Johannine letters, we find the context is one where a group of connected communities exists within and connected to a wider network of Christian groups. We do not have the evidence to make substantial claims about the economic or ethnic makeup of these groups, beyond the fact that there is no evidence that ethnic concerns were central. Rather, Christology is central, and provides the primary boundary marker for the group. Ethics is similarly prominent within the letters, albeit without the same role in defining group identity. Reading the Gospel in light of this context points to at least three important implications for how we interpret the Gospel, with regard to conflict with the Jews, Christology, and ethics. While the model advocated here does not have the drama of some approaches, arguably it gets us closer to what the issues of concern were in the original context of the Gospel.

NOTES

1. Raymond E. Brown, *The Community of the Beloved Disciple* (London: Cassell, 1979). Similarly, Reinhartz can describe her own suggestion as "a construct and a highly speculative one at that." Adele Reinhartz, "Forging a New Identity: Johannine Rhetoric and the Audience of the Fourth Gospel," in *Paul, John, and Apocalyptic Eschatology: Studies in Honour of Martinus C. de Boer,* ed. J. Krans, L. J. Lietaert Peerbolte, Peter-Ben Smit, and Arie W. Zwiep, NovTSup 149 (Leiden: Brill, 2013), 131.

2. Martinus C. de Boer, "The Story of the Johannine Community and its Literature," in *The Oxford Handbook of Johannine Studies*, ed. Judith M. Lieu and Martinus C. de Boer (Oxford: Oxford University Press, 2018), 63–66, 75.

3. I use the term "context" initially rather than "community" in the attempt to avoid concluding before investigating whether there is a community, as the term may imply a coherent, defined group identity. While "community" does imply a group identity and some degree of unity, Stowers gives too narrow a definition, arguing that it implies a group that is "highly cohesive with commonality in belief and practice." Stanley Stowers, "The Concept of 'Community' and the History of Early Christianity," *MTSR* 23 (2011): 245.

4. J. Louis Martyn, *History and Theology in the Fourth Gospel* (New York: Harper & Row, 1968); Brown, *The Community of the Beloved Disciple*. A similar use of the gospel as window also features in Paul Anderson's reconstruction in Paul N. Anderson, "On 'Seamless Robes' and 'Leftover Fragments'—A Theory of Johannine Composition," in *The Origins of John's Gospel*, ed. Stanley E. Porter and Hughson T. Ong (Leiden: Brill, 2016), 205, 209–10.

5. For some scholars, the reference to being put out of the synagogue remains the launching point for any consideration of a Johannine community. However, if the unwarranted assumption that it refers to a widespread official exclusion of Christians

instigated by a central authority is set aside, there are alternative explanations for the use of this expression in the gospel, including historical and rhetorical arguments. See Jonathan Bernier, *Aposynagōgos and the Historical Jesus in John: Rethinking the Historicity of the Johannine Expulsion Passages*, BInS 122 (Leiden: Brill, 2013); Paul Trebilco, *The Early Christians in Ephesus from Paul to Ignatius* (Grand Rapids: Eerdmans, 2007), 240; Christopher Seglenieks, "Desertion or Exclusion: Relationships with the Outgroup in the Johannine Writings," in *Figuring the Enemy: Socio-Scientific Approaches to Religious Enmity*, ed. Christopher Porter, Routledge Interdisciplinary Perspectives on Biblical Criticism (London: Routledge, forthcoming).

6. Adele Reinhartz, "The Johannine Community and its Jewish Neighbors: A Reappraisal," in *What Is John? Vol II: Literary and Social Readings of the Fourth Gospel*, ed. Fernando F. Segovia (Atlanta: Scholars Press, 1998), 111–38. Reinhartz also notes the tensions in Brown's reconstruction between seeing the community defined by a split from the synagogue on the one hand, and the community as including Gentiles and Samaritans, who would not have been part of the synagogue, thus would not have split from it. Reinhartz, "Forging a New Identity," 126–27.

7. Jörg Frey, *The Glory of the Crucified One: Christology and Theology in the Gospel of John* (Waco, TX/Tübingen: Baylor/Mohr Siebeck, 2018), 90–92; cf. Douglas Estes, *The Temporal Mechanics of the Fourth Gospel*, BInS 92 (Leiden: Brill, 2008), 243–46.

8. Richard Bauckham ed, *The Gospels for All Christians: Rethinking the Gospel Audiences* (Grand Rapids: Eerdmans, 1998). While challenging the common consensus, the idea of a broad intended audience was not a novel idea, as C. H. Dodd could write of "the work as addressed to a wide public consisting primarily of devout and thoughtful persons." C. H. Dodd, *The Interpretation of the Fourth Gospel* (Cambridge: University Press, 1968), 9.

9. David A. Lamb, *Text, Context and the Johannine Community: A Sociolinguistic Analysis of the Johannine Writings*, LNTS 423 (New York/London: Bloomsbury T&T Clark, 2015). For a critical, albeit more positive assessment of some of the issues around the term "sectarian," see Ruth Sheridan, "Johannine Sectarianism: A Category Now Defunct?," in *The Origins of John's Gospel*, 142–66.

10. Christopher A. Porter, *Johannine Social Identity Formation after the Fall of the Jerusalem Temple: Negotiating Identity in Crisis*; BInS 194 (Leiden: Brill, 2022).

11. Eve-Marie Becker, Helen K. Bond and Catrin H. Williams, *John's Transformation of Mark* (London: Bloomsbury T&T Clark, 2021); James W. Barker, *John's Use of Matthew* (Minneapolis: Fortress, 2015). Cf. Bauckham, *Gospels for All Christians*, 12–13.

12. Thus, David Sim in response to Bauckham argues for a regional network in Greece and Asia Minor that may have had less connections further south and east. David C. Sim, "The Gospels for All Christians? A Response to Richard Bauckham," *JSNT* 84 (2001): 14. Burridge similarly suggests the gospels were written for defined subsets of Christians, albeit not defined geographically. Richard Burridge, "About People, by People, for People: Gospel Genre and Audiences," in *The Gospels for All Christians*, 143.

13. Trebilco talks of the sorts of figures who would have written gospels as widely traveled, tied to the Christian community as a whole, not one local expression. However, while there may have been mobility within early Christian networks, there is no direct evidence that the author of the Gospel of John traveled widely. Trebilco, *Early Christians*, 238.

14. As Sim rightly points out, a gospel author would likely have been resident in a community for an extended period of time. Sim, "The Gospels for All Christians?": 21; cf. Pieter Botha, *Orality and Literacy in Early Christianity* (Eugene, OR: Cascade, 2012), 80. This point is not a new one, as Barrett states, "The Gospel must be considered as conditioned by the religious, ecclesiastical and theological convictions and disputes of its environment." C. K. Barrett, *Essays on John* (London: SPCK, 1982), 121.

15. Abraham J. Malherbe, *Social Aspects of Early Christianity* (Baton Rouge: Lousiana State University Press, 1977), 13.

16. Stowers, "Concept of 'Community'"; Sarah E. Rollens, "Does 'Q' Have Any Representative Potential?," *MTSR* 23 (2011); idem, "The Anachronism of 'Early Christian Communities,'" in *Theorizing 'Religion' in Antiquity* (ed. Nickolas P. Roubekas; London: Equinox, 2018).

17. Stowers, "Concept of 'Community'": 243–44.

18. Stowers, "Concept of 'Community'": 241–45.

19. Stowers, "Concept of 'Community'": 253.

20. Walter Bauer, *Orthodoxy and Heresy in Earliest Christianity* (Philadelphia: Fortress, 1971).

21. Rollens, "Does 'Q' Have Any Representative Potential?": 67.

22. Rollens, "Does 'Q' Have Any Representative Potential?": 70, 72; focusing on the work of William E. Arnal, *Jesus and the Villages Scribes: Galilean Conflicts and the Setting of Q* (Minneapolis: Fortress, 2001).

23. Rollens, "Does 'Q' Have Any Representative Potential?": 77.

24. Rollens, "Does 'Q' Have Any Representative Potential?": 76; with reference to Melissa (Phillip) Sellew, "'Thomas Christianity': Scholars in Search of a Community," *The Apocryphal Acts of Thomas*, ed. Jan B. Bremmer (Leuven, Peeters, 2001), 11–35.

25. Stowers, "Concept of 'Community'": 247.

26. The gospel as a community product is particularly explicit in the work of Culpepper and Cullmann. Oscar Cullmann, *The Johannine Circle* (London: SCM, 1976); R. Alan Culpepper, *The Johannine School*, SBLDS 26 (Missoula, MT: Scholars, 1975). Multi-stage models tend to imply that the text is the product of a community rather than a single audience, thus Anderson, "On 'Seamless Robes'"; Brown, *Community*; Martyn, *History and Theology*.

27. Recently, Robyn Faith Walsh has argued that the gospel authors are cultural elites writing for other cultural elites. However, unlike the Greco-Roman writers with whom she draws parallels, none of the gospels indicate writing for other writers. Indeed, the letters show themselves to be written for group(s) who would identify themselves as followers of Jesus, rather than others engaged in a literary enterprise. What is more, both 2 and 3 John reflect a preference for face-to-face interaction

over literary forms, further suggesting that these texts should not be allocated to a literary elite. Robyn Faith Walsh, *The Origins of Early Christian Literature* (Cambridge: Cambridge University Press, 2021), 6.

28. The fact that the audience can be referred to as a group (i.e., ecclesia) implies some degree of shared identity that makes it a group as opposed to a collection of individuals.

29. Thus Trebilco argues that they can be used as evidence for the life of a Christian community. Trebilco, *Early Christians*, 241.

30. John M. G. Barclay, "Mirror-Reading a Polemical Letter: Galatians as a Test Case," *JSNT* 31 (1987).

31. The Johannine letters have been investigated with respect to Greco-Roman rhetoric, notably by Duane Watson; see Duane F. Watson, "1 John 2.12–14 as Distributio, Conduplicatio, and Expolitio: A Rhetorical Understanding," *JSNT* 11.35 (1989): 97–110; idem., "Amplification Techniques in 1 John: The Interaction of Rhetorical Style and Invention," *JSNT* 51.1 (1993). Others to consider the rhetorical agenda of 1 John include: J. M. Lieu, "Us or You? Persuasion and Identity in 1 John," *JBL* 127 (2008): 805–19; R. Roitto, "Identity in 1 John: Sinless Sinners who Remain in Him," in *T&T Clark Handbook to Social Identity in the New Testament*, ed. J. B. Tucker and Coleman A. Baker (London: Bloomsbury, 2014), 493–510; Christopher Seglenieks, "The Rhetoric of Faith in 1 John," *BBR* 33 (2023), 186–203.

32. There are a range of views on the authorship of the three letters. Some advocate common authorship of all three along with the Gospel: so Trebilco, *Early Christians*, 265, 272; some just the letters, while at times being uncommitted on common authorship with the Gospel: Karen H. Jobes, *1, 2, & 3 John*, ZECNT (Grand Rapids: Zondervan, 2014), 27–29; John Painter, *1, 2, and 3 John*, SP 18 (Collegeville, MN: Liturgical Press, 2008), 52; Raymond E. Brown, *The Epistles of John*, AB 30 (New York: Doubleday, 1983), 14–19; while others leave the question open, thus Judith Lieu, *I, II, & III John*, New Testament Library (Louisville, KY: Westminster John Knox, 2008), 1–9. There are also those who suggest that all have different authors, with many locating the authors in the same context, as part of a Johannine school or community, thus de Boer, "Story of the Johannine Community," 64. Recently Méndez has argued that not only are they written by different authors, but also they are written in deliberate imitation. Hugo Méndez, "Did the Johannine Community Exist?," *JSNT* 42 (2020): 250–74. Ultimately, the question of authorship is difficult to resolve with any certainty, as observed by Barrett, *Essays on John*, 127.

33. Even if the more provocative proposal of Méndez is adopted, this project is still possible, albeit perhaps more tentative. For forged letters to be accepted, they would need to reflect enough of the real situation of the recipients for them to believe that these letters were in fact written to them.

34. Trebilco argues that 1 John was written to author's own community while 2,3 John were written to other communities in the Johannine network but geographically removed. Trebilco, *Early Christians*, 264–65. Second and Third John are similar to contemporary letters. While the homiletical style of 1 John does not fit neatly into conventions of the genre, the concern with specific events (1 John 2:19) indicates it is addressed to a specific group that has experienced this event.

35. De Boer, "Story of the Johannine Community," 65.

36. Trebilco, *Early Christians*, 272.

37. Kloppenborg addresses the many issues around identifying social and economic status of the members of Christian groups. John S. Kloppenborg, *Christ's Associations: Connecting and Belonging in the Ancient City* (New Haven, CT: Yale University Press, 2019), 162–208.

38. For a survey of economic models of the Roman Empire, see Kloppenborg, *Christ's Associations*, 170–80. Kloppenborg emphasizes that the evidence points to a significant proportion of middling incomes among the subtleties, rather than a simple binary of wealthy elites and poverty-stricken masses. Thus it is plausible that the audience of the letters had varied levels of income, but the evidence does not allow for firmer conclusions.

39. Early sources place "John" in Ephesus, although they may indicate two distinct people. See Polycarp, in Irenaeus, *Haer.* 3.1.2 and Papias, in Eusebius, *Hist. ecc.* 3.39.3–17.

40. Similarly, concerns with idolatry are fundamental to the telling of the Maccabean revolt (1 Macc 1:41–50; 2:23–25).

41. Paul Trebilco, *Outsider Designations and Boundary Construction in the New Testament* (Cambridge: Cambridge University Press, 2017), 172–73.

42. Advocates for a Jewish audience include Daniel R. Streett, *They Went Out from Us: The Identity of the Opponents in First John*, BZNW 177 (Berlin: De Gruyter, 2011); Terry Griffith, *Keep Yourselves from Idols: A New Look at 1 John*, JSNTSup 233 (London: Sheffield Academic, 2002).

43. While the written nature of 1 John implies that the author is similarly not present with his audience, the more homiletical style has led some to suggest that the author writes to a community which he is part of, but which he is not currently present with. Jobes, *1, 2, & 3 John*, 37; Brown, *Epistles*, 101.

44. Brown, *Epistles*, 651–5; Lamb, *Text, Context*, 185–87.

45. Barrett suggests a possible theological division, but that is only a hypothesis made in comparison to the Presbyter's exclusion of others on a theological basis. Barrett, *Essays on John*, 128.

46. Trebilco, *Early Christians*, 483–89.

47. Note though Trebilco sees Diotrephes and Gaius both as leaders of house churches. Trebilco, *Early Christians*, 270.

48. The rhetorical framing of the outgroup makes it likely that it represents a real departure rather than simply a rhetorical device. Thus Seglenieks, "Desertion or Exclusion," contra Hansjörg Schmidt, "How to Read the First Epistle of John Non-Polemically," *Bib* 85 (2004): 33.

49. The lack of identity to an outgroup may make it easier to cast them as outsiders rather than as misguided ingroup members. However, the lack of a concrete identity also indicates a rhetorical focus on the positive group identity of the ingroup and their shared theological standpoint. The ingroup focus is also evident in the theme of reassurance, which may be aimed at supporting the audience in what may have been a traumatic experience of schism, thus Wendy E. Sproston, "Witnesses to What Was ἀπ' ἀρχῆς: 1 John's Contribution to Our Knowledge of Tradition in the Fourth Gospel,"

in *The Johannine Writings*, ed. Stanley E. Porter and Craig A. Evans (Sheffield: Sheffield Academic, 1995), 146.

50. Thus Trebilco, *Early Christians*, 273; contra the Jewish focus of Streett, *They Went Out*; Griffith, *Keep Yourselves from Idols*.

51. Those identifying docetic or proto-Gnostic opponents include Ernst Wendland, "The Rhetoric of Reassurance in First John: 'Dear Children' versus the 'Antichrists,'" *Neot* 41.1 (2007): 174; Georg Strecker, *The Johannine Letters,* Hermeneia (Minneapolis, MN: Fortress, 1996), 75; Brown, *Epistles*, 104–6.

52. This does not need to imply theological uniformity, as the letters do not seek to define theological positions in detail.

53. While the actions of Diotrephes are condemned, his failings are individual, rather than those of the group.

54. I. Howard Marshall, *The Epistles of John*, NICNT (Grand Rapids: Eerdmans, 1978), 15; Brown, *Epistles*; John Painter, "The 'Opponents' in 1 John," *NTS* 32 (1986); Rudolf Schnackenburg, *The Johannine Epistles* (New York: Crossroad, 1992), 17; Colin G. Kruse, *The Letters of John*, PNTC (Grand Rapids: Eerdmans, 2000), 16–18.

55. Terry Griffith, "A Non-Polemical Reading of 1 John: Sin, Christology and the Limits of Johannine Christianity," *TynBul* 49 (1998): 257–60; Trebilco, *Early Christians*, 277–82. Cf. Barclay, "Mirror-Reading": 79–80.

56. Here we can contrast the context with that of some of the Pauline epistles. In those contexts, the Christian groups are often recently established, with Paul only spending limited time with them. As such, it is not surprising that diverse ethical perspectives remain. The Johannine epistles however are traditionally dated to late in the first century, and thus there is time to develop strong group norms defined by a leader who may have been present for decades. This would be particularly fitting if 1 John is more a sermon to the group where the author is resident.

57. Trebilco, *Early Christians*, 426–27.

58. A simple answer is that conflict with the Jews was a feature of Jesus' ministry. That is supported by the Synoptic tradition, which sets Jesus in conflict with Pharisees and Sadducees. However, it does not fully explain why John gives this motif greater emphasis, nor why it is generalised to "the Jews."

59. Reinhartz, "Forging a New Identity," 128; Seglenieks, "Desertion or Exclusion."

60. The argument that John's Christology is intentionally anti-docetic is strongly challenged in light of reception history by J. D. Atkins, *The Doubt of the Apostles and the Resurrection Faith of the Early Church*, WUNT 2/495 (Tübingen: Mohr Siebeck, 2019).

61. The framing of the origins of the gospel in terms of conflict with Judaism has been challenged more broadly in terms of whether it is appropriate to construe the gospel as something outside Judaism, or whether the gospel is better understood as reflecting the diversity of ways that Jewish identity could be negotiated in the first century. See Wally Cirafesi, *John Within Judaism: Religion, Ethnicity, and the Shaping of Jesus-Oriented Jewishness in the Fourth Gospel,* AJEC 112 (Leiden: Brill, 2022).

62. Stephen Motyer, *Your Father the Devil? A New Approach to John and 'the Jews'* (Carlisle, Cumbria: Paternoster, 1997).

63. See especially Jan van der Watt and Ruben Zimmermann eds, *Rethinking the Ethics of John: 'Implicit Ethics' in the Gospel of John,* WUNT 291 (Tübingen: Mohr Siebeck, 2012). Cf. Michael J. Gorman, "John's Implicit Ethic of Enemy-Love," in *Johannine Ethics: The Moral World of the Gospel and Epistles of John*, ed. Sherri Brown and Christopher W. Skinner (Minneapolis: Fortress, 2017); Jey J. Kanagaraj, "The Implied Ethics of the Fourth Gospel: A Reinterpretation of the Decalogue," *TynBul* 52 (2001): 33–60.

Chapter 3

The Language of John

Idiolect, Sociolect, Antilanguage, and Textual Community

David A. Lamb

THE HOLY GRAIL OF CONTEXT

When I first did a university course on Johannine Studies, I was introduced to Raymond Brown's community model, specifically that described in *The Community of the Beloved Disciple* (1979).[1] Prior to university, I had spent some time as member of a lay Christian community and it was perhaps that experience that led me to ask questions about what exactly was meant by this "Johannine Community," probably much to the frustration of my teachers. Now, I still wonder if for Brown and other Johannine scholars, the "Community" has always been a hermeneutical tool rather than a historical reality or else what Klink describes as an example of "reification," that is treating the abstract as if it were real.[2]

Of course, we would like to know the precise context in which the Gospel of John was composed as this would be a significant factor (a holy grail?) in its interpretation. It seems to me that in this task of reconstruction of context we have three main options:

1. We can use the writings of the early church fathers.
2. We can construct a broad socio-historical context from documents and archaeological evidence roughly contemporary with the Gospel.
3. We can focus on the text itself to see if its language implies a context. In this process, we can also draw on the Johannine Epistles, provided we accept that there is some relationship between them and the Gospel.

45

This is an oversimplification and, in reality, there is considerable overlap between these three options. In the process of reconstruction of context, I propose that up until roughly the mid-twentieth century the focus was on the *author* of the Gospel and, in particular, the question of "which John?," with much use being made of the external evidence found in the church fathers. This approach has certainly not been abandoned and still generates considerable debate.[3] If we were sure that it was John, the son of Zebedee, who was the Gospel's principal author, then that would influence our interpretation of the text and we would focus on the *idiolect* of someone intimately involved in the events recorded. However, since the influential work of Martyn and Brown, the focus has shifted markedly to the nature and role of a *community* as the primary context for this Gospel.[4] This community can be understood within a broad socio-historical context (or what we might label a *context of culture*) and comparison can be made with other groups, such as the comparison Culpepper makes with ancient schools.[5] Those who accept this notion of a Johannine community, still the majority in Johannine studies, despite Klink's belief in a paradigm shift,[6] tend to discuss the language of the Gospel as the *sociolect* of a particular school or community or sect within early Christianity. Indeed, this has led some scholars to make use of sociolinguistic writings to depict the language of John as an *antilanguage*, indicative of a sectarian outlook.

However, given uncertainty over the historical accuracy of the early church fathers' writings with respect to the Gospel's composition and given the variety of reconstructions of a Johannine community on the basis of a broad socio-historical context, my own focus has been on the third option, that is the text itself, and the application of insights from the field of sociolinguistics. In particular, I have made use of *register analysis*, which endeavors to understand the relationship between language and a *context of situation* that is narrower than the *context of culture*.

TEXT, CONTEXT AND THE JOHANNINE COMMUNITY

In *Text, Context and the Johannine Community* (2014), I employed a form of register analysis to determine what the *tenor* of the language used in the Gospel and Epistles might indicate about the situational context in which these writings were composed and specifically what it might suggest about a community involved in their production.[7] I drew particularly on the work of Michael Halliday and colleagues in the branch of sociolinguistics known as *systemic functional linguistics* (SFL) and Douglas Biber and colleagues in *text linguistics* and their *multidimensional* (MD) analysis. Broadly, my argument was that it is possible to analyze certain lexico-grammatical and discourse features of the Gospel and Epistles that are indicative of the interpersonal relations between the author and reader. To take one example: if the initial intended readers of the Gospel were members of the same tightly knit social group as the author/s, then it is likely that there would be much use of ellipsis or abbreviation and what Biber and Conrad label "vague references."[8]

In my analysis, I focused on those texts where the author appears to be addressing the reader directly and where the act of writing is consciously highlighted and I summarized my findings in terms of the categories used by the functional linguist Cate Poynton: *power, contact,* and *affective involvement.*[9] I proposed that in the texts analyzed:

1. The author has the *power* in relationship to potential readers. This power is most evident in the Gospel and 1 John and there may be some weakening of it in 2 John and more so in 3 John.
2. There is no evidence of prior *contact* between the author and reader in the Gospel. There is some evidence for it in 1 John, more in 2 John, and even more in 3 John.
3. There is no evidence of *affective involvement,* that is emotional involvement or commitment, in the Gospel and little evidence for it in the Epistles.

My overall conclusions were justifiably cautious. I rejected the idea that the Gospel was written for a closed community. However, I did accept the designation of a Johannine community in a limited sense to refer to a group of associates formed around the Gospel and reflected in the Epistles. Drawing on the terminology of the Canadian historian and philosopher Brian Stock, I proposed, "a 'Johannine Community' that is a loose network, an embryonic textual community or 'reading and interpretative community' (Stock) that gives particular status to the written text of the [Gospel of John]."[10]

I hoped that my study would encourage NT scholars to consider the relevance of certain methods from contemporary sociolinguistics as well as providing a critique of those who, in my view, have misused sociolinguistic terminology, particularly regarding the Gospel's so-called *antilanguage,* and that it would contribute to the continuing debate on the nature, indeed the very existence, of a Johannine community.

RESPONSES TO *TEXT, CONTEXT AND THE JOHANNINE COMMUNITY*

On balance, *Text, Context and the Johannine Community* has been positively received and it has even been used as a case study in methods of research

48   *David A. Lamb*

from the perspective of the writings of the Dutch philosopher Herman Dooyeweerd.[11] However, there have been criticisms from a variety of perspectives, such as from those who believe that I have misunderstood or misapplied the particular methodology of SFL.[12] A specific objection has been made by Philip Esler concerning my rejection of the language of the Gospel as an instance of *antilanguage*. It has also been suggested that my proposals regarding the nature of a Johannine community are framed primarily in negative terms, that is rejecting its sectarian character, without providing a more positive model in its place.[13]

In this chapter, I hope to engage with some of these objections, both by clarifying my arguments in the light of appropriate criticism and also by updating and developing some of the issues that I considered. I do this under the three headings of:

- Register: Idiolect and Sociolect
- Antilanguage
- Textual Community

REGISTER: IDIOLECT AND SOCIOLECT

My use of a form of register analysis to determine the possible tenor of the Johannine writings has attracted some criticism from those who see me as misusing the particular methodology of Hallidayan SFL. In response to this I would make two initial observations. The first is that SFL is only one of a number of methodologies within sociolinguistics and that, regarding register analysis within SFL, it should be recognized that this a developing and somewhat disputed field of study.[14] I do not believe that those who rightly, in my opinion, promote the use of sociolinguistic insights in the interpretation of ancient texts should be overreliant on one particular approach. As Nicholas J. Ellis perceptively observes in his essay "Biblical Exegesis and Linguistics: *A Prodigal History*," "An awareness of scholarly diversity . . . frees us from the perceived hegemony of a particular linguistic school within our guild."[15] My second observation is that as we live in an era of proliferating methodologies within NT studies, scholars cannot be expected to take on board yet another methodology, such as SFL with its complex terminology and range of understandings, unless its underlying principles are seen as clear and relevant. Indeed, as Chris Seglenieks points out, "When it comes to specialised fields such as sociolinguistics, many biblical scholars do not have the knowledge to assess claims that are made, and thus the scientific style of language associated with the claims can be convincing."[16] It is too easy with such interdisciplinary approaches to NT studies to "blind with science."

The Language of John   49

Nevertheless, it seems to me that one of the key insights of SFL and other schools of functional linguistics is that language, as a social phenomenon, always carries with it a social dimension.[17] This is the essence of *register*, that we learn to use words in particular contexts and, as our language use develops, we automatically adapt what we say to communicate effectively in different contexts. What is true of daily interaction in family conversations or shopping transactions or in scientific discourse and academic lectures is also true of the written communication of the NT texts and it is reflected in the authors' lexico-grammatical and discourse choices.[18] Accepting this general principle, my own approach has been to utilize a selective and simplified model of register, drawing on a range of sociolinguistic insights, that, I hope, goes some way to addressing the concerns of those who consider such an approach as somehow obscure, inappropriate or anachronistic.[19] However, what is central to my argument is that, unless we have clear evidence to the contrary, all language throughout history (spoken, written, "literary" or "non-literary") carries with it a social dimension. Maybe too many NT commentators treat its texts as a storehouse of sources to be arranged to provide material for dissection and debate, rather than being primarily means of communication written down at a particular time and place in a register that is appropriate for their purpose. This is not to deny that John used oral and/or written sources, but it is an acknowledgment that our focus should be on the final form of the text as can best be determined.[20]

I am well aware that, ideally, register analysis depends on the examination of a large corpus of texts in which we know what the context of situation is for many of the texts. Then, whatever the mode of analysis (SFL, MD or other), a correlation can be made between a text's lexico-grammatical and discourse features and the *context of situation* relating to its composition. In relation to written documents, I am not referring here to the situation of its actual inscribing, whether typed on a laptop during a train journey or dictated to a scribe writing on a clay tablet under the shade of a palm tree, but the situation as regards the interaction between author and (intended) reader. The value of register analysis of the NT documents would certainly be strengthened by comparative study within a large corpus of material in which the precise *context of situation* of at least some of its texts within a particular genre were known.[21] Brook O'Donnell, in *Corpus Linguistics and the Greek of the New Testament* (2005), commendably endeavors to provide such a corpus by including alongside the NT writings a selection of other Hellenistic Greek writings.[22] However, even here we are limited by our lack of knowledge of the situation in which many of these texts were composed.[23]

Despite these limitations and the need for caution, I still think that it is reasonable to suggest that certain linguistic features of the Johannine writings are indicative of a particular context of situation within the broad parameters of *power*, *contact,* and *affective involvement*. The lexico-grammatical and discourse features of the Gospel may not tell us precisely where and when it was written, but they can indicate that it was not written for a closed group. So, returning to the example of the discourse feature of "vague references" (Biber and Conrad), the principle is really a very simple one: our verbal communication with those we know well is often almost or completely unintelligible to those who lie outside that group. This is especially true of spoken discourse, but also applies to written communication. To take an example from the *Oxyrhynchus Papyri*, we have a (somewhat fragmentary) letter written in Greek and dated ca. 35 CE as follows:

> Thaisous to her mother Syras. I must tell you that Seleucus came here and has fled. Don't trouble yourself to explain. Let Lucia wait until the year. Let me know the day. Salute Ammonas my brother and . . . and my sister . . . and my father Theonas.[24]

We can determine some of the family relationships in this group, but who Seleucus is, why he has fled, why Thaisous' mother should not bother explaining and why Lucia should wait are *vague references*. Maybe Thaisous is proposing a postponed wedding between Seleucus and Lucia, but we cannot be sure as we are not "in the loop."

Similarly, when the author of the short letter 3 John writes to "Gaius" and refers to "Diotrephes" and "Demetrius" in relation to situations that are barely explained, then we can only conclude with Judith Lieu, that, "Presumably Gaius knew the circumstances well enough not to need further clarification, and the same allusiveness is true of most ancient letters."[25] The vague references in 3 John imply that the author has had previous contact with Gaius and this may imply "a fairly close network of church groups."[26] By contrast, in those passages in the Gospel of John where the author seems to be directly addressing the reader and consciously highlighting the act of writing, there is "little or no use of *ellipsis* or 'vague references' to suggest that close *contact* exists between author and readers."[27] So, for example, in John 2:21–22, the author makes it quite explicit that when Jesus spoke of the temple being destroyed and raised up in three days, he is referring to "the temple of his body" and that this only became clear to the disciples after the resurrection. There is no assumption that the readers or hearers will understand. Indeed, as Wendy North has observed, the author of the Gospel is at pains to provide explanations: "when it comes to getting his message across to his readers, John is a born pedant; everything necessary is explicitly communicated, false impressions are carefully ruled out, and nothing is left to chance."[28]

Of course, this still leaves us with the somewhat paradoxical possibility that the Gospel derives from a narrow sectarian group, a closed Johannine community, which nevertheless intended its core text for a wide audience. This raises the distinction between the *idiolect* of an individual author and the *sociolect* of a group and here we move into the realm of stylistics. The linguist David Crystal defines *idiolect* as, "A term used in linguistics to refer to the linguistic system of an individual speaker—one's personal dialect" and adds that, "Idiolectal features are particularly noticeable in literary writing, as stylistic markers of authorship."[29] There have been a number of studies of variation in language as a result of individual style rather than *context of situation*, but such studies depend for their validity on a corpus of material with closely defined situational parameters.[30] For the Gospel of John the only corpus we can credibly use for such comparison is the Synoptic Gospels, which have the same subject matter written in the same language at roughly the same time. Many scholars have noted the Gospel of John's distinctive language, noting such stylistic features as the use of repetition, or rather repetition with variety, and the simplicity of its lexico-grammatical choices.[31] Such observations are usually made in comparison with the Synoptics (and/or 1 John), but whether we can determine on a purely linguistic basis if the style of the Gospel is the product of a particular individual or a distinct Gospel community is problematic. We do not have a sufficient corpus of material to make a significant comparative study.[32] Moreover, even if it is the work of a particular individual, we have no reason for thinking that this individual was some kind of hermit, unattached to a variety of social groups.[33] Maybe the author was a "towering theologian" (to borrow Hengel's phrase),[34] but this need not imply a solitary figure. It seems eminently possible that the author's characteristic style (*idiolect*) was developed in conversation with others in a process of reflection over a long period. Language is social phenomenon. However, we do not have linguistic evidence for the *sociolect* of a closed Johannine community, which leads me to question the claim that the Gospel contains the *antilanguage* of an *antisociety*, as I consider in the next section.

ANTILANGUAGE

One of the chapters in *Text, Context and the Johannine Community* is "The Antilanguage Antisociety: The Contribution of Sociological Commentators." In this chapter, I traced how a number of Johannine scholars used a particular interpretation by Bruce Malina of an essay by Halliday in order to maintain that the language of the Gospel contains the "anti-language" of an "anti-society."[35] I suggested that Malina and subsequent scholars have fundamentally altered Halliday's thesis. In particular, I focused on two of the terms which Halliday used: *relexicalization* and *overlexicalization*. The basic understanding behind these terms is that certain groups within a society, who

52   *David A. Lamb*

wish to set themselves apart as "antisocieties," adapt that society's language
to produce new words or expressions (*relexicalization*) and that, for areas
important to these groups, they create many different expressions for the
same thing (*overlexicalization*).[36] I argued that these terms have been applied
to the Gospel with insufficient supporting evidence by scholars.

However, one of the scholars I highlighted for his use of the term *antilanguage*, Philip Esler, has responded vigorously to my critique regarding
relexicalization and *overlexicalization*.[37] He takes particular issue with my
observation that for Halliday *relexicalization* means the creation of "new
words," that is "a different vocabulary" in areas "that are central to the
activities of the subculture and that set it off most sharply from the established society" (Halliday's words, not mine).[38] Esler is insistent that Halliday
also includes new meanings for existing words, although I suggest that of the
three examples Esler gives to support his case, two would seem to be com-
binations of existing words to form novel terminology ("counterfeit crank"
and "bawdy basket").[39] He goes on to say that, "there is abundant evidence
in addition to that which Halliday mentions that anti-societies generate much
of their anti-language by attributing new meanings to existing words and not
just by creating new words." However, this "abundant evidence" is limited
to Malina and Rohrbaugh's use of the Omaha Police Department's *Gang
Slang Dictionary*.[40] Finally, Esler states, "social-scientific interpretation has
never been wedded to the unchanging use of a social-scientific perspective
in its original formulation; it has always been open to the need to modify
ideas in the light of the data."[41] If by this, he means that those who employ
social-scientific methodologies in NT interpretation are free to adapt these
methodologies, then to some extent I agree, provided there is data to support
the proposed modifications and that the impression is not given that their new
interpretation is widely accepted. There has been a considerable increase in
the literature on antilanguage in linguistics, literary theory and cultural theory
over recent years, but none of the studies I have read support the understanding of *antilanguage* found in those who have followed Malina's lead.[42]

The primary indicator of antilanguage is a playing with the standard language in novel ways and this is not the same as the widely recognized observation that the language in John frequently works on two levels: an everyday,
common meaning and a deeper spiritual reality.[43] Thus, David Ford, in his
recent "theological commentary," speaks of the "'deep plain sense'—the way
John uses carefully chosen ordinary words that turn out to have unfathomable
depths."[44]

Moreover, Esler does not engage with my more fundamental criticism that
if there were examples of antilanguage in the Gospel, that is the creation of a
new form of speech unavailable to those outside of the user group, reinforc-
ing the "us and them" barrier, then how do we access this speech world?

The Language of John 53

This point is echoed by Laura Hunt: "An antilanguage is, by definition, not understandable to those outside the community."[45]

A major recent essay on antilanguage is that of the linguists Natalie Lefkowitz and John S. Hedgcock, which focuses on the language play element and draws on their research on a variety of speech communities, such as users of *Verlan*, a French youth sociolect characterized by the inversion of syllables in words (e.g., "ziquemu" for "musique").[46] The features of antilanguage which Lefkowitz and Hedgcock highlight are: phonological and morphological innovation; relexicalization and overlexicalization; lexical borrowing (from outside the standard language); formal simplification (e.g., the use of abbreviations); taboo language (e.g., obscenities); and registerial blurring and crossover (i.e., violating appropriate norms for register choices).[47] In the light of Lefkowitz and Hedgcock's study and other recent research on antilanguage and its application to a range of sociolects, I am left wondering what significant (significant, that is, to the envisaged Johannine community) new forms of language are used in the Johannine writings to indicate an "anti-society." What "us and them" language is there that represents an "insider/outsider" relationship toward other Jewish, Gentile, and Christian groups? The only newly coined expression which might fit this description is ἀποσυνάγογος, a much-discussed term in Johannine scholarship.[48] In the Epistles there are the terms ἀντίχριστος and ἀντίχριστοι. Beyond these possibilities, there are, I think, no other lexical or discourse features of John's language that sociolinguists would recognize as examples of antilanguage. Whereas what Malina and others seem to be suggesting is that common terms such as "love" and "truth" have an antilanguage slant in John, indicative of an antisociety. Such an understanding is quite distinct from studies outside Johannine scholarship and may well derive from the "pre-theoretical motivations that underlie the coming-into-being of the [Johannine Community] paradigm," as Andrew Basden suggests in his recent study of research methods that uses my work as one of his case studies.[49]

In conclusion, what am I to make of Esler's assertion that his argument has "fatally undermined" my critique? I can only encourage people to read Halliday's original essay, to look at some of the more recent applications of the concept of antilanguage in the fields of linguistics and literature, and then decide for themselves whether this is an appropriate term to use for John's language. (A helpful brief presentation of antilanguage, written by David Robson, a feature writer for *BBC Future*, can be found online.[50]) If they do this, then I believe that they will agree with me that the meaning of antilanguage in Johannine scholarship has taken a novel trajectory, with an emphasis on dualism, metaphor and riddles that could be as much indicative of an idiolect as a sociolect. So, at best, we can say that Malina and those following him were inspired by Halliday's essay on antilanguages and borrowed

54 *David A. Lamb*

some of his terminology, but they have taken the idea in an entirely different direction from its development in sociolinguistics and other fields. There is, in fact, no sociolinguistic support for antilanguage in the Gospel or for modeling the Johannine community as an antisociety.

TEXTUAL COMMUNITY

Although I do not see any linguistic evidence for a community in the Gospel of John itself, I think that some case can be made for a group that formed after the composition of the Gospel and whose existence may be inferred from the Epistles, particularly 2 and 3 John. As stated earlier, in *Text, Context and the Johannine Community*, I drew on the work of Brian Stock to propose a community that is "a loose network, an embryonic *textual community* or 'reading and interpretative community.'"[51] However, I did not develop this idea and I think it may be helpful to reconsider it.

Stock's notion of textual communities was introduced in his *magnum opus*, *The Implications of Literacy* (1983), which considered the complex relationship between orality and literacy and the impact of written texts on cultural life in Western Europe in the eleventh and twelfth centuries (the high Middle Ages).[52] One focus of this work is on certain heretical and reformist religious groups arising in this period, which Stock defines as "textual communities," in that they are formed around the interpretation of particular texts, irrespective of the levels of literacy among individual members of these communities.[53] Stock concludes:

> Eleventh-century dissenters may not have shared profound doctrinal similarities or common social origins, but they demonstrated a parallel use of texts, both to structure the internal behaviour of the groups' members and to provide solidarity against the outside world . . . In this sense they were "textual communities." . . . What was essential to a textual community was not a written version of a text, although that was sometimes present, but an individual, who, having mastered it, then utilized it for reforming a group's thought and action.[54]

In *Listening for the Text*, a collection of essays published in 1990, Stock returns to the notion of textual communities, considering its theoretical foundations and also its possible application to "religious changes of the first six centuries after Christ," given that it was "invented to deal with medieval evidence."[55] He defines textual communities as "microsocieties organized around the common understanding of a script" and summarizes the process whereby a group of listeners to a text become educated and institutionalized into a community with "rules of membership."[56] However, Stock believes

The Language of John 55

that as expectations of literacy were significantly higher in antiquity compared with the high Middle Ages, his original scheme has to be modified.[57] In particular, whereas "in the Middle Ages, the text often started up the community," "in antiquity, the community preceded the critical text."[58] This needs to be understood correctly, for it might seem to support the idea that the Gospel of John derives from an existing community. However, somewhat confusingly, the "community" that Stock has in mind here is the "already existing self-conscious tradition" of Jewish and Christian history in which the interpretation of a particular text is part of its continuing storytelling, so that "the textual community . . . in this instance, may comprise the whole of a people."[59] It is true that Stock does reflect, in dialogue with Wayne Meeks's *The First Urban Christians*, on the Pauline churches as examples of textual communities with respect to "the textually organized education of the members in the groups," but it is not clear what "text" Stock has in mind here (the Hebrew scriptures? oral tradition? Paul's letters? the "Word," that is, Jesus?) or whether he envisages these churches as producing their own texts.[60] I suggest that there are in fact various unresolved ambiguities in Stock's application of the notion of textual communities to early Christianity.

Nevertheless, Stock's notion has been taken up by a number of NT scholars. Notably, in *Christian Identity in the Jewish and Graeco-Roman World* (2004), Judith Lieu refers to Stock to support her argument that "even before the invention of printing, written traditions could forge distinctive forms of community aware of their separation from the rest of the world," and she describes, "the early Christian communities as to a high degree 'textual communities,' centred around and shaped by the interpretation of particular texts."[61] Lieu makes specific mention of the "Johannine community" as an example of this process of interpretation, but it seems that she is referring primarily to its interpretation of the Hebrew scriptures and the conflict between Jewish and Johannine understandings.[62]

Regarding the Gospel of John, I am aware of a number of other authors who have used the term textual community. Esther Kobel (2011) follows Lieu's lead and states, "A 'textual community' refers to an interpretative community but it is also a social entity" and, as such, it "seems a helpful concept for thinking of the community behind the Fourth Gospel."[63] Ruth Sheridan (2015) believes that Stock's concept "has some usefulness for describing the so-called 'Johannine community'" and she understands the Prologue as an "exegetical narrative" that "evokes and forms a new reading community."[64] This is an "exclusive textual community," which distances itself from the voices of others.[65] Adele Reinhartz (2018), despite her "agnosticism about a historical Johannine community," also draws on Stock's work to suggest, "One cannot, however, rule out the possibility that the Gospel of John created a 'textual community' that was not only an interpretive community centered on this version of Jesus's story, but also a social entity."[66]

In view of applications such as these, I agree with Jane Heath, who, in a significant critical study of Stock's thinking (2018), states that "textual community" has become "something of a buzz term in recent years."[67] Heath analyses the work of a number of recent scholars who have used the term in studies of Christian, Jewish, and pagan antiquity and highlights some of the ambiguities of Stock's definition as well as the problems of its application to a diverse range of case studies. She argues that, "A model that is very flexible is always a risk, lest it be applied too readily to everything, such that it ceases to clarify anything at all."[68] She also perceptively notes that the expressions "textual" and "community" are highly appealing to scholars of religion and that "we feel as though talking of 'textual communities' makes sense, even if in reality it may be homogenising and simplifying complex social and religious phenomena."[69] She concludes, "On the whole, then, I regard the language of 'textual community' as problematic, and the concept it articulates as ill defined."[70] However, she does acknowledge that Stock's idea raises the important question of "*What does a text* do *in society, and how?*"[71]

As a "Theological Coda" to her essay, Heath helpfully draws on two images from Christian tradition: the "book of the heart" in monastic culture and Jesus as the perfect embodiment of the text.[72] I see in these images something of the ambiguity of the Gospel's own self-presentation, with its emphasis on the written text (ταῦτα δὲ γέγραπται, "these things are written . . . ," John 20:31) alongside an awareness of the limitations of the written word (21:25) in contrast to the one who is "the Word" of God (1:1, 14). So, in light of Heath's essay, it is important to consider afresh my own understanding of a "Johannine community" possibly reflected in the Epistles and, in particular, whether it is founded on the text of the Gospel or on the interpreter/s of that text or, as Heath suggests, on the person of Jesus as the embodiment of the text.

My own understanding of a "Johannine community" relates to the linguistic parallels between the Gospel and Epistles in both lexico-grammatical and discourse features, features which have long been noted. As Schnackenburg states, "there is an unmistakable 'Johannine' style, which shows itself as clearly in the epistles as in the Gospel."[73] These parallels do not necessarily imply common authorship by a particular individual and, indeed, they are seen by some scholars as a major argument for the existence of a Johannine community, so that Martinus de Boer writes, "the existence of the three canonical Letters of John alongside the Gospel of John provides *prima facie* support for the existence of such a community."[74] Of course, this requires that we accept that there is some historical connection between the Gospel and the Epistles that is the more than the "literary invention" that Hugo Méndez proposes.[75] My own analysis proposed stylistic similarities but differing registers: the register of the Gospel does not suggest a community; the Epistles, especially 2 and 3 John, do suggest some sort of group dynamic. However, I see limits to the benefit of applying Stock's textual community model to a hypothetical Johannine community, because his case studies imply that such a community exhibits distinctive behavior and ritual (the "rules of membership") linked to the interpretation of a specific text.[76] This may indeed be what many Johannine commentators envisage: a Johannine church shaped by its "us" against "them" mentality (whether "them" is the Jews, other Christian groups, or "the world" in general). So, would the Johannine community's reading of the text of the Gospel have resulted in forms of behavior and ritual that were distinct from other early Christian groups? Maybe celebrating the Lord's Supper on a different day of the week? Or else avoiding "sacraments" altogether and relying on Spirit-led forms of worship?[77] We have no evidence for such a Johannine group, yet this, it seems to me, is what Stock's model requires. So, I am led more to the idea of a "loose network" of Johannine Christians or a Johannine "reading and interpretative community" reflected in the Epistles. Stock uses the label "reading and interpretative communities" for rabbinic groups involved in the exegesis of Scripture, the Mishnah and "theological problems arising from the Jewish tradition."[78] They differ from textual communities as their "differing interpretations do not issue in rule-bound patterns of behavior that break with what has come before."[79]

I suggested in *Text, Context and the Johannine Community* that such a community may have arisen partly to maintain the authority of the Gospel as scripture.[80] I agree with Charles Hill that there is little or no evidence that the Gospel was regarded as heterodox in the early second century: it did not "snake its independent way through the period as a maverick and unaccompanied force."[81] However, as Hill suggests, there may have been some hesitancy in the acceptance of John, not because of a questioning of its orthodoxy, but because of its "narrative departures from the Synoptic Gospels."[82]

Nevertheless, even if there was a network of those who championed the Gospel in the face of some reluctance to accept it as authoritative and who adopted some of its linguistic features in their own writings, I am far less certain that this late first century/early second century "Johannine community" would have had rituals and liturgy noticeably distinct from other early Christian groups. Its focus would have been on the person who embodied their particular text, the same person who embodied the other Gospels, Jesus Christ.

58   *David A. Lamb*

CONCLUSIONS

In *Text, Context and the Johannine Community*, I drew on insights from sociolinguistics, specifically register analysis, to conclude that the Gospel of John was not written for a closed community, but that there may have been a "Johannine community" in the limited sense of a group which formed around the Gospel and which is reflected in the Epistles. I called this an embryonic *textual community*, drawing on Brian Stock's terminology. In this chapter, I have sought to address some of the issues raised by those who have responded to my register analysis of the Johannine writings and what it might indicate about such a community. I have looked again at my model of register analysis, its relation to *idiolect* and *sociolect*, and the use of the term *antilanguage* in Johannine scholarship. I have also reconsidered the appropriateness of the label *textual community* in the light of Jane Heath's recent critical study. In the course of my reexamination, I have stressed a number of matters:

- It is important to read the Johannine writings primarily as documents intended to communicate an *interpersonal* message and not treat them simply as sites for historical excavation. In this respect, it is best to focus on the final form of the text as we have it, rather than starting with the speculative attempt to isolate sources.
- The application of insights from contemporary sociolinguistic theory need not be obscure, inappropriate, or anachronistic, provided we make allowance for changes in language use across time and culture and we are cautious in our conclusions. It is also vital that such an interdisciplinary approach does not "blind with science," but that it makes itself accessible to a wide readership within NT scholarship.
- Conclusions about a *context of situation* for the Johannine writings, based on sociolinguistic analysis, can only be in terms of certain parameters, that is, what their lexico-grammatical and discourse features imply about the *power* in relationships, the *contact*, and the *affective involvement* between the author/s and intended readers. We do not possess the appropriate situationally annotated corpus of texts for comparative study which would lead to greater precision. This may be frustrating for those who want a fuller reconstruction of the Johannine writing's specific social context, but I think we have to be honest about limitations.

So, what sort of community are we left with from this simplified, cross-cultural sociolinguistic analysis of the Johannine texts? First, I would say that, despite Philip Esler's protestations, there is no evidence for a sectarian group lying behind the Gospel's production, an *anti-community* with its

The Language of John   59

own *antilanguage*. Indeed, the Gospel's literary construction and essential unity of style seem to point toward it being primarily the work of one person, an *idiolect* rather than a *sociolect*. On the other hand, an analysis of the language of the Epistles, specifically 2 and 3 John, does seem to imply a group of associates, a "community" in a very broad sense, that may have grown up around a particular interpretation of the Gospel. As Paul Anderson states in his modification of Raymond Brown's model, "The idea that the Johannine situation was *always* a community is flawed."[83]

However, I am now doubtful whether this broad community, reflected in the language of the Epistles, can be labeled a "textual community" in view of Stock's depiction of such a community as issuing in distinctive behavior and ritual linked to the interpretation of a specific text. We have no external evidence for such a Johannine group. This is not to deny that the writers of the Gospel and the Epistles belonged to Christian groups that had disputes with other groups, as the Epistles indicate, but we do not have evidence that these theological disputes resulted in behaviors and ritual (such as liturgy) that could be considered as distinctly "Johannine." Hence, my frustration with Raymond Brown's *The Community of the Beloved Disciple*, much as I admire this great scholar. So, it seems to me that Stock's alternative category of a "reading and interpretative community" is a more appropriate designation. This was the tentative conclusion I reached in *Text, Context and the Johannine Community* and now I am more convinced of it.[84] I envisage a collection of associates who wished to promote the Gospel of John's value as "scripture," a group that was aware of the differences of "their" gospel from other accounts of the ministry of Jesus (the Synoptics), but which was also aware that the true Gospel is more than any one written text. The "paper and ink" of this group's letters only have a certain value (2 John 12; cf. 3 John 13).

Support for this broad Johannine community that was not restricted to a particular brand of Christianity is found in a recent essay by Rikard Roitto, who employs *social network analysis* to the Epistles to conclude that "Johannine Christianity must have been a rather open-ended network . . . a loose heterogenous network of assemblies in contact with other forms of Christianity."[85] This, I think, is a reasonable understanding of a Johannine community and one that is supported by my own sociolinguistic reading of the texts.

NOTES

1. Raymond E. Brown, *The Community of the Beloved Disciple* (New York: Paulist Press, 1979).

2. Edward W. Klink III, *The Sheep of the Fold: The Audience and Origin of the Gospel of John*, SNTSMS 141 (Cambridge: Cambridge University Press, 2007), 52–53. Klink here draws on the work of the sociologist Joseph Gusfield.

3. See, e.g., the recent comprehensive work of Dean Furlong, *The Identity of John the Evangelist: Revision and Reinterpretation in Early Christian Sources* (Lanham, MD: Lexington/Fortress Academic, 2020).

4. I am referring here to J. Louis Martyn, *History and Theology in the Fourth Gospel*, third ed. (Louisville: Abingdon, 2003 [1968]); Raymond E. Brown, *The Gospel According to John*, 2 vols., AB 29–29A (New York: Doubleday, 1966–70); idem, *The Epistles of John*, AB 30 (New York: Doubleday, 1982), in addition to Brown, *Community*.

5. A recent and detailed such "history" of the Johannine community is Paul Anderson's reworking of Brown's model: Paul N. Anderson, "The Community that Raymond Brown Left Behind: Reflections on the Johannine Dialectical Situation," in *Communities in Dispute: Current Scholarship on the Johannine Epistles*, ed. R. Alan Culpepper and Paul N. Anderson, ECL 13 (Atlanta: SBL Press, 2014), 47–93. Anderson sees his outline as correcting some of the weaknesses of Brown's model, for example, by giving more emphasis to the demands of Roman Emperor worship (79–82). He rejects the view of Meeks and others that the community is highly sectarian, e.g., compared to the Qumran community (80 n. 27).

6. See Edward W. Klink III, "Gospel Audience and Origin: The Current Debate," in *The Audience of the Gospels: The Origin and Function of the Gospels in Early Christianity*, ed. Edward W. Klink, LNTS 353 (London: T & T Clark, 2010), 13.

7. See David A. Lamb, *Text, Context and the Johannine Community: A Sociolinguistic Analysis of the Johannine Writings*, LNTS 477 (London: Bloomsbury/T & T Clark, 2014).

8. Lamb, *Text, Context*, 100–101. The reference is to Douglas Biber and Susan Conrad, *Register, Genre, and Style*, Cambridge Textbooks in Linguistics (Cambridge: Cambridge University Press, 2009), 68.

9. Lamb, *Text, Context*, 95, 197. See Cate Poynton, *Language and Gender: Making the Difference*, second ed. (Oxford: Oxford University Press, 1989), 76–78. Poynton adapted her categorization from the influential paper of Brown and Gilmore on "The Pronouns of Power and Solidarity" (1960) and applied it to her argument that the use of language contributes to differences and inequality between men and women.

10. Lamb, *Text, Context*, 209. The citation is from Brian Stock, *Listening for the Text: On the Uses of the Past* (Philadelphia: University of Pennsylvania Press, 1990), 156.

11. Attridge concludes, "However one may view the results of his analytical effort, his careful critique of a strand of recent scholarship on John is extremely valuable." Harold W. Attridge, review of *Text, Context and the Johannine Community*, by David A. Lamb, *CBQ* 78 (2016): 557. Wendy North states that "this book makes a significant contribution to the present debate." Wendy E. S. North, review of *Text, Context and the Johannine Community*, by David A. Lamb, *RBL* 07/2015. David Ford notes his attraction to my "plea for caution" in modeling the Johannine community. David F. Ford, *The Gospel of John: A Theological Commentary* (Grand Rapids, MI: Baker

The Language of John 61

Academic, 2021), 41 n. 17. See also Andrew Basden, *Foundations and Practice of Research: Adventures with Dooyeweerd's Philosophy*, Routledge Advances in Research Methods (Abingdon: Routledge, 2020), 136–38, 152–54.

12. In a fairly lengthy critique, Wally Cirafesi, while supporting a sociolinguistic approach and agreeing with my conclusions, makes it clear that, in his view I have misunderstood or misrepresented aspects of Hallidayan SFL, so that my analysis "has numerous problems and deficiencies" and "lacks principle and theoretical robustness." Wally V. Cirafesi, "The 'Johannine Community' in (More) Current Research: A Critical Appraisal of Recent Methods and Models," *Neot* 48 (2014): 355, 356. Similarly Zachary Dawson states, "those who are familiar with modern linguistic theory, especially SFL, will find Lamb's model lacking." Zachary K. Dawson, review of *Text, Context and the Johannine Community*, by David A. Lamb, *Dialogismos* 1 (2016) 4. Hughson Ong is also critical of my use of the "Hallidayan register analysis framework." Hughson T. Ong, *The Multilingual Jesus and the Sociolinguistic World of the New Testament*, LBS 12 (Leiden: Brill, 2016), 90.

13. "In the end, Lamb is not able to make any strong assertions regarding the community behind the Gospel (or the lack thereof). His work does not provide the foundation for a new consensus on the Gospel context, but merely undermines some of the flawed evidence." Christopher Seglenieks, review of *Text, Context and the Johannine Community*, by David A. Lamb, *Colloquium* 50 (2018): 110.

14. See, e.g., Alison Rotha Moore, "Register Analysis in Systemic Functional Linguistics," in *The Routledge Handbook of Systemic Functional Linguistics,* ed. Tom Bartlett and Gerard O'Grady (Abingdon: Routledge, 2017), 418–37. Moore points out that "there has been surprisingly little explication and testing of Halliday's specific view of register" (418).

15. Nicholas J. Ellis, "Biblical Exegesis and Linguistics: *A Prodigal History*," in *Linguistics and New Testament Greek: Key Issues in the Current Debate*, ed. David Alan Black and Benjamin L. Merkle (Grand Rapids: Baker Academic, 2020), 244.

16. Seglenieks, review of *Text, Context*, 110.

17. Matthiessen, who in many ways has taken over the mantle from Halliday, describes register as "one of the absolutely central properties of language": Christian M. I. M. Matthiessen, "Register in Systemic Functional Linguistics," *Register Studies* 1.1 (2019): 11.

18. For a helpful overview of register, see the editorial article launching a new journal devoted to register studies: Bethany Gray and Jesse Egbert, "Editorial: Register and Register Variation," *Register Studies* 1.1 (2019): 1–3.

19. The danger of anachronism and the need for caution in historical linguistics, including in relation to social networks, is considered by the linguist Alexander Bergs, who points out some of the limitations of applying the "Uniformitarian Principle" to social sciences. Alexander Bergs, "The Uniformitarian Principle and the Risk of Anachronisms in Language and Social History," in *The Handbook of Historical Sociolinguistics*, ed. Juan M Hernández-Campoy and J. Camilo Conde-Silvestre (John Wiley & Sons, 2012), 80–98.

20. Of course, some commentators detect a variety of "voices" in the Gospel of John and possibly even contradictory "voices." See, e.g., Charles W. Hedrick,

"Authorial Presence and Narrator in John: Commentary and Story," in *Gospel Origins and Christian Beginnings: In Honor of James M. Robinson*, ed. James E. Goehring, Charles W. Hedrick, Jack T. Sanders and Hans Dieter Betz (Sonoma, CA: Polebridge, 1990), 74–93.

21. As Despotis correctly points out, my own "conclusion would be better attested from a broader textual basis." Athanasios Despotis, review of *Text, Context and the Johannine Community*, by David A. Lamb, *RelSRev* 42.1 (2016): 44. North also says that I use "too small a sample size" (review of *Text, Context*).

22. Matthew Brook O'Donnell, *Corpus Linguistics and the Greek of the New Testament*, NTM 6 (Sheffield: Sheffield Phoenix Press, 2005), 132–37, 164–65.

23. I also observe that in the case of the Gospels, O'Donnell follows Richard Burridge in allocating them to the genre of biography (βίος) and chooses texts such as Plutarch, *Cato Minor* for comparison. However, I would question whether this is an appropriate genre for the Gospel of John. See David A. Lamb and Thora Tenbrink, "Evaluating Jesus and Other 'Heroes': An Application of Appraisal Analysis to Hellenistic Greek Texts in the 'Lives' Genre," *Language, Context and Text* 4.2 (2022): 227–58.

24. Bernard P. Grenfell and Arthur S. Hunt (eds.), *The Oxyrhynchus Papyri: Part II* (London: Egypt Exploration Fund, 1899), 296.

25. Judith M. Lieu, *I, II, & III John*, NTL (Louisville: Westminster John Knox Press, 2008), 266.

26. Lamb, *Text, Context*, 195. As Justin Marc Smith states, from a genre perspective, "The letter or epistle genre would seem to be the most obvious genre through which to disseminate biographical or narrative information to a definite audience group." Justin Mark Smith, *Why Βίος? On the Relationship between Gospel Genre and Implied Audience*, LNTS 518 (London: Bloomsbury/T & T Clark, 2014), 13 n. 41. Although he does point out that writers such as the Apostle Paul and Pliny the Younger may also have a wider audience in view.

27. Lamb, *Text, Context*, 172.

28. Wendy E. S. North, *A Journey Round John: Tradition, Interpretation and Context in the Fourth Gospel*, LNTS 534 (London: Bloomsbury/T & T Clark, 2015), 149.

29. David Crystal, *A Dictionary of Linguistics and Phonetics*, sixth ed. (Oxford: Blackwell, 2008), 235.

30. One example is a recent study of the spoken output of US White House press secretaries, where an analysis of a wide range of lexico-grammatical features indicate clear idiolect differences in a shared context of situation. See Michael Barlow, "Individual differences and usage-based grammar," *International Journal of Corpus Linguistics* 18 (2013): 443–78. Another corpus study, this time using lemmata (words and their inflected forms) from particular semantic domains in literary texts and comparing the works of the Realist authors George Eliot and Charles Dickens and the Modernists Virginia Woolf and James Joyce, proves inconclusive in highlighting idiolects. The authors suggest that this may be owing to the "literary" nature of the texts they analyze. See Max M. Louwerse, "Semantic Variation in Idiolect and Sociolect: Corpus Linguistic Evidence from Literary Texts," *Computers and the*

Humanities 38 (2004): 207–21. It is also the case that it is difficult to define the situational parameters of such literary texts.

31. In his overview of the Gospel's "Language, Style, Movement of Thought," Schnackenburg emphasizes the simplicity, but also solemnity of the language. Rudolf Schnackenburg, *The Gospel According to St. John*, trans. Kevin Smyth, 3 vols. (London, Burns & Oates, 1968, 1980, 1982), 1:111–2. Cf. Craig S. Keener, *The Gospel of John: A Commentary*, 2 vols. (Peabody, MA: Hendrickson, 2003), 1:47–49.

32. Rodney Decker has considered certain grammatical features in assessing the idiolect of Mark's Gospel in comparison with the other Gospels and a selection of OT narrative texts, but he admits that "our sample sets are far too small to place a high degree of probability on our judgments." Decker is referring here specifically to his judgements concerning textual criticism, but the problem applies equally to the other areas he considers. See Rodney J. Decker, "Markan Idiolect in the Study of the Greek of the New Testament," in *The Language of the New Testament: Context, History, and Development*, ed. Stanley E. Porter and Andrew Pitts, LBS 6 (Leiden: Brill, 2013), 62.

33. See Lamb, *Text, Context*, 204.

34. Hengel states, "it seems to me unmistakable that the Gospel and the letters are not the expression of a community with many voices, but above all the voice of a towering theologian." Martin Hengel, *The Johannine Question*, trans. John Bowden (London: SCM, 1989), ix. Hengel nevertheless envisages this "towering theologian" as "the founder and head of the Johannine school" (ix).

35. Lamb, *Text, Context*, 103–44, referring to Bruce J. Malina, *The Gospel of John in Sociolinguistic Perspective*, 48th Colloquy of the Center for Hermeneutical Studies (Berkley, CA: Center for Hermeneutical Studies, 1985). The essay by Halliday was first published as "Anti-languages" in *American Anthropologist* 78 (1976): 570–84. It reappears as a chapter in one of his most influential works: Michael A. K. Halliday, *Language as Social Semiotic: The Social Interpretation of Meaning* (London: Arnold, 1978), 164–82; and in his collected works: Michael A. K. Halliday, *Language and Society: Volume 10 of the Collected Works of M. A. K. Halliday*, ed. Jonathan J. Webster (London: Continuum, 2007), 265–86. An example of the use of Malina's interpretation of Halliday subsequent to the publication of *Text, Context* is Ruth Sheridan, "Johannine Sectarianism: A Category Now Defunct?" in *The Origins of John's Gospel*, ed. Stanley E. Porter and Hughson T. Ong, Johannine Studies 2 (Leiden: Brill, 2016), 159–63.

36. Halliday, *Language as Social Semiotic*, 165.

37. Philp F. Esler, "Social-Scientific Readings of the Gospel and Letters of John," in *The Oxford Handbook of Johannine Studies*, ed. Judith M. Lieu and Martinus C. de Boer (Oxford: Oxford University Press, 2018), 237–58.

38. Halliday, *Language as Social Semiotic*, 165.

39. Esler, "Social-Scientific Readings," 243. In fact, in *Text, Context and the Johannine Community*, I pointed out that relexicalization *can* include new meanings for existing words (133 n. 144), but this is certainly not the main way that Halliday and other sociolinguists have understood the term.

40. Esler, "Social-Scientific Readings," 243; cf. 241–42. See Bruce J. Malina, and Richard L. Rohrbaugh, *Social-Science Commentary on the Gospel of John* (Minneapolis: Fortress, 1998).

41. Esler, "Social-Scientific Readings," 243.

42. In *Text, Context and the Johannine Community*, I noted its application to such diverse sociolects as hip-hop raps; Cockney rhyming slang; Rastafarian poetry; underground language in Communist-era Poland; gang graffiti in the Phoenix, Arizona, metropolitan area; language of the press in post-Communist Bulgaria; working-class Afrikaans; and South African township argots (Lamb, *Text, Context*, 116 n. 58; 138 n. 163). It has also been applied to the use of *Polari* in gay subculture; the gang language, *Nadsat*, in Anthony Burgess's *A Clockwork Orange*; cyber scammers in Nigeria; and various African urban youth languages; among others. See Paul Baker, *Fabulosa! The Story of Polari, Britain's Secret Gay Language* (London: Reaktion Books, 2019), 17–18; Benet Vincent and Jim Clarke, "The Language of *A Clockwork Orange*: A Corpus Stylistic Approach to Nadsat," *Language and Literature* 26 (2017): 247–64; Temitope Michael Ajayi, "Anti-language, Slang and Cyber Scam Subculture among Urban Youth in Southwestern Nigeria," *International Journal of Cyber Criminology* 13 (July–December 2019): 511–33; Andrea Hollington and Nico Nassenstein, "From the Hood to Public Discourse: The Social Spread of African Youth Languages," *Anthropological Linguistics* 59 (2017): 390–413.

43. Brant makes the distinction between Malina and Rohrbaugh's antilanguage approach and the use of metaphoric language. Her choice, as for most commentators, is for the latter. See Jo-Ann A. Brant, *John*, Paideia (Grand Rapids: Baker Academic, 2011), 96. In her earlier work *Dialogue and Drama*, she does seem to speak of the Gospel's distinctive language in terms of antilanguage (if I read her correctly), but then proceeds to say that its language is closer to that of ancient Greek tragedy. Jo-Ann A. Brant, *Dialogue and Drama: Elements of Greek Tragedy in the Fourth Gospel* (Peabody, MA: Hendrickson, 2004), 2–3.

44. Ford, *Gospel*, 434.

45. Laura J. Hunt, *Jesus Caesar: A Roman Reading of the Johannine Trial Narrative* (Tübingen: Mohr Siebeck, 2019), 19.

46. Natalie Lefkowitz and John S. Hedgcock, "Anti-Language: Linguistic Innovation, Identity Construction, and Group Affiliation among Emerging Speech Communities," in *Multiple Perspectives in Language Play*, ed. Nancy Bell, Language Play and Creativity 1 (Boston: De Gruyter Mouton, 2017), 347–76.

47. Lefkowitz and Hedgcock, "Anti-language," 349–50.

48. The word does not necessarily originate with the author/s of the Gospel. J. Andrew Doole provides linguistic arguments for his view that the term ἀποσυνάγωγος "must have been coined and used by a Greek-speaking synagogue community for people with a negative relationship to the group." J. Andrew Doole, "To Be 'An Out-of-the Synagoguer,'" *JSNT* 43 (2021): 399. It was only subsequently that this intended slur was adopted by outsiders and worn as a badge of honour. Doole concludes, "The label ἀποσυνάγωγος is not antilanguage but rather pure re-appropriation" (403).

49. Basden, *Foundations*, 153.

50. David Robson, "The Secret 'Anti-Languages' You're Not Supposed to Know," *BBC Future*, published February 12, 2016, https://www.bbc.com/future/article/20160211-the-secret-anti-languages-youre-not-supposed-to-know.

51. Lamb, *Text, Context*, 209.

52. Brian Stock, *The Implications of Literacy: Written Language and Models of Interpretation in the Eleventh and Twelfth Centuries* (Princeton, NJ: Princeton University Press, 1983).

53. Stock, *Implications*, 88–92.

54. Stock, *Implications*, 90.

55. Stock, *Listening*, 140.

56. Stock, *Listening*, 23, 150.

57. Stock, *Listening*, 151. This assertion of Stock has not gone unchallenged. See, e.g., David Brakke, "Parables and Plain Speech in the Fourth Gospel and the Apocryphon of James," *JECS* 7 (1999): 212–13. In fact, the levels of literacy in antiquity are notoriously difficult to assess. See Kim Haines-Eitzen, "Textual Communities in Late Antiquity," in *A Companion to Late Antiquity*, ed. Philip Rousseau, with the assistance of Jutta Raithal (Oxford: Wiley-Blackwell, 2009), 247–48.

58. Stock, *Listening*, 151.

59. Stock, *Listening*, 151–52.

60. Stock, *Listening*, 156–58.

61. Judith Lieu, *Christian Identity in the Jewish and Graeco-Roman World* (Oxford: Oxford University Press, 2004), 28, 300–1. Lieu also applies the term to the community associated with the Dead Sea Scrolls (34–35).

62. Lieu, Christian Identity, 41–4.

63. Esther Kobel, *Dining with John: Communal Meals and Identity Formation in the Fourth Gospel and its Historical and Cultural Context*, BInS 109 (Leiden: Brill, 2011), 32–33.

64. Ruth Sheridan, "John's Prologue as Exegetical Narrative," in *The Gospel of John as Genre Mosaic*, ed. Kasper Bro Larsen, SAN 3 (Göttingen: Vandenhoeck & Ruprecht, 2015), 188.

65. Sheridan, "John's Prologue," 189.

66. Adele Reinhartz, *Cast Out of the Covenant: Jews and Anti-Judaism in the Gospel of John* (Lanham, MD: Lexington/Fortress Academic, 2018), 151n6, 133. She cites Lieu in support of her belief that (contrary to Stock's view) even in antiquity texts could start up communities (152n7). She also notes my proposal of a "textual community" (130n67).

67. Jane Heath, "'Textual Communities': Brian Stock's Concept and Recent Scholarship on Antiquity," in *Scriptural Interpretation at the Interface between Education and Religion: In Memory of Hans Conzelmann*, ed. Florian Wilk, TBN 22 (Leiden, Brill, 2018), 15.

68. Heath, "Textual Communities," 29.

69. Heath, "Textual Communities," 30.

70. Heath, "Textual Communities," 32.

71. Heath, "Textual Communities," 32.

72. Heath, "Textual Communities," 33–34.

73. Schnackenburg, *Gospel*, 1:111. See Brown, *The Epistles of John*, 20–21, 755–59 for a comprehensive list of such features.

74. Martinus C. de Boer, "The Story of the Johannine Community and its Literature," in *The Oxford Handbook of Johannine Studies*, ed. Judith M. Lieu and Martinus C. de Boer (Oxford: Oxford University Press, 2018), 63.

75. "We have no external evidence for the network envisioned by the epistles because no such network existed." Hugo Méndez, "Did the Johannine Community Exist?" *JSNT* 42 (2020): 353.

76. Stock, *Listening*, 150.

77. Brown understood the primary characteristics of a distinct Johannine ecclesiology as its stress on the individual's relationship to Jesus and its egalitarianism (from his reading of the Gospel) and its reliance on the guidance of the Paraclete-Spirit (from his reading of the Epistles). See Raymond E. Brown, *The Churches the Apostles Left Behind* (New York: Paulist, 1984), 84–123. He does not, however, rule out a sacramental aspect to this ecclesiology (87–90).

78. Stock, *Listening*, 154.

79. Stock, *Listening*, 156.

80. Lamb, *Text, Context*, 203.

81. Charles E. Hill, *The Johannine Corpus in the Early Church* (Oxford: Oxford University Press, 2004), 475.

82. Hill, *Johannine Corpus*, 468.

83. Anderson, "Community," 61. Anderson believes that "multiple communities" developed in the later Asia Minor phase of the Johannine situation, but that there "might not have been an individuated community during its Palestinian phase" (61).

84. Lamb, *Text, Context*, 205.

85. Rikard Roitto, "The Johannine Information War: A Social Network Analysis of the Information Flow between Johannine Assemblies as Witnessed by 1–3 John," in *Drawing and Transcending Boundaries in the New Testament and Early Christianity*, ed. Jacobus Kok, Martin Webber and Jermo van Nes, BVB 38 (Zürich: LIT, 2019), 71.

Chapter 4

Disentangling "Mom's Spaghetti"

A Socio-Cognitive Approach to the Complexity of the Johannine Community

Christopher Porter

The majority of the past fifty years of Johannine scholarship has been based on background sociological models to the Fourth Gospel that have largely gone unquestioned—or at least mainly questioned in their details, rather than as a whole. Each layer of scholarship has built upon prior layers until the presumed sociological model is a completely entangled model containing layers of complicated and interrelated presumptions and conclusions. To interrogate this model, one could possibly ask the putative Johannine Community to "please stand up," although—as with this cultural reference—the referent of such a community is vague and unclear by the nature of the question.[1] Therefore, in order to interrogate the "Johannine Community" we must first attempt to disentangle the spaghetti-like sociological model that has built up on the sweater of scholarship.

Current incarnations of the primary incipient sociological model around the Johannine Community have mainly stemmed from the conflation of two sources. First, J. L. Martyn's two-level reading strategy—seeking to see some aspects of the Fourth Gospel as relating to the Jesus-era of the early first century, but many other aspects as related to the sociological context of the late first century. The second is Raymond Brown's notion of the Johannine community, hypothesizing that these late-first century readings stem from a sociologically identifiable community of the era. Upon this basis a swathe of Johannine scholarship has emerged. From Wayne Meeks' proposition of a religiously sectarian—rather than sociologically sectarian—community at the

68   *Christopher Porter*

heart of the Fourth Gospel; through to the allocation of tiers of text-critical evidence to various redactional communities in a multi-level reading strategy, such as that of Bultmann or von Wahlde. However, the problem at hand lies in the interrogation of the premise of these models. Namely, that there are definitively socially identifiable communities that lie behind each of the possible readings. To this end this chapter, rather than seek to simply dismantle each reading—thereby accruing data in support of a null-hypothesis—we will instead look at whether some of these readings are plausible, before spending the majority of the chapter looking at a socio-cognitive model of the social-construction that the Fourth Gospel is engaged in. To this end we will apply Social Identity Theory to the Fourth Gospel to build a deductive model of the social construction of the Fourth Gospel.

AN ENTANGLED SCHOLARLY BOWL

As we begin it is instructive to look briefly at two exemplars of interpretation, and how these are betrayed from within by the incipient sociological models they presume. The first model we shall investigate is that characterized by the work of Rudolf Bultmann and in later scholarship by Urban von Wahlde, and the assignment of various text-critical features in the Fourth Gospel to different redactional communities. As Bultmann expounds in his commentary on the Fourth Gospel, the Logos language and concept is unequivocally generated from a Gnostic source. As he writes "even if the reconstruction of this kind of thinking has to be carried out in the main from sources which are later than John . . . it is proved in the first place by the appearance of parallel forms of the basic ideas."[2] Thus, in Bultmann's exposition, proto-Gnosticism has been integrated into the Fourth Gospel in response to the "syncretistic Apocalyptic of Judaism [that] stands under the influence of Gnostic mythology."[3] Urban von Wahlde's commentary makes a similar sociological move, with a different orientation. As he presents it—firmly based on Martyn, Brown, and Culpepper—the Fourth Gospel consists of multiple "groups of material" each "exhibit[ing] a consistent ideological and theological orientation."[4] Each of these groups is based upon a prior group and is linked to a specific Johannine community that has generated the redactions.[5]

However, this becomes problematic as many of the supposed redactional layers in both cases do not present significant sociological distinctiveness. From a socio-cognitive perspective, redactors of each social group will be wishing to maximize inter-group positive distinctiveness, to present their social-category as distinct and superior to other social-categories. As French academic Pierre Bourdieu astutely—even axiomatically—observed: "social identity lies in difference, and difference is asserted against what is closest, which represents the greatest threat."[6] This is problematic as there is minimal evidence of distinction occurring in the redactional layers of the Gospel. While some redactions appear to be made in order to reinforce the social group, and others to harmonize oral tradition, few—if any—appear to be directed at other near-neighbor social groups. Nevertheless, those which do generate social difference are critical, and to these we shall return.

The second background observation comes from Wayne Meeks' proposal of Johannine sectarianism. In his strident essay *Man from Heaven in Johannine Sectarianism,* Meeks proposes that "One of the primary functions of the book, therefore, must have been to provide a reinforcement for the community's social identity, which appears to have been largely negative. It provided a symbolic universe which gave religious legitimacy, a theodicy, to the group's actual isolation from the larger society."[7] Thus he sees the Fourth Gospel as "describing the formation of a 'sect' of the sort we are discovering in the Johannine group."[8] To reinforce this point Meeks appeals to the sociological research of Berger and Luckmann,[9] where he finds a complementary framework for his perception of the Fourth Gospel as a sectarian tract. However, from a sociological perspective, Berger and Luckmann present little on sectarianism, rather using the term to designate sub-groups—as it is often used in social-science literature.[10] Nevertheless, for Meeks, the Fourth Gospel presents a sectarian perspective he perceives the discourse in the Fourth Gospel as relatively unintelligible for an outsider, but rather requires one to be integrated into the Johannine community to become intelligible. However, this is similarly problematic as the majority of the text presumes a shared schematic narrative based in a broadly shared Judaism, rather than one of a distinct sectarian bias.[11]

We will return to these two aspects of the theorized Johannine community throughout the rest of the chapter.

SOCIO-COGNITIVE APPROACHES

Given these challenges from incipient sociological models, it is worth introducing a robust socio-scientific approach to undergird our investigation. In the socio-scientific research on social-groups—or social-categories—arguably the most versatile approach is that of Social Identity Theory.[12] First set forth by Henri Tajfel and his protege John Turner in 1978, it recognized that while groups are indeed collectives of individuals, the social-category functions as more than the sum of its components. In their observations of social groups Tajfel and Turner noted that individuals ascribe membership to social groups where they derive "emotional and value significance."[13] Furthermore, through this social-category membership "individuals seek to achieve [significance] . . . by positively differentiating their in-group from a comparison out-group on a valued dimension."[14] It is this sense of "positive distinctiveness" that defines why people ascribe themselves to groups, and use "we" language, rather than "I" language. These early observations from Tajfel and Turner set forth the framework that would become Social Identity Theory, which has since been significantly expanded in scope and field to the broader category of Social Identity Approaches as a metatheory in use today.[15]

While many of the extensions to Social Identity Theory play a part in our understanding of social-category interaction, one is especially pertinent to our discussion here: that of the Structured Analysis of Group Arguments. To analyze how different social groups argued for their positions, and the subsequent impact on group social identity and self-categorization, Stephen Reicher and Fabio Sani sought to analyze how social groups—salient social identities—leveraged group dynamics to argue for their identity position, within existing group structures. This Structured Analysis of Group Arguments (SAGA) "sought to demonstrate that the rhetorical debates over self-categories are important because of their social-cognitive consequences."[16] Among a plethora of insights, this SAGA model highlights how social groups maximize inter-group and intra-group positive distinctiveness through the deployment of various types of group arguments. While the details of these arguments are overly complex for this discussion, in short each argument style serves to distance an out-group from the in-group—and any super-ordinate group—through the use of positive and negative descriptions of group behavior on "valued dimensions." Indeed, consonant with Reicher and Sani's intentions—and our purposes—SAGA assists us in "establishing the relationship between arguments about general category [social] identity and arguments about particular positions"[17]

The next socio-scientific aspect to consider is how to describe properly the basis—or social premise—for these group distinctiveness arguments. Indeed, these arguments are not simply abstracted concepts that seek to argue for a specific ideological position. But they are temporally situated in a particular time and space and use the history of the social group as a concrete framing point. Martha Augoustinos and Mark Rapley's work on argumentative use of schematic narratives can help us to see how these shared historical narratives are used in schematic form and deployed as part of inter- and intra-group arguments.[18] These schematic narratives, effectively the frames unlocked by a variety of mnemonic keys, provide the backdrop for the argumentative position that allows for the co-opting of contested identity markers, figures, and historical events to support the argument at hand.[19] This co-opting of shared overlapping historical narratives and identity markers serves as an attempt to either undermine or emphasize inter-group differences within the conversation and to promote in-group identity based on constructed social history.

Disentangling "Mom's Spaghetti"

Finally, these social identity arguments and constructions are cognitively construed within the range of social identity outcomes for the group, and members therein.[20] These possible future social identities are assessed as to their coherence and veracity against other options, allowing the group to opt for specific identity constructions on the basis of the group's past, present, and future. Therefore, parts of social categories may advocate for their own interpretation of the possible future for the group and envisage that as their end goal.

While there is far more within a robust socio-scientific model that could—and should—be addressed, this will have to suffice for now.

DISENTANGLING SPAGHETTI

Rather than only analyzing other models of sociological construction—effectively just gathering evidence for the null hypothesis—it will be more constructive to build a model of social-construction in the Fourth Gospel, to which we shall turn now. From our foundation in Social Identity Theory we can ask whether we may detect any sociological purpose within the Gospel. Given the purpose statement inherent within John 20:31 "these are written that you may believe that Jesus is the Messiah, the Son of God, and that by believing you may have life in his name" an initial hypothesis may be formed that there is some form of social category construction intended for the ideal audience of the Gospel. Examining the construction of this social category will further illuminate the broader social context and shed light on any putative Johannine Community.

From the perspective of a social identity model, we can look at the mechanism that the author(s) of the Fourth Gospel uses to engage the audience. The first step in this process is the identification of the shared schematic narrative that the author uses to build a background model for the social-construction work at hand. In the Fourth Gospel, this regularly takes a form that may be broadly interpreted within the framework of Judaism. This is presented at a macro level throughout the gospel, and also at a micro level the shared schematic narrative is repeatedly keyed through a series of location or temporal markers that emphasize Jewish festivals or locations in many of the scenes of the gospel.[21] A few brief examples of such smaller keys will have to suffice, even in the opening chapters we see a brief key of "Jewish purification jars" (2:6), a temporal key of it being "almost time for Jewish Passover" (πάσχα τῶν Ἰουδαίων; 2:13), a locative key of Jerusalem, the Passover itself in Jerusalem (2:23) as a key to the Nicodemus encounter, "one of the Jewish festivals" (ἦν ἑορτὴ τῶν Ἰουδαίων; 5:1), the Sheep Gate (5:2), and the key of

72 Christopher Porter

the Manna in the wilderness (6:31). Undoubtably the Fourth Gospel presents a distinctly Jewish shared schematic narrative for the events that it describes.

From this Jewish schematic narrative, the Fourth Gospel subsequently seeks to build a socially constructive narrative, and engage in identity formation in order to chase after the goal stipulated in 20:31. To this end after using the shared schematic narrative key to open a relevant frame for the audience a presenting problem is construed that engages with the both the schematic narrative and the audience to construe the super-ordinate group positively or negatively (SAGA stage 1). The Evangelist then presents the figure of Jesus to confront or resolve the problem introduced within the schematic narrative. This resolution or confrontation is often presented in two aspects as relating to the in-group and the out-group (SAGA stage 2). Finally, the Evangelist presents one or more social-category responses to the identity construction at hand.

While this pattern is repeated some fifteen times throughout the Fourth Gospel, we will examine here the first and last instances to demonstrate its utility.[22]

JOHN 2—THE CLEARING OF THE TEMPLE

In contrast to the Synoptics, the Fourth Gospel fronts the Jerusalem Temple incident and utilizes it as the basis for reading all of Jesus public ministry. The temple scene is located by a narrated chronological key associating the events with the Passover festival (2:13) and the Jerusalem Temple (2:14), which activates the cumulative memories of Passover and the associated cultic activity, along with the identity construction therein.[23] Given the likely late-first-century CE context this memorial frame would be strongly dissonant for a Jewish audience given the loss of annual remembrance linked to the destruction of the Temple.[24]

Within this cognitive frame of temple-based cultic activity the author places Jesus's temple clearing actions. To support Jesus making a whip and driving out the money changers and sacrificial animal sellers (2:15) the evangelist provides two justifications. The first is on the lips of Jesus: "Take these things out of here! Stop making my Father's house a marketplace!" (2:16), while the second presents a memorialization of Psalm 69:9: "Zeal for your house will consume me" (2:17).[25] In this action sequence the narrative provides two forms of identity construction in interaction with the broader shared schematic narrative. First, it presents Jesus as having a zealous concern for the ritual purity of the Temple precinct, and positively frames the intent of the cultic activity conducted in that place.[26] However, second, it also negatively associates the presented activity in the Temple precinct with

Disentangling "Mom's Spaghetti" 73

perceived abrogation of the intent of the place: an abrogation which must be cleared away.[27] Thus, in an environment of post-Temple destruction the intent of cultic worship is upheld, even if the reality is challenged. The narratival dissonance between these two perspectives internally culminates with the challenge from the Ἰουδαῖοι for Jesus's authority in clearing the temple: "What sign can you show us for doing this?" (2:18). The following challenge-response interchange and confusion presents the Ἰουδαῖοι as a narratively represented out-group to Jesus and the disciples.[28] Furthermore, the construal of the temple being represented by Jesus's body (2:21) functions to link the Jerusalem Temple—and associated memorial invocation—with that of Jesus and the disciples.[29] The scene closes out with a possible future social identity being presented for the audience, in the form of those who "believed in his name because they saw the signs" (2:23).[30]

From a Social Argument perspective this narrative functions as a "Type A" argument, presenting a positive assessment of super-ordinate group identity—that of ideal cultic worship in the Temple—followed by a negative evaluation of the out-group behavior—trading—and a corresponding positive evaluation of in-group actions—Jesus's zeal. This is reinforced by the possible future social identity characterized by belief because of the signs. However, this is placed in relief by the social reality of the audience, given the dissonance between the identity construction in the Temple scene and their post-Temple destruction environment. As James Dunn opines "it is hard to avoid the conclusion that John moved the account of the cleansing of the temple to beginning of the gospel narrative so as to provide a window through which the unfolding of Jesus's mission and revelation should be seen."[31] In this context Jesus-belief is presented as a social identity construction which can function as a temple replacement for an audience who associate themselves with the identity construction inherent within the Temple context.[32] This claim of identity coherence underpins the social arguments and claims of the Fourth Gospel, and therefore the social identities generated for its audience.

JOHN 18 AND 19—KINGDOM AND RULE

The other bookend of the Fourth Gospel's social identity construction takes place in the trial and crucifixion narrative of John 18 and 19. Here the construal takes on two forms, the first in the comparison of group representatives or exemplars in the interrogation scenes, and second in the narrated actions of social groups and their representatives.

The first of the prototypical exemplar confrontations comes with the discourse between the high priest and Jesus (18:19–23).[33] Here Jesus is not only construed as an individual, but also as the representative of a group which

74   Christopher Porter

includes his disciples and is gathered by the content of his teaching. For the ideal audience engaging this narrative the content of their belief about Jesus overlaps with the content of this questioning and incorporates their own social self-categorization within the frame of reference. In response the Evangelist records Jesus as reiterating the narrative of the Gospel, by not only locating its teaching content in public spaces, but also within significant structures for the super-ordinate group—and a Jewish audience—"in synagogues and in the Temple, where all the Jews gather" (18:20). The public nature of the teaching in important places of Jewish gathering reinforces the shared schematic narrative for that audience and locates it within the structures of the super-ordinate group. As Craig Keener observes, "the public nature of his teaching . . . also implicitly appeals to their failure to arrest him in public," and in comparison negatively portrays the office of the high priest.[34] This is further confirmed by the hostile response by the nearby assistant or official (18:22) that similarly dovetails with the Roman response in (19:3), and associates those representing the office of high priest as a Roman aligned out-group.[35]

Following this interrogation, the gospel bypasses the prefigured engagement with Caiaphas (18:24) in favor of a brief interlude with Simon Peter and returning to the longer exemplar engagement with Pilate (18:28). In this new scene the Evangelist again reinforces the temporal frame of Passover and its emphasis on ritual defilement, keying the memorial context for a Jewish audience: "They themselves did not enter the praetorium so as to avoid ritual defilement and to be able to eat the Passover" (18:28). In response Pilate enters into the socially liminal space outside of the *praetorium*, and emphasizes the social stability, and associated flexibility, that he operates from in negotiation between the groups.[36] Pilate's social stability in the narrative emphasizes the political hierarchy at play in the scene, as exemplified by the acknowledgment of the Roman right of pronouncing capital punishment: "We are not permitted to put anyone to death" (18:31). It is in this context that the audience finds that Pilate perceives Jesus as a member of the social category Ἰουδαῖοι, conflating the two previously highly distinct sub-groups from the high priestly interrogation scene, by perceiving these as an out-group member. Furthermore, this category allocation is emphasized by Pilate's examination of Jesus as "the king of the Jews" (ὁ βασιλεὺς τῶν Ἰουδαίων, 18:33).

By presenting to the audience Jesus as the exemplar of the social category Ἰουδαῖοι the Evangelist emphasizes the nature of the conflict as an intra-group concern.[37] As the interrogation continues this category allocation is compounded by Pilate's admission of his own self-categorization as an outsider, to both Jesus and the Ἰουδαῖοι—along with their representatives— "Pilate replied, 'I am not a Jew, am I? Your own nation and the chief priests have handed you over to me'" (18:35). Jesus, in response, attempts to delineate between the in-group of "my kingdom" (Ἡ βασιλεία ἡ ἐμὴ; 18:36) and

Disentangling "Mom's Spaghetti"   75

a broader kingdom of "the world" (18:36). This is reinforced in the temporal realm by noting his followers' lack of defense against Jesus being "delivered to the Jews" (παραδοθῶ τοῖς Ἰουδαίοις; 18:36), thereby rejecting Pilate's conflation of the two social categories. Despite this clarification, Pilate persists in categorizing Jesus as a social category exemplar Ἰουδαῖοι, by ascribing him the title of their king before the crowd of Ἰουδαῖοι in 18:38–39. This construction—especially as an ascription from an out-group member—reframes the group dynamics for the audience of the Fourth Gospel. By doing so it reframes the in-group as the salient super-ordinate category of Ἰουδαῖοι, along with the inherent power dynamics therein. As Lars Kierspel emphasizes: "Jesus is presented in a subtle way as a royal superior to the Jews as well as to the governor."[38] In response the narrative presents the crowd as redirecting their attention away from the super-ordinate category assignment to Barabbas (18:40), effectively replacing intra-group interaction by delineating sub-groups and treating them as separate categories in an inter-group context.

Pilate's construal of Jesus as a prototypical exemplar for the Ἰουδαῖοι continues after the interaction with the crowd as he continues to exercise political power and social stability by having Jesus flogged (19:1).[39] This representation is continued by the soldiers in 19:2–3, and then Pilate's re-presentation in mocking homage in 19:4–5: "Jesus came out, wearing the crown of thorns and the purple robe." The narrative reinforces the Evangelist's purpose here, by portraying Jesus as an exemplar for the super-ordinate group, Ἰουδαῖοι, not just as a member of a sectarian sub-group. In turn the presentation before the crowd leads to the leadership of that group—the chief priests and officers (οἱ ἀρχιερεῖς καὶ οἱ ὑπηρέται; 19:6) are narrated as coming to the fore in the push for crucifixion. For a Jewish audience of the Gospel, this changes the focus from the broader category of Ἰουδαῖοι, to a specific subset of that category, not only foreshadowing the following challenge, but also paves the way for further inter-sub-group permeability.

The subsequent discourse alters the parameters of the conflict, by reframing the content around the claim to be the Son of God and restricting the actors to those construed as group leaders. The claim shifts the power structures within the interrogation, leading to Pilate's fear (19:8), despite his social stability and external power.[40] As this power structure changes Pilate seeks to extricate himself and attempts to refuse to indict Jesus (19:12). Despite this attempt, the leaders of the Ἰουδαῖοι—reading from 19:6 to 19:12—entangle Pilate within his own social-category norms, by accusing him of renouncing his allegiance to Caesar if he releases Jesus.[41] This veiled threat leads to the tipping point in the narrative, as Pilate takes his place on the judgment seat (19:13). Here too the Evangelist reminds the audience of the chronology, noting that it was the "day of preparation for the Passover" (19:14), emphasizing the shared schematic narrative at play within the scene. Pilate makes another attempt to release Jesus, and the narrator seeks to emphasize the prototypicality of the characters for their social groups. This prototypicality comes to a head with Pilate's repeated description of Jesus as "your king" (ὁ βασιλεὺς ὑμῶν; 19:14, 15) culminating with the declaration from the chief priests: "We have no king but Caesar" (οὐκ ἔχομεν βασιλέα εἰ μὴ Καίσαρα; 19:15). In this declaration the Evangelist realigns the social-categorization of the chief priests outside of the realm of the Ἰουδαῖοι shared schematic narrative, and seeks to exclude them from the super-ordinate group construct. Yet for the audience the final proclamation of prototypicality comes from Pilate, as he erects a sign declaring: "Jesus of Nazareth, the King of the Jews" and the Evangelist recounts that members of the Ἰουδαῖοι read the sign. Along with the "fulfillment" pattern in 19:24,[42] this paints Jesus clearly as the super-ordinate group prototypical exemplar that even Pilate—as a Roman out-group representative—has recognized him to be.

Throughout this scene the Evangelist has taken great pains to present the culmination of the structured group arguments that have been built throughout their Gospel. Again, here the super-ordinate group narrative—especially around divine kingship—is presented in a positive light.[43] In that context Jesus is consistently presented as the realization of that positive assessment, linking him with framing of messianism and divine rule. On the other hand, the out-group is given a strongly negative outcome—as voiced by the chief priests—not only rejecting Jesus, and by implication the in-group, but declaring "we have no king but Caesar" (19:15). While the chief priests locate the fulfillment of their social identity within the Imperial regency the audience is invited to locate their own social identity in Jesus as the fulfilment of the super-ordinate group aspirations for divine kingship (e.g., 1 Sam 8:7). In the context of a post–70 CE environment, the presented Imperial alignment of the cultic apparatus would have been significantly galling for John's Jewish audience.

Therefore, given this pattern of Johannine identity engagement, let us now turn to pulling on individual spaghetti strands in turn.

OF COLOPHONS AND CO-EDITORS

One initial strand is entangled with concerns about the means of composition of the Fourth Gospel, given the common postulation that the Gospel stemmed from a sectarian Gentile Christian group, school, or community. As we have already seen, a broad range of scholars identify a variety of redactional layers within the received text, and associate these with various communities. Therefore, given the proposed structured group argument present in the

Disentangling "Mom's Spaghetti"   77

Fourth Gospel we must now assess the means of composition of this argument. Paul Anderson summarizes a variety of approaches to the codification of the Gospel in *"On 'Seamless Robes' and 'Leftover Fragments,'"* eventually proposing a five-stage and two-edition theory of composition.[44] While Anderson pushes back against a multi-stage sociological model of composition, nevertheless he does hypothesize a distinct difference in audience between his two textually codified editions. As he concludes:

> Within this theory, an earlier edition of John can be seen to have had an apologetic and evangelistic thrust, seeking to show Jesus as the authentic Jewish messiah, while the later material reflects more internal concerns with community maintenance and abiding in Christ and his community as the measure of faith.[45]

To this question of multiple audiences, we shall return anon, but in this initial disentanglement it is worth considering the question of multi-stage editorial composition. Inherent within the sociological presumptions of a multi-stage editorial composition is the tension between purpose and pastiche. Especially for documents with a declared purpose—such as that of John 20:31—presenting a coherent purpose is a high priority.[46] This prioritization of coherence presents a challenge to multi-audience or redaction models of composition, as often the hypothesized social circumstances require a variegation of attention and emphasis, as can be seen with Anderson's dual foci of external apologetics and internal community maintenance. The multiplicity of audience focal points has led a variety of scholars—such as Francis Watson—arguing for patterns of competitive textuality in order to address the pluriformity of gospel traditions. As Watson argues:

> Each attempt to write the gospel represents a new answer to the question of who Jesus is, on the assumption that the answers embodied in earlier gospels are either inadequate or misleading; and every gospel seeks its readers' endorsement of the answer it proposes, in preference to the alternative answers proposed by its competitors.[47]

Within the Fourth Gospel tradition this is best exemplified by readings of the Johannine colophons (20:30–31; 21:24–25) as attempts to compete with other gospel recountings. In this same vein Chris Keith has argued that the dual colophons in John not only highlight the Evangelist's knowledge of other gospel traditions but intends not only to supersede them but also to close off other gospel accounts. As he concludes:

> John 20:30–31 and 21:24–25 should thus function as supporting evidence for the theory that the Fourth Evangelist was familiar with the Synoptics. The author of the Gospel of John likely was not only aware of the trend of competitive

78   *Christopher Porter*

textualization of the Jesus tradition but intended actively to contribute to it in such a way that would render future contributions irrelevant.[48]

However, Keith himself—in the same article—treats the Fourth Gospel as a literary unity and downplays the apparent dissonance between these same two colophons that lead many other scholars to posit separated editions.[49] Key to Keith's approach is treating the dual colophons as non-conflictual, with John 21 simply expanding on the earlier themes within the Gospel.

This approach, as with others who have challenged the disunity of the Gospel, brings into relief the implicit sociological question at the heart of editorial redaction approaches: are all alterations necessarily competitive? To this question Logan Williams has offered a resounding "no," arguing, from the broader tradition of Greco-Roman literature, that varied recountings of events or persons need not act in competition. Rather, he argues that the Johannine colophons:

> Assertion of sufficiency need not be taken as an assertion of superiority or competition. "These things are written so that you would come to trust" does not mean "No other document on this topic is useful."[50]

Instead, to coin a phrase, we may consider the variegation of approaches as a form of "collaborative" or "complementary" textualization where multiple documents and editions hold the same or complementary purposes and hold the same social identity aims.

If we are not bound to consider textual editions as signs of variegated and competitive social groups, how may we then conceive of the authorial and editorial composition of the Fourth Gospel? Rather than requiring multiple communities to account for apparent redactions a simpler diachronic approach may be helpful. In Anderson's analysis of Gospel codification, he suggests an initial phase of oral tradition, focused around the "ministry of the Beloved Disciple."[51] While this association of oral tradent with the figure of the Beloved Disciple requires further scrutiny—and is outside the scope of this chapter—the proposition of the Fourth Gospel containing significant oral material coheres well with mechanisms of social identity formation. One possible reconstruction is to posit a series of narrative episodes[52] homiletically communicated[53] for audiences at the locations where the narrated events took place.[54] Working from this form of memorialization we can helpfully see the events of 70 CE and subsequent exclusion from the Jerusalem area as the impetus for the codification of the Gospel narrative. Without the physical environment for memory theater to take place, and the natural gathering places in a known context, the dispersal of the Gospel into the Diaspora in a written form allows for the same coherence of purpose expressed by John

Disentangling "Mom's Spaghetti"

20:31 and contextualized for the new environment. Therefore, we broadly suggest that a series of oral traditions were codified in an initial written form after the fall of 70 CE, with a possible second edition at a later stage.

A GOSPEL FOR WHOM

But this leads us to our next strand of implicit sociological model to disentangle, that of the audience for the Gospel. If the Fourth Gospel is comprised of Jerusalem memories contextualized for a Diaspora environment we must interrogate the intended and ideal audience for its reception.

One significant strain of Fourth Gospel scholarship has located the audience within the alleged *Birkat ha Minim* (Benediction against the Heretics), as suggested by J. L. Martyn's influential *History and Theology in the Fourth Gospel*.[55] Under this thesis the audience of the Gospel are those who have been ejected from synagogue worship by the force of the "Benediction" recited as part of "worship followed in every Pharasaic synagogue."[56] However, this approach is rendered problematic on multiple fronts. Historiographically, the evidence for the *Birkat* does not sustain robust interrogation, with the broad consensus forming that it does not appear until the middle of the second century, or even later.[57] Furthermore, evidence for widespread and authorized synagogue expulsion—à la the supposed ἀποσυνάγωγος application—has been strongly challenged, with many finding only evidence for individual and sporadic self-regulation of synagogue communities.[58] Finally, the use of the *Birkat* in any form of synagogal *haeresis* finds only scant evidence, suggesting its use as an mechanism for excommunication as unlikely.[59]

If the proposition of a limited and sectarian audience generated by synagogue expulsion—via the *Birkat* or other means—is unlikely, then the other end of the audience spectrum lies with Richard Bauckham's suggestion that the Fourth Gospel is intended for a broad audience. Bauckham argues that "the Gospels were written for general circulation around the churches and so envisaged a very general Christian audience"[60] and therefore the "readership is not a specific audience, large or small, but an indefinite readership."[61] Following in this train Edward Klink argues that the Fourth Gospel "functioned with a rhetorical invitation for an indefinite audience"[62] and that "the FG is not in a deep-rooted polemic with other Jesus traditions" but instead is evangelistic in focus.[63] However, positing such a broad audience for the Gospel raises a new set of challenges, especially given the specificity of language and sociolect present. As we have already seen in the Structured Group Argument analysis, the Fourth Evangelist specifically addresses their concerns within a framework construed from Jewish scriptures, and regularly integrated with positive assessments of a Jewish super-ordinate group.

80   *Christopher Porter*

But this raises a new problem, the Fourth Gospel is shot through with polemic and vitriol aimed squarely at the Ἰουδαῖοι. Is the presence of such vitriol incompatible with a Jewish audience, as some scholars have suggested?[64] While it is commonplace to presume that the presence of polemic would make such a document less palatable to members of the same group, this perspective usually presumes the polemic to be couched within a form of inter-group discourse. However, as many studies have indicated, this form of polemic is highly prevalent in close intra-group discourse. Indeed, as Lewis Coser found:

> A conflict is more passionate and more radical when it arises out of close relationships. The coexistence of union and opposition in such relations makes for the peculiar sharpness of the conflict. Enmity calls forth deeper and more violent reactions, the greater the involvement of the parties among whom it originates.[65]

Therefore, we should not immediately associate strong polemic with inter-group discourse, when intra-group discourses often show similarly "sharp" conflict. As Reicher and Sani discovered, groups enact social argument to "see themselves as defending [their] identity against the threat represented in the position of the other"[66] as "rhetorical debates over self-categories are important because of their social-cognitive consequences."[67] John Ashton interprets the polemic of the Fourth Gospel in this fashion, reading it as a series of "fierce family rows" with all of the inherent vitriol therein.[68] Furthermore, these textualized intra-group conflicts are not unique in the post–70 CE period. As Motyer writes: "Here is Jew speaking to Jew, in just the same way as the authors of 4 Ezra and 2 Baruch tried to minister to the needs of their fellow-Jews by publishing their solutions in written form."[69] To find these intra-group disputes in written form should be expected in a period of great social turmoil, as various groups contend to determine the identity of their group. Indeed, we should not be surprised to find this occurring with such vitriol in inter-group disputes, for—as we have seen—"social identity lies in difference, and difference is asserted against what is closest, which represents the greatest threat."[70]

If we take the Fourth Gospel as envisaging a Jewish audience, then this yields two further observations. First, the categorization of the "others" as members of the same shared—super-ordinate—group emphasizes the range of belief inherent within group membership. Despite the Fourth Gospel's reframing of the categories of belief around a broader Christocentric vision, it is still insistent on being a "Jewish" Gospel; with Jesus as the locus of the Jewish forms of worship and sacrifice. As Andrew Byers writes: "With John's Gospel, this Jewish author ironically labels 'Ἰουδαῖοι' those Ἰουδαῖοι who demand that one must become a Ἰουδαῖος to become a member of

Disentangling "Mom's Spaghetti" 81

Israel."[71] On this count the Fourth Evangelist is in good company, with heated contemporary debates about the degree to which one must be Ἰουδαῖος in order to be considered part of the people of God.[72] Furthermore, many of these debates share the same tenor of in-group polemic, vitriol, and even violence that is on display in the Fourth Gospel. 1 Maccabees records violent retribution against those perceived to violate the law, including forcible circumcision of all uncircumcised boys within the *eretz* (1 Macc 2:46). In 2 Maccabees the account of the revolt highlights the nature of the conflict as an intra-group separation, introducing "the word Ἰουδαϊσμός as a contrast term for Ἑλληνισμός"[73] and then highlighting the separation of those who remained ἐν τῷ Ἰουδαϊσμῷ (2 Macc. 8:1). From this intra-group separation, we read of the violence wrought upon towns and villages because of the perceived "impurity" of the high priest Jason, and those who followed him (2 Macc 4:7–22). The encouraging of purity via a "sectarian program" of Ἰουδαϊσμός is also visible within other Diaspora texts. Including *Joseph and Aseneth*, wherein the character of Joseph is reworked to portray him as upholding strict Jewish customs, such as that he "would not eat with the Egyptians, for this was an abomination to him" (JosAs 7:1), instead of one who is indistinguishable from his Egyptian context, as in Genesis 42. As an exemplary character Joseph becomes an example of "proper behaviour"[74] for the Diaspora community and encourages a form of intra-group distinction.[75] Therefore—with Motyer—we can read the Fourth Gospel, with its invective and polemic, as "Jew speaking to Jew," and attempting to provide "solutions" to the problems of a post–70 CE era.[76]

Second, however, we must also recognize the dangers of repurposed intra-group discourse, especially when reused in inter-group contexts. As Adele Reinhartz observes, the rendering of the Gospel in Greek increases its availability outside of the intra-group context, notably to Gentiles and Diaspora Jews.[77] Given the forcible migration driven by the 70 CE conclusion to the Jewish War, the use of Greek as a *lingua franca* for Diaspora communities is a natural conclusion.[78] Nevertheless, as can be seen *in nuce* by the probable use of the Septuagint in the Egyptian priest Manetho's anti-Jewish polemic, accessibility of texts presents significant risks.[79] Manetho recounts portions of the Exodus, specifically drawing on the leprosy excerpts, to cast the Jewish community as "lepers and other polluted persons" and those "wasted by disease."[80] This likely reuse of the narrative in Exodus 4:6–7 presents Manetho with a strong invective against the *Hyskos*—Shepherds—who end up settling in Jerusalem.[81]

Manetho gives us a brief—and ancient—example of the reuse of in-group narratives as inter-group polemic. The process of selection and stereotyping serves to demarcate and denigrate the other using their own identity formation mechanisms to do so. This is even more the case when the narrative already engages in intra-group polemic, as is often the case in the infamous receptions and reuses of John 8:44.[82] Much of this is due to the separation of the polemic from the shared identity construction of intra-group discourse, where the sharpness of polemic is required to generate difference between members of the same group. Without that shared identity these intensely vitriolic expressions are given meaning untethered from the inherent context of in-group entitativity and identification.[83] Some of these problems may be mitigated by reintegrating this form of polemic within its social audience and context. As Reinhartz reflects: "It is time to put [this form of polemic] back in its historical, literary, and rhetorical place, and to strip it of the destructive power that it has exercised for so many centuries."[84]

Therefore, overall, who may we consider as the audience of the Fourth Gospel? The target which makes best sense of the text and context is that of a broad Diaspora Jewish audience, as part of the post–70 CE migration away from Jerusalem. The melting pot of the existing Diaspora communities, along with the new arrivals, and wrestling with the religio-cultic impacts of the loss of the Jerusalem Temple provides fertile soil for intra-group discourse—and polemic—over Jewish identity. However, once these intense intra-group debates spread from a restricted Jewish audience, the firestorm of anti-Jewish polemic and vitriol takes form.

WHERE MAY A COMMUNITY BE FOUND?

Finally, then, with some strands of our spaghetti extracted, we can return to our opening question, on whither the Johannine Community may be found. From what we have disentangled we may conclude that the purpose of the Gospel is to bring an—implied Jewish—audience into the new social identity of Christ-followers (20:31). This aim is conducted primarily through a process of social group argumentation, which presents Jesus as a mechanism for cultic engagement in the aftermath of the destruction of Jerusalem—including the Temple—in 70 CE. The Gospel is not encoded for a specific sectarian group or community, it is aimed at a broader social group, that of the breadth of Diaspora Jewish communities. This form of prospective identity formation intrinsically drives toward a possible future social identity for the audience,[85] that of being part of the Christ-following social category.[86] This is what Raimo Hakola proposes as an "imagined community," the natural coalescing of members of a social category into a novel community.[87]

Indeed, the place where we are on firmer ground for such a community is not within the Gospel, but rather within the documents which evince their interaction with the Gospel: the Johannine Epistles.[88] There we find evidence of communities which seem to have formed around the tenets of Gospel

Disentangling "Mom's Spaghetti"   83

ethics and wrestling with their own set of concerns. However, as Christopher Seglenieks argues, it would be a mistake to simply equate any audience of the Epistles back into the sole putative Johannine Community.[89] Just as it would be short sighted to presume that a text with the social aims of the Fourth Gospel would not generate any social groups. But at the point of the Gospel, this novel community remains an imagined community, with the Gospel focused on the struggles and questions held by Diaspora Jews at large.

NOTES

1. The phrase "Will the real X please stand up" was initially popularized by the 1970s TV show *To Tell the Truth*, which concluded each episode by requesting the "real character" to reveal themselves in contrast to the two imposters also on the show. However, the lack of clarity is compounded by the modern presumption that the idiomatic referent is to the rap song "The Real Slim Shady" (2000) by Eminem, which utilizes the same phrase.

2. Rudolf Bultmann, *The Gospel of John: A Commentary*. Trans. G. R. Beasley-Murray (Oxford: Basil Blackwell, 1971), 27.

3. Bultmann, *The Gospel of John*, 27.

4. Urban C. von Wahlde, *The Gospel and Letters of John,* ECC (Grand Rapids, MI: Eerdmans, 2010), 43.

5. Wahlde, *The Gospel and Letters of John*, 50–55.

6. Pierre Bourdieu, *Distinction: A Social Critique of the Judgement of Taste*, trans. Richard Nice (Cambridge, MA: Harvard University Press, 1979), 479.

7. Wayne A. Meeks, "Man from Heaven in Johannine Sectarianism," JBL 91 (1972): 70.

8. Meeks, "Man from Heaven in Johannine Sectarianism," 70.

9. Peter L. Berger and Thomas Luckmann, *The Social Construction of Reality: A Treatise in the Sociology of Knowledge* (New York: Anchor, 1967).

10. Berger and Luckmann, *The Social Construction of Reality*, 144.

11. E. P. Sanders popularized the phrase "common Judaism" which expounds a form of this shared schema, or what Adele Reinhartz describes as the "essence of Jewish practice and belief." Adele Reinhartz, "'Common Judaism,' 'The Parting Of The Ways,' And 'The Johannine Community'" in *Orthodoxy, Liberalism, and Adaptation*, ed. Bob E. J. H. Becking (Leiden: Brill, 2011), 74.

12. A longer exploration of Social Identity Theory and its application within biblical studies is found in Christopher A. Porter and Brian S. Rosner, "'All Things to All People': 1 Corinthians, Ethnic Flexibility, and Social Identity Theory," *CBR* 19 (2021): 286–307, https://doi.org/10.1177/1476993X21990957.

13. Henri Tajfel et al., "Social Categorization and Intergroup Behaviour," *European Journal of Social Psychology* 1 (1971): 37.

14. S. Alexander Haslam, *Psychology in Organizations* (London: SAGE, 2004), 21.

15. Dominic Abrams and Michael A. Hogg, "Metatheory: Lessons from Social Identity Research," *Personal. Soc. Psychol. Rev.* 8 (2004): 98–106, https://doi.org/10.1207/s15327957pspr0802_2.

16. Stephen Reicher and Fabio Sani, "Introducing SAGA: Structural Analysis of Group Arguments," *Group Dynamics: Theory, Research, and Practice, Research Methods* 2 (1998): 270, https://doi.org/10.1037/1089-2699.2.4.267.

17. Reicher and Sani, "Introducing SAGA," 281.

18. Martha Augoustinos, "History as a Rhetorical Source: Using Historical Narratives to Argue and Explain," in *How to Analyse Talk in Institutional Settings: A Casebook of Methods*, ed. Alec W. McHoul and Mark Rapley (London: Continuum, 2001).

19. M. Rapley and M. Augoustinos, "'National Identity' as a Rhetorical Resource," in *Language, Interaction and National Identity—Studies in the Social Organisation of National Identity* (Aldershot, Hants, England: Ashgate, 2002), 201.

20. Marco Cinnirella, "Exploring Temporal Aspects of Social Identity: The Concept of Possible Social Identities," *European Journal of Social Psychology* 28.2 (1998): 227–48.

21. The term "Jewish" is used as a broad catch-all term for both cultural and religious aspects of this shared semantic narrative. While it is somewhat intrinsically anachronistic, here it seeks to balance perspectives of "Judean locale" (e.g., Mason and Esler) along with very pertinent concerns of a *"judenrein* New Testament." A. J. Levine, "Matthew and Anti-Judaism," *CurTM* 34.6 (2007): 415.

22. For an exploration of all fifteen instances see Christopher A. Porter, *Johannine Social Identity Formation after the Fall of the Jerusalem Temple: Negotiating Identity in Crisis.*, BInS 194 (Leiden: Brill, 2022), https://doi.org/10.1163/9789004469822.

23. Jacob Chanikuzhy, *Jesus, the Eschatological Temple: An Exegetical Study of Jn 2,13–22 in the Light of the Pre-70 C.E. Eschatological Temple Hopes and the Synoptic Temple Action* (Leuven: Peeters, 2012), 244–45.

24. Mary L. Coloe, *God Dwells with Us: Temple Symbolism in the Fourth Gospel* (Collegeville, MN: Liturgical Press, 2001), 69.

25. Chanikuzhy, *Jesus, the Eschatological Temple*, 276.

26. Alan Kerr, *The Temple of Jesus' Body: The Temple Theme in the Gospel of John*, JSNTSup 220 (London: Sheffield Academic Press, 2002), 79.

27. J. Andrew Overman, "The Destruction of the Temple and the Confirmation of Judaism and Christianity," in *Jews and Christians in the First and Second Centuries: The Interbellum 70–132 CE*, ed. Joshua J. Schwartz and Peter J. Tomson, CRINT 15 (Brill, 2017), 257.

28. Francis J. Moloney, "From Cana to Cana (Jn. 2:1–4:54) and the Fourth Evangelist's Concept of Correct (and Incorrect) Faith," *Sal* 40 (1978): 831.

29. Anthony Le Donne, "Memory, Commemoration and History in John 2.19–22: A Critique and Application of Social Memory," in *The Fourth Gospel in First-Century Media Culture*, ed. Anthony Le Donne and Tom Thatcher, LNTS 426 (London: T&T Clark, 2013), 198.

30. Raimo Hakola, *Reconsidering Johannine Christianity: A Social Identity Approach* (Florence: Taylor and Francis, 2015), 95.

31. James D. G. Dunn, "John's Gospel and the Oral Gospel Tradition," in *The Fourth Gospel in First-Century Media Culture*, 171.

32. Richard Horsley and Tom Thatcher, *John, Jesus, and the Renewal of Israel* (Grand Rapids, MI: Eerdmans, 2013), 163–66.

33. Whether the high priest is Annas or Caiaphas is secondary to the naming of the office in this passage. While the individual has historical significance, the social significance is carried by the office of high priest. Although some scholars have argued that Pilate functions as the specific "constant" in these scenes, the constant is not to be found in the out-group but in Jesus as the exemplar of the in-group in two different circumstances. Contra Warren Carter, *John and Empire: Initial Explorations* (New York: T & T Clark International, 2008), 279.

34. Craig S. Keener, *The Gospel of John: A Commentary,* 2 vols. (Grand Rapids, MI: Baker Academic, 2003), 2.1094.

35. Keener, *John*, 2.1095.

36. Haslam, *Psychology in Organizations*, 25.

37. In the approach of the Evangelist, if Pilate makes this association, so too should the ideal audience.

38. Lars Kierspel, *The Jews and the World in the Fourth Gospel: Parallelism, Function, and Context,* WUNT 2/220 (Tübingen: Mohr Siebeck, 2006), 70.

39. See for more on the exemplarity of leadership Haslam, *Psychology in Organizations*, 26; and S. Alexander Haslam, Stephen D. Reicher, and Michael J. Platow, *The New Psychology of Leadership: Identity, Influence and Power* (Hove, UK: Psychology Press, 2011), 83.

40. Warren Carter, "Social Identities, Subgroups, and John's Gospel: Jesus the Prototype and Pontius Pilate (John 18.28–19.16)," in *T&T Clark Handbook to Social Identity in the New Testament*, ed. J. Brian Tucker and Coleman A. Baker (London: T&T Clark, 2014), 247.

41. Carter, *John and Empire*, 308.

42. Keener, *John*, 1140.

43. Wayne A. Meeks, *The Prophet-King—Moses Traditions and the Johannine Christology*, NovTSup 14 (Leiden: Brill, 1967), 77.

44. Paul N. Anderson, "On 'Seamless Robes' and 'Leftover Fragments' – A Theory of Johannine Composition," in *The Origins of John's Gospel,* Johannine Studies 2 (Leiden: Brill, 2016), 200.

45. Anderson, "On 'Seamless Robes' and 'Leftover Fragments,'" 218.

46. Stephen Reicher, Nick Hopkins, and Susan Condor, "Stereotype Construction as a Strategy of Influence," in *The Social Psychology of Stereotyping and Group Life* (Malden: Blackwell Publishing, 1997), 116.

47. Francis Watson, *Gospel Writing: A Canonical Perspective* (Grand Rapids, MI: Eerdmans, 2013), 8.

48. Chris Keith, "The Competitive Textualization of the Jesus Tradition in John 20:30–31 and 21:24–25," *CBQ* 78 (2016): 327.

49. Keith, "Competitive Textualization," 323.

50. Logan Williams, "Was all Early Gospel Writing Competitive? Situating the Gospel of John within Greek Literary Culture." University of Nottingham Biblical Studies Seminar. March 2022.

51. Anderson, "On 'Seamless Robes' and 'Leftover Fragments,'" 200.

52. Culpepper identifies an episodic structure to the Fourth Gospel. R. Alan Culpepper, *Anatomy of the Fourth Gospel: A Study in Literary Design*, Foundations and Facets (Philadelphia: Fortress, 1987), 98.

53. Thomas Boomershine argues for a homiletical approach to the Gospel narratives. Thomas E. Boomershine, "The Medium and Message of John: Audience Address and Audience Identity in the Fourth Gospel," in *The Fourth Gospel in First-Century Media Culture*, 98.

54. Thatcher describes this as "memory theater." Tom Thatcher, "John's Memory Theater: A Study of Composition in Performance," in *The Fourth Gospel in First-Century Media Culture*, 87.

55. J. Louis Martyn, *History and Theology in the Fourth Gospel*, third ed., New Testament Library (Louisville, KY: Westminster John Knox Press, 2003 [1968]), 56–65.

56. Martyn, *History and Theology in the Fourth Gospel*, 58.

57. Reuven Kimelman, "*Birkat Ha-Minim* and the Lack of Evidence for an Anti-Christian Jewish Prayer in Late Antiquity," in *Jewish and Christian Self-Definition*, ed. Ben F. Meyer and E. P. Sanders, vol. 2 (Philadelphia: Fortress, 1981).

58. Jonathan Bernier, *Aposynagōgos and the Historical Jesus in John: Rethinking the Historicity of the Johannine Expulsion Passages*, BInS 122 (Leiden: Brill, 2013); Edward W. III. Klink, "Expulsion from the Synagogue?: Rethinking a Johannine Anachronism," *TynBul* 59 (2008): 99–118; Raimo Hakola and Adele Reinhartz, "John's Pharisees," in *In Quest of the Historical Pharisees*, ed. Jacob Neusner and Bruce Chilton (Waco, TX: Baylor University Press, 2007), 131–48.

59. Raimo Hakola, *Identity Matters: John, the Jews and Jewishness*, NovTSup 118 (Leiden: Brill, 2005); Philip L. Mayo, "The Role of the Birkath Haminim in Early Jewish-Christian Relations: A Reexamination of the Evidence," *BBR* 16 (2006): 325–43.

60. Richard Bauckham, ed., *The Gospels for All Christians: Rethinking the Gospel Audiences* (Grand Rapids: Eerdmans, 1997), 1.

61. Bauckham, *The Gospels for All Christians*, 45.

62. Edward W. III. Klink, *The Sheep of the Fold: The Audience and Origin of the Gospel of John*, SNTSMS 141 (Cambridge: Cambridge University Press, 2007), 238.

63. Klink, *The Sheep of the Fold*, 245.

64. See the extended review of historical audience in Adele Reinhartz, *Cast Out of the Covenant: Jews and Anti-Judaism in the Gospel of John* (New York/London: Lexington/Fortress, 2018), 94–98.

65. Lewis A. Coser, *The Functions of Social Conflict*, (London: Routledge, 1998), 71.

66. Reicher and Sani, "Introducing SAGA," 282.

67. Reicher and Sani, "Introducing SAGA," 270.

68. John Ashton, *Understanding the Fourth Gospel* (Oxford; New York: Oxford University Press, 2009), 137.

69. Stephen Motyer, *Your Father the Devil?: A New Approach to John and "The Jews,"* PBM 5 (Carlisle: Paternoster, 1997), 212.

70. Bourdieu, *Distinction*, 479.

71. Andrew J. Byers, *John and the Others: Jewish Relations, Christian Origins, and the Sectarian Hermeneutic* (Waco, Texas: Baylor University Press, 2021), 90.

72. See arguments over Ἰουδαϊσμός in Matthew Novenson, "Paul's Former Occupation in Ioudaismos," in *Galatians and Christian Theology*, eds. Mark Elliott, Scott Hafemann, N. T. Wright, John Frederick (Grand Rapids, MI: Baker Academic, 2014), 31; and Chris Porter, "Which Paul? Whose Judaism? - A Socio-Cognitive Approach to Paul within Judaism," in *Paul Within Judaism*, eds. Michael F Bird, Ruben Buhner, Jörg Frey, Brian S. Rosner WUNT 2/507 (Tubingen: Mohr Siebeck, 2023); and broader debates over the content of the social-category "Israel" in Jason A. Staples, *The Idea of Israel in Second Temple Judaism: A New Theory of People, Exile, and Israelite Identity* (Cambridge: Cambridge University Press, 2021), https://doi.org/10.1017/9781108906524.

73. Novenson, "Paul's Former Occupation in Ioudaismos," 24.

74. Jill Hicks-Keeton, *Arguing with Aseneth: Gentile Access to Israel's "Living God" in Jewish Antiquity* (New York: Oxford University Press, 2018), 23.

75. Christopher A. Porter, "'Hic Sunt Dracones' Mapping the Rebellious Social Dynamics of Bel and the Snake from the Daniel and Joseph Competitive Court-Tales," *BTB* 51 (2021): 80–81, https://doi.org/10.1177/0146107921997107.

76. Motyer, *Your Father the Devil?*, 212.

77. Reinhartz, *Cast Out of the Covenant*, 143.

78. See Josephus, *War* VII.10. Josephus, *The Jewish War, Volume III*, trans. H. St. J. Thackeray, LCL 210 (Cambridge, MA: Harvard University Press, 1928).

79. James K. Aitken and James Carleton Paget, eds., *The Jewish-Greek Tradition in Antiquity and the Byzantine Empire*, first edition. (New York: Cambridge University Press, 2014), 111.

80. Manetho, *Aegyptica*, Frag 54. See Manetho, *History of Egypt and Other Works*, trans. W. G. Waddell, LCL 350 (Cambridge, MA: Harvard University Press, 1940).

81. Manetho, *Aegyptica*, Frag 42.

82. Adele Reinhartz, "'Children of the Devil': John 8:44 and Its Early Reception," in *"Children of the Devil": John 8:44 and Its Early Reception* (Berlin/Boston: De Gruyter, 2020), 43–54, https://doi.org/10.1515/9783110671773-004.

83. Fabio Sani, "When Subgroups Secede: Extending and Refining the Social Psychological Model of Schism in Groups," *Personality and Social Psychology Bulletin* 31 (2005): 1078, https://doi.org/10.1177/0146167204274092.

84. Reinhartz, "'Children of the Devil,'" 52.

85. Marco Cinnirella. "Exploring Temporal Aspects of Social Identity: The Concept of Possible Social Identities." *European Journal of Social Psychology* 28 (1998): 227–48, 235–36.

86. See broader argument in Porter, *Johannine Social Identity Formation*; and Christopher A. Porter, "Will the Real Oἱ Ἰουδαῖοι Please Stand Up?," in *The Enduring*

Impact of the Gospel of John, ed. Dorothy Lee, Robert Derrenbacker, and Muriel Porter, Interdisciplinary Studies (Eugene, OR: Wipf & Stock, 2022), 62–80.

87. Hakola, *Reconsidering Johannine Christianity*, 153.

88. Reinhartz, Adele. "Women in the Johannine Community: An Exercise in Historical Imagination." Pages 14–33 in *Feminist Companion to John: Volume 2*, ed. Amy-Jill Levine with Marianne Blickenstaff (London: Bloomsbury, 2003), 17. *Pace* Méndez who also questions the possibility of reconstructing a Johannine Community from the Johannine Epistles. Méndez, Hugo. "Did the Johannine Community Exist?" *JSNT* 42 (2020): 352. https://doi.org/10.1177/0142064X19890490.

89. Christopher Seglenieks, "Desertion or Exclusion: Relationships with the Outgroup in the Johannine Writings," in *Figuring the Enemy: Socio-Scientific Approaches to Religious Enmity*, ed. Christopher Porter, Routledge Interdisciplinary Perspectives on Biblical Criticism (London: Routledge, forthcoming).

Chapter 5

Triangulating a Johannine Community from John 18:28–19:22

Laura J. Hunt

My approach to the Johannine community in this chapter involves triangulation between historical data and the text of the Gospel, using three different methodological tools.[1] In geometry, triangulation involves, for example, using similar triangles to precisely calculate a distance or a height from three pieces of data, such as two angles and the length of a straight line. In this chapter, Eco's Semiotics and Bayes's Theorem will provide, analogously to the angles, directions and constraints that require postulating historical groups evidenced from outside the Gospel text that might have formed a Johannine community, or at least John's addressees. Then, a Social Identity Analysis (SIT) of John 18:28–19:22 based on J. Brian Tucker's textual markers will provide, analogously to the length of the straight line, data describing the way John's Gospel negotiates the identity of the stipulated group. This social identity approach will be applied to the Johannine trial narrative, and the results will be proposed as a partial step toward triangulation of a Johannine community, or group (in SIT terms).

Unlike the precise results the ground of this triangulation metaphor might suggest, the resulting data will not pinpoint an answer.[2] Instead, methodological triangulation uses multiple methods, data sources, or researchers to provide convergence, inconsistencies *and* contradictions out of which the researcher can "construct meaningful propositions about the social world."[3] Thus, accumulating data from three different standpoints will inform the limited conclusion that a network of Jesus-followers in the region of Ephesus were nuancing at least Jewish and Roman identities in imitation of Jesus particularly with regard to obedience to law.

90   *Laura J. Hunt*

To speak into the existence of a possible Johannine community, however, the word *community* itself must be defined. In this chapter, I will follow the foundational definition of identity for social identity theory: "that part of an individual's self-concept which derives from his knowledge of his membership of a social group (or groups) together with the value and emotional significance attached to that membership."[4] Thus, I prefer the word "group" to "community." But what is a group? Tajfel notes that groups can have "a cognitive," an "evaluative," and/or an "emotional component," so one can know that one belongs to a group, one can evaluate that belonging on a scale from positive to negative, and one can have a range of feelings about one's belonging.[5] These three components (cognitive, evaluative, and emotional) are equally relevant about groups that one does *not* belong to, a factor which will become important to the analysis of John's trial narrative. However, while these three factors may come into play, Tajfel's minimal group experiments demonstrated that ingroup/outgroup behavior is prompted simply by "a classification and a perception of in-group/out-group membership."[6] So, while studies of ethnicity rightly include factors such as name, ancestry, history, culture, land, and sense of belonging, primarily that last factor in its cognitive, evaluative, and emotional aspects will be addressed in this chapter.[7]

A few brief comments about the history of Johannine community studies will helpfully establish the course of this chapter. Robyn Faith Walsh has recently traced the roots of the search for Gospel communities to German Romanticism.[8] More specifically on the Gospel of John, in 1968, J. Louis Martyn published his two-level reading approach, proposing that the text contained not only stories of Jesus but also the history of the community out of which it was written.[9] While his proposal shifted the paradigm of scholarly analyses, it was not without critics. In 1992, Frederik Wisse made some important observations about the assumptions behind Martyn's work.[10] On the one hand, Wisse helpfully distinguished between the community of the author (a network that Walsh, too, highlights) and the community of the audience.[11] Citing examples such as Milton's *Paradise Lost*, he pointed out that texts, and I might add specifically narratives, do not reveal as much about the author as we might hope: "style, taste, interests, beliefs and values," yes, but not historical data.[12] Less helpfully, Wisse challenged assumptions about a "wide geographical distribution" and a "great diversity of belief and practice" in early Christianity and asserted that "the historical conclusions warranted by the evidence . . . probably have already been reached."[13] Although I am sympathetic to cautions against over-reading, these last claims seem quite outdated in light of the subsequent thirty years of scholarship.

The elements of Wisse's essay that nicely introduce this chapter come up when he discusses the relationships between author, text, and audience. When scholars assume a textual community, he notes, they theorize that the text was written for a specific community and that that community shaped the text more than the author did.[14] Texts can, of course, be written for specific groups, but I believe Wisse is correct in his concerns that the author not be assimilated into the audience, nor that the shaping of the text be assumed to come from a point of view that includes both. It seems to me that authors are more likely to attempt to shape listeners in some way. The Fourth Gospel, at least, is explicit in this regard (John 20:31).

Adele Reinhartz, furthermore, points out that not only could a community not create a text, but instead the text creates the community, or at least a "social entity."[15] According to her, the Gospel of John propels polytheists into a transformational community with others who believe Jesus to be the Messiah, who expropriate Jewish markers of identity and repudiate Jews.[16] Further, she sees some intentionality on the part of "John" to create such a community.[17] While I argue for negotiation more than repudiation, I, too, read the Gospel as intentionally identity-creating rhetoric.

Previous approaches, then, have worked through the Gospel, looking for evidence of a social situation in a certain narrative, or determining the purposes of the text from a particular pericope. They have then imagined the situation that would call for such rhetoric.[18] My approach will instead postulate a group that seems relevant in some measure to the Gospel based on historical support, an *object* in semiotic parlance, and then propose a SIT reading of the Gospel with such a group in mind, asking about the identity-forming effects of the text on such a group. This approach does not aim at certainty, nor even at a preponderance of evidence, but instead offers some measure of plausibility to be used as data feeding into a Bayesian analysis.

THEORETICAL BASES FOR TRIANGULATION

Although I will not delve deeply into Umberto Eco's theories, I find his semiotic triad extremely useful in thinking about the meaning of texts, because it emphasizes both the importance and the limiting effects of sensory experiences on interpretation.[19] Eco calls the sensory world outside the text the object. But the understanding of that object is mediated through language, such that we sift our sensory data through the lens of language, and we limit our understanding of language through deictic references to sensory data. I know that the word "green" does not refer to the color orange, because when the people around me point and say "green," they never point to a color that I perceive as the real-world orange.

This explanation of communication highlights the necessity of having access to the historical situations within which texts are written to limit interpretation properly. It further demonstrates the difficulty of reading that situation from the text itself, when it is the situation that is required to interpret the text.[20] David A. Lamb and Rodolfo Galvan Estrada have pointed out that the text of John is often used to delineate a sectarian community, and then the sectarian community is used to interpret John.[21]

For example, Andrew T. Lincoln, in his 2000 book, *Truth on Trial*, discusses truth in the context of the Gospel of John.[22] Starting with Isaiah 40–55, he notes that truth is the correct judgment of Yahweh, in other words, the "effectiveness of the divine word in history," which then requires human witnesses to testify to it.[23] In the Gospel of John, the divine claim is extended: Yahweh's effective word is now revealed in Jesus, a claim testified to throughout the Gospel by Jesus himself, by the Spirit, by characters in the Gospel, but also, Lincoln writes, by "the beloved disciple."[24] This disciple "represents a community ('we') to which the actual narrator belongs, and this community also bears witness."[25] The community endorses the Gospel, and thereby adds its testimony to the truth of what is written.[26]

I mention Lincoln because I find his work so probative.[27] But in this case, the community has been entirely reconstructed from the text of the Gospel.[28] The semiotic triad is only two-legged when we have no access to data from the sensory world to push against our reconstructions.[29] Therefore, the truth to which Lincoln's community bears witness might be quite different from the truth as Lincoln uncovers it in the Gospel.

Issues of circularity come up frequently in analyses, although not every discussion addresses the same kind of circularity. Semiotic circularity occurs when we realize that an interpretation is communicated in signs which themselves have to be interpreted.[30] In other words, my own readers may misinterpret the signs I use to describe the signs John used.

Furthermore, there is circularity in the claim that "the community's witness to Jesus in its written testimony is self-authenticating," as Lincoln rightly notes.[31] But there is also circularity in assuming that the text reports exactly what the community believes. When author and audience are properly separated, one recognizes that a text could constitute a corrective to its audience rather than a reflection of it.[32] Navigating these two possibilities depends, though, on a priori assumptions about the historical state of John's audience. Does a narrative that seems to recommend being born "from above" (ἄνωθεν, John 3:7) do so in order to propose something new to its audience, or does it do so in order to confirm them in what they are already doing? To determine the effect of the narrative on the auditors, one needs more information about the intended audience than the text itself provides.

Eco's semiotics, then, have demonstrated some limitations in the search for John's Gospel's audience. Bayes's Theorem, however, offers another rule for triangulation. Although Eco pushes us beyond asking only, "What is the probability that this text was written to one particular group defined

Triangulating a Johannine Community from John 18:28–19:22   93

using the text?," three questions from Bayes' Theorem provide specifics: (1) What is the probability that a group so described might have existed at all in the ancient world? (2) If we stipulate its existence, what is the probability that someone would have written such a narrative to them? And (3) might someone have composed a text such as the Fourth Gospel for other reasons? That last question opens the door to comparative analyses of alternative proposals in the context of Bayesian analysis.[33] Without hard data for those probabilities, which we admittedly do not have, Bayesian analysis threatens to descend into scientific-sounding terminology for traditional subjective biblical interpretation.[34] But even without precise data (which Figure 5.1 does not pretend to communicate) Bayes does correlate certain questions often otherwise ignored.

The probability that a certain group existed given the fact that we have the Fourth Gospel *goes up* the stronger the probability that this specific group would have existed without reference to the Fourth Gospel at all. The probability that a certain group existed given the fact that we have the Fourth Gospel *goes up* the stronger the probability that this specific group would likely call forth an address such as the Fourth Gospel. And the probability that this certain group existed given the fact that we have the Fourth Gospel *goes down* the stronger the probability that the Fourth Gospel could have been written for some other recipients or in some other circumstance. This last question is built into interpreter's work as they write reviews and make comparative arguments with and against others' interpretations. In this sense, then, when Richard Bauckham looks at historical data for the existence of "a general Christian audience" and argues that these were the addressees

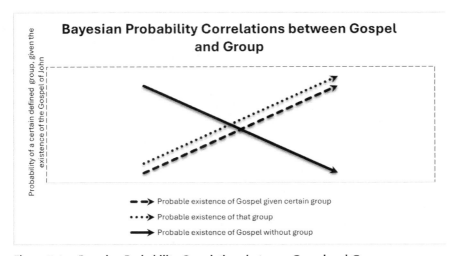

Figure 5.1. Bayesian Probability Correlations between Gospel and Group.

of John's Gospel, reviewers must compare the probability that a general Christian audience would have been addressed by such a text as the Gospel of John along with the historical evidence for this audience, against the probability that the Gospel of John might have arisen in various other ways.[35] The approach of this chapter, indeed, postulates the effects of the text on one particular historically plausible social group, in order to propose addressees more precise than his open-ended description.

To start triangulating, then, I will suggest a historically possible group of addressees; choose a section of the text for analysis; and, after setting up a framework, I will uncover some effects of that section on the social identity of the proposed group. At the same time, I offer this construction as one data point in a probability analysis that Bayes' Theorem suggests must take into account all other constructions, too.[36] After that, I will consider both corrective and reflective functions for the text.

HISTORICALLY PLAUSIBLE GROUP

I would like to propose, then, a network of Jesus-believers in about 100 CE or a little later, in and around Ephesus. My proposal is adduced from several pieces of evidence. First, of course, historical tradition locates John in Ephesus.[37] Second, while other Mediterranean cities cannot be ruled out, the evidence for the visible use of Latin in Ephesian inscriptions and archaeology may be reflected in the eighteen Latinisms that John uses thirty-two times.[38] Third, regarding dating, the use of πραιτώριον in John (18:28 [2x], 33; 19:9) to refer to a building (such as a governor's palace) rather than to the emperor's Praetorian Guard seems to reflect the assimilation of that Latin loanword still in process in the first century CE, although in general Greek tended to absorb Latin quickly.[39] The earliest data I have found outside of the New Testament for πραιτώριον as a reference to a building come from (1) a military letter, (2) an ostraca demanding the tax levy of bricks for building a πραιτώριον, and (3) in a Latin-Greek bilingual record of legal proceedings, all from Egypt in the early to mid-second century CE (P. Oxy. 58.3917; O. Bodl. 2.745 and P. Wisc. 2.48). The word also appears in Mark 15:16; Matt 27:27; Acts 23:35; and Phil 1:13. In Mark, πραιτώριον seems to require the explanation or specification of αὐλή (courtyard, dwelling [BDAG 150]), which admits the possibility the author was uncertain about his audience's ability to clearly understand the word. Matt 27:27 shows many similarities to Mark 15:16 and may have been chosen based on that contact. Luke does not use the term in his account of the Jerusalem trial (Luke 23:1–7), but he does when he describes Paul's trial in Caesarea (Acts 23:35). This uneven use suggests the word was not yet thoroughly integrated into Greek.

Triangulating a Johannine Community from John 18:28–19:22

However, Michael Flexsenhar III has recently raised questions about the use of πραιτώριον in Philippians (1:13), previously assumed to refer to the Praetorian Guard. If πραιτώριον was used early (mid-first century CE) to refer to a building, that could suggest that its later use in the Fourth Gospel (late first or early second century CE), having by then been thoroughly assimilated into Greek, could refer to Herod's palace in Jerusalem without necessarily bringing with it the strongly Roman cultural unit of an only partially assimilated loanword. Of course, a word for a building used by Romans, for Roman purposes, would likely carry a cultural reference to Rome no matter its level of integration into the language. However, this claim for cultural resonances based on historical data is not the same as the assumption Flexsenhar often makes that the meaning of the loanword in Greek brings with it the whole cultural encyclopedia of its Latin counterpart.[40] Furthermore, the many excellent examples he refers to where the Greek πραιτώριον is used to refer to a building often come from the late first century CE or later, or are simply dated to "the imperial period."[41] Thus, the evidence is less conclusive than one might assume. Flexsenhar also points out that the ending of the word (-ιον) categorizes it as a building rather than a group of people because of the regular patterns of the Greek lexicon in which "words ending in the neuter singular –(ε)ιον regularly refer to buildings."[42] However, the only other Latin loanword cited to support this point, ἀκροατήριον, can, like πραιτώριον, refer both to people (Plutarch, *Cat. Maj.* 22.2 "listeners" [Perrin, LCL]; *Mor.* 937 D "audience" [Cherniss, Helmbold, LCL]) and to a building (Acts 25:23).[43]

Standhartinger, though, successfully argues that the Greek phrase ἐν ὅλῳ (ἐν ὅλῳ τῷ πραιτωρίῳ in Phil 1:13) is never used to introduce a reference to people except, as here, metonymically; references to people start instead with ἐν παντί.[44] This practice is reflected in LXX usage, too; of the 256 uses of the phrase ἐν ὅλῳ, none provides a counterexample. Furthermore, Num 12:7 (ἐν ὅλῳ τῷ οἴκῳ μου, in my whole house/household) and 1 Kgdms 5:11 (ἐν ὅλῃ τῇ πόλει, referring to confusion in the whole city, in other words among the people of the city) parallel the metonymic use in Philippians that refers to a group of people by reference to a place associated with them. Thus, it seems clear that Phil 1:13 does refer to the whole *praetorium* rather than to the whole Praetorian Guard.

This early use must be viewed in context with the unevenness of some of the other evidence already mentioned. Furthermore, it is to the point that neither Philo nor, surprisingly given the Roman topics he discusses, Josephus ever uses the word. Josephus, for example, denotes a mobile general's tent on a campaign, *praetorium* in Latin (OLD, 1448), with στρατήγιον (*J.W.* 3.5.2 §82). The referent of πραιτώριον, thus, seems to have been under development in the first century CE, and only slowly assimilated into Greek use. Like referring to a town square using the word "piazza" in English, as Flexsenhar

96   *Laura J. Hunt*

also notes regarding Phil 1:13, πραιτώριον would have "pointed to a more distinctly Roman toponym in Paul's Greek city."[45] These three data points, that is, historical tradition about the provenance of John, the many Latin inscriptions in Ephesus, and the use of πραιτώριον in particular and other Latin loanwords more broadly within the Fourth Gospel, suggest Ephesus at around 100 CE as reasonable for the historical location of a proposed audience of John's Gospel.[46]

SOCIAL IDENTITY ANALYTICAL FRAMEWORK

The group proposed in the previous section would include Romans and Jews as overlapping identities.[47] While I am suggesting quite a loose network of Jesus-believers, it would include some subgroup identities around these two ethnicities at least. Ingroup/outgroup comparisons between these groups would develop using "markers" with which they could recognize and evaluate each other.[48]

The following SIT analysis will proceed by first noting the role of the law (νόμος in John) in the Roman cultural encyclopedia. Next, the role of *Torah* (also νόμος) as a Jewish marker from the first century CE will be briefly sketched. These discussions will provide the conceptual framework for examining the Johannine trial before Pilate. In that passage, Romans, "Jews," and Jesus negotiate νόμος.[49] Furthermore, by depicting Pilate (who crucifies Jesus) and certain "Jews" (who demand crucifixion), both as negotiating νόμος, John creates an exemplar for Jesus-believers that contrasts with the identity negotiations of the non-Christ-following Jews and Romans, and that insists that Roman and Jewish Jesus-believers themselves recategorize their own loyalties to Roman and Jewish laws under a larger, superordinate identity.[50]

Note that to create a superordinate identity is not to create a "universal" identity that is somehow less local or less ethnic than any other.[51] In fact, each subgroup within the larger group (in this case Roman and Jewish followers of Christ) tends to categorize itself as the best prototype for the larger group.[52] The difficulty, in a multi-ethnic group, is to convince each subgroup enactment of the superordinate identity that all of the other enactments are equally valid representations. Also, the analysis in this chapter about Christianity as a superordinate identity within the Gospel of John is not meant to construct Christianity as *the* superordinate identity of the world in any reified sense.[53] After all, Judaism, as a superordinate group, negotiates alternative subgroup expressions of Judaism, and Roman Imperialism, as a superordinate group, negotiates alternative subgroup expressions of Roman identity in similar ways, validating some expressions, correcting others, and perhaps excluding some as well.[54]

This superordinate/subgroup segmentation can be illustrated from the present day by advertisements seen in the London Tube in May–June 2015. Seeking to attract British visitors to its city, Las Vegas advertisers printed pictures of their recognizable skyline with the caption, "*Visit a place* where your *accent* is an aphrodisiac" (emphasis original). Despite the multiplicity of accents spoken by British citizens riding the Underground, the advertisers and the public were aware that distinctions meaningful in that social arena would not be relevant in the United States. And yet, the construction of "your accent" as one distinct from that spoken in Las Vegas, while creating a theoretically unified British accent, does not preclude that "aphrodisiac" from being enacted by Cockney, Geordie, Scouse, or any other UK accent once the visitors have arrived. What might rhetorically look like a universal identity is, in fact, enacted by a variety of subgroup identities who may even compete for the authority to represent the whole.

The following analysis of John 18:28–19:22 will detail some of the effects of the text on the identity of Roman and Jewish auditors around the marker of law. These two subgroups, however, are not completely distinct. In about 50 BCE in Ephesus, a group of Jewish Roman citizens received an exemption from military service.[55] Everyone in the Mediterranean world would be somewhat embedded within Roman culture. Romanness itself was theoretically offered as a superordinate identity that could encompass more local affiliations.[56] Romans understood themselves as mandated by the gods to spread the gift of civilization. In this way, Roman discourse recategorized local identities in "an attempt to bring intergroup peace by forming a superordinate identity while retaining subgroup salience."[57]

Aelius Aristides lays out Rome's ideology in his panegyric *To Rome*.[58] He covers three topics, as outlined by Rochette: "1) Rome established itself as the center of the world; 2) the Romans are by nature destined to command; 3) through the political qualities that its leaders demonstrated, Rome generated an era of peace and prosperity for the Greek cities, which it left with relative autonomy" (my translation).[59] Non-Romans who attracted Roman interest either submitted and were (at least partially) assimilated, or they demonstrated their barbarism by their refusal to submit to Roman law and thus "proved" that they deserved their destruction (Aristides, *Regarding Rome* 59).[60] Romans, then, welcomed outsiders into their law-governed midst and constructed those not welcomed as lawless barbarians.[61] Diodorus Siculus, in describing Herakles, says, "Travelling up and down the country [Keltike], he freed it from its lawless habits and ingrained hostility to strangers" (Diodorus, *The Library of History* 4.19).[62] The marker of "law" was thus quite important to Roman identity, although such an event would have looked quite different in regard to law and freedom from a Keltic perspective. In the *Aeneid*, Virgil has Anchises tell his son, Aeneas, "you, Roman, be sure to rule the world (be these your arts), to crown peace with justice (*mos*), to spare the vanquished and to crush the proud" (6.851–53, [Fairclough and Goold, LCL 63]). The reference is to *mos* ("custom") not *lex* ("law") or *ius* ("legal right"), and although Lewis and Short note that the distinctions were disappearing after Augustus, the foundation of Roman law is on tradition.[63] Quintilian, in a discussion about which of two laws (*lex*) to apply to a given situation, grounds law in the wisdom of the ancestors (*Decl.* 274).

There is tension in Roman thought, however, between natural and positive law. Natural law was "universal," "rational," "unwritten," "eternal," "unchanging," and the province of philosophers.[64] It was connected with the mandate that the gods had given the Romans to spread their civilization around the world, enacting their laws (in this mythical ideology) for the benefit of the conquered peoples.[65] Yet this rhetoric did not affect the positive application of the law.[66] Positive law was primarily enacted for the benefit of the elite and for the maintenance of the empire.[67]

In antiquity, government (and therefore law) depended on the gods.[68] This is particularly evident when discussing Jewish ethnicity which, although varied, usually included some relationship to belief in one God, chosenness, *Torah*, and Temple.[69] Yet using the transliteration of תורה can obscure the negotiations of *Torah* (νόμος) in Jewish identity (e.g., Philo *Creation* 1.1–3; Josephus *Life* 27.134). Within the Fourth Gospel, for example, in the debates over the Sabbath (John 5 and 9), Jesus's choices to heal are consistent with the healing brought by God through obedience in the Hebrew Bible (Exod 15:26), but John constructs them as inconsistent with some interpretations of that law. Yet healing even on the Sabbath was, in some views, consistent with the *Torah*'s concern for justice.[70] The legitimacy of healing on the Sabbath was a matter of dispute in Jewish sources.[71] Negotiations, then, both within and between Roman and Jewish identities, suggest that Jesus-believers' ingroup belonging might also frequently require debate.[72]

SOCIAL IDENTITY ANALYSIS

Eco's semiotics have pointed out the need for a historical referent outside of the text, and Bayesian analysis has shown that historical probabilities for the existence of an audience apart from Gospel evidence must be examined, as has been done above. J. Brian Tucker's six criteria for identifying a text that seeks to form the hearers' social identity will provide the third method to gather data for triangulation, addressing the second question from

Bayes: would the proposed group likely call forth an address such as the Fourth Gospel? I will measure that probability by the effects on the proposed group that a SIT analysis detects.

Tucker's criteria include that: (1) the text offers a rival narrative; (2) the text renames the auditors; (3) the text relates the new markers of identity to old markers in a way that recognizes the non-monolithic nature of identity; (4) the text addresses the implications of the new identity in areas of ethics (i.e., identity descriptors) and ethos (i.e., collective identity); (5) the text suggests performances that will embody the new identity; and (6) the text uses discursive practices from the environment to negotiate the new identity.[73] It is to the point that all of these criteria reference the development of a new identity in contrast to a previous one—in this case a Jesus-believing identity as Romans and Jews in some negotiated contrast with outsiders, Romans and Jews without connection to Jesus as the Christ/Messiah. For the purposes of this chapter, Tucker's criteria will be applied only to the Johannine trial narrative; a full study will require an analysis of the whole Gospel.[74]

Criteria 3 and 6 will be discussed in more detail below, but the other 4 criteria are immediately evident in John 18:28–19:22: Jesus claims an empire that rivals that of Rome (18:36) before whom he stands accused and also rivals "the Jews" who (according to the same verse) handed him over (criteria 1).[75] Jesus-believers are described as "those who listen to Jesus because they are from the truth" (18:37) (criteria 2). John 18:36 may also name Jesus-believers "servants of an empire that is not from this world," although because these are described in a contrary-to-fact conditional it is not certain whether the claim is that Jesus has no empire in this world (but does have servants in an empire he has elsewhere), or that Jesus has neither empire nor, therefore, servants.[76] Implications for ethics and ethos (criteria 4–5) of believing in Jesus are perhaps spelled out more clearly in other passages of the Gospel, such as the Farewell Discourse (John 14–17). Yet even in the trial narrative, hearers of the Gospel learn that Jesus-believers do not fight for Jesus's freedom (18:36), again contrasting with both Roman and Jewish identities.[77] Furthermore, Jesus himself models a man who chooses to be vulnerable for the sake of the people of God despite his power to do otherwise. These passages suggest, then, both a Johannine ethical stance as well as an identity intended to lead to its performance. The third criterion, the negotiation of non-monolithic identities, will be described through a brief spatial analysis of the trial. Then, for the sixth criterion, the element of Roman and Jewish discourse discussed above, νόμος, will be examined.

SPATIAL ANALYSIS OF JOHANNINE
TRIAL NARRATIVE

Spatial locations can be ethnically categorized through their physical descriptions, their conceptualization, and through the ways they are inhabited.[78] Based on the number of soldiers in the garden (a cohort, σπεῖρα), the conflict in John 18–19 starts out in a quite Roman space.[79] Even in that scene, however, Judas guides Roman soldiers *and* Jewish officials (ὁ χιλίαρχος καὶ οἱ ὑπηρέται τῶν Ἰουδαίων) to Jesus; they then take him to Annas (18:3, 12).

The chain of custody begins with "the Jews" who hand Jesus over to the Romans (18:30, 35, 36).[80] Romans and "Jews" separate inside and outside the Roman space, the *praetorium* (18:28), with Pilate travelling back and forth across the frontier.[81] The repetition of πραιτώριον, discussed above, marks the inside of the governor's palace as particularly Roman.[82] On the other hand, the refusal of "the Jews" to enter the palace for purity reasons (μιαίνω in 18:28), and the repetition of οἱ Ἰουδαῖοι (15 times in 35 verses) constructs the space outside the *praetorium* as ethnically Jewish.[83] However, Jesus starts on the Roman side, and while Pilate continually offers him to "the Jews" (18:31, 39; 19:6, 14), they reject him, suggesting that Jesus himself does not belong with "the Jews," despite his self-identification with them in John 4:20–22.[84] A key moment occurs in 18:35, when the surface answer to Pilate's question, "Am I a Jew?" is "No." However, I have argued elsewhere that all the Johannine questions formed with μή or μήτι have a double meaning.[85] The *Johannine* answer to Pilate's question is "Yes." So John, having already characterized Pilate as the one traveling between Roman and Jewish spaces, further blurs his identity.

In John 19:2, Roman soldiers offer a Roman salute to a Jewish king, somewhere in the *praetorium* (19:4). Although the crown and robe turn Jesus into Caesar, the pledge of loyalty to a Jewish king turns the Roman soldiers into ironic representatives of Judaism.[86] At this moment in the trial, then, Jesus is the only Roman left; he has never left Roman space, and he is repeatedly portrayed as a Roman emperor (19:2–5, 7, 12).[87]

The ethnicity of the two spaces is also blurred by the behavior of "the Jews," who begin to identify themselves as Romans by demanding crucifixion (19:6, 15). Pilate indeed offers to let "the Jews" crucify Jesus themselves (v. 6). Although the Romans were not the only people to use this method of execution, in the first century CE crucifixion was most often done by them. The generations alive after 70 CE would remember vivid stories of the crucifixions surrounding the fall of Jerusalem and the Temple.[88] Furthermore, when "the Jews" remind Pilate of his obligation as Caesar's friend (v. 11), they

Triangulating a Johannine Community from John 18:28–19:22 101

construct themselves as loyal to Rome.[89] Then, in 19:15, "the Jews" declare their allegiance to Caesar, completing their transformation into Romans.

In 19:16, the Johannine Pilate hands Jesus over, and whether he hands him back to "the Jews" or on to the Roman soldiers is ambiguous, at least temporarily, until v. 23. While the Roman Pilate seems to insist that Jesus *is* the ruler of "the Jews," "the Jews" insist that he is not.[90] Thus, the recategorization begins in 18:1–4, extends throughout John 18:28–19:22 and ends when the Romans become Jewish, Jesus becomes Caesar, and "the Jews" become Romans.[91] The two spaces, inside and outside the *praetorium*, could easily have been constructed with characters who acted according to the place they inhabited. Instead, Romans do not act like Romans, and "the Jews" do not act like Jews. The *titulus*, with its Aramaic, Latin, and Greek proclamation, "the king of the Jews," mirrors the Roman guards' hailing Jesus in the manner of an emperor. A narrative Jesus who is Caesar and at the same time a Jewish king establishes him as the exemplar for Romans *and* Jews who categorize themselves as Jesus-believers.[92] The uncertainty that might otherwise have surrounded the cognitive, evaluative, and emotional construction of the place of Roman citizenship and Jewish ethnicity within the group postulated near Ephesus is addressed with a claim for a continuing place for those ethnicities, a positive distinctiveness for their enactment, and (perhaps) an emotional connection to the exemplar (see below).

Thus, the third of Tucker's criteria for recognizing an identity-forming text, that of relating new markers of identity to old markers in a way that recognizes the non-monolithic nature of identity, is present in John 18:28–19:22. Using spatial divisions to highlight the unusual ethnic behavior of both Romans and "Jews" in the text, John presents a Jesus who moves between the two as an exemplar for Jesus-believers. This identity negotiation is confirmed through an analysis of elements of Tucker's sixth criterion, the use of discursive practices from the environment to negotiate the new identity. The marker of νόμος, which, as we have seen, is important to both groups, is recategorized such that it is not the exclusive resource of either Roman or Jewish identity but instead comes under the scrutiny of Jesus.

ROMAN AND JEWISH LAW

Scholars sometimes conclude that Jesus's crucifixion is carried out in violation of both Jewish and Roman law.[93] In Pancaro's study of the meaning of νόμος in the Gospel of John, he notes that "the Law should lead to the recognition of Jesus" and that, therefore, "the Law is violated by those who condemn Jesus."[94] Yet regarding the trial narrative, he also points out that both the law "in the eyes of the Jews" and the fulfillment of the law in the eyes of the evangelist demand the death of Jesus.[95]

Hallbäck notes this feature as well:

> There is . . . a conflict of interpretation between Jesus and the "Jews" respecting his person, a choice between belief and disbelief. But this is a conflict at the cognitive level of the narrative; at the pragmatic level there is no opposing programme. The "Jews" do not represent an opposing programme to the narrative assignment of Jesus. Evidently the "Jews" are behind the crucifixion of Jesus, and they themselves think of this as an opposing programme. But this is exactly where they are deceived, for it is in fact an auxiliary programme. It is the intention, the assignment, of Jesus to be crucified, and to that end the seemingly contradictory programme enters the principal narrative programme of the Gospel as an auxiliary programme. Jesus himself has to send off Judas during the last Supper; and when he is about to be arrested in Gethsemane, he almost has to insist on being caught.[96]

Although Thatcher writes that "the events of Jesus' death were predetermined not by the public transcript of Roman crucifixions, but rather by the imperative that God's word must be fulfilled," I suggest that from John's perspective they are both.[97] Indeed, "the emperor's *Lex* is an actor in the game."[98] Although Jesus has not transgressed Roman natural law, Pilate's need to ensure peace in the province, that is, the pragmatic application of Rome's power, positive law, demands that he must die.

So what happens to the νόμοι of "the Jews" and the Romans in the unfolding of the trial narrative?[99] As will be shown, the characters who are not disciples alternate in their claims to follow Roman or Jewish law, which deemphasizes both laws as identity markers and abrogates the use of either law to judge Jesus or to judge those auditors of the Gospel who want to embody the exemplar Jesus that John provides.

When the character of Pilate asks for the accusation against Jesus (18:29), he is following Roman legal procedure.[100] In the next verse, "the Jews" also present themselves as law-abiding, since they claim that Jesus has done "something wrong" (v. 30).[101] The law used as a standard for judging that wrong, however, is not specified. Nevertheless, when Pilate suggests that they complete their judgment "according to [their] own law" (v. 31), each group is abiding by their own proper code.[102] The rhetorical effect of the next phrase in v. 31, however, "we are not permitted to kill anyone," whether historically accurate or not, is a claim for a Jewish identity that abides by Roman law by bringing Jewish transgressors to Rome for execution.[103]

When Pilate declares a lack of αἰτία, grounds for accusation against Jesus (v. 38), this is not the same as a declaration of innocence.[104] Instead, Pilate is positioning himself as a law-abiding judge who will not try a case without reasonable grounds for Roman involvement.[105] He then refers "the Jews" to their own tradition (ἔστιν δὲ συνήθεια ὑμῖν) about releasing a prisoner at Passover (v. 39)—and for Romans, as already mentioned, tradition was the basis of law. Furthermore, Romans regularly upheld local laws, so Pilate is abiding by Roman law, by deferring to Jewish law.[106] At this point in the narrative, John has positioned "the Jews" as loyal to Roman law and Pilate as willing to follow Jewish law.

In John 18:40, "the Jews" for the first time declare themselves to be rebellious to Rome by choosing a rebel over Jesus.[107] This behavior becomes clearer when one disentangles the two levels of communication. Rather than putting the characterization of Barabbas in the mouth of Pilate or of "the Jews," John has the narrator step in and declare him to be a rebel.[108] The irony, then, as many have perceived, is that law-abiding "Jews" choose to set a rebel free.[109] So far, then, John has described Romans and "Jews" as outgroups to Jesus and his followers; they vie with one another in following each other's laws, and yet one is willing to support a rebel. The ingroup that John is constructing in opposition to these outgroups might therefore not prioritize obedience to either law while nevertheless *not* supporting rebellion against Rome.

The flogging and slapping in 19:1–3 are part of normal judicial processes in antiquity (*Dig.* 48.10.15.41), so Pilate is still following Roman law.[110] Pilate again follows Roman law by declaring a lack of grounds for Jesus's trial in 19:4, as in 18:38. Just as "the Jews" supported a Roman rebel, Pilate suggests Jewish rebellion (while characterizing himself as law-abiding) in v. 6 when he offers Jesus to "the Jews" for crucifixion. "The Jews," however, reject that suggestion and instead declare themselves to be law-abiding, specifically, here, to *Torah* (v. 7).[111]

John has Jesus, in v. 11, raise two questions relevant to a discussion of law: Who is the source of Pilate's authority? and Who has the greater sin? The first question pitting the Roman gods against the Jewish god (and his son Jesus) will be answered by the second.[112] The word for sin, ἁμαρτία, understood as a transgression of standards, implicates whichever gods provide that standard.

Present-day interpretations may want to distinguish between sin and the transgression of a legal code. In *Ant.* 16.1.1, Josephus accuses Herod of instituting a law that is "an offence against religion (ἁμαρτία πρὸς τὴν θρησκείαν) rather than a punishment," which sounds like a similar distinction. However, he goes on to point out that ordinary punishments are sanctioned by religion (Exod 22:1, 4, 7; Deut 15:12) whereas the punishment instituted by Herod (selling housebreakers into slavery) is judged excessive. Its enactment would require Jews to obey gentile masters and thus possibly to sin, a situation prohibited by *Torah* (Lev 25:47). Thus, both the punishment and the offense against religion are judged by what might today be called religious standards.

Who is the source of Pilate's authority? The Jewish god who has more authority than Roman gods (John 19:11a). Who can judge who has the greater sin? Jesus has abrogated to himself the divine sanction to recognize transgressors (19:11b). When he names "the one who handed me over to you," he judges someone neither Pilate nor "the Jews" have identified as guilty.[113] The exemplar Jesus that John sets forth, then, is given the authority to judge, and the outgroups' judgments are delegitimized.

In v. 12, when "the Jews" call Pilate's obedience to Caesar into question, they are now appealing to *his* law.[114] And verses 13–16 offer an ambiguous conclusion: Pilate sits himself or seats Jesus at the judgment seat (v. 13).[115] If Pilate is seated, he demonstrates his loyalty to Caesar's law, and in v. 15 "the Jews" join him as they declare their own loyalty to Caesar. When John 19:7 is read alongside 19:16, Jesus has now been condemned "according to both Jewish and imperial law."[116] But what if John, in a **double entendre**, has also seated Jesus at the judge's bench?

For Bro Larsen, the "weakness" of Pilate and the injustice of "the Jews" (18:40; 19:15) together "undermin[e] the legitimacy of both systems."[117] I have argued against a weak Pilate, and I do not conclude that the systems lack legitimacy.[118] Instead, this passage realigns both sources of law. In 19:11, John establishes Pilate's power as subordinate to another's.[119] While Jesus is condemned by both laws and does go on to suffer the consequences of that condemnation, his portrayal in this passage as emperor and judge (not to mention his later resurrection) aligns both rules of law as subject to him. As the exemplar for the Jesus-believers, the character of Jesus invites them to embody this power as well.[120] In the proposed group of Jews and Romans near Ephesus, the effects of such a text, then, would be to strengthen the group's confidence in the embodiment of a new identity, that, like Jesus, is not completely at odds with, but intersectional to previous Roman and Jewish identities.[121] In describing Jesus negotiating various groups' allegiances in the Johannine trial narrative, the Fourth Gospel provides for its audience three elements of group identification: (1) the knowledge that Jesus aligned himself sometimes with one and sometimes with another ethnicity, and (2) the evaluation of both laws as effective with an ambiguous stance toward rebellion, and yet (3) subsumed under Jesus's appraisal. The impassive way Jesus (as an exemplar) faces his opponents and eventually his death might also elicit feelings of admiration, adding an emotional component to the listeners' perception of the ingroup prototype.[122]

The question, then, is what kind of a Jew is Jesus? What kind of a Roman? This is a question better asked of the Gospel of John as a whole. However, I

Triangulating a Johannine Community from John 18:28–19:22 105

will suggest here two possibly fruitful leads: Jesus's words (cf. 1:17) and the Spirit (e.g., 3:34; 4:23–24; 14:17; 16:13; 20:22).[123] These become the appropriate arenas for identity negotiations in the new group.

CONCLUSIONS

For the purposes of this chapter, the Johannine community was described as a group with cognitive, evaluative, and emotional components. The group proposed was a network of Jesus-followers in the region of Ephesus consisting of various subgroup identities including Roman and Jewish. A social identity analysis of the Johannine trial narrative concluded that the identity marker of "law," whether Roman or Jewish, was under negotiation by all parties and ultimately under the evaluation of Jesus, the exemplar of the ingroup. Identity itself, particularly ethnic identity, was recategorized such that neither textual "Jews" nor textual Romans behaved in ways appropriate to those groups. Jesus emerged as the exemplar in this marker as well, as Roman Emperor and King of the Jews.

This SIT analysis constructed the effects the text of the Fourth Gospel would have on a network of Jesus-believers in the environs of Ephesus *ca.* 100 CE that was proposed based on semiotic demands and historical evidence. It seems likely that Jews and Romans, overlapping identities in any case, might have needed permission and support in developing an identity that allowed for the traditional elements of both ethnicities, but nuanced in imitation of Jesus. This analysis strengthens the probability that, given its existence, such a group could have required such a narrative, one ingredient of Bayesian analysis. However, Eco's semiotics revealed the impossibility of determining whether an identity-forming text is confirming or correcting its addressees (unless it says so specifically).[124] The above analysis reveals nothing about the enactments of an actual group identity, only the direction in which the Gospel pushes them. Furthermore, the power imbalance of Pilate over "the Jews" in the trial narrative might cause uneven results. A group in which Jewish followers of Christ are the strongest subgroup might be chastened and reminded by Jesus as Caesar that the Roman subgroup can also constitute a prototype of emerging Christian identity. But a group constituted only by Roman Christ-followers could overlook the importance of Jesus as a Jewish king, which is less prominent in the text, and denigrate all Jews for their role in the trial, in an emerging anti-Semitism that has proved all too real.[125]

Despite the lack of firm conclusions, this chapter has triangulated some information about the audience of the Fourth Gospel. I have constructed a SIT study of John 18:28–19:22 for Roman and Jewish identities, and with regard to law observance. Much more work remains to be done, but the presence of these negotiations does support the existence of people with Roman and Jewish identities among the audience of the Gospel. However, the two limitations just mentioned remain: First, the very fact that Reinhartz and Carter could suggest that the audience was too embedded in Roman identity while so many previous scholars had postulated a community completely cut off from the wider Roman culture demonstrates that while we may read social identity prototypes from the text, we cannot tell if they are being proposed or reinforced.[126]

Still, grounding the proposed Johannine group in historical data increases, according to Bayes, the probability that this group existed alongside the existence of the Fourth Gospel. The verisimilitude of the effects of the trial narrative on such a group strengthens the probability that this specific group would likely call forth an address such as the Fourth Gospel, thereby also raising the probability that this group existed given the existence of the Fourth Gospel. And more social identity proposals, not only for other markers across the whole Gospel, but also with other hypothetical audiences, ought to be compared and contrasted with this one, in the hope that more data will provide more nuanced conclusions. For now, this chapter has elucidated connections between a Johannine group minimally negotiating Jewish and Roman identities and the Fourth Gospel's trial narrative.

NOTES

1. Much of this chapter, particularly the second half, comes from unpublished sections of my dissertation, particularly chapter 7; Laura J. Hunt, "Jesus Caesar: A Roman Reading of John 18:28–19:22" (PhD diss., University of Wales Trinity Saint David, 2017).

2. Sandra Mathison, "Why Triangulate?" *Educational Researcher* 17.2 (1988): 15.

3. Mathison, "Why Triangulate?," 13–16. Note that Mathison rightly warns that such propositions must take into account the data, the project, and the current investigator's social world, and must all be located within the same theoretical approach. In the discussion that follows, I am theorizing an actual text written from and to first-century CE social locations (as stipulated in the chapter) by one or more ancient persons, as a rhetorically interested recounting of the life, death, and resurrection of the remembered Jesus. And I recognize that all my proposals are also rhetorically framed based on my own social location.

4. Henri Tajfel, *Differentiation between Social Groups: Studies in the Social Psychology of Intergroup Relations* (London: Academic Press, 1978), 63.

5. Tajfel, *Differentiation*, 28–29.

Triangulating a Johannine Community from John 18:28–19:22   107

6. A. Sue Russell, "A Genealogy of Social Identity Theory," in *T&T Clark Social Identity Commentary on the New Testament*, ed. J. Brian Tucker and Aaron Kuecker (London: T&T Clark, 2020), 11.

7. Anthony D. Smith, *The Ethnic Origins of Nations* (Oxford: Blackwell, 1986), 22–31; David G. Horrell, *Ethnicity and Inclusion: Religion, Race, and Whiteness in Constructions of Jewish and Christian Identities* (Grand Rapids, MI: Eerdmans, 2020), 71–72.

8. Robyn Faith Walsh, *The Origins of Early Christian Literature: Contextualizing the New Testament within Greco-Roman Literary Culture* (Cambridge: Cambridge University Press, 2021), 50–104.

9. J. Louis Martyn, *History and Theology in the Fourth Gospel* (New York: Harper and Row, 1968); Wally V. Cirafesi, "The Johannine Community Hypothesis (1968–Present): Past and Present Approaches and a New Way Forward," *CBR* 12.2 (2014): 17–93 (75).

10. Frederik Wisse, "Historical Method and the Johannine Community," *ARC: The Journal of the Faculty of Religious Studies, McGill University* 20 (1992): 35–42.

11. Cf. Walsh, *The Origins*, e.g., 6, 111.

12. Wisse, "Historical Method," 39.

13. Wisse, "Historical Method," 41, 42.

14. Wisse, "Historical Method," 40.

15. Adele Reinhartz, *Cast out of the Covenant: Jews and Anti-Judaism in the Gospel of John* (Lanham, MD: Lexington/Fortress, 2018), 133.

16. Reinhartz, *Cast out of the Covenant*, xvi, xxxi–xxxiii.

17. Reinhartz, *Cast out of the Covenant*, e.g., 148. "John" is used here and throughout the chapter as a stand-in for the Fourth Gospel's author/s.

18. E.g., Reinhartz, *Cast out of the Covenant*, xxvi–xxvii.

19. For my more detailed introduction into Eco's semiotics, see Laura J. Hunt, *Jesus Caesar: A Roman Reading of the Johannine Trial Narrative*, WUNT 2.506 (Tübingen: Mohr Siebeck, 2019), 6–13.

20. Hunt, *Jesus Caesar*, 54–55.

21. David A. Lamb, *Text, Context and the Johannine Community: A Sociolinguistic Analysis of the Johannine Writings*, LNTS 477 (London: Bloomsbury T&T Clark, 2014), 3–4; Rodolfo Galvan Estrada, III, *A Pneumatology of Race in the Gospel of John: An Ethnocritical Study* (Eugene, OR: Pickwick, 2019), 13.

22. Andrew T. Lincoln, *Truth on Trial: The Lawsuit Motif in the Fourth Gospel* (Peabody, MA: Hendrickson, 2000), 222–31.

23. Lincoln, *Truth*, 222.

24. Lincoln, *Truth*, 229.

25. Lincoln, *Truth*, 229.

26. Lincoln, *Truth*, 230.

27. He is one of the most quoted authors in *Jesus Caesar*.

28. Perhaps one might add the Hebrew Bible passages cited by the Gospel's author, but those are being read through the lens of one who already, in John's language, believes.

29. Hunt, *Jesus Caesar*, 17–21.

30. Gary P. Radford, *On Eco* (Australia: Thomson, 2003), 26.

31. Lincoln, *Truth*, 230.

32. Stephen C. Barton, "Can We Identify the Gospel Audiences?," in *The Gospel for All Christians: Rethinking the Gospel Audiences*, ed. Richard Bauckham (Grand Rapids, MI: Eerdmans, 1998), 176–79.

33. Christoph Heilig, "The New Perspective (on Paul) on Peter: Cornelius's Conversion, the Antioch Incident, and Peter's Stance Towards Gentiles in the Light of the Philosophy of Historiography," in *Christian Origins and the Establishment of the Early Jesus Movement*, ed. Stanley E. Porter and Andrew W. Pitts, TENTS 12, Early Christianity in Its Hellenistic Context (Leiden: Brill, 2018), 465–68.

34. Heilig, "The New Perspective," 466. Additionally, the theorem produces self-contradicting results when applied to extremely improbable events; thank you to Prof. Samuel Cohen from the Mathematical Institute at Oxford University, and to the Bayes and Bible group led by Christoph Heilig and funded by the Cogito Foundation, for these warnings.

35. Richard Bauckham, "For Whom Were Gospels Written?," *HTS Teologiese Studies/Theological Studies* 55.4 (1999): 865–82 (866, 874–80).

36. Cf. Reinhartz, *Cast out of the Covenant*, xxvii.

37. For an excellent discussion, see Marianne Meye Thompson, *John: A Commentary* (Louisville: Westminster John Knox, 2015), 20–21.

38. Hunt, *Jesus Caesar*, 91–141.

39. This paragraph and the next repeat, condense, and somewhat extend the discussion on Latin-Greek code-switching in Hunt, *Jesus Caesar*, 120–23. See, on the use of Latin loanwords in everyday Greek, Hugh J. Mason, *Greek Terms for Roman Institutions: A Lexicon and Analysis* (Toronto: Hakkert, 1974), 8.

40. Michael Flexsenhar, III, "The Provenance of Philippians and Why it Matters: Old Questions, New Approaches" *JSNT* 42.1 (2019): 18–45 (30n35, 37, 38; 31; 31n39, 40; 31n43; 34, 35). For example, Flexsenhar claims, "And yet if Paul wanted to use πραιτώριον as an allusion to a group of soldiers, then additional military designations would have appeared to make his meaning clear" and cites *OLD* s.v. praetorium 2, 1448 (see, similarly, 34).

41. Flexsenhar, "The Provenance of Philippians," 20; 30; 30n35; 31–32; 31n42, 43, 45; 33. His discussion of the *praetorium* and accompanying inscription at Dium (Dion, *Colonia Iulia Augusta Diensis*) is fascinating (35–36), but the building has not been securely dated; Anastasios Oulkeroglou, "Public Baths in Roman Dion (Colonia Iulia Augusta Diensis)," *Journal of Greek Archaeology* 2 (2017): 283–320 (283).

42. Flexsenhar, "The Provenance of Philippians," 29

43. Paul A. Holloway, *Philippians: A Commentary*, Hermeneia (Minneapolis, MN: Fortress, 2017), 21n166, partially cited in Flexsenhar, "The Provenance of Philippians," 29; 29 n. 29.

44. Angela Standhartinger, "Greetings from Prison and Greetings from Caesar's House (Philippians 4.22): A Reconsideration of an Enigmatic Greek Expression in the Light of the Context and Setting of Philippians" *JSNT* 43.4 (2021): 468–84 (476n35).

45. Flexsenhar, "The Provenance of Philippians," 34.

46. For Latin use in John, see Hunt, *Jesus Caesar*, 123–41. On the uncertainty of dating P52, see Brent Nongbri, "The Use and Abuse of P52: Papyrological Pitfalls in the Dating of the Fourth Gospel," *HTR* 98.1 (2005): 23–48.

47. Ephesus boasted an association of Roman citizens, a regular parade in celebration of Rome, and a location for the governor's courts; Hunt, *Jesus Caesar*, 94–97. For Jews in Ephesus, see Philo, *Legat.* 245; Josephus, *Ag. Ap.* 2.39; *Ant.* 20.256; Thompson, *John*, 21. I argue, further, for a Samaritan Israelite subgroup in Laura J. Hunt, "Samaritan Israelites and Jews under the Shadow of Rome: Reading John 4:1–45 in Ephesus," *Religions: Exploring the Complexity of Identities and Boundaries within the New Testament World* 14.8 (2023): 1149; https://doi.org/10.3390/rel14091149.

48. Aaron Kuecker, "Ethnicity and Social Identity," in *T&T Clark Handbook to Social Identity in the New Testament*, ed. J. Brian Tucker et al. (London: Bloomsbury, 2014), 67.

49. I use "Jews" or "the Jews" to refer to the textual construction of οἱ Ἰουδαῖοι within the Fourth Gospel; see further Hunt, *Jesus Caesar*, 65.

50. Anthony C. Thiselton, *New Horizons in Hermeneutics: The Theory and Practice of Transforming Biblical Reading* (Grand Rapids: Zondervan, 1992), 570; Laura J. Hunt, "Alternatives to Mirror Reading," in *Socio-Scientific Approaches to Religious Enmity*, ed. Christopher Porter, Routledge Interdisciplinary Perspectives on Biblical Criticism (London: Routledge, in press). Note that an exemplar in this chapter refers to a specific ingroup example (whether actual or textual), and a prototype refers to a cluster of characteristics. Each can be used for categorizing others and oneself; Eliot R. Smith and Michael A. Zarate, "Exemplar and Prototype use in Social Categorization" *Social Cognition* 8.3 (1990): 243–62.

51. Horrell, *Ethnicity*, e.g., 5.

52. Marilynn B. Brewer, "Social Identity Complexity and Acceptance of Diversity," in *The Psychology of Social and Cultural Diversity*, ed. Richard J. Crisp (Oxford: Wiley-Blackwell, 2010).

53. In appreciative response to Horrell, *Ethnicity*, 41–43.

54. For Jewish identity negotiations, see the correspondence between Elephantine, Jerusalem and Samaria; Gary N. Knoppers, *Jews and Samaritans: The Origins and History of Their Early Relations* (New York: Oxford University Press, 2013), 119–20. For Roman identity negotiation, see e.g., Aelius Aristides *To Rome*, 63–64.

55. Josephus, *Ant.* 14.10.13; Shaye J. D. Cohen, "'Those Who Say They Are Jews and Are Not': How Do You Know a Jew in Antiquity When You See One?," in *Diasporas in Antiquity*, ed. Shaye J. D. Cohen and Ernest S. Frerichs (Atlanta: Scholars Press, 1993), 31. Also, Luke claims that Paul was a Roman citizen (Acts 16:37–38; 22:25–29; 23:27).

56. Louise Revell, *Roman Imperialism and Local Identities* (Cambridge: Cambridge University Press, 2009), xi, 192. See, also, Greg Woolf, "Becoming Roman, Staying Greek: Culture, Identity and the Civilizing Process in the Roman East," *The Cambridge Classical Journal* 40 (1994): 116–43 (119); Richard Hingley, *Globalizing Roman Culture: Unity, Diversity and Empire* (London: Routledge, 2005), 62–64; Emma Dench, *Romulus' Asylum: Roman Identities from the Age of Alexander to the*

110 *Laura J. Hunt*

Age of Hadrian (Oxford: Oxford University Press, 2005), 31–33. Cf. Hunt, *Jesus Caesar*, 36–38.

57. Kuecker, "Filial Piety and Violence in Luke-Acts and the Aeneid: A Comparative Analysis of Two Trans-Ethnic Identities," in *T&T Clark Handbook to Social Identity in the New Testament*, ed. J. Brian Tucker, at al. (London: Bloomsbury, 2014), 211–33 (211).

58. Revell, *Roman Imperialism*, 14.

59. "1) Rome s'est imposée comme centre du monde; 2) les Romains sont destinés par nature à commander; 3) par les qualités politiques dont ses dirigeants on fait preuve, Rome a engendré une ère de paix et de prospérité pour les cités grecques, auxquelles elle laisse une relative autonomie"; Bruno Rochette, *Le latin dans le monde grec: Recherches sur la diffusion de la langue et des lettres latines dans les provinces hellénophones de l'empire romain* (Brussels: Latomus, 1997), 66.

60. See also Kuecker, "Filial Piety," 221–23.

61. Hingley, *Globalizing Roman Culture*, 61–67. For the construction of the Galatians into the "barbarian Other," see Brigitte Kahl, *Galatians Re-Imagined: Reading with the Eyes of the Vanquished* (Minneapolis: Fortress, 2010), 6–9, 42–75. See also Greg Woolf, "Inventing Empire in Ancient Rome," in *Empires: Perspectives from Archaeology and History*, ed. Susan E. Alcock, Terence N. D'Altroy, Kathleen D. Morrison, and Carla M. Sinopoli (Cambridge: Cambridge University Press, 2001), 319.

62. Translation from Greg Woolf, *Tales of the Barbarians: Ethnography and Empire in the Roman West* (Chichester: Wiley-Blackwell, 2011), 19.

63. N. M. Horsfall, "Virgil, History and the Roman Tradition," *Prudentia* 8 (1976): 73–89 (85); Wilhelm Kierdorf, *Mos maiorum, Brill's New Pauly* (Online: Brill, 2006).

64. Christine Hayes, *What's Divine About Divine Law? Early Perspectives* (Princeton: Princeton University Press, 2015), 92. Note that Hayes conflates Greek and Roman attitudes toward law over quite a long period of time (e.g., 86–87 where Hadrian, Stoicism, and Plato are all referenced).

65. Hayes, *What's Divine*, 61; P. A. Brunt, *"Laus imperii,"* in *Roman Imperial Themes* (Oxford: Clarendon, 1990), 291, 295; Brunt, "Roman Imperial Illusions," in *Roman Imperial Themes*, ed. P. A. Brunt (Oxford: Clarendon, 1990), 433–80 (438–40).

66. Hayes, *What's Divine*, 88.

67. Brunt, *"Laus,"* 316–22; P. A. Brunt, *Roman Imperial Themes* (Oxford: Clarendon, 1990), 509; Hayes, *What's Divine*, 81–86.

68. Martin Goodman, "Nerva, the *Fiscus Judaicus* and Jewish Identity," *JRS* 79 (1989): 40–44 (40).

69. James D. G. Dunn, *The Partings of the Ways: Between Christianity and Judaism and Their Significance for the Character of Christianity* (London: SCM, 2006), 24–48.

70. Warren Carter, *John and Empire: Initial Explorations* (New York: T&T Clark, 2008), 162.

71. Thompson, *John*, 211.

72. However, given the unequal status of Jews and Romans in Ephesus, and the uncertainty surrounding both an ingroup prototype for the newly developing group and the possibility of external threats to that group, the specifics of those negotiations remain uncharted. For some possible configurations, see John F. Dovidio, Samuel L. Gaertner, and Tamar Saguy, "Another View of 'We': Majority and Minority Group Perspectives on a Common Ingroup Identity," *European Review of Social Psychology* 18 (2007): 296–330.

73. J. Brian Tucker, *Remain in Your Calling: Paul and the Continuation of Social Identities in 1 Corinthians* (Eugene, OR: Pickwick, 2011), 51–57. For a justification of the relevance of social identity theory to the Gospel of John, see Philip F. Esler and Ronald A. Piper, *Lazarus, Mary and Martha: Social-Scientific Approaches to the Gospel of John* (Minneapolis: Fortress, 2006), 27, 38–40 (with exception taken to the characterization of John's language as an antilanguage, 39). Cf. also Hunt, *Jesus Caesar*, 33–38.

74. Laura J. Hunt, *John: A Social Identity Commentary*, T&T Clark Social Identity Commentaries on the New Testament (London: T&T Clark, forthcoming).

75. Hunt, *Jesus Caesar*, 143–297. It could be interesting, moreover, to argue that John's narrative also rivals those of the other canonical gospels, creating a narrative that seeks to form the identity of a group alternative to them.

76. Hunt, *Jesus Caesar*, 266.

77. Roman imperial conquest constructed as setting barbarians free is well known (Diodorus, *The Library of History* 4.19). For violence to obtain freedom as part of Jewish identity (even against oneself should violence against the other fail), see Exod 17:8–13; Josephus *Ant.* 2.44; *J.W.* 5.321; 7.255; 1 Macc 2:11; 14:25–26.

78. Gerhard van den Heever, "Space, Social Space, and the Construction of Early Christian Identity in First Century Asia Minor," *R&T* 17.3/4 (2010): 205–43 (222).

79. Stephen D. Moore, *Empire and Apocalypse: Postcolonialism and the New Testament* (Sheffield: Sheffield Phoenix Press, 2006), 53.

80. The verb παραδίδωμι cannot (*pace* Duke) be translated as "betray" wherever it occurs in the Fourth Gospel as one can hardly think that John 19:30 means that Jesus "bowed his head and betrayed his spirit"; Paul D. Duke, *Irony in the Fourth Gospel* (Atlanta: John Knox Press, 1985), 128.

81. This traveling between spaces is often noted, but the ethnic characterization of the spaces is not; Thompson, *John*, 371; Sherri Brown, "What Is Truth? Jesus, Pilate, and the Staging of the Dialogue of the Cross in John 18:28–19:16a," *CBQ* 77.1 (2015): 69–86.

82. Hunt, *Jesus Caesar*, 120–23.

83. *Pace* Carter who believes that the repetition of "the *Ioudaioi*" (18:31, 36, 38; 19:7, 12, 14) is done "to underline their opposition to Jesus"; Carter, *John*, 299. I am arguing instead that John is recategorizing them together with Romans (as represented by Pilate and his soldiers) as outgroups, who are incomplete prototypes for Roman *or* Jewish Jesus-believers.

84. Mark Stibbe notes also the sense of brotherhood between Jesus and "the Jews" that comes from their shared Father (8:41), although in that context, there is no

suggestion of *rapprochement*; Mark W. G. Stibbe, *John as Storyteller: Narrative Criticism and the Fourth Gospel* (Cambridge: Cambridge University Press, 1992), 135.

85. Hunt, "Samaritan Israelites," 6. Cf. David Rensberger, *Overcoming the World: Politics and Community in the Gospel of John* (London: SPCK, 1989), 93; Wayne A. Meeks, *The Prophet-King: Moses Traditions and the Johannine Christology* (Leiden: Brill, 1967), 63.

86. Hunt, *Jesus Caesar*, 211–40; 271–72.

87. Hunt, *Jesus Caesar*, 187–241.

88. David W. Chapman, *Ancient Jewish and Christian Perceptions of Crucifixion* (Grand Rapids, MI: Baker Academic, 2010), 94; for cultural memory see Jeffrey Andrew Barash, "Qu'est-ce que la mémoire collective? Réflexions sur l'interprétation de la mémoire chez Paul Ricoeur," *Revue de Métaphysique et de Morale* 2 (2006): 85–95.

89. Lance Byron Richey, *Roman Imperial Ideology and the Gospel of John*, CBQMS 43 (Washington, DC: Catholic Biblical Association of America, 2007), 167.

90. Raymond F. Collins, "Speaking of the Jews: 'Jews' in the Discourse Material of the Fourth Gospel," in *Anti-Judaism and the Fourth Gospel*, ed. R. Bieringer, D. Pollefeyt, and F. Vandecasteele-Vanneuville (Louisville: Westminster John Knox, 2001), 174.

91. See also François Genuyt, "La comparution de Jésus devant Pilate: Analyse sémiotique de Jean 18,28–19,16," *RSR* 73.1 (1985): 133–46 (134).

92. Van Tilborg also sees this blurring of alignment although he does not suggest a reason for it nor conclusions to be drawn from it; Sjef van Tilborg, *Reading John in Ephesus*, NovTSup 83 (Leiden: Brill, 1996), 166.

93. E.g., Severino Pancaro, *The Law in the Fourth Gospel: The Torah and the Gospel, Moses and Jesus, Judaism and Christianity According to John*, NovTSup 42 (Leiden: Brill, 1975), 130–57.

94. Pancaro, *Law*, 508–10.

95. Pancaro, *Law*, 510. Thus, *pace* Carter, there is no opposition between Jesus and the combined forces of Pilate and the Jewish leadership; Warren Carter, "Social Identities, Subgroups, and John's Gospel: Jesus the Prototype and Pontius Pilate (John 18.28–19.16)," in *T&T Clark Handbook to Social Identity in the New Testament*, ed. J. Brian Tucker et al. (London: Bloomsbury, 2014), 241–48.

96. Geert Hallbäck, "The Gospel of John as Literature: Literary Readings of the Fourth Gospel," in *New Readings in John: Literary and Theological Perspectives: Essays from the Scandinavian Conference on the Fourth Gospel, Arhus, 1997*, ed. Johannes Nissen and Sigfred Pedersen, JSNTSup 182 (Sheffield: Sheffield Academic, 1999), 45.

97. It is possible that Thatcher is also referencing a cognitive contrast in the meaning of these events. However, I would argue that both meanings are still present; Tom Thatcher, "'I Have Conquered the World': The Death of Jesus and the End of Empire in the Gospel of John," in *Empire in the New Testament*, ed. Stanley E. Porter and Cynthia Long Westfall, Mcmaster Divinity College Press New Testament Study Series (Eugene, OR: Pickwick, 2011), 155, 157–58.

Triangulating a Johannine Community from John 18:28–19:22   113

98. Kasper Bro Larsen, *Recognizing the Stranger: Recognition Scenes in the Gospel of John,* BInS 93 (Leiden: Brill, 2008), 175.

99. Although Pancaro looks at the function of the Jewish law in the Gospel of John, within the trial pericope he contrasts religious and political in a way that is anachronistic; Pancaro, *Law,* e.g., 315; Hunt, *Jesus Caesar,* 13–15. Genuyt notes the two laws in play as well; "Comparution," 135.

100. E. Bickermann, "*Utilitas crucis*: Observations sur les récits du procès de Jésus dans les évangiles canoniques," *Revue de l'Histoire des Religions* 112 (1935): 169–241 (198); D. Francois Tolmie, "Pontius Pilate: Failing in More Ways Than One," in *Character Studies in the Fourth Gospel: Narrative Approaches to Seventy Figures in John,* ed. Steven A. Hunt, D. Francois Tolmie, and Ruben Zimmermann, WUNT 1.314. (Tübingen: Mohr Siebeck, 2013), 584.

101. Lincoln, *Truth,* 37; Larsen, *Recognizing the Stranger,* 177–78.

102. Joel C. Elowsky, ed. *Commentary on the Gospel of John: Theodore of Mopsuestia,* ed. Thomas C. Oden and Gerald Bray, L., Ancient Christian Texts (Downers Grove, IL: IVP Academic, 2010), 152.

103. For an entrée into the historical debate, see Arthur M. Wright, *The Governor and the King: Irony, Hidden Transcripts, and Negotiating Empire in the Fourth Gospel* (Eugene, OR: Pickwick, 2019), 129–31. Note that Lincoln also examines the play of laws in this passage, although his analysis focuses more on results and mine on categories (*Truth,* 124–25).

104. Hunt, *Jesus Caesar,* 268–69.

105. Tolmie, "Pontius Pilate," 587–89.

106. For a discussion of Romans abiding by local laws, see Julien Fournier, *Entre tutelle romaine et autonomie civique: L'administration judiciaire dans les provinces hellénophones de l'empire romain, 129 av. J. C.–235 ap. J. C.* (Athènes: Ecole française d'Athènes, 2010), 594, 595 n. 7; Agnès Bérenger-Badel, "Formation et compétences des gouverneurs de province dans l'empire romain," *Dialogues d'histoire ancienne* 30.2 (2004): 35–56 (44–45).

107. Duke, *Irony,* 131; Carter, *John,* 304–305.

108. For the translation of ληστής as "rebel," see Hunt, *Jesus Caesar,* 269–70; Lincoln, *Truth,* 130.

109. Bruce Malina and Richard Rohrbaugh, *Social Science Commentary on the Gospel of John* (Minneapolis: Fortress, 1998), 263; Craig R. Koester, "Why Was the Messiah Crucified? A Study of God, Jesus, Satan, and Human Agency in Johannine Theology," in *The Death of Jesus in the Fourth Gospel,* ed. Gilbert Van Belle (Leuven: Peeters, 2007), 168; Helen K. Bond, "Barabbas Remembered," in *Jesus and Paul: Global Perspectives in Honor of James D. G. Dunn for His 70th Birthday,* ed. B. J. Oropeza, C. K. Robertson, and Douglas C. Mohrmann, LNTS (London: T & T Clark, 2009), 71.

110. Jennifer Glancy, "Torture: Flesh, Truth, and the Fourth Gospel," *BibInt* 13.2 (2005): 107–36 (125).

111. Barrett argues that a "particular statute," namely the "law of blasphemy" (Lev 24:16) is referred to in this verse, not Torah as a whole, but either meaning is sufficient for "the Jews" to be describing themselves as law-abiding; C. K. Barrett, *The*

Gospel According to St. John: An Introduction with Commentary and Notes on the Greek Text, second ed. (Philadelphia: Westminster, 1978), 541.

112. Larsen, *Recognizing the Stranger*, 179.

113. This judgment is different from that of Pilate or that of "the Jews," no matter who is thought to be the referent in this verse; Hunt, *Jesus Caesar*, 279–80.

114. Larsen, *Recognizing the Stranger*, 178.

115. Hunt, *Jesus Caesar*, 319–31.

116. Larsen, *Recognizing the Stranger*, 178.

117. Larsen, *Recognizing the Stranger*, 180.

118. Hunt, *Jesus Caesar*, 296.

119. Genuyt, "Comparution," 143.

120. Others also note the greater claim for Jesus's power, e.g., Tilborg, *Reading John*, 216; Thompson, *John*, 372.

121. Elizabeth A. Castelli, *Martyrdom and Memory: Early Christian Culture Making* (New York: Columbia University Press, 2004), 35. *Pace* Richey who recognizes that Jesus is "supreme" over Caesar yet sets the choice for believers in terms of an opposition "between Christ and Caesar" (*Roman Imperial Ideology*, 163–66).

122. For the concept of a noble death, see Hunt, *Jesus Caesar*, 153–54.

123. Lincoln, *Truth*, 109, 122, 237, 242–55, 248; Larsen, *Recognizing the Stranger*, 179. See also Genuyt, "Comparution," 136–37; Hunt, *Jesus Caesar*, 209; Estrada, *Pneumatology*, e.g., 23.

124. See, for example, 1 Cor 3:1–3, where Paul reveals his understanding of the state of the Corinthian Christ-followers; Laura J. Hunt, "Alien and Degenerate Milk: Embodiment, Structure and Viewpoint in Four Nursing Metaphors," *Journal for Interdisciplinary Biblical Studies* 4.1 (2022): 119–56.

125. For the way this unfolded among historical Jesus-believers, see David Nirenberg, *Anti-Judaism: The Western Tradition* (New York: Norton, 2013).

126. Others who argue that the Gospel of John seeks to create community include Tat-siong Benny Liew who describes it as "a site of struggle for community" and Warren Carter who argues that the Gospel's "antilanguage" creates a "rhetoric of distance" that calls for "less accommodation to imperial society" (Tat-siong Benny Liew, "Ambiguous Admittance: Consent and Descent in John's Community of 'Upward' Mobility," in *John and Postcolonialism: Travel, Space and Power*, ed. Musa W. Dube and Jeffrey L. Staley, The Bible and Postcolonialism 7 [London: Sheffield Academic Press, 2002], 191–224 [193]; Carter, *John*, 14–15, 81). For other Johannine narratives and techniques that seek to create community, see Liew, "Ambiguous," 195–202.

Chapter 6

The Johannine Community and the Johannine Community Vision

Historical Reflection, Rhetorical Construction, and Narrative Ecclesiology

Andrew J. Byers

JOHANNINE WORLD-BUILDING AND THE NECESSITY OF IMAGINATION

Modern writers of fantasy and science fiction practice "world-building," a craft that contextualizes a fictional narrative. Occasional references to complex histories and mythologies generate an "implied expanse"[1] that authenticates the story and situates the plot within textured layers of meaning that stir the curiosity of readers who, if the writer succeeds, long to know more and journey deeper into the text. Some authors grant access beyond the story proper to the details of their constructed worlds, whether through footnotes (as in Susannah Clarke's *Jonathan Strange & Mr. Norrell* or R. F. Kuang's *Babel*[2]), through scholarly addenda at the back of the book (such as maps, glossaries, overviews, or genealogies), perhaps through encyclopedic "wiki" sites (like Brandon Sanderson's "The Coppermind"), or even through informative companion texts (Tolkien's *The Silmarillion* is a prime example[3]). Other writers withhold their world-building documents and keep their readers guessing and intrigued enough to await the next installment in the series.

Authorial reticence, however, exerts little restraint on the collective imagination. Conjecturing and hypothesizing without recourse to the author still abound with fan-generated websites where communities of readers fill out unresolved plotlines, devise possible backgrounds, and venture backstories for mysterious characters. The readers become de facto builders of worlds, filling in gaps by reconstructing the narrative context out of clues dropped or guessed from the existing text. Verification only comes when the author releases the next book, writes a companion piece, or publishes a tweet or an online post confirming a theory or denying one that has gone wild.

Though J. Louis Martyn's image of an archaeological tell holds greater academic propriety than the pop-cultural activity on SFF wiki sites, the imaginative work of excavating literary layers in the Gospel of John and reconstructing their *Sitze im Leben* is not, in principle, unlike the elaborate hypothetical musings on Fandom or MuggleNet.com.[4] The Fourth Evangelist presents a story-world of "implied expanse." Narrative asides may function to a degree like today's footnotes. We also have the Johannine Epistles as companion texts, though these writings tantalize readers as much as they satisfy their curiosity, withholding or obfuscating answers to the Gospel's unresolved plotlines or thematic trajectories.

These parallels between today's world of popular fiction and the reconstructive work in Gospel scholarship are thinly drawn, of course. Johannine world-building is an enterprise that arises not from fan-based curiosity about fantastical elements but from scholarly interest in its historical setting (though many of us are indeed "fans," of a sort). And the world most intriguing for a recent generation of interpreters on whose giant shoulders we nimbly (shakily?) stand is not the world within the text or in front of it, but the world behind its composition. In the field of New Testament studies, this reconstructive world-building has produced one of the most iconic of scholarly products: the Johannine community.

As events in contemporary society bear out, though, the achievement of iconic status triggers the iconoclasm of later cultural moments. The construct of the Johannine community is currently facing dissident scrutiny, even dismissed recently as "an old and outdated idea" by a rising scholar assessing the state of Johannine studies.[5] The imaginative project of reconstructive world-building has been deemed by some as too fanciful (and perhaps more appropriate to the genre of fantasy than history).

Yet imagination is essential for interpretation and critical for the historical critic. To work with history is to work with incomplete data, so inferences must be drawn with the exercise of a disciplined and informed imagination.[6] In a critique of the Johannine community hypothesis, Adele Reinhartz has acknowledged and welcomed the place of imagination in biblical scholarship, even in the task of constructing "an ancient community, its experiences, and its way of looking at the world."[7] She notes that "not everyone will be satisfied with the labelling of scholarly construction as the exercise of imagination" then asks, "But how can it be otherwise?"[8] Though many will dismiss

The Johannine Community and the Johannine Community Vision 117

the imaginative fancy of a reconstructed community, others may more readily dismiss the imaginative fancy of reader-generated meanings unmoored from authorial intent. The point: imaginative faculties are an unavoidable and even necessary function of interpretation, regardless of angle or methodology. The quality of our scholarly findings is bound to how informed and disciplined we ply these faculties (Martyn wrote of exegesis as "more an art than a science" requiring both "scientific control" and "poetic fantasy"[9]). The Fourth Evangelist may even serve as an exemplar: in his Gospel we have access to a creative appropriation of the Jesus tradition engaged with multiple levels of historical context and deployed to stretch the theological, Christological, and ecclesial imagination of readers within different contexts altogether.

But what if John's own world-building, crafted from an ingenious interweaving of his narrative's temporal horizons and a creative interfusion of history with theology, circumvents the work of behind-the-scenes world-building? Has John so effectively closed off his implied (historical) expanse to later interpreters? For Martyn, the ἀποσυνάγωγος passages (9:22, 34; 12:42; 16:2) were recognized as slits in an opaque textual veil through which an historical datum might be glimpsed, supplying building blocks for imaginative reconstruction. Many have championed his work or at least his approach, posing similar or alternative reconstructions. Others have hedged off any interpretative resources beyond the text itself, finding diachronic analysis boorish or irrelevant to their disciplinary aims. Sociological and social-scientific models have also been applied, often with vastly divergent results.

My (attempted) contribution to the ongoing debate on the Fourth Gospel's audience and context is to attend to the evangelist's own creative world-building, redirecting focus from the Johannine community behind the text that has held such scholarly interest to the Johannine *vision of* community set forth within the text.[10] A redirection to the latter is not a dismissal of the former. The vision cannot be understood or even recognized apart from some sense of context. That said, our first point of contact to historical context may be theological vision. Theology thus offers more access to the Johannine background than aporias or presumed anachronisms. We will have to learn, however, to settle for the general over the specific. A close reading of John's vision of community has an offering to make, but it can only offer the historian a *general* portrait of Johannine Christianity's formative environment, not a specific profile of a community and its experiences.[11] Relinquishing the determination to penetrate the seams and cracks to secure concrete historical details may lead to a rereading of the textual clues to John's context: though often perceived as "mirrors of the present" directly corresponding to the Johannine community's experiences, those clues may actually be "vistas

118   *Andrew J. Byers*

to the future" that *cast a vision of community* only indirectly related to the Johannine setting.

Since the aim of this collection is to catalyze fresh ways of thinking about the Johannine context, I will provide in the section that immediately follows a cursory account of how the Johannine community hypothesis took root then identify two challenges to the model that tentatively hold promise for a way forward. In the third section, I offer a theological account of John's preemptive thwarting of eventual reconstructive work on his Gospel through the compositional features already named—the fusion of contextual horizons and the integration of theology with history. Taking these complications to reconstruction into account, I then turn to the hermeneutical work of examining historical reflection/description and rhetorical construction/prescription and discuss how they respectively correspond to the Johannine context (whether directly or indirectly). I will argue here that "John" composed a narrative recollecting the *einmalig* events of the historical Jesus (thus supplying "windows to the past") while *reflecting* concerns and situations in his own communal context (supplying "mirrors of the evangelist's present") and simultaneously *constructing* a communal vision (suppling "vistas to the future").[12] The study will close with a brief demonstration of how "narrative ecclesiology" (the cumulative presentation of John's theological vision of community) might aid the imaginative work of our Johannine world-building.

THE "LIFE, LOVES, AND HATES" OF THE JOHANNINE COMMUNITY HYPOTHESIS: TRACING THE TRENDS AND NOTING TWO KEY CHALLENGES

To situate my own arguments within the wider field of academic discourse, I launch into the fray with a brief account of how the community hypothesis was locked into place within Johannine scholarship (see the more detailed account in the introduction to this volume) then discuss two viable challenges to that model that relate to my claims in the following sections.[13]

The current climate seems conducive to the eventual demise of the Johannine community construct, as Robert Kysar predicted some years prior.[14] The discussions of our own moment, however, should not detract from the extraordinary nature of Kysar's oracular pronouncement—at the time of the prediction, the Johannine community had been a fixture for almost forty years in New Testament scholarship. Martyn was not an outlier. As his *History and Theology in the Fourth Gospel* (1968) began circulating, Raymond Brown was crafting his own contribution to the idea of a community behind the Johannine texts. Drawing on Martyn (his colleague at Union

The Johannine Community and the Johannine Community Vision   119

Seminary) and building on his own prior reconstructive work in his magisterial Anchor Bible Commentary on John, Brown's *Community of the Beloved Disciple* (1979) took the emerging skeletal frame and supplied seventy years' worth of hypothetical historical flesh. The "Johannine community" was thus established within mainstream New Testament studies.[15]

It was surely the explanatory (and some would argue *apologetic*) power of the Martyn-Brown hypothesis that so quickly solidified its dominance. Most scholars now take for granted that John's Gospel is a predominantly Jewish text. Martyn's investigations—alongside the wider recognition in scholarship that John shares affinities with other Jewish texts like the Qumran scrolls—helped lock into place the (mostly) axiomatic assumption that behind the Epistles and Gospel of John is a community of primarily Jewish Christians marked by a distinctive theology, Christology, and stylized idiom. As post-*Shoah* scholarship continues to wrestle uncomfortably with John's apparent anti-Jewish polemic, Martyn's account of an intramural debate resulting in synagogue expulsion did not necessarily justify the evangelist's harsh rhetoric, but it certainly provided a possible context in which the sharpness made historical sense.

The Johannine community hypothesis may have taken root so firmly for another reason: since John featured only marginally in the big debates on the historical Jesus quests that prized history over theology, Johannine scholars finally had viable historical details to work with once interest in the "Jesus behind the text" shifted to the "communities behind the text."[16] Sociological and social-scientific approaches could now abound as the Johannine community became a plausible social artefact from history.

Reconstructing a Gospel community, however, cannot escape a hermeneutical circle. Though Hans-Georg Gadamer argued that circularity is an unavoidable dynamic of hermeneutics, the problem for the Johannine community hypothesis is the unverifiable nature of the nodal points along which the circle orbits.[17] As the Gospel text is read diachronically for historical clues (paying close attention to the compositional breaks or disjunctures, often called "aporias"), the clues are synthesized into a hypothesis, which then becomes the perspective through which the text is reread. Since there is no hard historical evidence for a Johannine community outside the texts themselves, proponents of hypothetical reconstructions must live with the unavoidable vulnerability of their circular reasoning.

Despite its robust reception, the speed of the centripetal force within the Johannine community's hermeneutical circle has begun to slow, and voices are prodding and exploiting the weaknesses. I think we can roughly group these challenges into multiple categories (narrative-critical, historical, social-scientific, rhetorical, theological) or into multiple angles of approach (from the consideration of Gospel audiences, imperial politics, and even

120   *Andrew J. Byers*

pseudepigraphy). Since they relate more directly to my eventual proposals, I offer below a summary and subsequent evaluation of the critiques leveled against the community hypothesis by rhetorical and theological challenges.

Rhetorical Challenges

Rather than focusing on what is *historically reflected* or *mirrored* within the Gospel, some interpreters of the Johannine tradition have set their hermeneutical sights on that which may be *rhetorically prescribed* by the Gospel. Building on the lack of clear evidence connecting the twelfth Benediction and John's provenance, Adele Reinhartz has made a case for replacing Martyn's "expulsion theory" for a "propulsion theory." Attending to the Gospel's rhetorical style and techniques, she argues that the evangelist's references to being cast out of the synagogue do not reflect historical experiences suffered by the Johannine community but influence readers to undertake a volitional exodus from a wider Jewish community disparaged and demonized through Johannine artifice.[18] In discussing John's polemical presentation of "the Jews" (οἱ Ἰουδαῖοι), Reinhartz rightly points out that, though historical-critical investigations are of course key, interpreters must also examine "the Gospel's rhetorical intentions as they can be discerned in, or extrapolated, from the Gospel itself."[19]

Unconvinced by Martyn's understanding of the ἀποσυνάγωγος passages, Warren Carter takes a similar approach, arguing in *John and Empire* that these scenes are to be deemed as "consequential rather than descriptive, as performative rather than reflective."[20] Another scholar who understands John as a writer engaged more in the work of *prescribing* social identity rather than *reflecting* its historical expression is Raimo Hakola: "while many scholars have taken Johannine dualism as a direct reflection of historical reality, it should be primarily seen as a part of the construction of a stable symbolic world."[21] Some postcolonial readings also fit in this category, with focus often directed not so much on the world within or behind the text but beyond it.[22] In attending to what is rhetorically constructed over what may be historically reflected, Johannine world-building is recognized as a craft undertaken by the author of these texts to persuade and shape the audience.[23]

Evaluation: Rhetorical approaches are bolstered by the Fourth Evangelist's explicit revelation in his (initial) conclusion that the reader or auditor has been the target of a rhetorical agenda (John 20:30–31). John has at his disposal a trove of Jesus-material which he selectively presents to inspire particular convictions, (namely that Jesus is the life-giving Christ and Son of God). The author of 1 John writes self-consciously for multiple reasons, and rhetorical aims (explicit and implicit) may be detected across the entire Johannine

The Johannine Community and the Johannine Community Vision 121

corpus. Rather than treating these texts diachronically as opaque mirrors of the Johannine present, this rhetorical approach reads them synchronically as vistas from which the audience can imagine a possible future. That possible future is, of course, envisioned because of something deemed inadequate or lacking in the historical present. When that which is (potentially) prescribed rhetorically and (again, potentially) reflected historically are held together in tension, this approach holds promise, in my view, for reconsidering the Johannine context.

Theological Challenges

Martyn's two-level drama has often met with cold reception within conservative scholarship because the retrospective inscription of the Johannine community's experiences into the life of Jesus impinges on convictions about the historical veracity of Christian Scripture. If Martyn's model is correct, then John played fast and loose with history in such a way that his overall presentation of Jesus may be deemed inconsistently historical and thus unreliable and bound for slippage along slippery slopes.[24] Though I share some of these convictions, my concern here is to point to a different type of theological challenge, one raised by Jörg Frey's reorientation of Martyn's approach expressed eponymously in his 2018 monograph *Theology and History in the Fourth Gospel*.[25] Though appreciative of Martyn, and convinced that John is indeed a multi-level drama (he identifies three levels, actually[26]), Frey finds theology (that is, "Christology as theology") a more fruitful entrée into the Fourth Gospel than history—as I hinted earlier—since the historical constructions from which Martyn made theological assessments are so unverifiable.[27] Certain historical insights may be drawn from John's theological/ Christological convictions, which are jettisoned only to the disadvantage of interpreters hoping to comprehensively understand Johannine Christianity.

Evaluation: Many of the evangelical challenges to Martyn's two-level drama have been echoed or affirmed in wider academic circles, even if less motivated by confessional interests. Frey himself is not disturbed by the idea of a multi-level drama but anchors any discussion on the history behind the text in the theological convictions articulated within the text, an approach I am commending, and which seems more reliable and less fraught with guesswork than scrounging through the text for accidentally dropped contextual clues. In my own reflections on (the) Johannine community below, I will be combining a rhetorical approach along with Frey's directional recalibration, though focusing more on *ecclesiology* than theology or Christology.

Are Historical Reconstructions Inevitable?

Despite the vigorous critique of the community model, it is important to recognize that even the critics tend toward imaginative Johannine world-building and oscillate along the hermeneutical circle between text and imagined context. It is true that purely synchronic literary approaches, which locate meaning in the experience of reading the Gospel narrative, may avoid reconstruction and its circularity, but interpreters adopting this methodology are reliant on a self-engaged act of imagination just as subjective (if not more so) as the work of historical reconstruction. The most dominant responses to the community hypothesis may fire their shots while never transcending the hermeneutical circle between text and reconstructed context since posing alternative histories (including those based on rhetorical constructions) seems irresistible for the scholarly imagination, and perhaps rightly so. It is a curious factor in the ongoing debate that some of the Johannine community's most articulate critics end up following Martyn, Brown, and countless others into the same methodology. Hugo Méndez, for example, has provided a robust new challenge, questioning whether the Johannine community ever existed by reading the Fourth Gospel and Epistles of John as pseudepigrapha, literary works that present themselves as products of an authoritative figure (i.e., the Elder of 2 and 3 John and the beloved disciple of the Gospel) who is in fact a fabricated fiction (see his chapter in this volume).[28] Méndez's multi-phase history of the pseudepigrapher, however, is still a historical reconstruction. Likewise, Reinhartz's "propulsion theory"—in which the evangelist writes to a primarily Gentile audience to predispose them against Jews—remains an historical reconstruction. It is as if the only way forward is to pose an alternative within the Martyn-Brown approach, rather than to rethink how we conceive of the model itself.

Even so, the attention to what John seems to be rhetorically prescribing rather than just historically reflecting seems to provide not a key for unlocking or decoding the Johannine *Sitz im Leben*, but a dialectical tension between history and rhetoric out of which *modest* proposals about the *general* context may be responsibly made. And as Frey has argued, theological construction may be serviceable for historical *re*construction. As I hope to show, analyzing Johannine ecclesiology in a text so theologically infused provides the most suitable orientation for making any historical claims about an historical community.

But first, there is an additional hermeneutical reality to acknowledge and explore.

INCARNATION, INSCRIPTION, AND INSPIRATION: HOW JOHN PREEMPTS HISTORICAL RECONSTRUCTION BY FUSING CONTEXTUAL HORIZONS AND BY INTEGRATING HISTORY AND THEOLOGY

Before proceeding to my own modest proposals, it is worth taking a closer look at the two inevitable challenges undermining the exercise of any mode of historical reconstruction: John's fusion of the temporal horizons and his creative integration of theology and history. These temporal horizons interlock without obvious distinction. To combine language from both Martyn and Hans-Georg Gadamer, John may be writing a multi-level drama, but the horizons are so thoroughly fused that the building blocks for reconstructive work are too uncut or ambiguously edged to result in an edifice with well-defined layers or floorplans.[29] Moreover, each temporal horizon is theologically interpreted. History and theology are strands so inseparably plaited together by the narrative mode and rhetorical (pastoral) aims that a surgical retrieval of one without the other is a feat inoperable.[30]

In other words, John was not writing to drop contextual clues for clever readers in the distant future.[31] He wrote, rather, to present the historical significance and ongoing relevance of Jesus for his readers and to cast a social vision for how a community may be shaped around him. Because this project was as theological as it was historical, and as relevant for encounters with Jesus across the temporal span of the past and present as well as the future, the Fourth Gospel resists the scholarly impulses of disentangling the fused horizons of the text (the multiple levels of context) and of extracting kernels of history out of their dense integration with theology. The core theological ideas of incarnation, inscription, and inspiration help explain the fraught and elusive nature of reconstructive work.

Incarnation

For John, Jesus intersects all reality. He is never an artifact merely residual or vestigial. Jesus cannot be historicized apart from the present nor can he be contemporized apart from the past. And there is no Johannine future without him. With the self-proclaimed "I am," Jesus is not only co-identified with the God of Israel but presented as unbound to history (not "I was") and available before the eschatological future (not "I will be"). Johannine writing articulates this Christological intersection of the past, present, and future,[32] and these temporal stages can be theologically aligned with the acts of incarnation, inscription, and inspiration.

124   *Andrew J. Byers*

Because of the incarnation, John is not—and cannot be—aloof to history. He writes with a historical consciousness, situating Jesus beyond and then within a clear temporal sequence: "In the beginning was the Word . . . and the Word became flesh and lived among us" (1:1, 14). In the incarnation, Jesus enters the ongoing timeline. Though the specific time and particular place of birth is left ambiguous (see, e.g., 7:27–28, 41–42), Jesus's appearance in the narrative is linked to the timing of John the Baptist's ministry and placed "in Bethany across the Jordan where John was baptizing" (1:28). Note the references to time and place (italicized) in the following account, a few chapters later:

> *After this* Jesus and his disciples went into *the Judean countryside*, and *he spent some time there* with them and baptized. John also was baptizing *at Aenon near Salim* because water was abundant *there*; and people kept coming and were being baptized—*John, of course, had not yet been thrown into prison.* (3:22–24, emphases added)

Similar time and place indicators appear throughout John (leading some to regard the evangelist as more accurate on Palestinian geography than his Synoptic counterparts).[33] The incarnation establishes a Christological basis for John's historical consciousness and should therefore be taken seriously by exegetes.

Inscription

But John is also alert to his contemporary situation. The first colophon (20:30–31) makes explicit that Johannine writing is conscious of the present. At the time of inscription, Jesus is still "I am," still present and active. He cannot be reinscribed by a text into the historic past any more than he can remain sealed up within a tomb. The Christological "I am" fuses the horizon of the past with the horizon of the present when the evangelist writes. Martyn's two levels are present, but (as he acknowledged, at least for the most part) they are enmeshed. The retelling of Jesus's activity in the past has immediate bearing on its reception by the audience contemporary with the writer. The past of the "I am" intersects with the *Sitz im Leben*, infuses it with new meaning, provides its reinterpretation, and relativizes present experience to ὃ ἦν ἀπ᾽ ἀρχῆς ("what was from the beginning"—1 John 1:1). The audience is reinscribed into Jesus' past and he is re-presented as being in their future: Jesus prays "on behalf of those who will believe in me" (17:20) through the disciples' testimony, and he blesses "those who have not seen and yet have come to believe" (20:29). Though some evangelical interpreters have found this fusion of horizons inimical to a conviction of Scripture's truthfulness, the evangelist is

The Johannine Community and the Johannine Community Vision   125

plying what we might recognize as the homiletical craft of making the text come alive in the setting of modern-day congregations, and simultaneously helping congregations feel as though they have stumbled into the world of the the text.[34] If Jesus intersects the levels of history and the present, then so also must Johannine writing.

Inspiration

Perhaps the boldest feature of Johannine writing is the allowance for ongoing inspiration into the future. For John, incarnation and inscription are not Christological prisons. Jesus is not locked away into tomb-bound silence or engraved into time-bound pages. The bodily Jesus ascends, and thus Johannine ink is never fully dry. The Spirit-Paraclete will "will teach you everything, and remind you of all that I have said to you" (14:26). The "Spirit of truth" (14:17) will "guide you into all the truth." Because "you have been anointed by the Holy One," then "all of you have knowledge" (1 John 2:20), and "his anointing teaches you about all things" (1 John 2:27). Surely the anticipation for future revelation is that it will be fuller, not thinner or divergent or contradictory—there persists a διδαχή τοῦ Χριστοῦ, a "teaching of Christ" (2 John 9), that is grounded in the Johannine traditions about Jesus from which deviance signals communal departure (e.g., 1 John 2:19; 2 John 10).[35]

Incarnation, inscription, and inspiration—these are the nodal points at which Jesus is articulated in Johannine writing. And they intersect all levels of any timeline precisely because Jesus intersects all reality. Martyn is perhaps wrong to have limited his discussions on John's drama to only two levels, focusing on the past and present.[36] I am suggesting there are three (similar to Frey, but with some differences[37]). The Fourth Evangelist is engaged in a compositional exercise more complex than a de-historicizing or contemporizing of Jesus, and more robust than an over-realizing of eschatology. He has produced theological writ expressive of the "I am" so central to his narrative. No wonder narrative closure is a Johannine challenge (20:30–31 and 21:25).[38]

For our purposes here, these points of incarnation, inscription, and inspiration explain why reconstructive work is such a subjective and ultimately elusive enterprise: *the strands of context all intersect*. To defuse these horizons or unravel the strands is to read against the grain of the text and against the Johannine theology of writing. Also intersecting are theology and history. Though the Gospel writers' theological interpretation of the Jesus tradition is regularly deemed inhibitive of historical work, Johannine writing is not mischievously designed to conceal treasure from his readers. John values history but would surely struggle to understand why later readers would find it necessary to excavate it from the sloughs of his theology. The treasure is not

126   *Andrew J. Byers*

a reductionist version of Jesus, trimmed down to historical size, but the inter-preted Christ. And for John, the interpreted Christ is not an untrue or distorted version of the historical Jesus but the Jesus who is the "I am" and thus histori-cal, present, future, and only understandable within theological categories.

Hence the difficulty of reconstructing any level of Johannine contexts: no horizon can be purged of Jesus' activity or purified of theology.

THE HISTORICAL COMMUNITY AND THE IMAGINED COMMUNITY: TEXTS AS WINDOWS TO THE PAST (RECOLLECTION), MIRRORS OF THE PRESENT (REFLECTION), AND/OR PROSPECTIVE VISTAS TO THE FUTURE (CONSTRUCTION)

Fronted with these sobering (yet for me, exciting) complications to recon-struction posed by Johannine writing, we turn now to a more practical set of tasks. Though any confidence in Johannine world-building must be tempered by the theological reflections in section 3 and by the array of challenges discussed in section 2, recognizing that a Gospel writer may be promot-ing a communal vision rather than revealing historical reality may offer a more accurate (even if less precise) idea of what those historical realities were. Though I value synchronic readings over diachronic inquiries, I also acknowledge the importance of context in informing textual meaning. But as illustrated in the rhetorical challenges discussed briefly above, there may be alternative ways of handling the scenes and passages diachronic analyses take as clues to John's historical context. Since this early Christian figure is a self-consciously rhetorical writer unafraid to break the fourth wall as a narra-tor (Jn 1:14, 16; 19:35–36; 20:30–31; 21:24–25) and clear about his pastoral aims in writing 1 John (1:1; 2:1, 12–14, 21, 26; 5:13), we should expect to find scenes that function as "windows to the past" availing sight of (that is, recollecting) Jesus's historical ministry, alongside the incidental "mirrors of the present" of John's own context (which might reflect a local "historical community" or network), as well as scenes that provide "vistas to the future" envisioning aspirations for social identity and practices (and thus a rhetorical construction of an "imagined community," which may be translocal as well as local).[39]

The hermeneutical task I am considering here is using the contextual clues often used in diachronic studies but distinguishing between these "windows" that recollect the ministry of Jesus, "mirrors" that may reflect Johannine history, and "vistas" that articulate a future configured around Johannine theology (which still have at least an indirect bearing on Johannine history). Since the reconstructions of the Johannine community are not anchored in

The Johannine Community and the Johannine Community Vision   127

the actual ministry of Jesus (accessed through the "windows"), the focus here will be directed on those textual cues functioning as "mirrors" or "vistas." Though making these distinctions between material that is historically reflective/descriptive and what may be rhetorically constructive/prescriptive generates a wide range of interpretative possibilities, such a complex range provides a more realistic span of options to consider. The historical community and the imagined community are interrelated—though not the same—so our own speculative Johannine world-building may only proceed cautiously when we recognize the nature of their potential interrelation.

First, what are the clues used in diachronic study for reconstructing Gospel contexts? I am not drawing this list below out of a manual for crafting community hypotheses but providing my own taxonomy based on engaging with the literature over the past several years. I think we can roughly categorize the contextual clues in the following way:

1. *Compositional Breaks (aporias)*: See, e.g., John 2:23, 3:31, 4:54, 6:1, 10:1, 14:30–31, 20:30. Many scholars have looked for literary strata in the Gospel out of which historical reconstructions are made along a timeline of the Johannine community.[40]

2. *Extra-Literary Divergence*: By this phrase I am referring to John's departure from (primarily) the Synoptic accounts. For example, the presence of the Beloved Disciple is an addition to the cast of Gospel characters deemed directly related to the specific Johannine situation.

3. *Intra-Literary Divergence*: By this phrase I am referring to differences between the Fourth Gospel and the Johannine Epistles, which have been understood as reflecting different stages in the Johannine timeline or perhaps internal tensions.

4. *Conflict Scenes*: Since the *religionsgeschichtliche Schule* established conflict as a key to understanding Christian origins, possible evidence behind the text of social tensions has retained scholarly fascination (and sometimes for good reason).[41] When Gospels narrate conflict, the tendency has been to allegorize the scene into a reconstructed context (as in the mapping of the Peter-Beloved Disciple juxtaposition onto conflicts between various Christian traditions).

5. *Polemics*: Closely related to conflict scenes, and often included within them (though not always), polemical discourse has been viewed as a clue to some bugbear of the evangelist in his own context.[42]

6. *Hortatory Material*: When Jesus tells his disciples to collect a donkey at Passover or to stand up and walk, his instructions are normally understood as belonging to the narrative level of the text. Moral instructions, however, may be viewed as reflective of the historical situation (e.g.,

Matthew's Sermon on the Mount may reflect a Jewish audience trying to integrate the Jesus tradition with their torah practice).

7. *Anachronism*: This has been reckoned as one of the more obvious clues that a scene or statement is reflective of the evangelist's historical context, with synagogue expulsion serving as the most relevant Johannine example (even though its anachronic nature has been challenged[43]).

8. *Stylized Language*: Some evidence of the historical background may be detected when the evangelists use a special idiom or write a particular scene or section in a noticeably distinct style. Luke's Septuagintal style may be designed to authenticate his story for Jewish readers, and John's Prologue may be so poetic to draw attention to powerful theological convictions that counter heterodox ideas in the Johannine community.

In my modification of the diachronic approach, once a scene or passage is identified as a possible clue to the Johannine context, the next decision to be made is whether this clue is a "mirror of the (Johannine) present" or a "vista to the future." Again, with these phrases I am referring to the nature of the textual clue and the rhetorical aim of the passage. In the exercise of reconstructing the Johannine community, clues to the context have been treated primarily as mirrors glimpsing the evangelist's *Sitz im Leben*. The clues, therefore, are normally read as reflections of the community's experience, with a *direct link between clue and context*.

But the Gospel writers were not composing coded accounts of their present experiences. They were presenting Jesus to their contemporaries, cognizant of the social challenges and theological debates in their local environments and perhaps more broadly in the early Christian movement. Gospel writing was surely designed not merely to reflect these challenges and debates but to address them by casting vision for a possible future drawing on the historical past of Jesus' ministry. Rhetorical aims are thus future-oriented, engaging a current situation and envisaging an alternative way forward. When the future orientation of rhetorical material is taken into account, *access to the historical context may be less direct*. A prospective vista adds a layer of distance since textual clues to context may be prescribing something new rather than reflecting existing scenarios or concerns.

This subtle but I think important distinction between mirrors of the present and vistas to the future is demonstrated in two exemplar studies mentioned above: Raimo Hakola's *Reconsidering Johannine Christianity* and Adele Reinhartz's "propulsion theory," which is set out in multiple studies but most recently in *Cast Out of the Covenant*. As we have seen, Hakola argues that Johannine dualism is not to be historicized and thus read as directly indicative of a sectarian tradition at odds with the synagogue and world. Such contrastive language is used *precisely because* Johannine Christianity was too

The Johannine Community and the Johannine Community Vision 129

closely aligned with social groups in its context among whom the evangelist wanted to secure a more defined identity.[44] For Reinhartz, the Gospel's references to synagogue expulsion (9:22, 34; 12:42; 16:2) are not reflective of the Johannine community's historical experiences but part of a rhetorical program designed to promote disaffiliation with Jewish socioreligious life.[45] These two readings identify a prospective vista to a possible future (an imagined community) where others have identified a retrospective mirror of the evangelist's present (the historical community). Since reconstructive work has prodded the text in search of diachronic clues for accessing the Johannine context, scholars may be treating as history that which is merely rhetorical and thus aspirational, chronologically mistaking a vista for a mirror. To go with Hakola and Reinhartz, respectively, John's dualism may not indicate a sectarian community and synagogue expulsion may not reflect a (Jewish) Christian community oppressed by Jews. A supposed historical reflection may actually be a rhetorical prescription or construction for the future as John writes not to intentionally *describe* or incidentally *mirror* his historical community but to *reimagine* its aims, practices, and values (or perhaps even to maintain its social identity in light of new contextual hostilities).

But as already noted, historical reflection and rhetorical construction are hardly separable. The advantage of the proposals by Hakola and Reinhartz are not that they move the conversation outside the hermeneutical circle between text and context (which is unavoidable), but that they provide alternative angles for rethinking the points along which the circle spins. I am not suggesting that this dynamic is entirely lost on biblical scholars; on the contrary, connecting rhetorical and hortatory material to historical context is a standard feature of scholarly exegesis. For example, Jesus's prayer in John 17 that believers may be "one" is regularly interpreted as a promotion of social harmony (oneness being equated to unity), which in turn yields through mirror-reading the idea of a Johannine community marked by disunity. Extrapolating from other passages and texts confirms the logic—many of Jesus's disciples withdrew in John 6:66, a group seceded from the community in 1 John 2:19, and the repeated command to love one another must reflect a community struggling to do just that.

The difference, however, between this interpretation of John 17 and the interpretations of Reinhartz and Hakola of ἀποσυνάγωγος and dualism, respectively, is one of *direct versus indirect correspondence* between text and context. Martyn's reading of synagogue expulsion is taken as *directly* mirroring the Johannine context, whereas Reinhartz views it as a rhetorical device to effect something in the audience's future. Likewise, the standard sectarian reading understands John's dualistic language as a *direct* reflection (and thus reinforcement) of its existing separation from the world, whereas

130 *Andrew J. Byers*

Hakola perceives it as creating separation that does not yet exist. In summary, the methodological points I am making are these:

1. Textual clues to Johannine context may be rhetorical constructions/prescriptions, not just historical reflections/descriptions.
2. Rhetorical constructions do reflect historical context, but the correspondence is less direct. Put slightly differently, historical reflection and rhetorical prescription are always related, but their correspondence to context *is not the same*.

Returning to the example of John 17, the conventional (and largely diachronic) reading is to view the prayer for oneness as directly corresponding to a fragmented community behind the text. Yet, if we take seriously the synchronic readings championed by literary-critical approaches, we will note that John situates the prayer within a narrative context of threat that is not *internal* but *external* ("you will be scattered" reads 16:32, which is presumably effected by the Roman cohort and Jewish authorities moments later in 18:1–11). I have argued elsewhere that the rhetorical aim is not to address internal disunity but external challenges from a hostile setting.[46] The prayer "that they may be one" affiliates the audience (within and beyond the text) with the "one" God of Israel (from the Shema's confession of divine oneness in Deuteronomy 6:4) through the one Davidic shepherd (of Ezekiel 34/37) who will gather and unite God's dispersed people. This reading attempts to make sense of a sophisticated development of oneness that has been underway in John at least since 8:41. Holding an interpretative mirror up to John 17, many have directly correlated the prayer for oneness to a context of insular factionalism. But if this text is more of a vista to the future than a mirror of the evangelist's present, we may envision a more indirect correspondence in which the prayer gives aspirational hope to a largely Jewish audience of Christ-believers who find themselves at theological and social odds with their own tradition. For John, they are still the one people of the one God of Israel and aligned with his one messianic shepherd-king.

To be clear, I am less convinced of Reinhartz's propulsion theory than Martyn's expulsion theory, and I am still mulling over Hakola's alternative readings of John's dualistic language.[47] What I want to commend, however, is their methodological alertness to the rhetorical function of texts that are often treated as mere diachronic mirrors of the community's present. Since space is limited for a more detailed discussion on this dialectic between historical reflection and rhetorical construction, the figure below charts examples discussed in this section to illustrate the range of hermeneutical possibilities at play in our decisions over the possible clues to the Johannine context.

Though the Johannine community hypothesis has been constructed on the methodological approach of viewing the clues as direct reflections of context, exploring the possibility that the clues are future-oriented yields a less direct correspondence to context and broadens (and may in some cases sharpen) the reconstructive possibilities.

CONCLUSION: "NARRATIVE ECCLESIOLOGY" AND (THE) JOHANNINE COMMUNITY

I began this chapter commenting on Johannine world-building. This phrase has referred to the scholarly exercise of reconstructing the Johannine context and has also pointed to John's own rhetorical work of shaping his context with a future-oriented vision of community. Imagination and circularity are inevitable, and both may be understood as helpful hermeneutical resources for understanding the meaning-making relationship between text and context. Yet the imagination in crafting the community hypothesis has been critiqued as too fanciful at times, and the hermeneutical circle has been too rigidly set along unverifiable historical nodes. After categorizing, summarizing, and briefly evaluating two key challenges to the Johannine community construct, I ventured theological reflections on Johannine writing (on the ideas of incarnation, inscription, and inspiration) that resist an uncoupling of history from theology and the severing of the Gospel's fused horizons. I then commended rhetorical approaches for being alert to how John may be constructing a vision for a community's future rather than merely reflecting the experiences of a community's present (acknowledging that these are related, though often in a way more indirect than avowed in the reconstructive models).

I also commended Jörg Frey's emphasis on Johannine *theology* as the exegetical starting point for exploring Johannine *history*. Convinced that ecclesiology is the more specific dimension of Johannine theology for any reconstructive work, I sketch here concluding reflections on how "narrative ecclesiology" may provide insights into the Fourth Gospel's broader context. In other words, reading Johannine ecclesiology (the vision of community *within* the text) may lead to modest observations about Johannine history (the possible community or social network *behind* the text). My approach of narrative ecclesiology—explored elsewhere and part of a larger project underway on all four canonical Gospels—is synchronic in that it traces the incremental presentation of the identity of the people of God around Jesus. For the sake of space, I limit my discussion to the Prologue, the opening passage that launches the sequential presentation of Johannine community.

Though we rightly treat John's Prologue as a text focused on Christology, we are wrong to miss its robust foundations for ecclesiology. This opening

Table 6.1. Windows to the Past and Vistas to the Future.

Event, Scene, or Phenomenon in the Text	Type of Textual Clue	*Windows to the Past*		*Vistas to the Future*	
		Possible Rhetorical Construction (Context-Oriented)	Possible Historical Reflection (Direct)	Possible Rhetorical Construction (Future-Oriented)	Possible Historical Reflection (Indirect)
Awkward transitions	Compositional Breaks (Aporias)	Comfort and exhortation in varying times of crisis	Conflicts and crises over a (multi-decade) timeline	(Probably none if the redactor/writer hoped the audience would not notice them)	Ongoing theological reflection on the developing tradition (that may or may not reflect dramatic crises)
Aposynagōgos	Anachronism	Be comforted after expulsion	There is an Intra-Jewish Conflict	Leave the Jewish context	Johannine believers are too closely affiliated with Jewish social and cultic life
Johannine Dualism	Polemics; Stylized Language	Synagogue and world are dangerous and inimical	The JohCom is insular and sectarian.	Become more distinctive in your social relations and religious convictions	Johannine believers are too integrated with their social and religious contexts
Prayer for oneness in John 17	Conflict; Extra-Literary Divergence	Be unified	The JohCom is divided	Identify with Israel's "one" God and a Christological and ecclesial embrace of Scriptural oneness	Johannine believers are being persecuted within their Jewish context for departing from orthodox faith by worshipping Jesus alongside the "one" God.

The Johannine Community and the Johannine Community Vision   133

text does not just launch a narrative Christology; for John there is no messiah without Israel, no Christ without an ἐκκλησία.[48] We are immediately notified that the evangelist is concerned as much about the identity of God's people as he is about the identity of Jesus when he describes not only how this social entity is formed but also how it is *not* formed: "But to all who received him, who believed in his name, he gave power to become children of God, who were born, not of blood or of the will of the flesh or of the will of man, but of God" (1:12–13). Reception of Jesus as the Word generates a community. Alternatively, the related ideas of genetics, parentage, ancestry, biology, and bloodline are *not* to be viewed as determinative of covenant membership. These initial statements about the identity of God's people are not necessarily attacks on Jewish ethnicity.[49] Jesus will soon be identified as a Ἰουδαῖος in 4:9, and John the Baptist's vocation is to present him to "Israel" as "the Messiah, which is translated as Christ" (1:41, AT). John 1:13 does, however, undermine attempts to rigidly limit covenant membership on racial or ethnic grounds, which is an important feature of the harsh debate in John 8:31–59.

This "Johannine genealogy" of John 1:12–13 can only be properly understood when read within the broader vision of ecclesiology that the evangelist cumulatively develops along the narrative sequence. But what might we venture about the Johannine context from the foundational convictions of Johannine ecclesiology in the Prologue? First, it seems relatively safe to suggest that John is writing within a Jewish framework. The scriptural tradition of Israel is instantly prominent. We may also suggest that John is hoping to expand (1) Jewish ideas about God (by correlating θεός and ὁ λόγος) so as to accommodate a divine Christ; and (2) Jewish ideas about community (by challenging biological descent as solely constitutive of covenant membership) to accommodate a more diverse community. To be clear, John is not necessarily challenging all Jewish modes of identity construction—as John Barclay and others have pointed out, Jewish identity in the ancient world could be construed along more polythetic categories.[50] But since the Temple's destruction compelled decisive rethinking about Jewish identity, John may be situated as one of the voices within this wider debate promoting a reconfiguration of social belonging. His own vision is more inclusive of those from wider ethnic backgrounds (as evidenced in the positive reception by Samaritans and Greeks), but still undeniably exclusive in a different way in that membership seems limited to those who receive Jesus as the Logos.[51] The specifics of the Martyn-Brown hypothesis cannot be so tidily substantiated by mirror-reading a narrative ecclesiology that is as invested in rhetorical construction as it is in historical reflection. But we can certainly observe from the Prologue that this is an ancient narrative determined to say something about community identity. And that communal vision is surely grounded in a set of ongoing debates prompted by the crises not only of the Temple's destruction but also

134   *Andrew J. Byers*

the bizarre phenomenon of Christ-belief in a very strange Christ who dies on the cross owned by the powers that crushed the Temple but who still finds a following in dark times.

My treatment of narrative ecclesiology needs more work than space allows, of course. The concluding point here is that attempts to de-theologize the Fourth Gospel will also de-historicize it because the evangelist's context is most readily available in his rhetorical and theologically informed construction of identity. As the Johannine community hypothesis has shown, prodding the text primarily for diachronic insights into the past produces shaky foundations for imaginative world-building. Accessing the world of the text requires exploring the Johannine imagination of a world (context) different yet still inseparable from his own.

NOTES

1. The phrase is from sci-fi/fantasy author Adrian Tchaikovsky—"Adrian Tchaikovsky Interview: Writing Mind-Blowing Worlds," on Wizards, Warriors, and Words: A Fantasy Writing Advice Podcast, Episode 1.19 (https://youtu.be/UWR7GxexhFw) (accessed 25/7/2023).

2. Susanna Clarke, *Jonathan Strange & Mr Norrell* (London: Bloomsbury, 2004); R. F. Kuang, *Babel: An Arcane History* (London: Harper*Voyager*, 2022).

3. J. R. R. Tolkien, *The Silmarillion*, ed. Christopher Tolkien (London: HarperCollins, 2013 [1977]).

4. See his essay, "Glimpses into the History of the Johannine Community" in J. Louis Martyn, *History and Theology in the Fourth Gospel*, third ed. (Louisville, KY: Westminster John Knox, 2003 [1968], 145–67; here 145. Of course, Martyn was specifically referring to the strata of literary layers within the existing text (John's Gospel).

5. Toan Do, "The Epistles of John," in *The State of New Testament Studies: A Survey of Recent Research*, ed. Scot McKnight and Nijay K. Gupta (Grand Rapids, MI: Baker Academic, 2019), 444–58; 446.

6. In a robust defense of the Johannine Community hypothesis, Martinus C. de Boer provides quotes from R. G. Collingwood on "the historical imagination." See de Boer's "The Johannine Community Under Attack," in *The Ways That Often Parted: Essays in Honor of Joel Marcus*, ed. Lori Baron, Jill Hicks-Keeton, and Matthew Thiessen, ECL 24 (Atlanta: SBL Press, 2018), 227n82. See also R. G. Collingwood, *The Idea of History* (Oxford: Oxford University Press, 1956), 242–46. Collingwood's use of imagination and reenactment in the work of history has been criticized, of course. See the nuanced defence in William H. Dray, *The Historical Imagination: R. G. Collingwood's Idea of History* (Oxford: Oxford University Press, 2011), 191–228.

7. Adele Reinhartz, "Building Skyscrapers on Toothpicks: The Literary-Critical Challenge to Historical Criticism," in *Anatomies of Narrative Criticism: The Past,*

Present, and Futures of the Fourth Gospel as Literature, ed. Tom Thatcher, Stephen D. Moore, RBS 55 (Atlanta: SBL Press, 2008), 55–76; 71.

8. Reinhartz, "Building Skyscrapers," 71.

9. J. Louis Martyn, "A Law-Observant Mission to Gentiles: The Background of Galatians," *SJT* 38 (1985): 313. In a review discussion on Martyn's essay "Glimpses into the History of the Johannine Community" (now included in the third edition of *History and Theology*, pp. 145–67), David Aune wrote (tongue in cheek) that "he will certainly not be faulted for lacking imagination." See David E. Aune, Review of *The Gospel of John in Christian History: Essays for Interpreters*, by J. Louis Martyn, *CBQ* 43 (1981): 138.

10. Similarly, Andrew J. Byers, *Ecclesiology and Theosis in the Gospel of John*, SNTSMS 166 (Cambridge: Cambridge University Press, 2017), 3.

11. This approach is taken by Jörg Frey (*Theology and History*), in contrast to Martyn whose study roughly moved in the reverse direction (*History and Theology*). See Jörg Frey, *Theology and History in the Gospel of John: Tradition and Narration* (Waco, TX: Baylor University Press, 2018), 1–12.

12. Martyn used the German term *"einmalig"* to refer to originating historical events that John often stretches out into the experience of his community life (*History and Theology*, 40).

13. In this section, I am reproducing with permission (and adapting) material in Andrew J. Byers, "Is the Johannine Community Hypothesis Still Viable?" *Didaktikos* 6.3 (2023): 33–36. The phrase "Life, Loves, and Hates" in the heading are taken from the subtitle of Raymond E. Brown, *The Community of the Beloved Disciple: The Life, Loves, and Hates of an Individual Church in New Testament Times* (New York: Paulist Press, 1979).

14. Robert Kysar, "The Whence and Whither of the Johannine Community," in *Life in Abundance: Studies in John's Gospel in Tribute to Raymond E. Brown, S. S.*, ed. John R. Donahue (Collegeville, MN: Liturgical Press, 2005), 65–81.

15. There were other contributions. See, e.g., Oscar Cullmann, *The Johannine Circle: Its Place in Judaism, Among the Disciples of Jesus and in Early Christianity* (trans. John Bowden; London: SCM Press, 1976).

16. For an account (and critique) of this move in NT scholarship, see Francis Watson, "Toward a Literal Reading of the Gospels," in *The Gospels for All Christians: Rethinking the Gospel Audiences*, ed. Richard Bauckham (Grand Rapids: Eerdmans, 1998), 195–217.

17. Hans-Georg Gadamer, *Truth and Method*, rev. tr. Joel Weinsheimer, Donald G. Marshall (London: Bloomsbury Academic, 2021 [1960, 1975]), 302–6.

18. Though Reinhartz has been working on this alternative reading throughout several publications, see most recently Adele Reinhartz, *Cast out of the Covenant: Jews and Anti-Judaism in the Gospel of John* (Lanham, MD: Lexington/Fortress, 2018), 131–57.

19. Adele Reinhartz, "The Jews in the Fourth Gospel" in *The Oxford Handbook of Johannine Studies*, ed. Judith M. Lieu and Martinus C. de Boer (Oxford: Oxford University Press, 2018), 134.

20. Warren Carter, *John and Empire: Initial Explorations* (London: T & T Clark, 2008), 26.

21. See esp. Raimo Hakola, *Reconsidering Johannine Christianity: A Social Identity Approach*, BibleWorld (London: Routledge, 2015), 4.

22. See, e.g., Tat-Siong Benny Liew, "Ambiguous Admittance: Consent and Descent in John's Community of 'Upward' Mobility," in *John and Postcolonialism: Travel, Space, and Power*, ed. Musa W. Dube, Jeffrey L. Staley (London: Bloomsbury, 2002), 193–242; Yak-Hwee Tan, "The Johannine Community: Power and Identity as a New Lens of Interpretation," in *Soundings in Cultural Criticism: Perspectives and Methods in Culture, Power, and Identity in the New Testament*, ed. Francisco Lozada Jr. and Greg Carey (Minneapolis, MN: Fortress, 2013), 83–95. For a broader discussion on the diverse approaches of postcolonial studies to Johannine history, see Jin Young Choi, "John's Writings and Empire: Views of Empire Studies and Postcolonial Criticism," in *The Oxford Handbook of Postcolonial Biblical Criticism*, ed. R. S. Sugirtharajah (Oxford: Oxford University Press, 2018), 162–89.

23. Carter also uses the language of describing a historical situation versus prescribing a desired outlook (*John and Empire*, 11).

24. For measured critiques, see Edward W. Klink III, "Expulsion from the Synagogue? Rethinking a Johannine Anachronism" *TynBul* 59 (2008): 99–118; D. A. Carson, *The Gospel According to John*, PNTC (Grand Rapids, MI: Eerdmans, 1991), 360–61, 369–72; Craig L. Blomberg, *The Historical Reliability of John's Gospel* (London: Apollos/Inter-Varsity Press, 2001), 153–57; and, more recently, Mark Zhakevich, *Follow Me: The Benefits of Discipleship in the Gospel of John*, Interpreting Johannine Literature (Lanham, MD: Lexington/Fortress, 2021), 156–69.

25. See n. 11 above.

26. Frey, *Theology and History*, 120.

27. See the summary account of his modus operandi in *Theology and History*, 10–12.

28. Hugo Méndez, "Did the Johannine Community Exist?" *JSNT* 42 (2020): 350–74.

29. The language here draws on both Martyn and Gadamer, *Truth and Method*, 313–18.

30. Martyn would not disagree with the idea that diverse strands are inextricably entangled in John—he writes that the Gospel's "seams" are "sewed together so deftly" that the dramatic levels are forged into one drama. Martin, *History and Theology*, 131.

31. Byers, *Ecclesiology and Theosis*, 20.

32. See the extended treatment of John and time in Jörg Frey, *The Glory of the Crucified One: Christology and Theology in the Gospel of John*, tr. Wayne Coppins and Christoph Heilig, BMSEC (Waco, TX: Baylor University Press, 2018), 73–99.

33. See, e.g., 5:2; 6:59; 9:11; 10:40; 11:54; et al.

34. While developing this material, I came across Jörg Frey's substantive discussion on John's fusion of contextual horizons, drawing on Gadamer. See *The Glory of the Crucified One*, 89–99 and *Theology and History*, 8–12. He notes other writers drawing on Gadamer in interpreting John include Ferdinand Hahn, "Sehen und Glauben im Johannesevangelium," in *Studien zum Neuen Testament 1*, ed. Jörg Frey, Juliane Schlegel, WUNT 191 (Tübingen: Mohr Siebeck, 2006), 521–37; Takashi

The Johannine Community and the Johannine Community Vision   137

Onuki, *Gemeinde und Welt im Johannesevangelium: Ein Beitrag zur Frage nach der theologischen und pragmatischen Funktion des johanneischen 'Dualismus,'* WMANT 6 (Neukirchen-Vluyn: Neukirchener, 1984). For Gadamer's discussion of horizons and their fusion, see *Truth and Method,* esp. 313–18.

35. For more on this, see Andrew J. Byers, "Johannine Readings of the Johannine Gospel: Reception Theology and Practice in John's Epistles" in *Gospel Reading and Reception in Early Christian Literature,* eds. Madison N. Pierce, Andrew J. Byers, and Simon Gathercole (Cambridge: Cambridge University Press, 2022), 190–214.

36. Martyn: "John's two stages are past and present, not future and present" (*History and Theology,* 131).

37. Jörg Frey also calls for a three-level drama but configured somewhat differently: (1) "the time and ministry of the earthly Jesus"; (2) "the history of the early communities of his followers in Jewish Palestine and then in the Diaspora"; and (3) "the time and perspective of the evangelist, his communities, and the addressees he has in view" (*Theology and History,* 120).

38. On this dynamic, see Beverly Roberts Gaventa, "The Archive of Excess: John 21 and the Problem of Narrative Closure," in *Exploring the Gospel of John: In Honor of D. Moody Smith,* ed. R. Alan Culpepper and C. Clifton Black (Louisville, KY: Westminster John Knox, 1996), 240–52.

39. For the phrase "imagined community" I am drawing on Hakola's use of this phrase (*Reconsidering Johannine Christianity,* 153–54), which he takes up from Benedict Anderson, *Imagined Communities: Reflections on the Origin and Spread of Nationalism,* rev. ed. (London/New York: Verso, 1991).

40. Perhaps the most sophisticated, comprehensive, and respected example of this approach is Urban C. von Wahlde, *The Gospel and Letters of John,* 3 vols., ECC (Grand Rapids, MI: Eerdmans, 2010).

41. See Ferdinand Christian Baur, *The Church History of the First Three Centuries,* trans. Allan Menzies, 2 vols, third ed; (London: Williams and Norgate, 1878); and Walter Bauer, *Orthodoxy and Heresy in Earliest Christianity,* eds Robert A. Kraft, Gerhard Krodel, trans. David Steinmetz (Philadelphia: Fortress Press, 1971 [1934]). For recent critiques, see Christoph Markschies, *Christian Theology and its Institutions: Prolegomena to a History of Early Christian Theology,* trans. Wayne Coppins, BMSEC (Waco, TX: Baylor University Press, 2015), 303–31; and Markus Bockmuehl, *Simon Peter in Scripture and Memory: The New Testament Apostle in the Early Church* (Grand Rapids, MI: Baker Academic, 2012), xv.

42. I have separated Conflict Scenes and Polemics since at times polemical language may occur when there seems to be little reason for conflict (as in John 8 when Jesus gets into fierce debate with Ἰουδαῖοι who had believed in him) and conflict may occur with virtually no polemics (as in John 6:66 when "many of his disciples turned back and no longer went about with him").

43. See Jonathan Bernier, *Aposynagōgos and the Historical Jesus in John: Rethinking the Historicity of the Johannine Expulsion Passages.* BInS 122 (Leiden: Brill, 2013).

44. Hakola, *Reconsidering Johannine Christianity,* 1, 4, 26.

45. Reinhartz, *Cast Out of the Covenant,* 131–57.

46. See Andrew J. Byers, "One Flock, One Shepherd, One God: The Oneness Motif of John's Gospel" in *One God, One People: Unity and Oneness in Early Christianity*, ed. Stephen C. Barton and Andrew J. Byers, RBS 104 (Atlanta: SBL Press, 2023), 195–215; idem, *Ecclesiology and Theosis*, 103–152; and idem, *John and the Others*, 106–9.

47. Note also the critique of this approach (that "synagogue" functions as a stand-in for Judaism in John, and without anchoring such a link in recent synagogue studies) offered in Wally V. Cirafesi, *John Within Judaism: Religion, Ethnicity, and the Shaping of Jesus-Oriented Jewishness in the Fourth Gospel*, AJEC 112 (Leiden: Brill, 2021), 272–77.

48. Byers, *Ecclesiology and Theosis*, 14.

49. See my extended discussion on John and the Ἰουδαῖοι in *John and the Others*, 45–94.

50. John M. G. Barclay, "Ἰουδαῖος: Ethnicity and Translation," in *Ethnicity, Race, Religion: Identities and Ideologies in Early Jewish and Christian Texts, and in Modern Biblical Interpretation*, ed. Katherine M. Hockey and David G. Horrell (London: T & T Clark, 2018), 46–58.

51. See Byers, *John and the Others*, 55–59; John M. G. Barclay, "Universalism and Particularism: Twin Components of Both Judaism and Early Christianity," in *A Vision for the Church: Studies in Early Christian Ecclesiology in Honour of J. P. M. Sweet*, eds. Marcus Bockmuehl and Michael B. Thompson (Edinburgh: T & T Clark, 1997), 207–24.

Chapter 7

Renewing Johannine Historical Criticism

A Proposal

Hugo Méndez

In 2005, Robert Kysar, a leading historical critic of John, reflected on his own growing disillusionment with historical studies of the Gospel of John. Lamenting that "our historical investigations were becoming more speculative and (even worse) taking our attention off the text as it stands before us," he suggested that the future may simply require a move away from diachronic studies altogether: "I now believe that literary studies are the wave of the future," Kysar writes, "and that historical-critical studies will become fewer and fewer in this new century."[1] Now, nearly two decades later, it is hard to escape the impression that the field has largely followed Kysar's prescription. Although historical-critical and social-scientific studies of John continue to be produced, a brief scan of the major venues of the field—book titles, conference presentations—will quickly reveal that these approaches do not dominate the study of John as they once did. On the contrary, a recent survey of the state of Johannine studies has gone so far as to speak of "the dominance of literary or narrative readings" of the Gospel in the twenty-first century, "especially in North American circles."[2] It is also hard to escape the impression of a general stagnation of historical-critical and social-scientific approaches to the Gospel. While the 1960s–1980s saw an explosion of novel and imaginative reconstructions of the Gospel's origins, more recent studies offer little to enrich the models of old. As a rule, a majority of historical-critical studies are distinguished more by restraint and agnosticism.

In this chapter, I would like to offer my own assessment of this decline—my own diagnosis of why the diachronic study of the Johannine texts has

140 *Hugo Méndez*

lost momentum. As I see it, the problem does not lie in the historical or social-scientific criticism itself. Rather, the problem lies in the inability of Johannine historical critics to think outside certain entrenched frameworks for this research.

The historical and social-scientific criticism of John has long been dominated by an interconnected cluster of undertheorized and unhelpful models that have led scholars into unproductive trajectories. I will scrutinize three interconnected projects in particular, diagnosing what I perceive to be the individual weaknesses and limitations of each—specifically: (a) the idea of a Johannine community, (b) the idea of institutional or personal links between the supposed Johannine community and Gnosticism, and (c) the idea of a Johannine "sociolect" or social dialect. In my view, the task of renewing Johannine historical criticism—of reigniting research into the origins and contexts of the Gospel and Epistles of John—requires that we frankly confront the failure of these older projects and imagine new projects in their place.

THE JOHANNINE COMMUNITY

Over the past fifty years, no single idea has played as central a role in the historical and social-scientific criticism of John than the notion of the Johannine Community. In fact, by the late 1970s, Kysar himself would remark that the study of John was "moving in one general direction, namely, toward the elucidation of the Gospel in relation to the community which gave birth to the document and to which the document itself was addressed."[3] The best days of the community hypothesis appear to be behind us, however. Most scholars today have retreated from the most detailed reconstructions of the community's history—for example, Martyn's idea of a community affected by the *Birkat Ha-Minim* or Brown's five-stage model.[4] Although most scholars today agree that "the reconstruction of a Johannine community rests on a much more secure foundation than do the other theoretical gospel communities," Johannine scholars no longer see it as viable "to reconstruct its history with the same rigor and precision as [others] have attempted."[5]

Most scholars may greet this shift as a turn to a healthier project: a more restrained search for the Johannine Community—one more cautious in its claims and humble in its conclusions. But I would argue that this turn should be read a different way—that is, as a sign that the idea of a "Johannine community" may not be a viable and productive framework for future research. Scholars have no obligations to the models they extract from their data. On the contrary, it is their burden to test and interrogate each model with regularity, asking: Is this model generative, yielding new insights into existing

Renewing Johannine Historical Criticism   141

data? Does this model find further support in emerging data sets? Does it predict what data will surface in the future? The trend line of the Johannine community hypothesis is negative on all these counts. The hypothesis does not illuminate the interpretation of the Johannine texts so much as parasitically impose itself upon them, constraining their interpretation in what Adele Reinhartz has called a "circular hermeneutical process."[6] The hypothesis' most specific forms have been flatly falsified. For that matter, the hypothesis' core claim—that a definable "Johannine Christianity" once existed—still finds no external support or corroboration either in the literary or archaeological record.

As I see it, what Johannine historical criticism needs is not a retrenchment around a vaguer, less imaginative, and (rather deliberately) less falsifiable community hypothesis. Rather, it should explore and test new models, entertaining a broader set of possible matrices for the Johannine texts. As Stanley Stowers insists, it is precisely "the uncritical assumption that early Christianity . . . consisted of communities" that "precludes and occludes the possibility of finding other social formations" that might lie behind New Testament texts.[7] A renewed Johannine historical criticism should boldly weigh the possible merits of other imagined contexts for the Gospel and Letters of John. That search might as well begin by dismantling the core assumption of the community hypothesis—namely, its unreflective claim that the Johannine authors must have hailed from the same social or geographical matrix.

Multiple Matrices

For the last fifty years, Johannine scholars have insisted that the similarities between the Gospel and Epistles of John indicate that they must have been produced within the same localized "community."[8] That community is, of course, the "Johannine Community." And yet, through the entire period in which the community hypothesis has dominated Johannine studies, scholars have held two other ideas that suggest more than one matrix for these works.

First, Johannine scholars agree that the similarities between the Johannine texts are too close to be merely coincidental convergences. They are, instead, signs of a direct and sustained program of literary borrowing; some Johannine texts are directly modeled on earlier texts. More specifically, the "vast majority of scholars" maintain that the Gospel was written first and that it served as a linguistic model for the later Epistles.[9] Remarkably, 1 John contains over 70 linguistic correspondences with the Gospel despite being only 105 verses long.[10] Even more strikingly, 2 and 3 John, with a combined 28 verses in total, contain 54 points of contact with the Gospel and 74 with 1 John.[11] The problem is that Johannine scholars have neglected to bring this empirically grounded

142 *Hugo Méndez*

insight into conversation—even collision—with the community hypothesis. If scholars generally agree that the four Johannine texts show signs of literary contact, then their similarities would no longer require nor demonstrate their origins in a single, localized network of churches. Scholars do not claim that Mark, Matthew, and Luke were written within a single community; literary contact provides a sufficient explanation for their overlap.

But there is more. Scholars recognize that Mark, Matthew, and Luke do not hail from the same matrix because of the presence of subtle but important differences in their outlook, ideas, and phraseology. Of course, scholars have also long recognized that the Gospel and Epistles also harbor subtle differences in outlook, ideas, and phraseology. These differences were crucial to establishing that these texts were not written by the same author.[12] But as Raimo Hakola notes, the same "marked differences" also "suggest that the gospel and the epistles have emerged in different situations."[13] What Hakola calls evidence of "different situations" (ostensibly in the life of a single community) might as well be something else, however—namely, evidence that they were produced in different matrices, different "communities" (to use that expression).[14] That is, the subtly different profiles of the text may suggest different social and geographical locations—different "communities," if you will—for their authors.

If we build upon these insights, then we should not constrain ourselves to imagine only a single "community" setting for the Gospel and Epistles. Instead, we can imagine other sorts of matrices for these texts as well as links between their respective authors. For one, we can speculate that the Johannine authors, like the Synoptic authors, might have operated without any sort of direct relationship, precisely as readers and consumers of one another's works, who opted to imitate one another's products.[15] What similarities exist between their writings would simply be due to literary contact and imitation.

Dubious Authorial Claims

We can enhance this image with yet a third insight of recent Johannine scholarship emerging in the past several decades—namely, the growing recognition that the Johannine texts contain dubious authorial claims. Especially after the literary turn in Johannine studies (1980s–present), multiple writers have argued that the implied author of the Gospel of John—the "disciple whom Jesus loved"—is probably only a literary invention.[16] Other writers have cast suspicion on the authorial claims of 1 John and 2 John.[17] We know that ancient Christians doubted the authenticity of 2 and 3 John.[18] Of course, disguised authorship was a mode of composition that typically did not entail public, visible authors working in a coordinated fashion. It usually involved authors effacing their contributions to literary works.[19]

More to the point, I have argued that there is impressive evidence that all four Johannine texts share the same false authorial construct—that is, they are all written as if they were works of the same anonymous eyewitness to the life of Jesus.[20] It is worth recalling that early Christians inferred that the Gospel and Epistles did share a common writer, attributing them all to a single person (ergo, why they are all named "John"). Many who disagreed with this view did so on the grounds that at least some Epistles might be spurious works.[21] Rather than reconstruct the Johannine authors as writers working within a single ancient Christian "community," then, we might do better to imagine them as a chain of writers who successively contributed to the same literary tradition of disguised authorship. What emerges is a new, different model to test in place of the older "community" model—and new, compelling research trajectories. We can experiment with reading each of John, 1 John, 2 John, and 3 John as pseudo-historical works and weigh the plausibility of those readings. And we can set certain features of the Epistles in conversation with other examples of disguised authorship in antiquity, determining their plausibility.

Whatever alternatives to the community hypothesis emerge, they should be data-driven rather than model-driven. Historical criticism of John has already produced important, empirically grounded results that are not currently in wide dispute among critical scholars.[22] The texts themselves are also filled with pools of data neglected or marginalized in the traditional "community" model. A renewed Johannine historical criticism should grapple with all this data more freely, unafraid to create, test, and even discard any number of new hypotheses from it. If, as Kysar says, "our historical investigations" have taken "our attention off the text," then the correct prescription is to return to the text, developing more empirically grounded and resilient models from it.

THE JOHANNINE "ORIGINS" OF GNOSTICISM

As I noted earlier, the Johannine Community was not merely one thread of Johannine historical criticism. It was, instead, the center or hub, suspending other, corollary projects. As the community hypothesis gives way to new and imaginative alternatives, then, other ideas long presupposing it should be reconsidered and retired as well. One idea is especially worth discarding—namely, the surprisingly tenacious thesis that the Johannine community, as a discrete, historical, social group, has social or institutional links to so-called Gnostic Christianities.

The idea that the Johannine tradition represents something of a "missing link" between Jesus and Gnosticism has a long pedigree.[23] That thesis, however, found new life with the advent of the community hypothesis, which suggested a stronger, even institutional, link between the two ideological currents. In an especially prominent proposal by Raymond Brown, Gnosticism's imagined origins no longer simply lay in Johannine tradition but in the Johannine community itself.[24] Specifically, Brown proposed that "the Johannine secessionists"—a group reconstructed from 1 John 2:19—"eventually became Gnostics and, indeed . . . their Johannine background may have catalyzed the development of early Gnostic systems."[25] These sorts of speculations continue to cling to the edifice of Johannine historical criticism, as seen in recent reference works in the field.[26] An entry in the *Cambridge History of Christianity* (2006) claims that certain "representatives of Johannine Christianity, nurturing alternative strands of tradition [than those in 1, 2, and 3 John], influenced various second-century movements, characterized by their opponents and much modern scholarship as 'Gnostic.'"[27] The same piece goes on to situate the *Apocryphon of John* and the *Acts of John* as witnesses to "some second century 'Johannine' Christians with 'Gnostic' characteristics."[28] Similarly, a chapter in the still more recent *Oxford Handbook of Johannine Studies* (2018) speculates that "the early gnostic Cerinthus" was "a Gentile Christian member of the Johannine Community who took his teacher's ideas further, under the influence of Platonic popular philosophy . . . and [Paul's] spirit-flesh dualism, and was led to break away," "taking some of John's pupils with him, and forming a rival sect."[29] Similar speculations appear in major New Testament textbooks.[30]

Rather than sustain these ideas, a renewed Johannine historical criticism should lead the charge against them. It should problematize both ends of this contrived family tree, highlighting the lack of concrete historical evidence for both an institutional "Johannine Christianity" on the one hand and a coherent, reified "Gnosticism" on the other. Contemporary scholars recognize that "what is today usually called ancient 'gnosticism' includes a variegated assortment of religious movements," of very different extractions, with different outlooks, and social forms.[31] Some may never have represented definable social groups; so-called Thomasine Christianity, for example, might be better conceptualized as a literary tradition augmented by authors with distinct intellectual syntheses.[32]

By the same token, Johannine historical critics should also be prepared to tell the story of the Gospel of John's relationship with these intellectual trajectories in a more nuanced way. They should situate the Gospel within and beside some of these works—as a text shaped by the same fluid sea of influences and currents informing late-first and early second-century Christian thought (e.g., *Logos* speculations, flesh/spirit binaries, realized-eschatological

Renewing Johannine Historical Criticism 145

ideas, etc.). They should project that fluidity outward as well, casting the Gospel's influence on later, so-called Gnostic works not in teleological terms—that is, as institutional succession or intellectual evolution—but as the result of numerous, undirected readerly engagements with the Gospel in various postures (creative synthesis, resistance, and competition). The Gospel of John circulated widely among readers positioned across a broad spectrum of early Christian thought, some of whose engagements with the Gospel fostered their eventual consolidation into the groups documented by later heresiologists (e.g., Valentinians, Proto-Catholics, Montanists, Sethians, etc.). These engagements, in turn, triggered the composition of many of the most popular and influential literary works of the second century, including a significant share of the Nag Hammadi library.

As I see it, then, what we need are not more social histories of the Johannine Community's dissolution and supposed continuations—histories built on limited data and questionable models. Rather, what we need is a richer reception and cultural history of the Gospel of John—one that probes the many readerly engagements and syntheses of the text by those Christian authors we know existed and read the Gospel.[33] This would be a far more productive project than the one that preceded it.

THE JOHANNINE SOCIOLECT

Although the Johannine community hypothesis emerged in a decidedly historical-critical matrix, "the concept of the Johannine community also generated a number of social-scientific studies," which were "built upon the assumptions of historical criticism."[34] One especially prominent line of research in this area has been sociolinguistic in nature. Its aim has been to interpret and analyze the language of the Gospel and Letters of John as a living social dialect (sociolect) spoken by Johannine Christians near the turn of the second century CE.[35]

Even from a cursory glance, it is obvious that the four Johannine texts share a distinctive "vocabulary . . . and even . . . fixed phrases and habits of speech."[36] These "fixed phrases" include twenty-six expressions that appear in multiple Johannine texts but nowhere else in first-century Christian literature:[37]

1. the light shines
2. the true light
3. walk in the light/darkness
4. do what is true
5. know the truth

6. be of the truth
7. the Spirit of Truth
8. know the true one/God
9. be of/from [ἐκ] God
10. be born of/from God
11. be of/from the devil
12. be of/from the world
13. overcome the world
14. the world hates you
15. abide in Jesus/God
16. Jesus/God abides in a person
17. word of God abides in you
18. to love Jesus/God is to keep commandments
19. a new commandment
20. lay down one's life for others
21. Jesus takes away sin
22. to pass from death to life
23. water and blood
24. we have known and believed
25. joy fulfilled

As it became natural to anchor the distinctive outlook of the Johannine texts in the life of a particular community, it also became natural to credit these expressions—the vehicle for communicating this outlook—to the same community. In his 1968 volume *Rätsel und Missverständis*, Herbert Leroy analyzes the Johannine *"Sondersprache"* as the "theological language of the community."[38] So too, Meeks's celebrated essay "The Man from Heaven in Johannine Sectarianism" interprets "the special patterns of language" in the Gospel of John within a social frame, precisely as the language of "the Johannine Christians."[39] For both Leroy and Meeks, however, the language of the Johannine texts was not simply a literary form of expression. Rather, both authors imagined that the "special language" represented in the Gospel and Epistles was used in other, non-literary contexts as well—especially, "preaching . . . catechesis, and . . . ritual."[40] With this move, Leroy and Meeks lifted the Johannine language off the page, transposing it into the imagined world of the first century as a living system of speech and converse—and, in turn, a meaningful object of sociolinguistic analysis.

Sociolinguistics was a nascent discipline in the 1960s–1970s—one only beginning to break into the landscape of Western academe. Within a decade, however, Johannine scholars had begun making active use of its theoretical resources to describe the language of imagined spoken language of the Johannine community—a trend that continues to the present. The Johannine community has been neatly interpreted as a "speech community." In turn, the language of their life and converse has been analyzed as "what sociolinguistics would call . . . the dialect of an in-group, a . . . subdialect not only of Koine Greek but even of early Christian discourse."[41]

The idea of a Johannine sociolect has not attracted the same level of scrutiny as the Johannine community hypothesis—at least not an independent scrutiny. Nevertheless, this prominent *topos* of Johannine social-scientific criticism harbors problems of its own. At least three deserve careful consideration—namely, (a) the failure, once again, to grapple with literary contact between the Johannine writings, (b) the failure to consider the place of individual voice or "idiolect," and (c) the failure to consider other speech contexts for the Johannine language.

Failure to Grapple with Literary Contact

It is true that the four Johannine texts have a strong set of verbal similarities. What the sociolect model fails to recognize, however, is that these similarities are literary in nature, in part if not in whole. As I noted earlier, the majority of scholars already posit literary contact and borrowing between the Johannine texts. Unfortunately, the present study of the Johannine literature has failed to connect this observation with the question of whether a Johannine sociolect as such existed. If the Gospel did serve as a kind of literary and linguistic model for the author(s) of the Epistles, one does not need to also posit a sociolect to explain the similarities of all these texts. The literary explanation suffices.

Failure to Grapple with Idiolect

Taken in isolation, the insight that certain Johannine authors copied other Johannine authors does not necessarily rule out the idea of a "Johannine sociolect." After all, social-scientific studies of John have always suggested that the distinctive language of any single Johannine author—including, presumably, a single Johannine author whose language was emulated by others—requires its own social and dialectical explanation.[42] The leap from author to community is more precarious than social-scientific critics recognize, however.

At its core, the idea of the Johannine sociolect assumes that the language the Johannine authors used in their writings is, in some way, representative of the language spoken by their peers. Missing from this model is the possibility that any part of this language is, in fact, unrepresentative—that is, that this language was in any way idiosyncratic and individual. In other words, in their rush to interpret the Johannine language as sociolect, social-scientific critics failed to consider how much of the language might instead reflect what sociolinguistics are more accustomed to calling "idiolect"—that is, the distinctive speech of an individual.[43]

To be fair, this oversight is not so much a failure of the Johannine scholars as a limitation of their tools. In the 1960s–1980s, the formative period of Johannine social-scientific criticism, structuralist assumptions still pervaded the field of sociolinguistics—assumptions that privileged abstract systems over speakers. A field focused on the delineation of systemic rules had little interest in the exceptional and idiosyncratic, all but bracketing out idiolect as a meaningful object of study:

> The lack of concern with . . . individual variation is the result of the fundamental incompatibility of the linguistic individual with Sausserean structuralism (as linguists have interpreted it). Linguists who study *langue* study something that is by definition superindividual and self-replicating. *Langue* is seen as the property of the community, not the individual. The object of study for structuralist linguistics is thus social: societies and social groups, dialects, and languages. These are sometimes treated not as convenient abstractions but as real entities . . . [and] often referred to in the discourse of structuralism as agents languages: languages drop pronouns, for example; dialects influence other dialects.[44]

Indeed, none other than William Labov, the father of modern sociolinguistics, would notoriously insist that "idiosyncratic habits are not a part of language so conceived."[45] It is little wonder, then, that social-scientific critics of John ignored the possibility of individual particularity and creativity in the language of the Johannine texts. The methods and models they harvested permitted only a single analysis: one that identified that language with a society, social group, or community—specifically, the Johannine community. Johannine speech, in short, was and could only be a dialect.

Since the 1980s, however, the field of sociolinguistics has re-centered idiolect and the individual in its conceptualization of dialect, especially in "the interactional turn" and "third wave sociolinguistics."[46] Where earlier studies saw group speech as the determiner of individual speech, contemporary studies see individual speech as the determiner of dialect. Individual speech is the site of linguistic innovation and the matrix of dialectical variation and change. Individual speakers develop new speech habits and forms, and individual speakers transmit these forms to other speakers by interaction. If Johannine scholars want to take these trends seriously, they should abandon, or at least nuance, models that would see the Johannine authors as mere mirrors and conduits of a community's dialect. They should also be open to seeing possible innovation, creativity, and individual genius in the language of the Johannine texts.

Failure to Consider Other Speech Contexts

A further flaw of the traditional "Johannine sociolect" model further underscores why it is so important to center the individual author when describing Johannine language. Previous studies identify the formative speech matrix of the Johannine authors with one and only one entity: the Johannine community, a specific, local network of assemblies, gatherings, or house churches. But to cite Stowers again, Christian assemblies were hardly the only networks in which an early Christian author might have been embedded:

> Why should community or even households-plus-communities be the only social formations that can be used in the explanation of early Christianity? Why should social formations such as neighborhoods, merchant networks, patterns of social connection based on religious places, artisan networks, religious entrepreneurial-consumer relations and networks, circles of slave friends, linked levels of social dominations, coalitions of friendship and enmity, age and gender sets (e.g., elderly men, early teenage girls), many sorts of markets, patterns and practices of linked levels of social domination, coalitions of friendship and enmity, age and gender sets (e.g., elderly men, early teenage girls), many sorts of markets, patterns and practices of ethnic identification and non-identification and many other social formations not be important for the social explanation of early Christianity?[47]

Since these formations/identifications are hardly exclusive, we can and should imagine that the Johannine authors participated in several of these.

This point is not incidental to the study of Johannine language. From the beginning, sociolinguists have insisted that dialects can be articulated around a wide range of variables, including geography, gender, ethnicity, and age. Thus, "any population . . . may be expected to contain a very large number of speech communities indeed, with overlapping memberships and overlapping language systems."[48] In turn, each of these language systems can express in a single individual's speech habits, if not in particular situations—i.e., instances of code-switching—then in multiple contexts. With respect to the Johannine authors, then, we cannot simply assume that a particular speech pattern found in a given text was determined by the author's participation in his local Christian "community," assembly, or house church. That speech pattern could have been as easily derived by the author's (former or continuing) participation in other simultaneous identifications—ones not shared by his Christian peers.

To take a concrete example: in John's reference to Christ as "Logos," Harold Attridge detects a "riff" on "fundamental Philonic strategy or rhetoric."[49] But by what vector would the author of John come in contact with Philonic (or pre-Philonic, or para-Philonic) language and thought? Did this

150   *Hugo Méndez*

contact occur because he worshipped in a Christ-confessing assembly deeply committed to synthesizing Philonic thought with Christian messianism? Or was our writer situated in another kind of network or association that incubated this philosophical tradition—perhaps a local philosophical guild or network of corresponding literary elites? After all, "the social spaces . . . of highly literate writers, interpreters and consumers of specialized writings held together and cut through many other social formations."[50] Could it be instead that our writer was an individual engineer of this kind of synthesis—perhaps as a literate, educated consumer of Philo's treatises, which he acquired in the bookseller's shop, the ancient library, or the gift exchange? As a rule, "speech communities . . . need not have any social or cultural unity" and can very well encompass isolated readers.[51]

Even if we could identify a given network as the source of our author's "Logos" speculation, this network would hardly represent the source of other signature themes and images in John. There is no unambiguous connection between Philonic thought and our author's conceptualization of the indwelling "Spirit of Truth" as παράκλητος (John 14:17). In all probability, this idea was inherited from yet another sphere of engagement. The image of baptism as a "rebirth" may derive from the same source or another altogether.

This bewildering array of branching possibilities is certainly "a vastly more complex . . . context than the writer-community model allows."[52] But it is not an unwieldy one. All these possibilities find unity and concreteness precisely in the person standing within them all—the person of the author. It is the individual author, then, who should be the primary object of our linguistic description—not any one of the many unknown and unknowable social formations around him, impossible to cleanly discriminate from others.

Failure to Grapple with Counterindications

Re-centering authors in the study of Johannine language of the Johannine texts stands to provide one more benefit to scholars. Simply, it can help us better account for data that the sociolect model has difficulty integrating. In her commentary on the Johannine Epistles, for example, Judith Lieu writes that while "the Johannine literature . . . [is] otherwise . . . characterized by a consistent . . . set of language patterns" 3 John seems to have an "uneven relationship with the Johannine literature"; at least in some verses. "3 John uses its own vocabulary [and idioms], some shared with other, and perhaps particularly with Pauline, traditions."[53] The opening greeting of 3 John is remarkably un-Johannine in language and form: "I pray that all may go well with you and that you may be in health; I know that it is well with your soul." Third John is also the only Johannine text to use the term "ἐκκλησία," and it does so several times (vv. 6, 9, 10). It is also the only Johannine text to call itinerant preachers συνεργοί ("co-workers"; v. 8), and to refer to gentiles as "ἐθνική" (v. 7).

To make sense of these divergent elements, Lieu is forced to fall back on a sociolinguistic explanation. She speculates that there were certain situations in which Johannine Christians might choose not to write in the community's sociolect. Specifically, she writes, "the intra-Johannine 'dialect' was perhaps reserved for internal purposes and would be inappropriate for a normal letter."[54] There is, however, a far more satisfying explanation for these supposed lapses in Johannine speech. In all likelihood, the reason 3 John breaks from the Johannine idiom is simply that its author reached the limits of what was available to imitate. It was there, in those gaps, that the author turned to other linguistic resources—that is, to whatever other expressions s/he ordinarily possessed—to communicate his/her ideas. It is in those gaps, I would argue, that we should be searching for the actual linguistic profiles and other literary influences of the multiple Johannine authors—a worthy new project for the field.

CONCLUSION

In the Synoptics, Jesus insists on the necessity of pouring "new wine" into "new wineskins" (Mark 2:22; Matt. 9:16–17). What the diachronic study of the Johannine texts needs is precisely "new wineskins"—new projects, new frameworks, new models to elaborate, test, critique, and refine. It needs an agenda for research that does not merely turn back to older frameworks—either in defensive, conservative, or critical postures—but that can think outside and beyond them.

In this chapter, I have proposed some possible trajectories for this research. Some of these models may fare no better under scrutiny than the older ones. All the better—we can discard those models as well. Although we have an obligation to handle the textual data with care, we have no obligations to our scholarly models. But we should be willing to experiment with new frameworks—even at the risk of being wrong again. In this way, we can get back to what Johannine historical criticism once was and can be again: not a staid orthodoxy, but the stage for some of the most compelling inventiveness in our field.

NOTES

1. Robert Kysar, *Voyages with John: Charting the Fourth Gospel* (Waco, TX: Baylor, 2005), 146.

2. Alicia D. Myers, "The Gospel of John," in *The State of New Testament Studies: A Survey of Recent Research*, ed. Scot McKnight and Nijay K. Gupta (Grand Rapids, MI: Baker, 2019), 334.

3. Robert Kysar, "Community and Gospel: Vectors in Fourth Gospel Criticism," *Int* 31 (1977): 355. The same survey introduces the quest for the sources of John under the heading: "traditions of the Johannine Community" and the analysis of "the Jewish character of" the Gospel as "the situation of the community" (Kysar, "Community and Gospel," 357, 362).

4. See discussion in Martinus C. de Boer, "The Johannine Community Under Attack in Recent Scholarship," in *The Ways That Often Parted: Essays in Honor of Joel Marcus*, ed. Lori Baron, Jill Hicks-Keeton, and Matthew Thiessen, ECL 24 (Atlanta: SBL Press, 2018), 211–41. Critics of the hypothesis fall into two camps. The first targets the Johannine Community within a broader challenge to the idea of "gospel communities." Representative studies include Richard J. Bauckham, "For Whom Were the Gospels Written?," in *The Gospel for All Christians: Rethinking the Gospel Audiences*, ed. Bauckham (Grand Rapids, MI: Eerdmans, 1998), 9–48; idem., *The Testimony of the Beloved Disciple: Narrative, History, and Theology in the Gospel of John* (Grand Rapids, MI: Baker Academic, 2007); Edward W. Klink, III, *The Sheep of the Fold: The Audience and Origin of the Gospel of John*, SNTSMS 141 (Cambridge: Cambridge University Press, 2007). Others assume a community but insist on its strictly conjectural status, e.g., Adele Reinhartz, "The Johannine Community and Its Jewish Neighbors: A Reappraisal," in *What Is John?*, ed. Fernando F. Segovia, 2 vols., SymS 7 (Atlanta: Scholars Press, 1998), 2:111–38; idem., "Building Skyscrapers on Toothpicks"; idem., *Cast Out of the Covenant: Jews and Anti-Judaism in the Gospel of John* (Lanham, MD: Lexington Books, 2018), 111–57; Robert Kysar, "The Whence and Whither of the Johannine Community," in *Life in Abundance: Studies of John's Gospel in Tribute to Raymond E. Brown, S.S.*, ed. John R. Donahue, S.J. (2005), 65–81; Judith M. Lieu, "The Audience of the Johannine Epistles," in *Communities in Dispute: Current Scholarship on the Johannine Epistles*, ed. R. Alan Culpepper and Paul N. Anderson, ECL 13 (Atlanta: SBL Press, 2014), 123–54.

5. Christopher W. Skinner, *Reading John* (Eugene, OR: Cascade, 2015), 44.

6. On this circularity, see Reinhartz, "Skyscrapers on Toothpicks."

7. Stanley Stowers, "The Concept of 'Community' and the History of Early Christianity," *MTSR* 23 (2011): 249; a call echoed in Sarah E. Rollens, "The Kingdom of God Is Among You: Prospects for a Q Community," in *Christian Origins and the Establishment of the Early Jesus Movement*, ed. Stanley E. Porter and Andrew W. Pitts, Early Christianity in its Hellenistic Environment 4 (Leiden: Brill, 2018), 224–41.

8. Martinus C. de Boer, "Johannine Community," in *The Oxford Handbook of Johannine Studies*, ed. Judith M. Lieu and Martinus C. de Boer (Oxford: Oxford University Press, 2018), 176.

9. George L. Parsenios, *First, Second, and Third John,* Paideia (Grand Rapids, MI: Baker Academic, 2014), 13.

10. Raimo Hakola, *Reconsidering Johannine Christianity: A Social Identity Approach* (New York: Routledge, 2015), 69–71.

Renewing Johannine Historical Criticism 153

11. J. Marty, "Contribution à l'étude des problèmes johanniques: Les petites épîtres 'II et III Jean,'" *RHR* 91 (1925): 202–3. As Raymond Brown notes, "70% of the significant words of III John are found in I John or GJohn, as are 86% of those in II John" (Raymond E. Brown, *The Epistles of John: Translated, with Introduction, Notes, and Commentary*, AB 30 [New Haven: Yale University Press, 1982], 16).

12. On these differences, see Brown, *Epistles*, 19–30; Hakola, *Johannine Christianity*, 67–95.

13. Hakola, *Johannine Christianity*, 73.

14. On the problems of the term "community," see Stowers, "Concept of 'Community.'"

15. As Stowers also notes, "fields or networks of literate and specialized cultural producers" "formed highly specialized social arenas" that "contested their own norms, forms of power, practices and products of literacy," precisely as they "produced, circulated and consumed writings" ("Concept of 'Community,'" 250).

16. On the history of this view, see James H. Charlesworth, *The Beloved Disciple: Whose Witness Validates the Gospel of John* (Valley Forge, PA: Trinity Press International, 1995), 134–41. Recent contributions include H.-M. Schenke, "The Function and Background of the Beloved Disciple in the Gospel of John," in *Nag Hammadi, Gnosticism, and Early Christianity*, ed. C. W. Hedrick and R. Hodgson Jr. (Peabody, MA: Hendrickson, 1986), 119; Barnabas Lindars, *The Gospel of John*, NCBC (Grand Rapids: Eerdmans, 1987), 33–34; Joachim Kügler, *Der Jünger, den Jesus Liebte*, SBB 16 (Stuttgart: Katholisches Bibelwerk, 1988), 429–38; Ismo Dunderberg, "The Beloved Disciple in John: Ideal Figure in an Early Christian Controversy," in *Fair Play: Diversity and Conflicts in Early Christianity: Essays in Honour of Heikki Räisänen*, ed. Ismo Dunderberg, Christopher Tuckett, and Kari Syreeni ed, NovTSup 103 (Leiden: Brill, 2002), 243–69; Harold W. Attridge, "The Restless Quest for the Beloved Disciple," in *Early Christian Voices: In Texts, Traditions, and Symbols: Essays in Honor of François Bovon*, ed. David H. Warren, Ann Graham Brock and David W. Pao (Leiden: Brill): 71–80; David Litwa, "Literary Eyewitnesses: The Appeal to an Eyewitness in John and Contemporaneous Literature," *NTS* 64 (2018): 343–61; Hugo Méndez, "Did the Johannine Community Exist?" *JSNT* 42 (2020): 350–74.

17. On 1 John as a falsely authored work, see Bart D. Ehrman, *Forgery and Counterforgery: The Use of Literary Deceit in Early Christian Polemics* (Oxford: Oxford University Press, 2013), 419–25. On 2 John, see Rudolf Bultmann, *The Johannine Epistles: A Commentary on the Johannine Epistles,* Hermeneia; (Philadelphia: Fortress Press, 1973), 1; Judith Lieu, *I, II, & III John: A Commentary*, NTL (Louisville, KY: Westminster John Knox, 2008), 4., 7, 18, 239–65; Ruth B. Edwards, *The Johannine Epistles* (Sheffield: Sheffield Academic, 1996), 50.

18. For example, Origen, the first writer to mention 3 John at all, reports that "not all say [2 and 3 John] are genuine" (quoted in Eusebius, *Hist. Eccl.* 6.25.10; Greek text and Eng. trans. from Eusebius, *Ecclesiastical History, Volume II: Books 6–10*, trans. J. E. L. Oulton, LCL 265 [Cambridge, MA: Harvard University Press, 1932], 76–77). Eusebius himself would rank 2 and 3 John among "the disputed books" (Eusebius, *Hist. Eccl.*, 3.25.1–5; Greek text and Eng. trans. from Eusebius,

Ecclesiastical History, Volume I: Books 1–5, trans. Kirsopp Lake, LCL 153 [Cambridge, MA: Harvard University Press, 1926], 256–7).

19. On the practice and strategies of disguised authorship in antiquity, see Ehrman, *Forgery and Counterforgery*, 93–148. Like other ancient works, falsely authored texts could be distributed in a number of ways, even at some remove from the author (Raymond J. Starr, "The Circulation of Literary Texts in the Roman World," *CQ* 37 [1987]: 216). Individual Johannine authors could have sent their text(s) under false pretenses to individuals in other cities with the resources to copy them; they could have deposited them in a library; or they could have surreptitiously introduced their text(s) into an accepted literary collection through intercalation.

20. Méndez, "Johannine Community," 360–66.

21. See n. 18.

22. These results would include the idea that John must date no later than the mid-second century and the conclusion that John, the son of Zebedee, could not have authored the Fourth Gospel as envisioned by tradition.

23. See history in Urban von Wahlde, "The Johannine Literature and Gnosticism," in *From Judaism to Christianity: A Festschrift for Thomas H. Tobin, S.J., on the Occasion of His Sixty-fifth Birthday*, ed. Patricia Walters, NovTSup 136 (Leiden: Brill, 2010), 221–22.

24. Brown, *Epistles*, 55–68, 104–6.

25. Raymond E. Brown, *The Community of the Beloved Disciple* (New York: Paulist, 1979), 182.

26. Fortunately, this speculation is well in decline (Urban C. von Wahlde, *Gnosticism, Docetism, and the Judaisms of the First Century: The Search for the Wider Context of the Johannine Literature and Why it Matters* [LNTS 517; New York, Bloomsbury, 2015], 61).

27. Harold W. Attridge, "Johannine Christianity," *The Cambridge History of Christianity*, 9 vols., ed., Margaret M. Mitchell, Frances M. Young, and K. Scott Bowie (Cambridge: Cambridge University Press, 2006), 1:125.

28. Attridge, "Johannine Christianity," 128.

29. Alistair H. B. Logan, "The Johannine Literature and the Gnostics," *The Oxford Handbook of Johannine Studies*, ed. Judith M. Lieu and Martinus C. de Boer (Oxford: Oxford University Press, 2018), 176.

30. For example, an earlier edition of prominent textbook in the field taught that "the sect" of Johannine Christians might have "disappeared from the face of the earth by being integrated into a larger society of Gnostically-minded individuals" (Bart D. Ehrman, *The New Testament: A Historical Introduction to the Early Christian Writings*, seventh ed. [Oxford: Oxford University Press, 2019], 213).

31. Michael Allen Williams, *Rethinking "Gnosticism": An Argument for Dismantling a Dubious Category* (Princeton, NJ: Princeton University Press, 1996), 3. Landmark studies questioning "Gnosticism" as a scholarly category include Williams, Rethinking "Gnosticism"; Karen L. King, *What Is Gnosticism?* (Cambridge, MA: Harvard University Press, 2003).

32. Melissa (Phillip) Sellew, "'Thomas Christianity': Scholars in Search of a Community," in *The Apocryphal Acts of Thomas*, ed. Jan B. Bremmer (Leuven, Peeters,

Renewing Johannine Historical Criticism   155

2001), 11–35. Of course, I believe that the Johannine tradition is also only a literary tradition.

33. On the aims of a cultural-historical approach to the New Testament, see Timothy Beal, "Reception History and Beyond: Toward the Cultural History of Scriptures," *BibInt* 19 (2011), 370.

34. Kysar, "Whence and Whither," 69–70.

35. A history of scholarship on the Johannine sociolect appears in David A. Lamb, *Text, Context, and the Johannine Community: A Sociolinguistic Analysis of the Johannine Writings*, LNTS 477 (New York: Bloomsbury, 2014), 103–44. Representative studies include Wayne A. Meeks, "The Man From Heaven in Johannine Sectarianism," *JBL* 91 (1972): 44–72; Herbert Leroy, *Rätsel und Missverständnis: ein Beitrag zur Formgeschichte des Johannesevangeliums*, BBB 30 (Bonn: Peter Hanstein, 1968), 167; Bruce J. Malina, *The Gospel of John in Sociolinguistic Perspective* (48th Colloquy of the Center for Hermeneutical Studies, Berkeley, CA: Center for Hermeneutical Studies, 1985); idem., "John's: The Maverick Christian Group: The Evidence of Sociolinguistics," *BTB* 24 (1994): 167–82; Bruce J. Malina and Richard L. Rohrbaugh, *Social-Scientific Commentary on the Gospel of John* (Minneapolis: Fortress, 1998); Norman R. Petersen, *The Gospel of John and the Sociology of Light: Language and Characterization in the Fourth Gospel* (Valley Forge, PA: Trinity, 1993).

36. Lieu, *I, II, & III John*, 4.

37. Hakola, *Johannine Christianity*, 69–71; Hakola's list organizes Raymond Brown's more exhaustive catalogue (*Epistles*, 755–59).

38. Leroy, *Rätsel und Missverständnis*, 167.

39. Meeks, "Man from Heaven," 44, 57. The term "Johannine Christians" first appears on p. 45.

40. Meeks, "Man from Heaven," 49.

41. Lieu, *I, II, & III John*, 4.

42. See, for instance, Michael Labahn, *Jesus als Lebensspender: Untersuchungen zu einer Geschichte der johanneischen Tradition anhand ihrer Wundergeschichten*, BZNW 98 (Berlin, New York: DeGruyter, 1999), 106–9.

43. On the distinction between "sociolect" and "idiolect" in Johannine studies, see Jörg Frey, *Die johanneische Eschatologie*, 3 vols., WUNT 96, 110, 117 (Tübingen: Mohr Siebeck, 1997–2000), 1:439–41; Labahn, *Jesus als Lebensspender*, 106–9.

44. Barbara Johnstone, *The Linguistic Individual: Self-expression in Language and Linguistics* (Oxford: Oxford University Press, 1996), 11.

45. William Labov, *Sociolinguistic Patterns* (Philadelphia: University of Pennsylvania Press, 1972), 277.

46. Landmark or pioneering discussions include Hans-Heinrich Lieb, *Linguistic Variables: Towards a Unified Theory of Linguistic Variation* (Amsterdam: John Benjamins, 1993); Johnstone, *Linguistic Individual*; James Milroy, "Internal vs. external motivations for linguistic change," *Multilingua* 16.4 (1997): 311–23; Salikoko S. Mufwene, *The Ecology of Language Evolution* (Cambridge: Cambridge University Press, 2001); Joseph W. Kuhl, "The idiolect, chaos, and language custom far from equilibrium: Conversations in Morocco" (PhD thesis; Athens: University of Georgia, 2003); Peter Auer and Frans Hinskens, "The role of interpersonal accommodation in

a theory of language change," in *Dialect Change: The Convergence and Divergence of Dialects in Contemporary Societies*, ed. by Peter Auer, Frans Hinskens, and Paul Kerswill (Cambridge: Cambridge University Press, 2005), 335–57.

47. Stowers, "Concept of 'Community,'" 249–50.

48. Dwight Bolinger, *Aspects of Language*, second ed. (New York: Harcourt, Brace, Jovanovich, 1975), 333. Indeed, just as "there is no limit to the ways in which human beings league themselves together for self-identification, security, gain, amusement, worship or any of the other purposes that are held in common: consequently there is no limit to the number and variety of speech communities that are to be found in society."

49. Harold W. Attridge, "Philo and John: Two Riffs on One Logos," in *Essays on John and Hebrews*, WUNT 264 (Tübingen: Mohr Siebeck, 2010), 47. Attridge leaves open the question of how the author of John knew (at least predecessors or strains of) Philonic thought ("Philo and John," 58).

50. Stowers, "Concept of 'Community,'" 249.

51. Richard Anthony Hudson: *Sociolinguistics*, second ed. (Cambridge: Cambridge University Press, 1996), 24.

52. Stowers, "Concept of 'Community,'" 248.

53. Lieu, *I, II, & III John*, 277–78.

54. Lieu, *I, II, & III John*, 278.

Chapter 8

The Legacy of the Beloved Disciple

The Johannine Letters as Epistolary Fiction

Elizabeth J. B. Corsar

The hypothesis of a Johannine Community from which the Gospel of John and the Letters of John emerged has a long history in Johannine scholarship.[1] However, it was not until the publication of J. Louis Martyn's seminal work on the gospel in 1968 followed by the important work of Raymond Brown in 1969, in which he advanced the work of his colleague to include the letters, that the hypothesis of the Johannine Community truly took its place in Johannine scholarship.[2] While for over half a century this hypothesis has been hugely influential in shaping Johannine scholarship, the proposal has recently been met with criticism.

In this chapter, I follow this recent scholarly trend and offer an alternative proposal regarding the production of the letters that does not rely on a community hypothesis. To do this, I consider the literary environment within which the letters were written and propose that the letters are examples of epistolary fictions. Specifically, I suggest that the Johannine Letters fit within the form of pseudo-historical letters. A type of letter that is pseudonymously penned in the name of a notable figure in order to continue the legacy of the individual. Thus, I suggest that the letters are pseudonymously written in the name of the Beloved Disciple in order to continue his legacy as an authoritative witness. This line of enquiry builds on a similar argument recently put forward by Hugo Méndez who proposes that the Johannine Gospel and the Letters "are not the independent products of a single community of like-minded churches.

Rather, they are successive pseudepigrapha, which present themselves as the work of the same invented figure [the Beloved Disciple]."[3]

EPISTOLARY FICTION

In Graeco-Roman literary culture the production of letters was prolific, to the extent that Patricia Rosenmeyer remarks "letters can be found lurking in every corner of ancient writing."[4] Moreover, the letter genre had several different subgenres, as Ruth Edwards notes,

> The Graeco-Roman world knew many different kinds of epistolary writing. There were short philosophical treatises in the form of letters; fictional letters written as creative literary exercises; official letters reporting on events or asking for advice, pastoral and ecclesial letters . . . And there were private letters, sometimes quite literary . . . sometimes informal and almost illiterate.[5]

It is the fictional letter written as a creative literary exercise which Edwards mentions that is of interest in this present essay. The fictional letter perhaps has its origin in the form of Bellerophon's tablet in Homer's *Iliad* with the subgenre subsequently establishing itself and becoming a popular choice among authors of the ancient Mediterranean.[6] One particular type of letter within this subgenre is the pseudo-historical letter, a form of fictional letter that was prevalent at the time in which the Johannine Letters were composed.

One of the key functions of the letter in antiquity was to reveal the character of its author. This objective is stated in the literary treatise attributed to Hermogenes. For in a section dedicated to the style of letters, the literary critic explains that "the letter should be strong in characterisation. Everyone writes a letter in the virtual image of his own soul. In every other form of speech, it is possible to see the writer's character, but in none so clearly as in the letter" (Demetrius, *Eloc.* 227).[7] This aim is true for both real and fictional letters, for pseudo-historical letters are interested in the character of notable figures in as much as the letters are intent on maintaining the legacy of "ancient celebrities"[8] in whose name the letters are penned. This form of fictional letter is further described by Rosenmeyer:

> The principal impulse behind the work of a pseudonymous letter writer may have been the desire to illuminate a figure from the glorious past through a more intimate character portrait than a standard biography would allow. The letter writer presents an "apology" for the hero's life, or challenges a later generation to admire his accomplishments, viewing historical events through the lens of one man's personal correspondence.[9]

The Legacy of the Beloved Disciple 159

There are a number of examples of these pseudo-historical letters in ancient literature. For instance, there are letters attributed to well-known historical figures such as the philosopher Plato, the rhetorician Isocrates, or the writer Xenophon; as well as letters of individuals whose historicity is less certain such as the philosopher Apollonius of Tyana, the philosopher Anacharsis, or the tyrant Phalaris.[10] Pseudonymous writings, such as these pseudo-historical letters, have often been misjudged and misunderstood as being deceptive counterfeits. However, as Irene Peirano observes, pseudonymous texts are "creative readings and interpretations of master-author's texts" for they are an "expansion and creative refashioning of canonical texts" and ultimately, they are "reception texts."[11] This creative approach to source material is true also of pseudo-historical letters. For Claire Rachel Jackson and Janja Soldo note that these letters "embellish and rewrite traditional biographical narratives about famous figures."[12] Similarly Rosenmeyer observes that authors of these letters "were at once scholar and artist, researching historical materials for the basic facts, and then using their imagination to elaborate creatively and dramatically on those facts."[13]

The practice of writing in the name of another figure and reworking the source material written by or associated with that figure is evident in both literary education and compositional culture. For the practice of literary impersonation began in the classroom with the exercises of *ethopoeia*. This exercise involved taking a well-known historical or mythical figure and writing a speech in the voice of the selected figure. A pupil would be expected to imitate the figure in so far as they would need to consider what choice of words (content of the speech) would be fitting for the character of the figure they had selected and for the chosen audience. For instance, rhetoricians recommend that pupils reflect on "what would Cyrus say when marching against Massagetae?" (Theon, *Prog.*, 115)[14] or "what words Achilles would say to Deidamia when about to go to war" (Hermogenes, *Prog.*, 20)[15] or "what words Agamemnon would say after taking Ilium" (Nicolaus, *Prog.*, 64).[16] Moreover, the exercise of ethopoeia is creative in nature, for the rhetorician Aphthonius describes the practice of invention as playing a key part in the exercise of ethopoeia:

> Ethopoeia has a known person as speaker and only invents the characterization, which is why it is called "character-making"; for example, what words would Heracles say when Eurystheus gave his commands? Here Heracles is known, but we invent the character in which he speaks. (Aphthonius, *Prog.*, 44)[17]

To undertake this exercise, a pupil would acquaint themselves with the character of Heracles, perhaps by consulting the mythical tradition concerning the legendary hero.[18] Then, with this knowledge, the pupil would construct a speech by imagining what Heracles might say in response to the commands of his rival Eurystheus.

The rhetorical handbooks make clear that the exercise of ethopoeia served to train pupils to compose in various genres. For instance, Theon notes "under this genus of exercise fall the species of consolations and exhortation and letter writing" (Theon, *Prog.*, 115)[19] and Nicolaus observes "this progymnasmata is useful for three kinds of rhetoric. . . . encomium, prosecuting, and giving consul. To me, it seems also to exercise us in the style of letter writing" (Nicolaus, *Prog.*, 66–67).[20] Furthermore, in his commentary on Aphthonius' *progymnasmata*, John of Sardis writes "practice in ethopoeia is most useful everywhere; for it does not contribute to only one species of rhetoric, but to all" (John of Sardis, *Comm. Aph.* 200).[21]

The rhetorical practice of ethopoeia evidently influenced the composition of pseudo-historical letters. For pseudonymous authors wrote in the names of well-known figures, drew on material written by or about their selected figure, and reworked the gathered material offering a recognizable yet distinct portrayal of the figure. A Greek example of this type of letter is the epistle collection of the poet Euripides. The pseudonymous author writes in the name of Euripides, draws material from Satyrus's biography on Euripides, and reworks the material to offer a positive presentation of Euripides.[22] Moreover, a Jewish example of this form of letter is the epistle of the prophet Jeremiah. The pseudonymous author writes in the name of Jeremiah, draws material from the canonical book of Jeremiah, and reworks the material to depict Jeremiah addressing a created situation (e.g., idols) concerning the exiles in Babylon.[23] Furthermore, a Christian example of this type of letter is the third epistle of Paul. The pseudonymous author writes in the name of Paul, draws material from the authentic Corinthian Letters and the Pastoral Letters, and reworks the material to portray Paul addressing an imagined situation (e.g., false teachers) facing the Christians in the Corinthian church.[24]

The idea of reworking written material for the composition of pseudo-historical letters is part of the broader compositional practice of literary imitation. Literary imitation is the practice of drawing on the works of one's literary predecessors, adapting the work, and creating a new piece of writing, but nevertheless to some degree reflecting the literary work of the predecessor. The practice of literary imitation was crucial in the production of new literature in the ancient world, as Quintilian in the *Institutio Oratoria* states, "it cannot be doubted that a large part of art consists of imitation" (Quintilian, *Inst.* 10.2.1).[25] The practice of literary imitation was initially introduced to aspiring literati in the classroom of the rhetor. As Javier Martínez observes, "education was based on imitation of canonical models."[26] Teresa Morgan similarly discerns that in the educational setting, "texts oscillated between two statuses: that of the particular canonical version of the story, and that of a tool which could be used and altered."[27] As part of the preliminary rhetorical exercises (*Progymnasmata*), Quintilian advises that pupils should take texts such as *Aesop's Fables* and they should "break up, then interpret in different words, then make a bolder paraphrase in which they are allowed to abbreviate and embellish some parts, so long as the poet's meaning is preserved" (Quintilian, *Inst.* 1.9.2). Later in their rhetorical training, he suggests that pupils should imitate the works of great authors. Quintilian offers a reading list of authors with commentary on the quality of their works and highlights those that are particularly worthy of imitation. With the identification of these works as the starting point, Quintilian discusses the theory and the practice of imitation. He explains that simple "imitation is not sufficient on its own" (Quintilian, *Inst.* 10.2.4), with it being "a disgrace to merely to attain the effect you are imitating" (Quintilian, *Inst.* 10.2.7); rather, the texts should be adapted. To adapt a text, Quintilian proposes using the practice of paraphrase. He explains that paraphrase is not "mere passive reproduction" but rather it is utilized in order "to rival and vie with the original [while] expressing the same thoughts" (Quintilian, *Inst.* 10.5.5). Moreover, within his reading list, Quintilian discusses authors' successful imitation of texts, for example, Cicero "succeeded in reproducing the forcefulness of Demosthenes, the abundance of Plato, and the elegance of Isocrates. But he did more than reproduce by study the excellences of each: most, or rather all, of his virtues re the self-generated product of the happy richness of his immortal genius" (Quintilian, *Inst.* 10.1.109).

Thus, the pseudo-historical letter was a popular literary form at the time that the Johannine Letters were composed. These letters were pseudonymously penned in the name of a well-known figure and by borrowing and reworking material written by or written about the selected figure, pseudonymous authors composed letters that offered an intimate portrayal of the figure to continue the legacy of the figure.

THE BELOVED DISCIPLE AND THE RELATIONSHIP BETWEEN THE GOSPEL AND LETTERS

The Beloved Disciple, according to the gospel, was a disciple of Jesus who was present with his master at various significant moments. For instance, the Beloved Disciple sat next to Jesus at the last supper (John 13:23), he waited outside the High Priest's palace for Jesus (John 18:15), he stood at the foot of Jesus's cross (John 19:26), he saw Jesus's empty tomb (John 20:5–6), and he followed the resurrected Jesus (John 21: 20).[28] Therefore, his testimony concerning Jesus is understood as being "true" (John 21:24); his witness is authoritative. Proponents of the Johannine Community hypothesis

162   *Elizabeth J. B. Corsar*

suppose that the Beloved Disciple was the head of the community and that his eyewitness testimony and subsequent interpretation of Jesus' revelation was the source of the tradition on which the gospel and letters are based. For Raymond Brown understands the Beloved Disciple to be a historical disciple of Jesus who was the "hero of the community." He supposes that the gospel and the letters emerge from a "Johannine School of writers" who have a "shared theological position" based on the eyewitness testimony of the Beloved Disciple and as a community they are the "heir" to his tradition.[29] Similarly, R. Alan Culpepper interprets the Beloved Disciple as a historical companion of Jesus who was the "founder of the community." He assumes that for the authors of the gospel and the letters, the Beloved Disciple was the "source of [their] traditions" and that the texts draw on this tradition and "represent [different] periods of the community's life," the gospel reflecting an earlier period and the epistles a later one.[30]

Moreover, advocates of the Johannine Community hypothesis have assumed that the similarities and differences between the gospel and the letters point toward the existence of a community. As Raimo Hakola observes, "it is the coexistent similarities and subtle differences in the style and theology between the Fourth Gospel and the Johannine Epistles that originally formed a crucial building block in the emergence of the theory of a specific Johannine group or school."[31] Michael Labahn has recently argued "the similarities along with the differences point to different authors from the same milieu who shared a fund of common ideas and language. These authors then were possibly members of a Johannine school."[32] However, by considering the role of the Beloved Disciple and the relationship between the Johannine texts in light of ancient compositional practice, particularly in respect of pseudo-historical letters, it becomes possible to argue against the Johannine Community hypothesis. In the gospel, the Beloved Disciple is presented as an intimate companion of Jesus who witnessed his master's ministry (public/private), death, and resurrection and who with this authoritative witness composed the gospel (John 21:24). In regard to the historicity of the Beloved Disciple, I follow the proposal of Méndez and his predecessors Barnabas Lindars, Harold Attridge, and Andrew Lincoln, in assuming that the Beloved Disciple is a "literary invention."[33] Yet despite his fabricated character, I suggest that the Beloved Disciple became a legendary figure after the publication of the gospel and his character captured the imagination of early Christian authors who employed the genre of pseudo-historical letters to continue his legacy as an authoritative witness. This proposal assumes Richard Bauckham's position that the Gospel of John was intended for and was read by a "general Christian audience."[34] Thus, the figure of the Beloved Disciple would have been well known among early Christians and not simply an insular Johannine Christian group, and authors would have been eager to

The Legacy of the Beloved Disciple 163

utilize the form of the pseudo-historical letter to continue the legacy of the Beloved Disciple. If the Beloved Disciple is a fabricated character as I have suggested, it follows that the audience of the epistles is also invented. The pseudonymous authors of the letters present the Beloved Disciple writing to a believing community (e.g., 1 John 5:13; 2 John 4; 3 John 3) just as the pseudonymous author/redactor of the gospel presents the Beloved Disciple writing to an already believing community (John 20:31).

Furthermore, I suggest that the similarities and differences between the gospel and the letters do not reflect tradition grounded in the Beloved Disciple's witness and shared by the Johannine community. But rather, in line with the practice of writing pseudo-historical letters and indeed broader compositional practice, they represent the borrowing and reworking of predecessor texts by the pseudonymous authors of the letters. Such a view was held by Rudolph Bultmann who suggested that "the author of 1 John had the Gospel before him and was decisively influenced by its language and ideas" and that "2 John is dependent on 1 John."[35]

Therefore, in the next section, I will follow the commonly held assumption of gospel priority and interpret the letters as later documents that were literarily dependent on the gospel.[36] Several commentators suggest that the three letters were composed by the same author.[37] While it is possible that there is one author who wrote two very different styles of letter, I suggest that it is more likely that there were two authors, one who wrote 1 John and another who wrote 2 and 3 John on the basis of the over similarities between 2 and 3 John and their overall difference to 1 John. Thus, I suggest that in composing their pseudo-historical letters, the pseudonymous author of 1 John borrowed and reworked material from the gospel and the author of 2 and 3 John borrowed and reworked material from the gospel and 1 John.

THE LETTERS AS EPISTOLARY FICTIONS

The Beloved Disciple as Author

The pseudonymous author/redactor of the gospel presents the Beloved Disciple as an intimate companion of Jesus who witnessed his master's ministry, death, and resurrection. In addition to this, the Beloved Disciple is also portrayed as the author of the gospel, the one who committed his authoritative witness to writing, in the form of a biography of Jesus.[38] The gospel's second epilogue mentions "the disciple who Jesus loved" (John 21:20) and confirms that "this is the disciple who is testifying to these things and has written them." (John 21:24a). This builds on the gospel's first epilogue which specifies what "these things" are and states the gospel's purpose:

164   *Elizabeth J. B. Corsar*

> Now Jesus did many other signs in the presence of his disciples, which are not written in this book. But these are written so that you may *continue to believe* (πιστεύητε) that Jesus is the Messiah, the Son of God, and that through believing you have life in his name. (John 20:30–31)[39]

Additionally, the gospel's prologue implies that the one who selected and compiled these signs was a witness to the miracles of Jesus, for in the prologue it states, "we have seen his glory" (John 1:14), as Jesus's glory is revealed to the disciples through his signs (cf. John 2:11; 11:4). Therefore, by reading the prologue and double epilogue in combination, the Beloved Disciple is depicted as an authoritative witness-author, the one who witnessed and wrote about Jesus' signs.

The Beloved Disciple is not named as the author of the letters, however, his identity as the author is strongly implied in the prologue of 1 John and the epilogues of 1, 2, 3 John. Although the author of 2 and 3 John is named as "the elder" (2 John 1; 3 John 1), the Beloved Disciple as author is nevertheless inferred through the letter's epilogues. For, by borrowing from the gospel, the pseudonymous authors of the letters, identify the author of the letters as one and the same as the gospel, the Beloved Disciple.

1 John

The pseudonymous author of 1 John identifies the Beloved Disciple as the author of the letter in the prologue and the epilogue and does so by borrowing from the gospel's prologue and double epilogue. In the gospel's prologue, the Beloved Disciple is presented as one of a group who saw Jesus (John 1:14), the Son of the Father who was made known (John 1:18), and who is the Word and the life (John 1:1, 4). In comparison, in the letter's prologue, the author is portrayed as one of a group who saw, heard, and touched Jesus (1 John 1, 3, cf. John 20:27—Thomas), the Son of the Father, and the word of life who was revealed (1 John 1:2). Additionally, in the gospel's epilogues, the Beloved Disciple is presented as writing the gospel and including "these things" that he has witnessed to bolster belief in Jesus the Son of God and to emphasize the gift of life (John 20:31; 21:24). In comparison, in the letter's epilogue, the author is portrayed as writing the letter and including "these things" that he has witnessed to sustain belief in Jesus the Son of God and to highlight the gift of eternal life (1John 5:13). Through this borrowing, the pseudonymous author of the letter identifies the author of 1 John as the Beloved Disciple.

2 and 3 John

The pseudonymous author of 2 and 3 John identifies the Beloved Disciple as the author of both letters in the epilogues and does so by borrowing from the

The Legacy of the Beloved Disciple

gospel's double epilogue. As in the gospel's epilogues, the Beloved Disciple is depicted as mentioning "many other things" that could not be included in the book, and which were excluded due to exceeded capacity (John 20:30; 21:23). In comparison, in the epilogue of 2 John, the author is portrayed as having "much" to write about but due to exceeded capacity, he chooses not to write using pen and ink but to visit face to face (2 John 2:12) and in the epilogue of 3 John, the author is presented as having "much" to write about yet on account of exceeded capacity, he decides not to write with paper and ink but to visit face to face (3 John 13). By means of this borrowing, the pseudonymous author portrays the author of 2 and 3 John as the Beloved Disciple.

Therefore, in line with the practice of composing pseudo-historical letters, the pseudonymous authors of the epistles present the Beloved Disciple as the author. Moreover, they offer a more intimate portrayal of the Beloved Disciple as the letters are written in the first person: "I write to you" (1 John 2:1, 7–8, 12–14, 21, 26; 5:13; 2 John 1, 4, 5, 12; 3 John 1–4, 9–10, 13–14). Thus, the Beloved Disciple is depicted as personally sharing his authoritative witness in the form of a letter.

A Continued Legacy of the Beloved Disciple

The pseudonymous author/redactor of the gospel portrays the Beloved Disciple as an authoritative witness and as the author of the gospel, and the pseudonymous authors of the letters present the Beloved Disciple as the author of the letters and portray him personally sharing his authoritative witness. Additionally, the material which constitutes the Beloved Disciple's authoritative witness has been borrowed from the gospel or 1 John and reworked by the pseudonymous authors. The points of contact particularly between the gospel and 1 John are extensive, so I have selected a representative selection of examples which demonstrate borrowing and reworking.

1 John

Children of God: The pseudonymous author presents the Beloved Disciple writing about the children of God, for seeing himself and his audience as believers and children of God, the Beloved Disciple notes "everyone who believes that Jesus is the Christ has been born of God" (1 John 5:1a) and he explains that it is through the love of God "that we should be called children of God" (1 John 3:1a), yet he warns that "the reason the world does not know us is that it did not know him" (1 John 3:1b). These ideas of belief resulting in the status of children of God and the status being possible through God's love, and the world responding to the children of God in the same negative way that it responded to Jesus are found in the gospel. For in the gospel, it states that "all who received him, and believed in his name, he gave the power to become children of God" (John 1:12) and it explains that because God loved he sent his Son into the world so that the world might believe in him (John 3:16), yet Jesus warns that the world will respond to the children of God in the same negative way that it responded to him, for he explains that the "world" which represents unbelief (John 1:10–11) hates believers because it had hated him (John 15:18).

Love: The Beloved Disciple is presented by the pseudonymous author as reflecting on the commandment to love (1 John 2:7), for the Beloved Disciple emphasizes that "we should love one another" (1 John 3:11) and clarifies that "we know love by this, that he laid down his life for us and we ought to lay down our lives for one another" (1 John 3:16). These concepts of the commandment to love and the laying down of one's life out of love for another are present in the gospel. For in the gospel, Jesus says, "I give you a new commandment, that you love one another" (John 13:34b cf. 15:12) and he clarifies that "no-one has greater love than this to lay down one's life for one's friends" (John 15:13).

Moreover, the Beloved Disciple is portrayed as more specifically discussing God's love, for he writes, "God's love was revealed to us in this way: God sent his only son into the world so that we might live through him" (1 John 4:9) and emphasizes that "since God loved us so much, we also ought to love one another" (1 John 4:11). These notions of God's love being made manifest through the sending of his Son who brings life and also the call for believers to emulate the love of their deity are found in the gospel. As in the gospel, it states, "for God so loved the world that he gave his only Son, so that everyone who believes in him may not perish but may have eternal life" (John 3:16) and Jesus calls his disciples to "love one another. Just as I have loved you" (John 13:34; 15:12).

Furthermore, the Beloved Disciple is depicted as further discussing the importance of love and noting, "we must not be like Cain who was from the evil one and murdered his brother" (1 John 3:12). These ideas of not showing love to those close to you and rather being a "murder" and being from the "evil one" are present in the gospel on two occasions. For in the gospel, "the Jews" who are Jesus's "own" (John 1:10) who seek to kill him (John 5:18; 7:19) and who hand him over to death (John 18:28) are described as having the devil as their father (John 8:44); and Judas who was a disciple of Jesus handed his master over to death (John 18:3) and is described as having the devil in him (John 13:2, 27). Neither "the Jews" or Judas show love toward Jesus despite being "his own" people or disciple, in fact "the Jews" are described as hating Jesus (John 15:25) and both bring about his death (murderers) and are associated with the devil (evil one).

The Legacy of the Beloved Disciple 167

Eternal life: The pseudonymous author portrays the Beloved Disciple discussing the gift of eternal life, for the Beloved Disciple writes, "and this is the testimony: God gave us eternal life, and this life is in his Son. Whoever has the Son has life; whoever does not have the Son of God does not have life" (1 John 5:11–12). This notion of God giving the gift of life through his Son who in himself had the life by being the life is present in the gospel. As in the gospel, it states that God gave eternal life as he sent his Son to enable the bestowal of eternal life upon believers (John 3:16). Additionally, Jesus declares, "I am the resurrection and the life. Those who believe in me even though they die, will live" (John 11:25) and he explains "this is the will of my Father, that all who see the Son and believe in him may have eternal life" (John 6:40).

Opponents: The Beloved Disciple is presented by the pseudonymous author as addressing the problem of opponents, for he writes, "everyone who commits sin is a child of the devil" (1 John 3:8) and he speaks of "antichrists" who deny that Jesus is the Christ and deny the Father and the Son, and he explains that these individuals "[do] not belong" (1 John 2:18–19, 22). These ideas of sinning, being a child of the devil, and not belonging are found in the gospel. For in the gospel, Jesus associates sin with unbelief as he says "if I had not come and spoken to them, they would not have sin" (John 15:22) and "if I had not done among them the works that no one else did, they would not have sin" (John 15:24). Here Jesus is speaking of "the Jews" who did not receive or believe in him (e.g., John 1:11). "The Jews" in the gospel are Jesus opponents and are described by Jesus as having the devil as their father (John 8:44). Additionally, they deny that Jesus is the Christ and that he is the Son of the Father (e.g., John 5:18) and are depicted by Jesus as not "belong[ing] to my sheep" (John 10:26). The idea of belonging also relates to the idea of abiding found in the gospel, for Jesus asks for those who believe in him to abide in him and says, "I am the vine, and you are the branches. Those who abide in me and I in them bear much fruit . . . whoever does not abide in me is thrown away like a branches and withers" (John 15:5–6). Jesus explains that those who abide, those who believe and belong to him, while those who do not abide, who do not believe do not belong to him, they are not part of his vine.

2 and 3 John

Love: The pseudonymous author of 2 John presents the Beloved Disciple reflecting on the love commandment, for he writes, "I ask you, not as though I were writing a new commandment, but one that we have had from the beginning, let us love one another" (2 John 5). The concept of the love commandment and having the directive to love from the beginning is found in the

168   *Elizabeth J. B. Corsar*

gospel and 1 John. As in the gospel and 1 John, Jesus urges the disciples to love one another (John 13:34; 15:12) and the Beloved Disciple encourages believers to love one another (1 John 3:11). Additionally, in 1 John the love commandment is referred to as being "from the beginning" (1 John 2:7).

Opponents: The Beloved Disciple is presented by the pseudonymous author as addressing the problem of opponents in 2 John, for he writes "many deceivers have gone out into the world, those who do not confess that Jesus Christ has come in the flesh any such person is a deceiver and the antichrist" (2 John 7). These ideas of antichrists, refusal to confess belief in Jesus as the Christ, and separateness of unbelievers are found in 1 John. For in the letter, the Beloved Disciple warns against antichrists who do not confess that Jesus is the Christ and who are separated from believers on account of their unbelief (1 John 2:18–19, 22).

Moreover, the pseudonymous author of 3 John portrays the Beloved Disciple again addressing the difficulty of opponents, for he contrasts the created figures of Demetrius who is good with Diotrephes who is evil (cf. 3 John 11). Diotrephes is evil as he "spread[s] false charges" (3 John 10a) and "refuses to welcome the friends, and even prevents those who want to do so and expels them from the church" (3 John 10b). These ideas of false charges and expulsion from places of worship are present in the gospel. As in the gospel, "the Jews" falsely charge Jesus (John 18:32) and they cast out from the synagogue all those who were confessing that Jesus was the Messiah (John 9:22).

Therefore, in line with the practice of composing pseudo-historical letters, the pseudonymous authors of the epistles portray the Beloved Disciple as the author who personally shares his authoritative witness, and the material which constitutes the Beloved Disciple's authoritative witness (Children of God, Love, Eternal Life, and Opponents) is borrowed from the gospel and 1 John and reworked by the pseudonymous authors.

CONCLUSION

In this chapter, I have put forward a proposal concerning the production of the Johannine Letters that does not rely on a community hypothesis. I have proposed that the Johannine Letters are pseudo-historical letters composed by pseudonymous authors to continue the legacy of the Beloved Disciple. In line with the practice of writing pseudo-historical letters, I have suggested that the pseudonymous authors of the letters present the Beloved Disciple as the author of the epistles and offer a more intimate portrayal of him by presenting him as personally sharing his authoritative witness.

The Legacy of the Beloved Disciple   169

Therefore, I have proposed that the pseudonymous author/redactor of the gospel presents the Beloved Disciple as the author of the gospel which is a record of his authoritative witness in the form of a biography of Jesus. Thus, I suggest that the pseudonymous authors of the letters portray the Beloved Disciple as the author of the letters which are a personal sharing of his authoritative witness. The pseudonymous authors of the letters borrow and rework material from their predecessor texts (gospel and 1 John) to identify the Beloved Disciple as the author and to present his authoritative witness. Therefore, they compose pseudo-historical letters which continue the legacy of the Beloved Disciple.

NOTES

1. Ludwig F. O. Baumgarten-Crusius was perhaps one of the first to propose a Johannine Community. He speaks of John's gospel being "the property of an Ephesian Community, which was only later given over to common use." Ludwig F. O. Baumgarten-Crusius, *Theologische Auslegung der Johanneischen Schriften*, 2 vols (Jena: Fredrich Luden, 1843), xxv.

2. J. Louis Martyn, *History and Theology of the Fourth Gospel* (New York: Harper and Row, 1968); Raymond E. Brown, *The Community of the Beloved Disciple: The Lives, Loves and Hates of an Individual Church in New Testament Times* (New York: Paulist Press, 1979).

3. Hugo Méndez, "Did the Johannine Community Exist?," *JSNT* 42 (2020): 353.

4. Patricia Rosenmeyer, *Ancient Greek Literary Letters: Selections in Translation* (New York: Routledge, 2017), 2.

5. Ruth B. Edwards, *The Johannine Epistles* (Sheffield, UK: Sheffield Academic Press, 1996), 22.

6 Patricia A. Rosenmeyer, *Ancient Epistolary Fictions: The Letter in Greek Literature* (Cambridge: Cambridge University Press, 2001), 42.

7. Demetrius, *On Style*, ed. and trans., W. H. Fyfe, S. Halliwell, D. C. Innes, and W. Rhys Roberts, LCL 199 (Cambridge, MA: Harvard University Press, 1995), 479–80.

8. Claire Rachel Jackson and Janja Soldo, "Introductions: Fictions of Genre," in ›Res vera, Res ficta‹: *Fictionality in Ancient Epistolography*. Trends in Classics—Supplementary Series 149, ed. Claire Rachel Jackson and Janja Soldo (Berlin: De Gruyter, 2023), 1.

9. Patricia A. Rosenmeyer, *Ancient Epistolary Fictions: The Letter in Greek Literature* (Cambridge: Cambridge University Press, 2001), 42.

10. Émeline Marquis, "Introduction: Epistolary Fiction vs Spurious Letters," in *Epistolary Fiction in Ancient Greek Literature*, Philolougus 19, ed. Émeline Marquis (Berlin: De Gruyter, 2023), 1, 5.

11. Irene Peirano, *The Rhetoric of the Roman Fake: Latin Pseudepigrapha in Context* (Cambridge: Cambridge University Press, 2012), 9.

12. Jackson and Soldo, "Introductions: Fictions of Genre," 1.

13. Rosenmeyer, *Ancient Greek Literary Letters*, 98.

14. George A. Kennedy, *Progymnasmata: Greek Textbooks and Prose Composition* (Atlanta: SBL Press, 2003), 47.

15. Kennedy, *Progymnasmata,* 85.

16. Kennedy, *Progymnasmata*, 156.

17. Kennedy, *Progymnasmata*, 115.

18. In his *Confessions*, Augustine reflects on his rhetorical education and his practice of ethopoeia as an exercise. For he writes, "a task was assigned to me . . . it was to perform the speech of Juno when she was angry and hurt because she could not divert the Trojan king from Italy, words that I had never heard Juno utter. Instead, we were obliged to go astray by following the footsteps of poetical inventions, and to declaim in prose something similar to what the poet had written in verse" (Augustine, *Confessions*, 1.17). Augustine, *Confessions*, ed. and trans, C. J. B. Hammond, *LCL* 26–27 (Cambridge; MA: Harvard University Press, 2016), 49. Augustine explains that he was expected to invent a speech to reflect the hurt and anger of Juno and he was to do this by reworking material from the poetical tradition, likely the *Aeneid*, but his reworking needed to be done in a fashion whereby Juno's speech was still fitting of her character.

19. Kennedy, *Progymnasmata*, 47.

20. Kennedy, *Progymnasmata*, 166.

21. Kennedy, *Progymnasmata*, 217.

22. Orlando Portela, "The Letters of Euripides," in *Epistolary Narratives in Ancient Greek Literature*, ed. Owen Hodkinson, Patricia Rosenmeyer, and Evelien Bracke (Leiden: Brill, 2013), 156–57; Johanna Hanink, "The *Life* of the Author in the Letters of 'Euripides'" *Greek, Roman, and Byzantine Studies* 50 (2010): 548–49.

23. Reinhard G. Kratz, "Die Rezeption Von Jeremia 10 Und 29 Im Pseudepigraphen Brief Des Jeremia," *JSJ* 26 (1995): 2–31.

24. Benjamin L. White, "Reclaiming Paul? Reconfiguration as Reclamation in 3 Corinthians," *JECS* 17 (2009): 497–523.

25. English translations taken from Quintilian, *The Orator's Education: Volume IV*, ed. and trans. D. A. Russell, LCL 127 (Cambridge, MA; Harvard University Press, 2002), 322.

26. Javier Martínez, "Pseudepigraphy," in *A Companion to Late Antique Literature*, edited by Scott McGill and Edward J. Watts (New York: Wiley, 2018), 403.

27. Teresa Morgan, *Literate Education in the Hellenistic and Roman Worlds* (Cambridge: Cambridge University Press, 1998), 224.

28. I am assuming that "another disciple" in 18:15 is the Beloved Disciple.

29. Brown*, The Community of the Beloved Disciple*, 31, 32, 96.

30. R. Alan Culpepper, *The Johannine School: An Evaluation of the Johannine-School Hypothesis Based on an Investigation of the Nature of Ancient Schools,* SBLDS 26 (Atlanta: SBL Press, 1975), 264, 270.

31 36 Raimo Hakola, *Reconsidering Johannine Christianity: A Social Identity Approach* (New York: Routledge, 2015), 6–7.

32. Michael Labahn, "Literary Sources of the Gospel and the Letters of John," in *The Oxford Handbook of Johannine Studies*, ed. Judith M. Lieu and Martinus de Boer (Oxford: Oxford University Press, 2018), 25–26.

33. Méndez, "Did the Johannine Community Exist?": 366; Barnabas Lindars, *The Gospel of John* (Grand Rapids, MI: Eerdmans, 1972), 31–34; Harold W. Attridge, "The Restless Quest for the Beloved Disciple," in *Early Christian Voices: In Texts, Traditions, and Symbols. Essays in Honor of François Bovon,* ed. David H. Warren, Ann Graham Brock, and David W. Pao (Leiden: Brill, 2003), 71–80; Andrew Lincoln, "'We Know that His Testimony Is True': Johannine Truth Claims and Historicity," in *John, Jesus, and History, Volume 1: Critical Appraisals of Critical Views*, ed. Paul Anderson, Felix Just, and Tom Thatcher (Atlanta: SBL Press, 2007), 180–83.

34. Richard Bauckham, "For Whom Were Gospels Written," in *The Gospel for All Christians: Rethinking the Gospel Audiences*, ed. Richard Bauckham (Grand Rapids, MI: Eerdmans, 1998), 26 (26–44).

35. Rudolph Bultmann, *The Johannine Epistles: A Commentary on the Johannine Epistles* (Philadelphia: Fortress, 1973), 1.

36. On gospel priority see, George L. Parsenios, *First, Second, and Third John,* Paideia (Grand Rapids, MI: Baker, 2007), 11–13.

37. Charles H. Dodd, *The Johannine Epistles* (Hodder & Stoughton: London, 1946), lxvi. Raymond E. Brown, *The Epistles of John,* AB 30 (Garden City, NY: Doubleday, 1982), 15; Colin G. Kruse, *The Letters of John,* TNTC 4 (Grand Rapids, MI: Eerdmans, 2000), 7; Parsenios, *First, Second, and Third John,* 26.

38. For a proposal for interpreting the Gospel of John as a biography of Jesus, see Richard A. Burridge, *What Are the Gospels? A Comparison with Graeco-Romans Biography* (Baylor: Baylor University Press, 2018), 213–51.

39. Πιστεύητε—Present, Active, Subjunctive (א, B, Θ). For English translations of biblical texts, I use the NRSV.

PART II

The Way Forward?

Responses to the Proposals

Chapter 9

Who Are the Children of God?

Rhetoric, Memory, and Creating Communities with the Johannine Writings

Alicia D. Myers

The present collection offers a variety of methods and suggested conclusions for the perennial question of the "Johannine community." In my work on the Gospel and Letters of John I have never sought to reconstruct a specific Johannine community. This is not because I think such an endeavor is not valuable, but rather because I question our ability to do so with a great deal of confidence with the evidence we currently have. Instead, I have used the heuristic of a "community" in a flexible way, employing an audience-centered approach that focuses on rhetorical and literary elements of the Johannine writings.[1] Certainly, I recognize myself among the scholars trained and, thus, predisposed to assume historical communities from which NT writings, particularly the gospels, came and for which they were written. At the same time, my training also made me skeptical of precise community reconstructions and claims of "authorial intent," leading me to focus on potential audiences based on comparative external evidence, especially rhetorical and genre expectations. In this, I sense a great deal of agreement between myself and the contributors to this volume in acknowledging the limits of we can *know* about the origins (or "community") of the Gospel and Letters of John. What sets the scholars in this collection apart is *where* and *how* we determine those limits.

Although this is a response chapter, I will not summarize and reply to each chapter separately. Instead, I will begin with an overview of some broad areas of agreement between the proposals offered here before offering another possible way forward, building on the insights of my colleagues. Rather than

175

176 *Alicia D. Myers*

simply a window to the past or mirrors to a community's past, I agree with my colleagues that the Johannine writings project different interpretations of past, present, and future. I will focus, however, on how these writings offer a mixture of potential realities and experiences that they work with audiences to reflect on and to create. Thus, one reason our constructions of the Johannine communities vary so much is because reality in and of itself is in ways quite fluid, being continually reshaped, reinterpreted, and lived into by different individuals and groups situated in different contexts. Written works participate in this process of reality-shaping and interpreting, using rhetoric to work with audiences to construct a world in which their epistemologies make sense. The Gospel and Letters of John are epistemological and equip audiences not only to accept their rhetoric, but to take action by living it out and, in so doing, reframe their own identities as children of God. Such rhetoric may be the result of an already extant community or, certainly, felt pressures, but it also shaped those who received these writings, whether they agreed or disagreed with them, initiating effects that we continue to experience to this day.

ENGAGING THIS COMMUNITY: POINTS OF CONNECTION

In his introduction, Christopher Skinner rightly notes the diversity of perspectives presented in this collection. While these contributors have different approaches, and some come to very different conclusions, these chapters also have several broad areas of agreement. My colleagues note the indebtedness of this conversation to the work of J. Louis Martyn and Raymond E. Brown.[2] Yet, more than just retelling Martyn's and Brown's theories, many of them emphasize that Martyn and Brown crafted their stories of a Johannine community with full awareness that such work was ultimately imaginative and speculative. It is later interpreters who have relied on their works and transformed these theories into facts and foundations for the Gospel and Letters of John. As David Lamb aptly shows, when we approach the writings with the assumption of a sectarian context, for example, we will likely find and reproduce that outcome, cherry-picking linguistic evidence to support a previously determined conclusion. In her scholarship, Adele Reinhartz has likewise made this observation as a part of her larger argument that all history writing is imaginative work.[3] This does not mean that there are no methodological moorings or evidence on which we might rely; rather, it means there is always much more lost to time than we can recover and re-narrate with full certainty in the present. As a result, scholars should remain humble in our reconstructions. We should offer potential contexts and readings, but with

Who Are the Children of God? 177

the recognition that our colleagues will read the same evidence and the same Johannine texts and come to different conclusions as this volume attests.[4]

In challenging Martyn and Brown, Reinhartz showed another potential pitfall of reading John's Gospel as a window to the past. While John's story depicts Jesus's disciples as being cast out from synagogues (9:22, 41), or at least threatened with this outcome (12:42; 16:2), it does not necessarily mean this is an accurate representation of life in Jesus's day or after. Instead, she demonstrated that one could read the Gospel as *producing* a community of Christ-followers who left some local synagogues rather than being cast out. Thus, repeatedly in this collection authors have wrestled with the question of whether and how transparent the texts of the Johannine writings are; do they offer a clear view of the past, simply reflect a community's present, or project an ideal future. Rather than choosing just one of these modes, Andrew Byers emphasizes that John blends all three in light of its own Christocentric worldview. Parsing these various vistas, however, remains a tricky business with scholars disagreeing on which horizon dominates at which points. While in his conclusion, Christopher Seglenieks highlights the need to remain "in the text" to "constrain" our scholarly imaginations, the reality is that all these scholars use diverse methodologies and contextual evidence along with the text to support their conclusions. Thus, Seglenieks's earlier observation that scholars need to negotiate "text and context" with clearly identified methodological strategies is more helpful.[5] When we proceed in this manner, we will certainly still offer different conclusions, but we will be in a better place to understand why and how we got there.

The chapters in this collection incorporate insights from comparative literatures and struggles from the ancient Roman world to understand better the cultural contexts of the Johannine writings.[6] Hugo Méndez argues that when we turn to this external material, we should admit there is no evidence of a Johannine community that was separate from other Jesus-followers. For Lamb, this means there is no evidence of a community of believers with different language and rituals from other extant groups; thus, he cautiously posits a "loose network" of groups that composed and received these writings. For Méndez, however, it means we should return to historical-critical methods while open to completely different possibilities and a wider body of evidence for reconstructing the origins of these works. Focusing on 2 and 3 John, Méndez argues that they are later, pseudo-historical works that imitate known works, thus reflecting common literary practices. Working with Méndez's theory, Elizabeth Corsar integrates more explicit language from rhetorical handbooks on practices of *ethopoiia*. It would be helpful to add more on this topic, however, and see its connection to *prosopopoeia* as well as the fact that these practices cover much more than simply written works imitating another, but also inform how speeches and dialogues were written within works. For *prosopopoeia* (also called *ethopoiia*) to be effective, it was meant to reflect what an audience believed a certain person would say based on their identities and contexts. Nevertheless, Corsar's work offers a helpful grounding for reading 2 and 3 John, increasing the literary context Méndez has provided in other publications.[7]

While all the contributors note the dilemma of circular reasoning in historical reconstructions, Laura Hunt's work includes a self-conscious discussion of these pitfalls and her attempt to move beyond the bottleneck with triangulation. She uses inscriptional and literary evidence to suggest a test-case of an Ephesian audience. As the site of multiple ethnicities under the totalizing Roman regime, Hunt notes that Ephesus was a place that prompted reflection on ethnic identity as people negotiated both self-understanding and systems for survival. Hunt, then, agrees with Christopher Porter insofar as they both see ethnicity as a key contested site in John's Gospel, though Hunt avoids placing the events of 70 CE at the center of this debate. This is, in part, because Hunt is open to a more diverse intended audience than Porter, who focuses on dispersed Judeans. Rather than asserting one ethnicity over the other, Hunt concludes John's Gospel could act as a means to "strengthen a group's confidence in the embodiment of a new identity, that, like Jesus, is not completely at odds with, but intersectional to Roman and Jewish identities." John's Gospel blends particular social locations in order to show how they are all compatible with, and potentially subsumed by, a new identity created by Jesus.

As I move to offer my own take on the question of the Johannine community, I am thankful for the work of my colleagues and for their diverse results. Regardless of their different conclusions, the consistent emphasis on identity constructions and negotiations was particularly fruitful for reflection. These chapters, along with additional research, have reinforced for me the importance of audience-centered approaches to reading the Johannine writings, which I will continue below. Instead of reading John's works as working on behalf of a predefined group, this collection shows how the Johannine writings work with their audiences to craft realities past, present, and future. These realities include reframing identities, especially ethnic identity, straddling the particularities of peoplehood in a universalizing Roman world. Instead of erasing all these particularities entirely, I will argue that John's writings selectively use and reframe them under a different empire led by Jesus as king, lord, and, indeed, God. This rhetoric can offer hope to some marginalized groups even as it encourages the marginalizing of others.

RE-NARRATING THE PAST: WORLD-MAKING WITH THE JOHANNINE WRITINGS

Harold Attridge has recently argued that John's Gospel is "primarily epistemological" because it seeks to persuade audiences of its truth that Jesus is the Son of God and Christ (20:30–31) through narrative and dramatic rhetoric.[8] Moreover, Attridge concludes, once persuaded audiences will believe they have access to *the Truth*. In my own recent work, I have noted how this claim is perhaps all the more striking given the reality of Jesus's physical absence from the lives of Christ-followers.[9] The Gospel presents Jesus as the epistemological key to the cosmos *and* argues that he remains accessible to believers by means of the Holy Spirit. The Letters take up this theme of access in different ways, but each one asserts that remaining aligned with their authors is what guarantees access and life. Rather than just asserting this through rhetoric to a passive audience, I suggest that the Gospel relies on audience participation to achieve its epistemological goals.[10] Both ancient and contemporary rhetoricians agree that audiences are not inert recipients, but rather are participating subjects. When hearing or reading John's writings, audiences engage with the works by filling in gaps, answering open-ended questions, exploring multiple meanings, and being rewarded by dramatic irony. Focusing on ancient expectations of audience participation, Kathy Reiko Maxwell writes: "Audience participation is as vital to rhetoric as the second player is to a game of catch. The creation of rhetoric is *not complete* until the audience fills its active role."[11] For the Johannine writings to be persuasive, then, audiences must be moved not only to agree, but to help create the realities in which their epistemologies work.

The role of audiences in world-making along with and through the Johannine writings obscures our ability to reconstruct the earliest contexts of these writings outside of broad strokes. The author and implied audience seem to be either Jewish or closely affiliated with Jewishness, and they live in an imperial world where negotiating identity is fraught. Rather than picturing the Johannine community as a separate and sectarian group, it is more fruitful to consider the potential contexts of an author and their audiences using internal and external evidence. The consistent appearance of Jewish authorities and traditions, and the fact that these works were composed and consumed in the Roman imperial world, will shape my reflections. In what follows, I will use elements of historical-criticism, social memory, and social identity theories, alongside an awareness of audience participation in rhetoric, to offer potential ways the Johannine writings could reflect their contexts and work with audiences to create new ones or to reinforce existing power structures.

180 *Alicia D. Myers*

Methodological Considerations

Like others in this collection, I have benefited from Reinhartz's emphasis on the communal and imprecise nature of history writing. Rather than working with facts or full narratives, we build histories by highlighting certain things and omitting others. Moreover, history writing is a fluid process as we review, reread, and reinterpret sources to make sense of them in our present situations. In the Gospel of John, Jewish traditions and writings are continually reinterpreted to make sense in light of its position that Jesus is God's unique son and Christ (1:14–18; 3:16–18). Using Barry Schwartz's concept of social memory, Catrin H. Williams explores the ways the Gospel incorporates memories of Moses, Abraham, and Isaiah selectively, reshaping them into ideal witnesses to the Gospel's portrayal of Jesus as God's exclusive means of direct revelation.[12] No one else has seen God except for him (1:18; 3:13). Williams's observations resonate with ancient rhetorical handbooks that instruct their users to incorporate known figures and events in support of their arguments.[13] Bringing shared knowledge into one's rhetorical world makes an argument more persuasive because it seems more real, tethering the new to the "known." Yet such integration is not one to one; traditions, language, and people are reshaped so they fit into a new reality.[14] Indeed, the practices of *ethopoiia/prosopoiia* encourage such remolding, paraphrasing, and comparisons to persuade audiences that one's presentation is informed and truthful. As Maia Kotrosits observes, writing histories requires ruination and rebuilding to cope with ruptures that have displaced old narratives of "the real."[15]

In the Johannine writings, the rupture at the center is Jesus, who acts as a gravitational point pulling all other narratives toward him. I place Jesus at the center of this rupture instead of the destruction of the Jerusalem Temple because the Gospel and Letters explicitly focus on Jesus's identity throughout even if the Gospel makes implied references to the temple's demise (John 2:19–22; 11:45–53). It is not the temple's fate necessarily, but rather, debates about Jesus that cause the conflicts in the Gospel and the internal tension in 1 and 2 John. By placing Jesus at its center, then, the Gospel reframes the crises of its readers from whatever pressing experiences and memories they have (including of the temple's destruction) to focus on Jesus. For John's Gospel, the real trauma is not Jerusalem's destruction but Jesus's arrival, which revealed the apocalyptic conflict between God and the devil, and Jesus's departure, which threatens to leave believers bereft of divine connection.[16] The Gospel's depiction of Jesus in exclusive terms necessitates the destruction of old narratives alongside the building of new ones even as it claims to offer the oldest and most transcendent story of all, that of the Logos who was in the beginning with and as God (1:1–5).

Who Are the Children of God?   181

Kotrosits's work is helpful in exploring John's tension between the particular and transcendent in light of the Roman imperial world. Kotrosits argues "[e]thnic peoplehood, . . . was arguably one of the most salient categories, if not *the* most salient category for self-understanding in antiquity" because it was "imagined in unequivocally physical and geographical terms" even as religious practice, language, and culture could shift.[17] Rome's claims of universalism, moreover, do not undermine this emphasis. As Hunt shows, Rome's self-presentation as the arbiter of "law" casts it as a universal good desiring an assimilation that could erase different ethnicities. At the same time, it is precisely this move to universalize that ultimately reinforces not only Roman distinctiveness (even if assumed "superior"), but also that of "others" who display ethnic difference, casting those who resist assimilation and domination as "lawless barbarians."[18] The simultaneous erasure and emphasis, then, makes ethnicity an especially contentious topic as colonized and diasporic people sought to remain authentic even as they adjusted previous narratives to fit present realities.

When approaching the Gospel and Letters of John in the next section, then, I focus on how these writings negotiate Jewishness as they work with audiences to create a new identity as children of God. The Gospel of John in particular appeals to Jewishness throughout with frequent references to the Jews (οἱ Ἰουδαῖοι) along with other scenes that discuss or debate Jesus's ethnicity. These conversations are a part of the larger theme of Jesus's origins, which highlights the paradox noted above: he is both a specific Galilean, Jewish man while also the transcendent Logos. In addition to Jesus's ethnicity, however, that of his followers is also open for discussion as Jews, Samaritans, Greeks, and Romans engage with him and wonder if he really offers truth. Even though 1–3 John do not highlight Jewishness in the same way, they continue asserting a particular way of being part of God's family: namely, through loyalty to Jesus as the Christ demonstrated through love for other believers (1 John 3:1–10; 2 John 4; 3 John 4–5). First John even goes so far as to offer a vivid analogy of conception and generation by God's sperm in contrast to that of Abraham's in the Gospel (1 John 3:9; John 8:33, 37). While this portrait does not offer a robust picture of a Johannine community per se, it recognizes the Johannine writings in the midst of a larger imperial milieu that put pressure on people's sense of belonging. When ethnicities were threatened, they could both be erased and heightened by the specific universal of "Romanness." The Johannine writings, then, offer audiences new or adjusted realities centered on their understandings of Jesus. In this way, these writings create communities in their performative moments and beyond as audiences puzzle over the "truths" described and what they mean for daily life.

Re-Narrating Jewishness in John's Gospel

Rome's preoccupation with conquest and assimilation uncovers and reinforces ethnic distinctions even as it seeks to assimilate and erase. Imperial forces must identify what is "barbaric" in order to establish the borders of what is "civilized." Kotrosits pays attention to the grief and anxieties this caused for different people groups as evidenced in a range of ancient and contemporary writings.[19] The Gospel of John, too, describes and depicts a range of emotions attesting to the intensity that negotiating and asserting identity and group association engenders. In these negotiations, there are perceived "winners" and "losers" as the new identities asserted can alienate even those from one's own marginalized group. In the case of the Gospel, Jewishness is a negotiated identity that people claim and seek to preserve underneath Rome's might. Jesus's reframing of this identity both comforts and threatens characters within the narrative, depending on whether they agree with his epistemology. In the same way, audience members could be comforted by the Gospel's claims of a new begetting as God's children even as the narrative distances others from God's family. While scholars can claim either one side or the other of these conclusions reflects the Gospel's historical situation and intent more, the fact that audiences interpret in multiple ways makes a single conclusion impossible. Moreover, the impacts of writings stretch far beyond the limits of "intention." Space prevents a full exploration of John's reframing of Jewishness in the Gospel, so here I will explore only two examples in conversation with recent scholarship: first, I will note the ways John's story of Jesus uses Jewish notions of divine embodiment to create its exclusive emphasis on Jesus; second, I will reflect on discussions of practices in ancient Greco-Roman assemblies as a lens through which to view the ἀποσυνάγωγοι passages.

As argued above, the Gospel of John's epistemology centers on its identification of Jesus as God's supreme means of revelation. It is this core belief that shapes its presentations and debates of Jewishness. Jesus's exclusivity does not erase Jewish traditions, however, but rather uses them as a foundation and reframes them to reinforce its conclusions. Indeed, using these traditions is part of the Gospel's larger theme of remembrance that reaches out to audiences when describing disciples' later remembering Jesus's actions and words reinterpreted in light of his death and resurrection (2:22; 12:16). In this way, the Gospel effectively trains its audiences to participate in this re-narrating process, which it presents as divinely guided by the Holy Spirit (14:26). The Gospel teaches audiences how to view the world, how to understand their own identities and, therefore, how to live within that world. Like other apocalyptic writings, John's Gospel asserts that its perspective is superior, that it offers the *real* real in spite of all appearances to the contrary.[20] Thus, Jesus's

Who Are the Children of God?

death is not defeat, but the fulfillment of God's will and a fate purposefully orchestrated and chosen by Jesus himself as the obedient and unique Son.

Deborah Forger's and Brittany Wilson's recent studies focus on one way in which interpretations of Jesus as God's unique point of revelation both reflect and diverge from other Jewish traditions and expectations about divine revelation.[21] While Martyn and Brown suggested a division in synagogues over the increasingly high Christology of Jesus-followers, Forger and Wilson add important nuance. Often this "high Christology" has been said to challenge Jewish monotheism, especially Jesus's incarnation that unites the incorporeal divine with human flesh.[22] As Forger and Wilson demonstrate, however, Jewish sources from the Second Temple period and earlier present God in different corporeal forms and depict angelic and human figures as divine and yet distinct from the one God.[23] Thus, God is not incorporeal or invisible, but takes different forms and remains unseen unless intentionally self-revealed. With this context in mind, Forger argues Jesus's incarnation does not separate "Judaism" from incipient "Christianity," but reflects Jewish ways of understanding God's interaction with humanity. What potentially causes conflicts is not Jesus's incarnation per say, but the exclusivity of it; John's Gospel denies that anyone else has seen God, it is only "Unique-one God who is in the bosom of the Father, that one made [him] known" (John 1:18, my translation; cf. 3:13; 5:37; 6:46). Thus, it is not that Jewish monotheism was threatened because of a sort of Jewish exclusivity that denied divinity's revelation in corporeal form.[24] Rather, it is that the Christ-followers prioritized Jesus and reframed Jewish narratives to the extent that they did, leaving very little room for other revelations. As Williams notes, Moses still matters, but he did not see God face to face (1:17–18; 3:13); instead, he is a witness to Jesus (1:45; 5:45–46).[25] Moreover, Jacob's wrestling with God is diminished by the one giving living water (4:12–14). Isaiah, too, sees Jesus's glory (12:41) and Abraham rejoiced when he saw Jesus's day (8:56). For John's Gospel, seeing Jesus is the way to see God (14:6–10). With this view of reality at its core, all other theophanies must be reframed.

Could such a reframing ultimately result in the expulsion of Christ-followers from local synagogues or expulsion of other Jews from their midst? Both outcomes are possible from the text alone. We can gain a better picture by exploring ancient synagogues in light of Greco-Roman associations more broadly.[26] Although these studies initially started to illuminate Paul's ἐκκλησίαι in his letters, the applications to other NT writings are immediately apparent. Rather than specifically Jewish religious gatherings similar to contemporary uses of the term "synagogue" (or "church"), these studies have shown that συναγωγή was used by Jews and non-Jews alike to describe public gatherings at which a variety of matters were discussed.[27] Wally Cirafesi argues that John's stories of expulsion are better understood in these contexts, and he highlights the political conflicts that took place in ancient Jewish synagogues.[28] Using lines and scenes from Sirach, Luke, and Josephus's *Vita*, Cirafesi concludes that expulsions from local synagogues were primarily over political rather than ethnic or religious matters. Comparing these scenes to other political assemblies, he argues that synagogues were "highly competitive and deeply contentious" and that "[p]olitical actors in this arena had to work hard and be clever in order to win the favor of the people. Ad hoc alliances and political interest groups within the assembly tried to sway the people in a particular direction."[29] When speakers failed to win favor, they could be rejected and even violently removed.

Cirafesi's comparative work is helpful for our understanding of John's Gospel in several ways. Most importantly, it broadens our understanding of synagogues and reinforces the conclusion that expulsions could happen sporadically without official decrees against people or groups. Yet Cirafesi's conclusion that these types of expulsions have nothing to say "about individuals or groups being 'outside' of Jewishness, 'un-Jewish,' or betraying the Jewish *ethnos*" is shortsighted. Although he concludes that in these exchanges "there are just political winners and losers," this conclusion oversimplifies the debates of identity happening in these public gatherings. The expulsion Jesus experiences in Luke 4:14–30, for example, concerns his interpretation of God's work in and through him using the writings of an authoritative Jewish prophet living in imperial times (Isa 58:6; 61:1–2). Can such a rejection only be "political"? Certainly no one in the narrative accuses Jesus of being "un-Jewish," but they do reject *his* interpretation of Jewishness and deem him worthy of death. That Jesus's application of Isaiah focused on his affiliation with other ethnic groups apart from Jews also seems significant, as it does for reading Josephus's *Vita*. Luke works hard to reinforce Jesus's Jewishness, just as Josephus does for himself in his writings, perhaps because there were challenges to this understanding due to increased non-Jewish connections.[30] The writings only provide internal constructions of identity rather than the perceptions of outsiders.

Cirafesi's focus on the internal "self-identification" of John's Gospel leads him to conclude that the Gospel presents Jesus and his followers as still Jewish. The debates in John, then, are intra-Jewish rather than the product of a past separation.[31] They are Jewish because John's Gospel never explicitly declares them otherwise. He writes: "In antiquity, breaking away from Jewishness would have entailed more than being thrown out of the public assembly. It would have meant no longer *self-identifying* with the Jewish *ethnos*, or, to use the language of Tacitus (*Hist.* 5:5), 'despising' one's ancestral traditions. We get no sense that John intends to shape such an identity."[32] At the same time, however, the focus on self-definition in Cirafesi's work overlooks the fact that identity is not entirely self-crafted, it is communal. Who

Who Are the Children of God? 185

we "are" is continually observed and evaluated by those around us as well as by ourselves. All these evaluations impact how we present ourselves, whether individually or as groups. Self-identity, like other realities, is continually constructed, ruined, and rebuilt. Thus, while John's Gospel may not explicitly claim "un-Jewishness," its focus on Jewishness reveals ethnicity is a key site of conflict and reframing.[33] Could some of John's audience members or those in their larger context, whether Christ-followers or not, have argued for Jesus's non-Jewishness? Or for that of his followers? John's (re)claiming Jewishness for Jesus and his followers, then, could respond both to external and internal perceptions whether believers had been expelled from gatherings, left on their own, or expelled others from their midst. As even contemporary debates show us, John's Jewishness is also a reality its audiences determine, not just the text alone.

So, what can we confidently assert about a Johannine community receiving or listening to the Gospel narrative? While there is no evidence of a separate Johannine group who received this story, I suggest the Gospel creates a community in its consumption. Moreover, its author certainly envisioned audiences who would engage with this narrative and work with it to create a world in which its epistemology makes sense. As Porter notes, the Gospel's story could have provided Jews it convinced that Jesus was an anchor after the First Jewish War and its further dispersion of Jewish people. By reframing divine access apart from a physical temple, John reflects common conversations among Jewish authors in this milieu who were part of a dispersed ethnic group which had experienced the loss of a temple before.[34] What makes John's view distinct is its emphasis on Jesus's body as the sanctuary (ναός, 2:19–21); it is *only* through their association with Jesus that believers access God (1:18; 4:20–24; 14:6–7). Moreover, since loyalty to Jesus is the primary marker of inclusion, the Gospel also shifts Jewishness away from genealogy, thereby making room for non-Jews in its epistemology. It is not being born as the offspring of Abraham that one is a child of God, but rather, through re-begetting and birth made possible only through Jesus's death, resurrection, and giving of the Holy Spirit (cf. John 8:37–41).

In this way, John simultaneously emphasizes Jewishness and undermines it, detaching it from what Kotrosits calls the "unequivocally physical and geographical" nature of the term.[35] Thus, it makes sense that John's Gospel moves away from "Jews" (or "Judeans") as a name for Jesus's followers. Instead, they are "children of God" and "friends" or "siblings" of Jesus (1:12; 11:52; 15:13–14; 20:17). This move not only corresponds to its transcendent depiction of Jesus, but it also imitates the universalizing move of empires as well as of people groups subsumed and dominated by them. Smaller groups of people divided by ethnic and other differences can gather together (11:52), united by another common identity that anchors them and encourages them to

186   *Alicia D. Myers*

resist Rome's imperial assimilation and erasure. Furthermore, John promises not only an earthly peoplehood for Christ-followers, but also a unique and complete connection to God. Belief in Jesus has its goal in creating one-ness between believers and God that transcends even Rome's reach (17:23). But this one-ness is, nevertheless, the product of another empire (or "kingdom," 3:1–8; 12:15–16; 18:33–37; 19:3).[36] And while Jesus's empire may be open to (or, ultimately, conquering of) people of all ethnicities, providing them a place of inclusion and refuge against Rome, it too assimilates and erases distinctives in service of its new "universal." The main requirement for participation in John's world is the belief in and loyalty to Jesus's exclusivity. One-ness with God is on offer, but only for those who access the Father through Jesus as Christ and Son. As a result, John's Gospel effectively presents all others, including other Jews, as outsiders if they do not believe in Jesus and access God in this way.

Constructions of Belonging in 1–3 John

Extending this conversation to include the Letters of John increases the complexity but also offers a chance to see how Johannine audiences, whether already extant or created by these works, continued to shape Jewish traditions and stories of Jesus. Before delving into the questions of how these works construe belonging, a few words about their possible compositional chronology and historicity are in order. As the discussion of method above would indicate, my conclusions here are tentative and offer just one way of reading the evidence from these writings as well as from their reception. While a narrative can be constructed wherein the Letters were composed prior to the Gospel of John, I am more disposed to see these works as later compositions if only because of the way in which they were received by later Christians, particularly 2 and 3 John. I am open to readings of the Gospel and 1 John being completed around the same time since references to both these works appear in early to mid-second-century works. As Méndez notes, however, tracing the reception of 2 and 3 John is more difficult.

It is possible that Polycarp's *Letter to the Philippians* includes a reference to 2 John 7, but the language is equally close to 1 John 4:2–3. Evidence from Irenaeus is likewise murky. He quotes 2 John 11 in *Haer.* 1.16.3 crediting it and the Gospel to "John, the disciple of the Lord." Later Irenaeus introduces a quotation of 1 John 2:18–19 with the phrase, "For this reason he [John] has testified to us in his Epistle" (*Haer.* 3.16.8).[37] Some interpreters suggest that Irenaeus conflates 1 and 2 John as a single epistle, but he never quotes from 3 John. This could be because 3 John was not useful to his arguments, he did not know of it, or he thought it spurious. The eventual acceptance of 2 and 3 John, however, shows that later audiences found their descriptions of earlier

Who Are the Children of God? 187

community disputes plausible, perhaps especially in light of other letters that also became part of the New Testament. Reading through the contributions in this collection, it seems that discussion of whether or not 2 and 3 John are "real" or not has come to a bit of a bottleneck; conclusions are based on what evidence is included and considered more compelling to the debate. Instead of positing a certain conclusion on these works, then, what follows will again focus on the audiences who received these works and the ways in which the rhetoric of 1–3 John encourages their participation in crafting identities and realities.

Identity and belonging in 1–3 John are both similar to and different from the Gospel as well as from one another. While Jewishness does not feature in these discussions explicitly, it is assumed in 1 John with its use of authoritative Jewish traditions, most explicitly with its version of Cain's story. The debate is not over whether use of these traditions is legitimate for audience members, but where they are to see themselves and others within the typological narrative of Cain and his unnamed brother in 1 John 3:11–17. As in the Gospel, this Jewishness is reframed with Jesus at its center, resulting in a new collective memory and new priorities for an audience's self-understanding and epistemic constructions. When 1 John leaves out Abel's name, for example, it leaves a gap for audiences to fill with Jesus, themselves, or others depending on their experiences.[38] If Genesis 4 is a subtle intertext for John 8, then, we see how 1 John reuses a story alluded to in the Gospel and builds it out to fit a new context and create a new contrast that is nevertheless rooted in a circular supposition: the children of God act like God's children.[39] In the Gospel of John, children revealed their parentage by accepting or rejecting Jesus as God's Son. First John highlights the sibling relationship to reflect the internal conflict of division and maltreatment described by the proclamation. While the rejection this "we" faces from the world is to be expected, hatred from fellow believers is compared to Cain's murder of the unnamed sibling. Instead of ones who "have passed from death to life" (3:14; John 5:24), these murderous siblings "abide in death" and kill others by selfishly refusing to help when they are in need (1 John 3:14). Moreover, rather than imitating a named "Abel," 1 John removes Abel from the story and instead reminds audiences to imitate Jesus's laying down his life by giving to one another (3:15–17). As in the Gospel of John's keying and reframing of Moses, Jacob, Abraham, and Isaiah, 1 John keys and then reframes Cain and Abel's story to make it yet one more example that coheres with Jesus's model.

The development and reframing of the Cain and Abel narrative in 1 John, however, is but one example of this proclamation's use of material also found in the Gospel for its own rhetorical and epistemic ends. Space precludes a full examination here, but in addition to the quotation from John 5:24 above, one can also find elements from John 6 and 18 in 1 John's story of the antichrists who deny Jesus, as well as John 3 with its insistence that "we testify about what we know and speak about what we have seen" and 1 John's opening words.[40] Yet it is Jesus's final discourse to his disciples in John 13–17 that seems most to have influenced 1 John. William Loader suggests that 1 John expands upon these traditions and applies them to its present situation.[41] In terms of social memory theory, 1 John keys and reframes memories of Jesus's words to speak to the audiences' present moment, a moment that seems especially focused on determining who is a "real" child of God or not based on one's behavior. In this way, 1 John not only challenges its audiences to examine those around them, but it also prompts self-examination to see if one is behaving as a true child of God ought, including in their acceptance of this paternal teacher's instruction. The audience is taught to believe and reinforce *this* teacher's version of reality, their reframing of not only other Jewish traditions but of Jesus's words as preserved in the Gospel. Thus, while Corsar is right that 1 John imitates the Gospel which would certainly add to its authority, we can push the rhetorical move a bit further. In John's Gospel, the narrator often blends their voice with that of other figures sent by God, including John (the Baptist) and, of course, Jesus (e.g., 3:11–21, 31–36). The blending of voices in 1 John, then, is more than simply an imitation of the author of the Gospel, it is an imitation or *prosopopoiia* (or *ethopoiia*) of Jesus.[42] As ones taught by the anointing of the Holy Spirit rather than the spirit of the antichrist, 1 John's author claims "real" children of God will recognize the truth proclaimed because it confirms what they have known from the beginning (1 John 1:1; 2:7, 11–14, 24; 3:11).

The situation of 2 and 3 John is more difficult because of their convoluted reception history, but also because of their brevity. Second John posits a similar situation as 1 John by describing antichrists who reject Jesus's "coming in the flesh" (2 John 11) and likewise highlights what its audience has known "from the beginning" (2 John 5–6). Third John, however, moves the conversation away from doctrinal issues to a personal conflict over the care of the Elder's emissaries. The unique context and vocabulary of 3 John sets it apart from 1 John, but George Parsenios suggests 2 John acts as a bridge between these texts, showing them all to be interrelated.[43] Yet, if 3 John is a later imitation of 2 John, then its differences from 1 John make even more sense. Even if a "fake" letter, though, 3 John likewise posits a reality, crafting a scenario of what the Elder would say to a rival leader who rejected his messengers. Although not necessarily a historical situation, then, 3 John must have seemed real enough to convince later readers that its scenario was possible, even if just in positing what could or would have been said.

When 3 John is added to the collection with 1–2 John and the Gospel, then, it creates a story of early Christ-followers navigating their identity in a world that cannot understand them. Whether or not the story happened in this way has become largely irrelevant for audiences who have created the narrative and, subsequently, the world in which this story makes sense. Detached from a place and having various ethnicities, these children of God find a new story in which they are God's chosen victors because of their perseverance in the face of opposition. Like Jesus, they too face misunderstanding, rejection, and abandonment in the world. Conforming Christ-followers are comforted to remain in fellowship with the teacher delivering this message, whether in its original settings or centuries later. As such, the story places checks on those who might dare to "go beyond" in their interpretations of Jesus (2 John 9), justifying the hierarchy of elders who can pass judgment against them. In this way, the story creates and reinforces divisions between insiders and outsiders, the real children of God versus the children of the devil. Indeed, in both the Gospel and the Letters opposition comes from places one might least expect it—from fellow Jews who rely on the same scriptures as Jesus and worship at the same temple, or from siblings who confess to believe in Jesus and love the Father. In the end, the story of the Johannine writings encourages ongoing surveillance of self and others to determine who is *really* a child of God living in the *real* world and who is not.

FINAL THOUGHTS TO CONTINUE
THE CONVERSATION

Overall, I am grateful to the authors of these chapters for their thoughtful and engaging work that prompted me to continue my own reflections on the Johannine community. While we have offered a diverse range of conclusions, there is nevertheless a consensus that the Johannine writings help their audiences create and navigate different identities. We cannot confidently retroject a precise history of "the" Johannine community, but we can see how the Johannine writings create communities when audiences engage with them. Rhetoric is communal and ultimately audience-focused; the words suggest a world, but that world is only real when it is lived out by receptive audiences who apply it. This application, however, is both destructive and constructive. It tears down, borrows, and reshapes significant traditions in light of its own epistemic center.

Thus, John's Gospel and 1 John are broadly Jewish and participate in larger debates of Jewishness in the Roman world, but this history does not diminish the rhetoric against Jews or others who reject their claims. Instead, situating the Johannine writings in the larger imperial context of Rome helps us to see how and why ethnicity is such a significant point of conflict. When read together, the Johannine writings offer an anchor for displaced and threatened people either forced into migration or colonized. Yet they also craft another empire, one that absorbs colonizers and displaces dissenting people groups even further. Rather than only exploring the past and suggesting potential origins for the Johannine writings, then, it is my hope that we continue asking about the types of realities these works have helped and continue to create. While the horizons offer hope for life-giving readings, we should not overlook the destructive past and potential of these works. Instead, we ought to ask ourselves what motivates our reconstructions, who is included in our conversations, and what our stories might generate in the future. Martyn and Brown could not have predicted where discussions of the Johannine community have gone, but their desire to address the difficult issue of the Gospel's presentation of the Jews has prompted a generation of scholars to grapple with this past and present topic. Postcolonial scholars, too, have called on interpreters to see the underside of inclusion, how it erases even as it offers salvation. By widening our own communities of readings and readers, we will discover more about the messy mixing and fluidity of realities, but we might also gain a greater glimpse of the truth.

NOTES

1. E.g., Alicia D. Myers, *Characterizing Jesus: A Rhetorical Analysis on the Fourth Gospel's use of Scripture in its Presentation of Jesus*, LNTS 458 (London: T&T Clark, 2012), 17–20.

2. J. Louis Martyn, *History and Theology in the Fourth Gospel*, third ed., NTL (Louisville: WJK, 2003); Raymond E. Brown, *The Community of the Beloved Disciple: The Life, Loves and Hates of an Individual Church in New Testament Times* (New York: Paulist Press, 1979).

3. Adele Reinhartz, "Building Skyscrapers on Toothpicks: The Literary-Critical Challenge to Historical Criticism," in *Anatomies of the Fourth Gospel: The Past, Present, and Futures of the Fourth Gospel as Literature*, RBS 55 (Atlanta: SBL, 2008), 55–76; Reinhartz, *Cast Out of the Covenant: Jews and Anti-Judaism in the Gospel of John* (Lanham, MD: Lexington/Fortress, 2018), xxvii–xxxi. See also Colleen M. Conway, "New Historicism and the Historical Jesus in John: Friends or Foes?" in *John, Jesus, and History, Vol 1: Critical Appraisals of Critical Views*, ed. Paul Anderson, Felix Just, and Tom Thatcher (Atlanta: Society of Biblical Literature, 2007), 199–216.

4. Reinhartz, *Cast Out*, xxviii.

5. The language of "remaining in the text," like the term "community," is a slippery phrase that can be (and has been) used in ways to limit what is deemed legitimate scholarship and what is not based on unnamed and unrecognized ideological grounds. While I am not suggesting this is what Seglenieks intends to do, we should use extreme caution concerning whom we identify and exclude as "scholars" lest we

limit the conversation and ignore evidence that would otherwise help us understand the objects of our study (and ourselves) better.

6. Lamb also encourages the use of comparative literatures and archaeological finds in his suggested methodology.

7. See especially Hugo Méndez, "Did the Johannine Community Exist?" *JSNT* 42 (2020): 350–74.

8. Harold W. Attridge, *History, Theology, and Narrative Rhetoric in the Fourth Gospel*, The Pére Marquette Lecture in Theology (Milwaukee: Marquette University Press, 2019), 71. See also Tyler Smith, *The Fourth Gospel and the Manufacture of Minds in Ancient Historiography, Biography, Romance, and Drama*, BInS 173 (Leiden: Brill, 2019); Michael R. Whitenton, *Configuring Nicodemus: An Interdisciplinary Approach to Complex Characterization*, LNTS 549 (London: T&T Clark, 2019); Deborah Forger, "Jesus as God's Word(s): Aurality, Epistemology and Embodiment in the Gospel of John," *JSNT* 42 (2020): 274–302.

9. Alicia D. Myers, "We Speak the Truth: Rhetoric, Epistemology, and Audience Participation in John 3:1–21," *Int* 77 (2023): 325–35.

10. Myers, "We Speak the Truth," 327–28.

11. Kathy Reiko Maxwell, *Hearing Between the Line: The Audience as Fellow-Worker in Luke-Acts and Its Literary Milieu*, LNTS 425 (London: T&T Clark, 2010), 48, emphasis added.

12. Catrin H. Williams, "Patriarchs and Prophets Remembered: Framing Israel's Past in the Gospel of John," in *Abiding Words: The Use of Scripture in the Gospel of John*, ed. Alicia D. Myers and Bruce G. Schuchard, RBS 81 (Atlanta: SBL Press, 2015), 187–212, esp. 191–92. See also Tom Thatcher, ed., *Memory and Identity in Ancient Judaism and Early Christianity: A Conversation with Barry Schwartz*, SBL Semeia Studies 78 (Atlanta: SBL Press, 2014).

13. Myers, *Characterizing Jesus*, 47–49, *passim*; e.g., Aristotle, *Rhet.* 1.9.39–40; 2.20.8; Quintilian, *Inst.* 5.11.6, 82; 8.3.72–73; Cicero, *Top.* 20.78; Ps.-Cicero, *Rhet. Her.* 4.49.62.

14. Williams, "Patriarchs and Prophets Remembered," 210–12.

15. Maia Kotrosits, *The Lives of Objects: Material Culture, Experience, and the Real in the History of Early Christianity*, New Studies in Religion (Chicago: University of Chicago Press, 2020), 44–46.

16. See Adele Reinhartz, "Incarnation and Covenant: The Fourth Gospel through the Lens of Trauma Theory," *Int* 69 (2015): 35–48, esp. 39–47. In addition to Jesus's incarnation, his departure effectively re-inflicts the trauma for disciples who are left without him. Jesus's insistence that he will not leave them "orphaned" (14:18) perhaps reflects this impact.

17. Kotrosits, *Lives of Objects*, 16.

18. Kotrosits, too, notes that "[u]niversalism and particularity are not opposites; they rather operate in a dependent relationship with one another" (*Lives of Objects*, 17). Not only does "universalism" highlight differences, but it also relies on differences to exist. The deception of universalism lies, in part, in its ability to convince those shaped by its narrative that some identities are "normal" while other are not. Those who fit these molds of normalcy have the privilege of not consciously

192 *Alicia D. Myers*

negotiating spaces because of supposedly aberrant gender, race, class, or physical ability, for example. Yet such privilege belies the fact that all lives are particular and that universalism itself describes a particular (and never fully realized) reality.

19. Kotrosits, *Lives of Objects*, 53–66. Commenting on 1 Corinthians, Kotrosits writes, "Paul's collapse into anxiety, into hierarchy, into hard lines, and into a future eschaton rather than a present one presents problems for certain ethical and politicized interpretations of the letters. It is also on par for the diasporic course, as the ground beneath his feet is not just shifting and unsteady, but full of the vestiges of the fragmentation of other peoples, the fractured figures and forms of bygone eras" (65). John's Gospel presents an emotional Jesus encountering emotional characters who are all walking on fractured ground. The Gospel, however, seeks to offer steadiness by emphasizing Jesus's role as the fracturing force rather than as another victim (or criminal) consumed by Rome.

20. On apocalypticism and John see Catrin H. Williams and Christopher Rowland eds., *John's Gospel and Intimations of Apocalyptic* (London: Bloomsbury, 2014); Benjamin E. Reynolds, *John Among the Apocalypses: Jewish Apocalyptic Traditions and the "Apocalyptic" Gospel* (Oxford: Oxford University Press, 2020), 117–43.

21. Deborah L. Forger, "Divine Embodiment in Jewish Antiquity: Rediscovering the Jewishness of John's Incarnate Christ" (PhD diss., University of Michigan, 2017); Brittany E. Wilson, *The Embodied God: Seeing the Divine in Luke-Acts and the Early Church* (Oxford: Oxford University Press, 2021).

22. Space precludes a full analysis and engagement with Forger's and Wilson's works. Both, however, helpfully problematize an unnuanced notion of monotheism as a category for Second Temple Judaism that leads scholars to assume God is incorporeal and invisible despite clear texts that express the contrary (Forger, "Divine Embodiment," esp. 53–83; Wilson, *Embodied God*, 7–11). Forger and Wilson are influenced by the work of Benjamin D. Sommer, *The Bodies of God and the World of Ancient Israel* (Cambridge: Cambridge University Press, 2009). While Sommer agrees that "monotheism" is a concept that *can* apply to the Hebrew Bible, he argues that the absolute "polarity 'monotheism-polytheism'" is often overstated and "obscures connections that transcend this polarity" (145, cf. 172–74). Instead, he offers the definition of monotheism as "the belief that there exists one supreme being in the universe, whose will is sovereign over all other beings" who live in various places in the cosmos. Some of these beings ("gods" or "angels") might even be immortal "but they are unalterably subservient to the one supreme being" who alone is "God" (146–47). See Forger, "Divine Embodiment," 56–57; Wilson, *Embodied God*, 95–106. Forger and Wilson also rely on Mark S. Smith's (*Where the Gods Are: Spatial Dimensions of Anthropomorphism in the Biblical World*, AYBRL [New Haven: Yale University Press, 2016]) concept of "divine fluidity" for describing the diverse forms in which God appears in Second Temple Jewish literature and the NT.

23. E.g, Gen 2–3; 18; 23; Exod 24, 33–34; Isa 6; 1 Enoch 48; Philo, *Abr.* 273; *Mos.* 1.156, 158; *Ebr.* 94; *Migr.* 45; *Somn.* 1.193. Forger also includes examples of the Jewish high priest as a divinized figure who manifests God's presence on earth ("Divine Embodiment," 120–64). Wilson traces God's embodiment and theophanic

appearances in portrayals of God's divine attributes (e.g., "Name," "Power," or "Word"), angels, and exalted humans (*Embodied God*, 106–21).

24. The ways in which this assumption resonates with stereotypes of "legalistic" Judaism should not be overlooked. As Forger notes, by working backward and presupposing the split between later Judaism and Christianity, scholars have retrojected assumptions from their own time onto the Gospel of John ("Divine Embodiment," 51–52). I suggest that this includes ingrained narratives of Jewish exclusivity versus Christian inclusivity that is also replicated in other studies (such as Jesus's interaction with Jewish purity laws or the inclusion of the Gentiles in Acts and Pauline Letters).

25. Catrin H. Williams, "(Not) Seeing God in the Prologue and Body of John's Gospel," in *The Prologue of the Gospel of John*, ed. Jan G. van der Watt, R. Alan Culpepper, and Udo Schnelle, WUNT 1/359 (Tübingen: Mohr Siebeck, 2016), 79–98; Forger, "Divine Embodiment," 259–60; Brittany E. Wilson, "Seeing Jesus, Seeing God: Theophany and Divine Visibility in the Gospel of John," in *Early High Christology: John among the New Testament Writers*, ed. Chris Blumhofer, Diane Chen, and Joel B. Green (Minneapolis: Fortress Press, forthcoming 2024), 59–62.

26. For a recent overview of this conversation and new proposals see Bruce W. Longenecker, ed., *Greco-Roman Associations, Deities, and Early Christianity* (Waco, TX: Baylor University Press, 2022). On συναγωγή see Ralph J. Korner, "συναγωγή and Semi-Public Associations," in Longenecker, ed., *Greco-Roman Associations*, 225–46.

27. Korner, "συναγωγή," 230–41.

28. Wally V. Cirafesi, "Rethinking John and 'the Synagogue' in Light of Expulsion from Public Assemblies in Antiquity," *JBL* 142.4 (2023), 683. See also John S. Kloppenborg, "Disaffiliation in Associations and the ἀποσυναγωγός of John," *HTS Theological Studies* 67.1 (2011): Art. #962, 16 pages, doi: 10.4102/hts. v67i1.962. Kloppenborg offers a number of examples of expulsions from clubs in the Greco-Roman world. In light of this evidence, he argues that expulsions from clubs and synagogues were the product of deviant behavior rather than of differing beliefs. Thus, he suggests, the Johannine believers could have been expelled because of their factionalist behavior (e.g., not observing Sabbaths and washing each other's feet) and not because of their "high Christology."

29. Cirafesi, "Rethinking John," 689. Cirafesi is operating with Anders Runesson's understanding of "political/civic synagogues" found in rural Judea (*The Origins of the Synagogue: A Socio-Historical Study*, ConBNT 37 [Stockholm: Almqvist & Wiksell], 2001). On the outskirts of the Roman Empire, these synagogues had more political and civic responsibilities since Rome encouraged local communities to govern themselves so long as they were not a threat to Roman power. Christopher J. Fuhrmann, *Policing the Roman Empire: Soldiers, Administration, and Public Order* (Oxford: Oxford University Press, 2012), 6–12, 45–88.

30. On Josephus's intersectional identity as a Judean and Roman see William den Hollander, *Josephus, the Emperors, and the City of Rome: From Hostage to Historian*, AJEC 86 (Leiden: Brill, 2014).

31. See also Wally V. Cirafesi, *John within Judaism: Religion, Ethnicity, and the Shaping of Jesus-Oriented Jewishness in the Fourth Gospel*, AJEC 112 (Leiden: Brill, 2022), 19–21.

32. Cirafesi, "Rethinking John," 697; emphasis added.

33. Cirafesi's longer project emphasizes that John's Gospel is negotiating a certain type of Jewishness. For Cirafesi, John's Jewishness is inclusive of people of other ethnicities and critiques priestly oriented Jewishness (*John within Judaism*, 123–26). While I agree with Cirafesi that the Gospel highlights Jesus's continuation with Jewishness, its focus on this issue suggests it was a topic of some debate for insiders and outsiders alike.

34. See, for example, Kotrosits, *Lives of Objects*, 48–53 where she discusses the durability of the imagery of Babylon in Isaiah and Revelation.

35. Kotrosits, *Lives of Objects*, 16.

36. Musa W. Dube and Jeffrey L. Staley, eds., *John and Postcolonialism: Travel, Space, and Power, Bible and Postcolonialism* (Sheffield: Sheffield Academic, 2002); Musa W. Dube, "John 18:2–19: A Postcolonial Trickster Reading of the Arrest and Trial of Jesus," *Tubinger Theologische Quartalschrift* 2 (2022): 54–73; Sung Uk Lim, *Otherness and Identity in the Gospel of John* (Cham: Palgrave Macmillan, 2021), 31–36. Lim argues that Jesus is both imperial and anti-imperial in his conversation with the Samaritan woman and designation as the "Savior of the world" (4:42) that anticipates his crucifixion as the paradoxical "King of the Jews" (92–93). Lim writes, "What is intriguing is that the more Jesus is portrayed as anti-imperial, the more imperial he appears" (92). Perhaps a better way to understand this intrigue is to notice that when Jesus is most *anti-Roman* imperial, he is most stridently championing *God's empire* instead. In this sense, Jesus is not so much "anti-imperial" as he is "anti-Roman Empire" or "anti" any leadership that denies what he presents as God's reign.

37. In this section, Irenaeus also introduces a quotation of 1 John 5:1 in the same way to cast it as a parallel to John 1:14.

38. On leaving gaps as a means of facilitating audience participation, see Maxwell, *Hearing Between the Lines*, 72–78.

39. On Cain and Abel traditions in John 8 and 1 John, see especially Tom Thatcher, "Cain the Jew the AntiChrist: Collective Memory and the Johannine Ethic of Loving and Hating," in *Rethinking the Ethics of John: 'Implicit Ethics' in the Johannine Writings*, ed. Jan G. van der Watt and Ruben Zimmermann, WUNT 1/291 (Tübingen: Mohr Siebeck, 2012), 350–73.

40. For more on the overlap between 1 John, John 6, and 18 see Alicia D. Myers, "Us and Them: Lessons from 1 John's Antichrist Polemic," *WW* 41.1 (2021): 42–50.

41. William R. G. Loader, *The Johannine Epistles*, Epworth Commentaries (London: Epworth, 1992), xx. See also David M. Reis, "Jesus' Farewell Discourse, 'Otherness,' and the Construction of a Johannine Identity," *SR* 32.1 (2003): 39–58.

42. Alicia D. Myers, *Reading John and 1, 2, 3 John: A Literary and Theological Commentary*, Reading the New Testament, Second Series (Macon, GA: Smyth & Helwys, 2019), 224.

43. George Parsenios, *First, Second, and Third John*, Paideia (Grand Rapids, MI: Baker Academic, 2014), 26–28.

Chapter 10

The Johannine Situation

An Advance over Imagined Communities

Paul N. Anderson

One of the most robust of theories in New Testament studies over the last half century has been the emergence of views regarding "the Johannine Community." As required by his developing thought and understanding between his Anchor Bible Commentaries on the Gospel (1966–1970) and the Johannine Epistles (1982), Raymond Brown put forth his own vision of what Johannine Christianity must have been like, as a means of understanding contextually the authors and audiences of these writings within a particular sector of early Christianity.[1] Here we see Johannine historical and literary interest shifting from authorship and personalities to situations and contexts as a new and critical set of inquiries in the history of New Testament and Early Christianity studies.

As outlined in Christopher Skinner's excellent introduction to the present volume, Brown's Community-Paradigm built upon and alongside the synagogue-expulsion theory of his colleague at Union Theological Seminary, J. Louis Martyn. However, Brown's vision of the Johannine movement was far more dialectical and expansive, including a number of other context-specific engagements, as well.[2] In contrast to Martyn, Brown also saw the Gospel as an independent account of the actual ministry of Jesus of Nazareth. It was engaged with the Synoptics but not dependent on them. And yet the ways John's Gospel developed also engaged issues and audiences within the developing situation over seven decades, informed also by the issues addressed by the Epistles.

Within the relationship between the Gospel and Epistles, it is clear that some sort of a relationship existed, but which came first, the Gospel or the Epistles? Or both? If there were two or more editions of the Gospel, might the Epistles have been written between them? And, if the finalizing of the Gospel followed the death of the evangelist (John 21:20–24), might the author of the Epistles have served as the final compiler? A number of scholars have thought so, and such a relationship reflects a growing consensus among several Johannine scholars,[3] with important implications for understanding the history and character of "The Johannine Community that Raymond Brown Left Behind."[4]

In my judgment, the Gospel's "Dialogical Autonomy" is the best way to envision the history, character, and contexts of the Johannine tradition and its development. Within that overall approach, I see "the Johannine Situation" as a critical improvement over "the Johannine Community" for a number of reasons, having argued such since the completion of my 1989 Glasgow thesis, and since my SNTS 1993 presentation on the *Sitz im Leben* of the Johannine Bread of Life Discourse, performing with John 6 what Martyn had done with John 9.[5] The present assignment is timely, as it avails me the opportunity to define my approach to *The Johannine Situation* as a broader perspective than *The Johannine Community*.

"THE JOHANNINE COMMUNITY" OR "THE JOHANNINE SITUATION"?

Within the larger discussion of these issues, appreciation for the ways and reasons that Raymond Brown constructed his overall Johannine theory—involving his theory of John's composition, relations to other traditions, and contextual features—facilitates a foundational basis for evaluating his work. In my judgment, Brown deserves to be regarded as the greatest American biblical scholar of all time, and yet his views did not emerge in a vacuum. Brown built constructively upon his judgments regarding the best of Johannine theories, and as this volume has shown, his work has continued to precipitate developments for years to come. While my overall theory is more indebted to Brown's than other interpreter, I also depart on a number of scores.

First, with Brown, I see the Gospel as an autonomous tradition developing alongside Mark and the other Gospels, but not dependent upon them literarily. John has its own story to tell, as 92 percent of John is not in Mark, and every single connection—for more than a word or a phrase—is also different. Further, 85 percent of John is unique among the Synoptics altogether, although no fewer than six dozen times Luke departs from Mark in Johannine directions. This requires, in my view, a Bi-Optic Hypothesis.[6] Nor does

The Johannine Situation 199

John's narrative depend on alien sources; it developed from the evangelist's preaching and teaching about Jesus. With Brown, the compiler was conservative—not intrusive—in finalizing and preserving the evangelist's work after his passing.[7]

Second, with Brown, the Johannine Elder—author of the three Johannine Epistles—echoed the teachings of the Beloved Disciple within the Epistles, especially 1 John. The "new commandment" of Jesus to love one another in John 13:34–35 has eventually become the "old commandment" that has been heard from the beginning in 1 John 2:7, and the author of 1 John appropriates the eyewitness-authority of the Johannine evangelist for himself in 1:1–3. This would explain the similarities of phrase and expression between the Johannine writings, while also some of the differences. Perhaps, as Brown conjectured, the Elder may also have been an eyewitness, though not one of the Twelve. I see the first edition of John's narrative being drafted around 80–85 CE, with chapters 6, 15–17, and 21 being added later, along with the Christ-hymn and the eyewitness attestation around 100 CE after the death of the Beloved Disciple. Contra Brown, though, I do not see the compiler adding duplications and variations; those were likely part and parcel of the evangelist's own self-repetitions.

Third, following or during the destruction of Jerusalem by the Romans (66–73 CE), the Beloved Disciple and associates moved to Asia Minor, joining other believers—both Jewish and Gentile—who would have encountered those reached in the first and second generations of the Pauline mission. Within this cosmopolitan setting, engagements with local synagogues were common, as they were with other communities of Jesus-adherents. Here, Brown's longitudinal approach is more compelling than Martyn's, identifying multiple individuals and groups in dialogue with the Johannine believers, ranging from earlier Judean-Galilean dialogues and engagements with Baptist-adherents, to engagements with synagogue leaders, schismatic members, docetizing visitors, and hierarchical leaders. Brown neglects to include in his historical situation sketch the impact of the Roman presence under Domitian (81–96 CE), who required participation in the imperial cult on pain of persecution, exile, and even death.[8]

Fourth, the Johannine Situation thus likely involved no fewer than seven crises (or dialectical engagements with different audience targets) over seven decades, involving three periods with two or more somewhat sequential but overlapping engagements within each period.[9] These include:

- Period I: A Palestine Setting, 30–70 CE
  - Crisis 1—engaging the followers of the Baptist
  - Crisis 2—Galilean struggles with the *Ioudaioi* and centralizing Judeans
- Period II: A Hellenistic (Asia Minor?) Setting A, 70–85 CE

- Crisis 3—give-and-take with the local Synagogue leaders
- Crisis 4—struggles with the roman imperial cult under Domitian (81–96 CE)
- Period III: A Gentile Setting B, 85–100 CE
  - Crisis 5—Docetizing Gentile believers teaching assimilation with culture
  - Crisis 6—Diotrephes and his kin—rising institutionalism in the larger church
  - Crisis 7—(extending over all three periods) dialectical engagements with synoptic presentations of Jesus and his ministry (esp. Mark and Matthew)

Fifth, while Brown questions the apostolicity of the Beloved Disciple due to his juxtaposition with Peter, I query whether the exact opposite is more likely the case. In light of the inhospitality of Diotrephes and his kin (3 John 9–10), scholars for over a century have seen the Fourth Gospel as a corrective to rising institutionalism in the late first-century situation, not against apostolic memory, but precisely rooted in a more primitive, egalitarian, familial ecclesiology—including women in leadership roles and all having at least potential access to the Light of Christ and the guidance of the Holy Spirit—as an alternative apostolic memory of Jesus and his original intention for the church.[10] While some conflict between friends and good partners in apostolic ministries together (with Brown, note the ministries of Peter and John in Acts 3–8) may be reflected here as personalities, their prototypical ecclesial visions may also have come into competitive relation in the later decades of the first century CE. Thus, from personalities to prototypes, the Matthean and Johannine ecclesial memories reflect dialogues before the turn of the first century CE; they certainly have continued to be for over the next two millennia, perhaps for historical reasons.

ENGAGING THE PRESENT ESSAYS

Now for an engagement with the chapters in the present volume, I shall comment on the contributions of each of the chapters, while also raising a number of questions with each.

Chris Seglenieks's New Method: Reading the Johannine Community in the Letters

In reviewing sociological approaches to understanding early Christianity, Chris Seglenieks argues that the best method for understanding the Johannine

The Johannine Situation

Community is to do so through the lens of the Letters. I agree. This gets us out of the speculative conundrum of imagined "mirror-readings" of gospels, although the lack of specific issues being addressed in the Letters (except for the idols-reference in 1 John 5:21) still creates a challenge. Nonetheless, Seglenieks notes that the dearth of explicit references to Jewish-Johannine references in the Letters calls into question the inference of synagogue-Johannine tensions behind the Johannine writings, overall. And, this would also include the Gospel's backdrop.

When the contextual thrusts of 2 and 3 John are considered, as well as those of 1 John, several insights into "the Johannine Community" emerge. First, palpable tensions with Jewish communities do not appear to be present. Rather, engagements with other believers' communities in the region are more readily apparent, and they are presented as largely agreeing with each other on most things. Second, the primary debates seem to orbit around Christology, although there are also tensions with Diotrephes over hospitality and perhaps ecclesial issues. Third, debates over ethical concerns are also referenced, although the particulars of ethical concerns are not explicitly stated.

As I consider Seglenieks's argument, I find myself in basic agreement with his more modest approach to what Brown described as the "The Life, Loves and Hates of an Individual Church in New Testament Times," with the eaglets under the Johannine eagle tearing at the nest. And, as the Epistles suffer from a dearth of direct references to Jewish-Johannine tensions, this might also account for Martyn's reasons for distancing the Epistles from the Gospel, as their content would have threatened his single-issue approach. Rather, it is precisely because Christological and ethical issues are in play in the Letters that the Gospel might be seen also as addressing some of those particulars.

That being the case, a number of questions follow. First, while explicit tensions with Jewish neighbors are absent from the Letters, does this really mean they are absent? What it might suggest is that Judean-Jesus and Judaism-Johannine tensions in the Gospel may have been earlier, with the Letters representing a later situation. Historically, Judean leaders were clearly divided over Jesus of Nazareth, and tensions with his followers likely continued for some time after his ministry had ended (cf. e.g., Acts 3–22).[11] Thus, the references to synagogue-exclusion in John 9:22; 12:42; 16:2 may primarily represent memories of earlier tensions that had not entirely disappeared, even later in Diaspora settings.[12] Distanced tensions would be a different inference than absent tensions with local synagogues.

A second question follows: might there also be veiled references to Jewish-Johannine tensions in the Letters, even if subtle? When the reasons for the schism of 1 John 2:18–25 are considered contextually, the Johannine schismatics (labeled ἀντίχριστοι) should not be confused with the visiting false prophets (ψευδοπροφῆται) of 1 John 4:1–3 and 2 John 7. The flawed

Christology of the schismatics is that they refuse to believe that Jesus is the Christ; the flawed Christology of the false prophets is that they refuse to believe (teach) that Jesus came in the flesh. The secessionists will thus forfeit the pleasure of the Father, but, if they receive the Son, they will retain the pleasure of the Father.[13] Such interests relate squarely with Jesus's debates with the Judean leaders in John 5 and 7–10, where Jesus defends his ministry and authority as rooted in the Prophet-Like-Moses agency schema, featured in Deuteronomy 18:15–22.[14]

Thus, the Jewish–Johannine tensions reflected in 1 John appear to be rooted not in expulsions from synagogues. Rather, they appear to be factors of Jewish former community members who were proselytized back into synagogue fellowship—perhaps departing from house churches—whether or not the Johannine Community had totally individuated from local Jewish synagogues. It may well be that some Johannine believers worshiped in local synagogues on Sabbath and in the homes of Gentile believers on First Day. So, earlier Pauline and later Johannine "communities" likely would have been worship-participants in believers' homes, led sometimes by women ministers, and this may be why 2 John is written to "the Chosen Lady and her children," sharing greetings also from the Elder's "sister community" as a different house-church or a female leader.

A third question centers upon particular relations between theology and ethics in New Testament Christianity. It is not enough to note the "what" of Christological debates; one must ask the question "why" a problematic view was embraced. Regarding the split, the refusal to confess that Jesus was the Jewish Messiah allowed Jewish associates to preserve Jewish monotheism while still appreciating Jesus as a prophetic leader, perhaps like John the Baptist. They could thus remain in good standing with Jewish family and friends, and not be vulnerable to allegations of ditheism. Here Brown's inference of "Crypto-Christians" might come into play, although Nicodemus is also presented as a convinced supporter of Jesus in John 7 and 19 as a positive example, not simply a negative one.

The other explicitly Christological flaw involves the refusal to believe that Jesus came in the flesh (1 John 4:1–3 and 2 John 7): a clearly different set of beliefs from those denying the Son's divine relationship to the Father. If the false-prophet traveling ministers advocate a docetizing Christology, the question is "why?" Rather than seeing later Gnosticism as being in play, the existential implications of a non-suffering Jesus alleviated expectations of the Way of the Cross for his later followers.[15] Thus, if Jesus did not suffer, neither need his followers, especially under the rise of imperial cult requirements of Domitian. The admonition to "love not the world" (1 John 2:15–17) called for resistance to Greco-Roman cultural pressures and cultic festivities, and that is precisely what the assimilative Gentile ministers were likely teaching,

The Johannine Situation 203

which is also what would obviously have scandalized Jewish community members, causing them to defect. Practical issues always are more abrasive and winsome than theoretical ones. In light of these contextual realities, 1 John 5:21 is not simply an add-on; it may well reference the dominating ethical and theological challenge of the Johannine Community, which related to the imperial-cult requirements under Domitian (81–96 CE), rather than synagogue-expulsion issues.

David Lamb's Exploration of the Language of John: Idiolect, Sociolect, Antilanguage, and Textual Community

David Lamb's exploration of John's language begins with noting the reason for the emergence of Johannine community hypothesis over the last half century and more; it is a direct factor of authorship particulars—the identity of the Beloved Disciple, "which John" was involved in writing, and so on—supplanted by historical school and community theories. Lamb thus proposes a register analysis addressing idiolect and sociolect as a means of understanding the relationship between language and a context of situation within the larger context of culture. The Johannine writings are best seen as communications between persons and groups rather than an archaeological tel. In applying Brian Stock's paradigm of a textual community, Lamb raises the question as to whether the Gospel's status might have been elevated to the authoritative status of "scripture" within the Johannine situation, thereby providing clues to particular dynamics within and beyond a particular community.

While the Gospel does not confirm the existence of a textual community, the second and third Epistles do reflect a cluster of communities in touch with each other, seeking to address the implications of following Christ within their contextual situations. In that sense, Lamb argues that idiolect (theology) was more important than sociolect (sociology). What we see in the Epistles is the formation of embryonic communities that valued the Gospel—likely composed by a single authoritative individual rather than reflecting a diachronic history of composition—in seeking to embody adherence to its subject: Jesus.

I like Lamb's restrained, less speculative approach to understanding the rhetorical thrust of the Gospel without expanding too much upon how many issues and audiences might have been addressed by the Gospel. Thus, the Johannine writings likely emerge from a Johannine Situation, but that does not imply that they were targeted only to a singular Johannine Community. The language of "from a community" is more compelling an inference than "for a community" (with Bauckham) in envisioning the intended audience. And Lamb's modesty of inference regarding the antilanguage in the narrative points to reflections upon earlier memory rather than later projections only.

204   *Paul N. Anderson*

True or false? There were no adversaries of Jesus of Nazareth until a post-70 Diaspora relocation. Obviously, "false," and tensions with Jesus and the movement that followed him are corroborated expansively in the Synoptics, the Acts of the Apostles, and the Pauline and Petrine Epistles. So, what if the Fourth Gospel served the primary purpose of telling the story of Jesus—his ministry, teachings, and last days—including positive and negative receptions back in that day? In that sense, the Gospel conveys theology *and* history, not just history and *theology*.[16]

Along these lines, a number of questions follow. First, how did John's Gospel play alongside the Gospel of Mark and the other Synoptics? Is John providing something of an augmentation of Mark, or is John dependent on the Synoptics with no individuated memory to convey, on its own? With Bultmann, Brown, Borgen, Smith, and others, such is critically implausible. Thus, while community interests may have motivated the selection and crafting of the Gospel, they alone cannot account for the origin of its content, which appears to be rooted in an individuated memory of Jesus, alongside and in dialogue with other accounts.

A second question invites further expansion on the plausible idea that the Epistles not only reflect the emergence of embryonic communities within the Johannine Situation; they also reflect the interest in remembering the witness of the Gospel as an authoritative text. This move, and likely evidence of a difference of authorship between the Gospel and Epistles, is reflected in 2 John 9. While the evangelist emphasizes abiding in Christ (John 15:1–8), the Elder emphasizes abiding in the teaching about Christ, which has been heard from the beginning. This implies an affirmation of a communal embracing of what Johannine believers have been hearing about Jesus "from the beginning" (1 John 1:1; 2:7, 24; 3:11; 2 John 5, 6, 9).

A third question follows. If (with Brown) the Epistles appear to be echoing familiarity with the evangelist's teachings over the years, even if written by a different leader, the prologue to 1 John (1:1–3) clearly echoes familiarity with what has been "seen and heard" from the beginning. The eyewitness and hand/side-touching reports of John 19:34–35 and 20:20–28 are echoed here, "concerning the word of life," couched in a poetic form similar to the Christ-hymn of John 1:1–5, 9–14, 16–18. That being the case, if the prologue of 1 John reflects a confessional response to the evangelist's witness over the years, might the Johannine Christ-hymn reflect the same, as a hymnic overture to the narrative? It might even be composed by the same person (the Elder) rather than the evangelist. Thus, the references to John the Baptist in vv. 6–8 and 15 were not "added later" to address Baptist-adherents in Ephesus; they reflect the first edition of John's Gospel, echoing the beginning of Mark, providing an alternative perspective to the Baptist's witness (vv. 19–42), while also affirming its importance. Interestingly, Acts 4:19–20 presents John the Apostle (not the Elder) as testifying to "what we have seen and heard." Might this be an overlooked key to the Johannine Question?

Christopher Porter's Reflections on Complexity, Socio-Cognitive Approaches, and Spaghetti

Given the literary complexities of inferring the backgrounds of the Johannine corpus, Chris Porter raises the playful question as to how to "untangle spaghetti" in Johannine studies. While focusing more on the Gospel than the Epistles, Porter appeals to Social Identity Theory as a means of getting at the groups and issues in play within the Johannine Community and its environs. In his analysis, Porter focuses also on the temple incident of John 2 and the trial and crucifixion of Jesus in John 18–19. These texts present the authority of Jesus over and against Jewish institutions and leaders, and the colophons at the ends of John 20 and 21 suggest distinctive purposes between the narrative's first edition and its final ending.[17]

Within Porter's use of Structured Arrangement of Group Analysis (SAGA), identifications of intra-group identities and inter-group features in the Gospel provide insights into what the Johannine Community may have been like. Along those lines, though, contrastive operations may well be addressed toward similar groups rather than groups that are totally different. In that sense, the inherent Jewishness of the Gospel is presented at the outset, as the temple incident of John 2 relocates the center of Jewish identity—*the temple*—in the body of Jesus.[18] Porter thus argues that Jesus (and the community of his "body") is presented as the locative social identity of Johannine Jewishness in post–70 CE Diaspora settings. The closing bookend for instantiating this new Jewish identity—in contradistinction with Jerusalem-centric opposition to Jesus and alignment with Pilate—is the kingly reign of Jesus: one of *truth*.

Porter then identifies the two colophons of John (20:30–31; 21:24–25) as marking two endings of the Gospel, with the first edition featuring narrations of Jesus and his ministry in a post-70 setting, with other material added later; I agree. With Chris Keith, John's narrative appears to acknowledge other gospel traditions competitively, but it asserts its own insider perspective even versus other renderings.[19] Thus, presentations of Jewish leaders in the narrative reflect the desire to draw post-70 Judaism into new communities of believers in Jesus as the Jewish Messiah—Judaism's new "temple"—in fellowship with Gentile believers, as well. With Raimo Hakola, the imagined Johannine Community is not sectarian; rather, it advances a vision of a Jewish Messiah-centered fellowship addressing the social struggles and identity concerns of post-70 Diaspora Jews, and Gentiles, at large.

Here, Porter's introduction of Social Identity Theory with reference to Group Identities (insiders and outsiders) provides helpful ways forward, including Cognitive-Critical implications for how post-70 Jewish identities might be helped to construct a new sense of Jewish faithful identity in the light of Gentile responses to Jesus as the Jewish Messiah.[20] It might even be the case that *if* there were post-70 curses issued against followers of the Nazarene (more apparent in John 16:2 than in 9:22 and 12:42),[21] these disciplinary measures may have been motivated by more conservative Diaspora synagogue leaders feeling that the distinctive features of faithful Judaism among the Gentiles were being threatened by Jews and Gentiles sharing fellowship around Jesus-adherence, compromising the socio-religious distinctives of conservative Judaism in more liberal and assimilative directions.

As social psychologists have reminded us, territoriality exists only between members of like species. Thus, the presentation of tensions between Jesus and Jewish authorities in the Gospel, in reality, reflects intra-Jewish tensions rather than intra-faith polemics.[22] Whereas Paul argued for extending the boundaries of Judaism, John argued for its center. Indeed, the Johannine "I-Am sayings" fulfill the typologies of biblical Israel, and Jesus fulfills a dozen biblical texts explicitly as well as the typologies of Moses and Elijah implicitly. Uncontrovertibly, the Johannine author is devotedly Jewish, but the struggles of Jewish family and friends come with welcoming Gentile believers into a cross-cultural and inter-faith movement.

In addition, other "friendly targets" of the Gospel included Markan-Johannine dialectics, friendly competition with followers of the Baptist, and even with other apostolic leaders. I might like to see Porter's SAGA analysis be applied in these directions also. After all, one of Barrett's reasons for not going along with the Martyn/Brown synagogue-expulsion theory was his conviction that the juxtaposition of Peter and the Beloved Disciple was the primary contextual target of the Gospel.[23] In presenting Peter as continuously non-comprehending, with Mikhail Bakhtin, stupidity in narrative is always rhetorical.[24] Thus, the presentation of multiple individuals and groups within the Gospel function to create imaginary—corrective *and* confirming—dialogues with Jesus over several decades within the longitudinal Johannine Situation.

Laura Hunt's Triangulating a Johannine Community Based on the Trials and Crucifixion of Jesus

Laura Hunt continues the quest for the Johannine Community, seeing "group"—reflecting insiders and outsiders—as preferable language. In so doing, she builds on historical background information as a means of inferring identity formation as furthered by the Gospel. The narrative first shows clear evidence of being finalized in a Roman context, given its many Latinisms. Second, features of "law"—both Jewish and Roman—are shown to have been transgressed in John's presentation of the trials of Jesus in

John 18:28–19:22. Third, in terms of Social Identity Theory, the kingship of Jesus is shown to be a superior alternative to Jewish and Roman authorities, inviting audiences around 100 CE in Ephesus to join the in-group as followers of Jesus, welcoming Jewish and Gentile audiences into a new group of Jesus-adherents as an advance over lesser alternatives.

As a response to Hunt's work, I like her triangulation of semiotics, probabilities, and Social Identity Theory. That sort of interdisciplinary approach offers corroborative ways forward in seeking to understand the development of Johannine communities and groups over decades and across geographical settings. Especially helpful is her pointing out of law-transgressions among authorities in the narrative—Jewish and Roman alike—pointing to the "Kingdom of Jesus" which is ever one of truth (John 18:36). The formation of group-identity through the narrative's development and circulation among the churches also plays well, in seeing the Gospel as circulated among the churches, thus inviting the coming together of Jewish and Gentile believers in Jesus as the Messiah, in forming Jesus-adherent communities throughout the Mediterranean world.

My questions with her analysis are simply to explore further how the Gospel might have functioned rhetorically in drawing Jews and Gentiles alike into new communities of faith as a means of fulfilling a Christocentric view of extending the blessings of Abraham to the nations. For instance, the Johannine Jesus travels among the Samaritans in John 4, and they offer hospitality to Jesus and his band, declaring him to be "the Savior of the world" (v. 42). Such a confession is also rendered in 1 John 4:14. Second, the mission of Jesus is presented as fulfilled when the Greeks come to Jesus in John 12:20–23. Jesus then declares the time is come for the Son of Man to be glorified. Third, the Light of Christ enlightens everyone—at least potentially—and despite being rejected by some of his own, as many as received Jesus are welcomed into the divine family as children of God, born not of human operational schemes, but born of the divine initiative, responded to in faith (1:9–13).[25] Fourth, the purpose of the narrative is to draw audiences into belief that Jesus is the Christ, the Son of God, and that believing, they (Jews and Gentiles alike) might receive eternal life in his name (20:31).

Thus, as an augmentation of the Markan narrative, the five distinctive signs of Jesus (all in John's first edition) present an alternative to the five books of Moses. Jesus also fulfills the writings of Moses, as Moses wrote of Jesus (5:31–47), so the Law of Moses is fulfilled in Jesus. Likewise, the confession of Thomas in John 20:28—"My Lord and my God!"—presents Thomas as making an anti-Domitian confession.[26] And when Jesus declares that he *is* a king, but his kingdom is one of truth, Pilate himself confesses to be an outsider to that sovereign reign, uttering whimsically, "What is truth?" (18:36–38). In fulfilling the way of Moses, the truth of Torah, and the lifeline of Abraham, Jesus declares himself to be the way, the truth and the life (14:6), and Jesus declares to "the Jews who believed" that they will know the truth, and that revelation will set them free (8:31–32). Thereby do believers in Jesus—Roman and Jewish alike—receive a new social identity as a Jewish extension of Abrahamic blessing to the world within a cosmopolitan Anatolian setting.

Andrew Byers and the Johannine Vision in the Light of Historical Reflection, Rhetorical Construction, and Narrative Ecclesiology

In his approach, Andrew Byers focuses on the Johannine vision of its community, whether or not such a community actually existed in reality. Byers thus argues that the evangelist "composed a narrative recollecting the *einmalig* events of the historical Jesus (supplying 'windows to the past') while reflecting concerns and situations in his own communal context (supplying 'mirrors of the evangelist's present') and simultaneously constructing a communal vision (supplying 'vistas to the future')." This represents a "narrative ecclesiology," informing an understanding of the sorts of issues the Johannine Community was engaging in the ways that Gospel was presented.

Along these lines, Byers advocates a theological approach to assessing the Gospel's rhetoric, and with Frey, Johannine theology is couched in the rubric of Christology. More specifically, Johannine theological concerns are seen to be addressing aspects of incarnation, inscription, and inspiration. Incarnationally, the fleshly suffering of Jesus is emphasized; the Johannine inscription appeals to what has happened in history (John 20:30–31). Inspirationally, the Gospel connects that memory with later issues in the future as experienced by Johannine believers. Thus, theology and Christology are ultimately connected with Johannine *ecclesiology*: the difference Jesus as the Christ makes within the Johannine Situation.

Once more, the chapters featured in this volume represent valued advances in understanding the Johannine Situation, and this one by Byers is no exception. I agree entirely with his situating the Johannine corpus within first-century Judaism, as the Parting of Ways has not yet been actualized.[27] He also judiciously evaluates the Martyn-hypothesis of synagogue expulsion, although he is not convinced by Reinhartz's theory of propulsion. Rather, he sides with Hakola's view of the Johannine Community developing within a cosmopolitan situation with multiple partners in dialogue, not simply Jewish family and friends.[28] To me, that seems realistic. I also like his ecclesiological inferences about Christology and theology, as it is nearly always the practical implications of a doctrine that drive its energized thrust.

The Johannine Situation 209

Along these lines, questions also emerge. In particular, *why* does John's narrative highlight the importance of the incarnation? If the Epistles provide any backdrop, it may be that docetizing false prophets have been teaching a non-suffering Jesus, as they were likely Gentile traveling ministers teaching a doctrine of salvation by grace through faith, affirming assimilative liberties with pagan culture. Within the second generation of the Pauline mission to Asia Minor, the debates between Galatians and James had by no means disappeared. Further, if the admonition to "love not the world" (1 John 2:15–17) had to do with local festivities in Ephesus—Artemis worship, the imperial cult under Domitian, cultural festivities and pagan processions—those may have been precisely the divisive issues addressed in the last verse of 1 John (5:21). "Little children, stay away from idols!"

Venial sins may abound, but confessing Caesar as Lord and denying Christ (see the situation two decades hence in Pliny's *Letters* 10.96–97) are directly referenced as the death-producing sin (v. 16). Thus, those claiming to be "without sin" are walking in the dark instead of the light, making God a liar, as the first two Commandments explicitly forbid worshiping other gods and venerating graven images (1 John 1:5–10; Exod 20:2–7). In these ways, the Elder and the evangelist would have been siding with Jewish Torah-concerns. Jesus-adherents must be willing to suffer for their faith, and to refuse imperial cult requirements (as well as cultic festivities) in their allegiance to Jesus as the Jewish Messiah/Christ.

A second question has to do with John's high Christological features as well as its incarnational thrusts. If John 20:31 reflects the purpose of the first Gospel's draft, the signs, the witnesses, and the fulfilled word of the text are crafted to convince hearers and readers that Jesus is the Christ, the Son of God, availing believers life in his name. Additionally, the Father-Son relationship in the Gospel shows that Jesus carries forth the will of the Father as a fulfillment of the Mosaic agency-schema of Deuteronomy 18:15–22. Therefore, while the incarnational and pastoral thrust of John's later material emphasized abiding with Christ and his fellowship and embracing the way of the cross in the midst of adversity (John 1:10–14; 19:34–35; 6:51–66; 15:18–25; 16:1–33; 21:18–24), John's earlier material was crafted to bring people to faith—Jews and Gentiles—in Jesus as the Jewish Messiah.[29] John's later material calls for solidarity with Jesus and his followers within a hostile Greco-Roman world.

A third question relates to the ecclesial function of inspiration within the Gospel. As chapters 15–17 reflect the compiler's gathering of the later ministry and teachings of the Beloved Disciple, this accounts for their emphases on the Holy Spirit's guidance and protection of believers, dealing with the world's tribulation. In my judgment, the hostile world is *not* Jewish pressures or authorities; it is directly related to cultural and folkloric pressures of Artemis and other cults in the region, exacerbated by the imperial cult raised

210 *Paul N. Anderson*

under Domitian (81–96 CE). Since the days of the physical voice of Jesus are past for Johannine believers, the abiding voice of his Spirit is seen as bringing existentially to remembrance memories of his teaching for the present day later, among later trials and tribulations. Thus, Jesus breathes on his followers and invites them to receive the Holy Spirit (John 20:19–23). He also promises that the παράκλητος will lead his followers into liberating and comforting truth (16:4–15), and that the guidance of the Spirit will also assist them in discerning the spirits of the times, as they receive or reject traveling ministers with questionable teachings and practices (1 John 4:1–3).

Hugo Méndez and Renewing Johannine Historical Criticism

While other critiques of the Johannine Community have questioned whether there was a single community or several, or whether the Gospel was written *for* a community or *from* a community, Hugo Méndez questions the entire enterprise of community inferences behind the Johannine writings. Seeing the Martyn-Brown paradigm and following discussions as both undertheorized and unproductive, Méndez also questions the presence of Gnostic actors in the Johannine situation as well as the concept of a Johannine "sociolect." Given the fact that second- and third-century Christians questioned the authorship of 2 and 3 John, Méndez follows Robert Kysar in questioning the viability of diachronic speculations about Johannine authorship and composition histories, and he extends that skepticism to "historical investigations" of the Johannine Community rather than focusing on the contents of the writings.[30] That being the case, focusing on the literary content (idiolect) rather than sociological features (sociolect) poses a surer way to proceed critically, in his view.

As a number of quips and phrases are noted between the Johannine writings, Méndez questions whether they reflect socio-historical connections, or whether they might reflect literary copying, or perhaps even pseudepigraphal feigning, of authorship. Most compellingly, Méndez states, "One idea is especially worth discarding—namely, the surprisingly tenacious thesis that the Johannine community, as a discrete, historical, social group, has social or institutional links to so-called 'Gnostic Christianities.'" Thus, criticizing Brown's speculation that the secessionists were proto-Gnostic heretics—the likes of Cerinthus—deserves to be abandoned in the interest of adopting a more modest (and accurate) inference of the issues being addressed, perhaps even by those feigning false authorship, when the thrusts of the Johannine writings seem to be quite different. Too easily do later discussions of how texts were engaged in following centuries distort our understanding of what was really happening back then and there, so reading the New Testament writings with greater epistemic neutrality may lead to some new and helpful insights.

In responding to the work of Méndez, this is not my first round. He and I exchanged a robust set of engagements in the *Biblical Interpretation* online journal, as I responded to his essay in the *Journal for the Study of New Testament*.[31] In that engagement, I objected to inferred pseudepigraphy of anonymous writings, as that reflects a categorical mistake. Such could be alleged of Revelation (claiming four times the name "John" as author), but 1 John makes no authorial claims, and "the Elder" behind the second and third Epistles remains unnamed.

A second objection focused on claiming that there was "no community" involved because of alleged pseudepigraphy. Even false authorship claims were done by persons within communities, so the questioning of authorship does not imply the absence of a community. In fact, the community-related features of a text invariably inform guesses as to who the real author might have been, hiding behind pseudonymity, even if such were the case. Nonetheless, Méndez follows Kysar's questioning of our diachronic approaches and inferred certainties regarding imagined reconstructions of literary processes and historical situations, and on that score, Reinhartz and I agree.[32]

One of the strengths of Méndez's work is his bold questioning of long-standing paradigms, of which Brown's *Community of the Beloved Disciple* has been one of the most robust in recent biblical studies. For sure, just because there may have been *one community*, this does not mean that there was only one community in the larger Johannine Situation. On that matter, these questions have struck a chord with questions other scholars have had, to which even this present book-length project is indebted. On the matter of idiolect and content interests versus sociolect and community concerns, Méndez makes a good point, but I still think both must be held together, in tension, with sociolect controversies most often driving idiolect concerns. In particular, when people were abandoning the community of 1 John, the basis for their sociolect failure was their idiolect flaw. The schismatics refused to believe that Jesus was the Messiah, thus forfeiting the approval of the Father; but this was precisely a problem because they left a fellowship—likely a second-generation house-church in the Pauline situation—as a factor of their flawed theological commitments (1 John 2:18–25). If they had not departed, their low Christology would not have been a problem.

Likewise, the warnings about visiting traveling false prophets (1 John 4:1–3; 2 John 7) imply that it was a community they were visiting, requiring their exclusion. And the problem with Diotrephes is that he refused to welcome Johannine believers into his community, even willing to expel his own community members who took them in (3 John 9–10). Therefore, Méndez is

212 *Paul N. Anderson*

wrong in claiming that there were no communities involved in relation to the composing, sending, and receiving of the Epistles. It would be like saying that the seven knowing letters to the named churches in Revelation 2–3 were not intended to be received by any communities in particulars, even if they were sent to Macedonia instead of Anatolia.

Perhaps the most important thrust of Méndez's essay, though, and it may well be the most important point made among all seven of the seven papers reviewed, is his call for the total abandonment of Gnosticism-inferences behind the Johannine adversaries. On this score, I want to make several points as to the veracity and importance of this claim.

First, while all Gnostics were Docetists, not all Docetists were Gnostics. Yes, some among the audience of 1 John 1:5–10 claimed not to be sinning, but this was not a reflection of Gnostic perfectionism. As the beginning of the next chapter clarifies, the Elder writes so that people *would not sin* (1 John 2:1). Thus, those "walking in darkness" rather than light were likely disagreeing about what was sinful and what was not: a disagreement between Gentile and Jewish Jesus-adherents within the Johannine Situation. On this score, Brown's translation of 1:8 is wrong. The meaning of ἐὰν εἴπωμεν ὅτι ἁμαρτίαν οὐκ ἔχομεν is not "If anyone says, 'We are *free from the guilt of sin*' . . ." (thus rejecting the propitiation of Christ); the claim more literally is: "If we say we *have no sin* . . ." (thus claiming their actions were not sinful). Like bookends, the Elder comes back to the specifics of sinful behaviors in 1 John 5, naming the death-producing sin (v.16) in the last verse (v. 21).

If Greco-Roman traveling ministers were teaching assimilation with culture (loving the world) and participation in the imperial cult and cultic festivities (embracing idols), their flesh-denying Christologies functioned to reject the way of the cross and the cost of discipleship. Again, it is invariably the experiential and ethical implications of a doctrine that determine its pressing urgency—sociolect, not its abstract nationalities—idiolect. A closer set of false-teaching threats may be referenced by 2 Peter 3:14–18 and other writings: those who distort Paul's teachings on grace through faith, not righteousness obtained Jewish customs, works, and sociolect norms as warned about pointedly in Jude 4: "For certain intruders have stolen in among you, people who long ago were designated for this condemnation as ungodly, who pervert the grace of our God into debauchery and deny our only Master and Lord, Jesus Christ."

Thus, there is no need to infer later Gnosticism as the leading source of ethical disagreement among the Pauline, Petrine, and Johannine churches; on this score, nineteenth-century German scholarship was wrong. Teachings of the likes of Cerinthus could be involved here, but they were not the secessionists; they were "invasionists" as false teachers and prophets. Acts 15 did not settle everything, as the edict of Claudius in 49 CE showed, and ethical

The Johannine Situation 213

disagreements between Jewish and Gentile Jesus-adherents continued for centuries.

A second important implication of this challenge to the Martyn-Brown paradigm is that it rejects a single-adversary inference of the larger Johannine Situation, as the crises were not singly Jewish-Johannine tensions nor Gentile-Docetizing heresies. Again, the secessionists of 1 John 2:18–25 are clearly not the same persons as the false prophets of 4:1–3 and 2 John 7. On the latter references, their "going out" does *not* imply "going out *from us.*" They simply are "out there" as a false-teaching threat. On this score, Brown fails to distinguish these two crises, as the Elder labels them both "Antichrists." Note, however, the differences between these two labeled antichristic threats:

1. Movement: crisis 1—secession; crisis 2—invasion
2. Timing: crisis 1 actualized and past; crisis 2—impending and future
3. Content: crisis 1—refusing to believe that Jesus is the (Jewish) Messiah/Christ; crisis 2—refusing to believe that Jesus (suffered) came in the flesh.

Thus, with Méndez, not only are the second antichrists not Gnostics; they are also not secessionists.

A third value of this call for reevaluation of the Johannine Community by Méndez is that it forces us to reject simplistic inferences of Johannine pneumatism as the basic flaw of the adversaries. If some later Gnostics embraced pneumatism as the basis for their perfectionism and incorrigibility, some scholars have resorted to terribly flawed inferences of such as a catch-all basis for understanding a number of the Johannine riddles. First, "those incorrigible Gnostic schismatics" are assumed to imagine their own views of what is acceptable behavior and what is not. No, we more likely have disagreements between what is acceptable and what is not between Jewish and Gentile Jesus-adherents. Second, incorrigible pneumatists must not have obeyed authority—like later charismatics and Protestants splitting off from the Mother Church—"You just can't deal with those enthusiasts claiming spirit-led authorization." No, they do not reject theological propitiation; they reject the way of the cross and costly discipleship. Third, why is John different from the Synoptics? "Obviously," (a claim often made in the absence of evidence) "the Beloved Disciple must have been a Hellenistic mystic, who superimposed his own transcendental visons of what Jesus must have done and said." That explains why he wrote "a spiritual gospel" as opposed to the "the facts" of the Synoptics, according to Clement. I disagree. John has more mundane and archaeologically attested content than all the other gospels combined; John is "the Mundane Gospel" as well as "the Spiritual Gospel."

214   *Paul N. Anderson*

So, while I do see the Epistles as written by the Elder, the call for a new appraisal of the Johannine Situation is timely, calling for new thinking and considerations and approaches the Johannine riddles.[33]

Elizabeth Corsar's Exploration of the Legacy of the Beloved Disciple and the Johannine Letters as Epistolary Fiction

In her chapter exploring the yoking of the Beloved Disciple's legacy to the Letters as epistolary fictions, Elizabeth Corsar introduces recent pseudepigraphal studies as potential ways of accounting for problematized issues related to the vexing questions of Johannine authorship. In her view, rather than inferring a Johannine Community, 1–3 John can otherwise be seen as appropriating the legacy of the Gospel's Beloved Disciple as a legendary figure, borrowing and making use of the Gospel's language and themes within these fictive compositions. In the light of ancient practices of literary fictive pseudepigraphy—*ethopoeia*—Corsar applies these contemporary practices as a means of posing new ways forward in understanding not only Johannine authorship perplexities, but also accounting for the telling relationships between the Gospel and Epistles.

The primary strength of this approach is that it applies insights of ancient literary studies to the Johannine writings, seeking to account for similarities and differences without making extended speculations regarding imagined communities or situations. The unnamed purported author of the Gospel (John 21:20–24) thus plays into additional questions regarding the authorship of the Epistles. As an unnamed legendary figure, "the Beloved Disciple" as an independent eyewitness to Jesus with his own story to tell would certainly have caught the imagination of others, and the relations between the Gospel and Epistles could have developed in such a fictive way, independent of the existence of a historical figure. Nonetheless, when new solutions to familiar problems are themselves problematized, advances may be more modest than first imagined. Put otherwise, to challenge an earlier view is not to overturn it; neither does a challenge to one view confirm an alternative view. Such must also be established based on evidence and reason if it is to survive as an alternative advance. The mere noting of an ancient literary parallel does not confirm its use in particular cases.

Nonetheless, the main strength of Corsar's work is that she notes numerous similarities between the Epistles and the Gospel of John. These include such memorable themes as: children of God, love, eternal life, and opponents. These themes are ubiquitous in all four of these writings, so, with Brown, at least some sort of connection is clear. Robust also is the idea of the Christ-hymn added to the first edition of the Gospel,[34] with the Christ-hymn

The Johannine Situation 215

added to the initial opening of the Johannine account (John 1:6–8, 15, 19–42) as an overture based on the Elder's assimilation of the evangelist's teachings over the years. So, Corsar's work reinforces the connections between the Johannine writings, whatever they might have looked like, historically.

Then again, problematizing new solutions to earlier views leads also to further questions. As referenced above, the inference of pseudonymous Johannine authors advanced by Méndez, when proper names are not used, falls short of plausibility as a critical inference. One might question whether an author was "actually a Presbyter," or whether 2–3 John were written by the author of 1 John, but to say that one feigning positional authority was not a real person within a real community—or a pseudonymous or fictive writer with no community involved—is hard to imagine.

Likewise, inferring that the legacy of an authoritative community leader or founder existed, but that there never was such a figure as a historical reality, makes it hard to imagine how such phenomenology developed. Far more compelling would be the inference of a real, memorable, patriarchal leader of a community—whoever he might have been—whose authority is borrowed by others. Thus, Corsar's theory would be more compelling if the authority of *a real figure*—not an imagined one—was being co-opted by others and appealed to for rhetorical reasons. So, abandoning the pseudonymity element of the Gospel's authoritative basis would bolster the likelihood of the fictive appropriation of its authority by the Epistle writer(s).

A second question problematizes the function of anonymity in the Gospel. As a leading figure in the narrative, the unnamed Beloved Disciple—intimate with Jesus, companion of Peter, present at the crucifixion, recognizer of the resurrected Lord, apparently deceased—is credited as the authorial source of the Gospel. Does anonymity itself, though, prove non-identity, given that those of Zebedee are referenced earlier in the chapter (John 21:2) along with other disciples? Critics have argued such, claiming that the Beloved Disciple is a "literary invention," as Corsar has acknowledged, but how is this known, critically? How is it known with historical or literary certainty that the Beloved Disciple was *not* a real person, referenced by the final compiler, if such a figure never existed? Does anonymity itself disprove the existence of a real person, or even a known reference to a univocally traditional-referenced individual?[35] Perhaps, but not necessarily.

Take, for instance, the fact that "the mother of Jesus" is not mentioned by name in John. Does this prove, or even imply, that that person was *not* Mary, wife of Joseph, one of the parents of Jesus who are reportedly known personally by actants in the Gospel (John 6:42)? Thus: "The mother of Jesus in John, because her name is not mentioned, cannot have been Mary, wife of Joseph, but she simply was a 'literary invention'—like the Beloved Disciple—because Johannine anonymity proves traditional views to have

216   *Paul N. Anderson*

been just plain wrong." If critics argue such for the unnamed Beloved Disciple, must they also be forced to do the same for the unnamed mother of Jesus? Problematizing solutions to other problems give one pause, critically.

If, however, the anonymity of the unnamed mother of Jesus is accounted for otherwise, it could be a factor of three other possibilities. First, the mother of Jesus was *known by all*; she did not need to be named. Second, her authority was not a function of her name; it was a factor of her relationship to Jesus: his beloved mother. Third, as there were many "Marys" in the narrative (Mary Magdalene, Mary sister of Lazarus, Mary wife of Cleopas), her name was not as important as distinguishing her from other figures in the narrative with the same name. If these three bases for anonymity are applied to the Beloved Disciple, how might they support or challenge Corsar's thesis? First, the Beloved Disciple was a known figure, indeed a historical, key persona within the Johannine Situation. Second, his "beloved-ness" references his proximity to Jesus—the "special disciple" with an inside perspective, as a contrast to alternative memories—and also his having recently departed. Third, his non-naming may be a factor of the need to distinguish his identity from the most common male name in the narrative and context: John the Baptist, Peter son of John, John the Elder, John the Apocalyptist, and so forth. Thus, if Mary's unnamed reference is any indicator, anonymity might well point directly to someone named "John" *as* the Beloved Disciple—a known, respected, departed, eyewitness figure—whose legacy was appropriated in the Epistles, even if they were written by another, or others.

Ironically, in our scholarly advances over the last half century over historical authorship views, moving to historical community views, when the latter is called into question on the basis of authorial issues, we are thrown right back into authorial/non-authorial inferences. Harry Attridge makes the point that the identity/non-identity of the Beloved Disciple in relation to Johannine authorship continues is a vexing interest.[36] Nonetheless, we must engage the Johannine writings *as they stand*—regardless of who authors and editors might or might not have been—so particular identities remain less than relevant. Then again, claiming to know who an author was not also requires problematization, if we are faithful critically to truth-seeking scholarship. Thus, what is needed is *Second Criticality*, not simply *Second naïvete*.

An Overview of These Chapters: New Windows into the Johannine Situation

As I reflect on the chapters in the present volume in the light of my overall theory of *the Dialogical Autonomy of the Fourth Gospel*, and whether my mind has changed or remained the same, I conclude that none of my overall judgments have changed, although I do find several of them bolstered or

The Johannine Situation   217

refined in some profitable ways. I now comment on some of the most compelling perspectives in the seven chapters as they inform my set of critical ways forward regarding the Johannine Situation.

- With Seglenieks, the Johannine Situation should indeed be approached through the lens of the Epistles (and I would add some contextual content of Rev 2–3, for instance), as they reflect multiple players internal and external to communities of Johannine believers. Thus, Jewish-Johannine dialectics are rather muted in their intensity, rather than centrally impactful upon the Gospel.
- With Lamb, what if the Gospel simply reflects an individuated memory of Jesus and his ministry, crafted to address emerging issues within the longitudinal Johannine situation, crafted for believers simply trying to be faithful to their understanding of what it meant to follow Jesus within a dialectical Diaspora situation? A modest inference, but not too far-fetched.
- With Porter, social identity—in relation to faith and practice issues—would clearly have been an issue for virtually all Jesus-adherents in the first-century Greco-Roman world, as Jewish communities. Thus, seeing John within Judaism is most helpful in understanding fraternal tensions in the Johannine Situation, with implications for ecclesiology.
- With Hunt, Johannine Latinisms build bridges between the ministry of Jesus and Greco-Roman audiences in the Diaspora. In addition to the Jewish and Roman law-breaking, note that the two Kingdom-references in John are both corrective (versus Synoptic constructive Kingdom sayings), pushing back against Nicodemus and religious sensibilities (John 3:1–8) and against Pilate and political hegemony (18:36–38).
- With Byers, the Gospel builds on the past, addresses the present, and prepares the way for the future—within the cosmopolitan Johannine Situation—as history and theology are drawn into play in terms of ecclesiology. And when the works of the παράκλητος are cited in relation to the prayer of Jesus as a programmatic manifesto of church unity (John 14–17), Johannine historical memory is selectively ordered as a means of connecting earlier meanings with later needs, providing guidance for the present and future.
- With Méndez, the speculative imaginings of secessionists in every closet or Gnostics around every corner deserves to be abandoned. Likewise problematic, there never was *just one* Johannine Community, although there must have been *at least one*, as well as many others. Especially needed is the demarcation of who the Antichrists were, and were not, based on critical analysis. No, they were not all secessionists, and the secessionists were not the same threat as the visiting Docetists. We need

218 Paul N. Anderson

to address errors of antichristic interpretation in seeking to discern the diverse errors of the Antichrists.

- With Corsar, the yoking of the Gospel's language and authority into the rhetoric of the Epistles is important to consider. It may also be that the authority of the Epistle writer(s) is felt to be less operationally potent than the remembered legacy of another departed leader, so that consideration may well also inform understandings of how second-generation leadership differs—in its challenges and its strategies—from first-generation founders of a community or a movement. Ecclesiology again presents itself as a primary concern of the Johannine authors and editors.

CONCLUSION

In reflecting on the vision and contributions of the present volume, I am grateful to have been drawn into the project and hope our explorations continue. While the epoch-turning contributions of Martyn, Brown, and others have formed our views of the Johannine Situation, viewing its dialectical character and development in longitudinal and multicultural perspective is instructive. As the above chapters suggest, scholars have successfully questioned a single Johannine Community beset by secessionist Gnostics and railing from synagogue expulsions. Nonetheless, relations between the Gospel and Epistles remain in play, with serviceable analyses going in both directions.

Within my own overall theory, the Johannine Situation viewed in longitudinal perspective presents an advance over a singular Johannine Community. Thus, the quest for a singular crisis, when the Johannine tradition developed over seven decades, is historically implausible. Nor do two-level readings of the text supplant the historical likelihood that Jesus of Nazareth actually engaged Judean leaders, followers of the Baptist, Samaritan neighbors, Roman authorities, Hellenistic seekers, nationalistic revolutionaries, and disciples with different perspectives. Then again, all historical narratives hinge upon memories of the past, perspectives of an author, and perceived needs of an audience.

Thus, while the middle and later Johannine Situation is most clearly understood by starting with the Epistles, the pre-70 period, as well as the Johannine memory of Jesus of Nazareth, is best conveyed via the Gospel. And yet, John's Gospel represents an individuated account, despite some overlap with the Synoptics. Thus, it is not simply the issues within the Johannine Situation that formed the narrative of Jesus and his ministry; it was also John's augmentation and modest correction of Mark in its earlier phases, followed by the final compiler's adding later and harmonizing material, that accounts for the Fourth Gospel's finalized and circulated account. Thus, in affirming the

The Johannine Situation 219

witness of the Beloved Disciple, the compiler/Elder and his community attest that his and our "testimony is true" (John 21:24; 3 John 12).

NOTES

1. Raymond E. Brown, *The Gospel According to John I-XII*, AB 29 (New York: Doubleday, 1966); *The Gospel According to John XIII-XXI*, AB 29a (New York: Doubleday, 1970); *The Community of the Beloved Disciple (*Mahwah, NJ: Paulist, 1979); *The Epistles of John*, AB 30 (New York: Doubleday, 1983).

2. J. Louis Martyn, *History and Theology in the Fourth Gospel,* third ed., NTL (1968, 1978; Louisville: Westminster John Knox, 2003); *The Gospel of John in Christian History: Seven Glimpses into the Johannine Community* (Revised and Expanded), ed. Paul N. Anderson. Johannine Monograph Series 8 (Eugene, OR: Wipf & Stock, 2019).

3. At least three scholars in this volume see the Epistles being written between a first and final edition of the Gospel: *Communities in Dispute: Current Scholarship on the Johannine Epistles,* Paul N. Anderson and R. Alan Culpepper, eds. ECL 13 (Atlanta: Society of Biblical Literature, 2014).

4. See my analysis within *Communities in Dispute*: "The Community that Raymond Brown Left Behind—Reflections on the Dialectical Johannine Situation," 47–93.

5. Paul N. Anderson, *The Christology of the Fourth Gospel: Its Unity and Disunity in the Light of John 6*, third ed. (Eugene: Cascade, 2010), 195–265; *idem*, "The Sitz im Leben of the Johannine Bread of Life Discourse and its Evolving Context," in *Critical Readings of John 6*, ed. R. Alan Culpepper, BInS 22 (Leiden: Brill, 1997), 1–59.

6. Paul N. Anderson, "A Bi-Optic Hypothesis—A Theory of Gospel Relations," *From Crisis to Christ: A Contextual Introduction to the New Testament* (Nashville: Abingdon, 2014), 102–26.

7. While Brown's view of Johannine composition was left somewhat vague, Barnabas Lindars put forward the most plausible view: a modest two-edition theory, seeing a first edition of John developing around 80–85 CE, which was finalized by the Elder around 100 CE after the death of the Beloved Disciple. Barnabas Lindars, *The Gospel of John*, NCBC (Grand Rapids: Eerdmans, 1972).

8. See here the works of Richard J. Cassidy, *John's Gospel in New Perspective: Christology and the Realities of Roman Power*, ed. Paul N. Anderson, Johannine Monograph Series 3 (Eugene, OR: Wipf & Stock, 2015); Warren Carter, *John and Empire: Initial Explorations* (London: T&T Clark, 2008); Tom Thatcher, *Greater than Caesar: Christology and Empire in the Fourth Gospel* (Minneapolis: Fortress, 2009).

9. I have posted this outline in several of my writings, including Paul N. Anderson, *The Fourth Gospel and the Quest for Jesus: Modern Foundations Reconsidered*, LNTS 321 (London: T&T Clark, 2006), 196–99.

10. Among others, see Adolf von Harnack, "Uber den dritten Johannesbrief," *Texte und Untersuchungen zur Geschichte der altchristlichen Literatur* 15:3

(Leipzig, 1887), 3–27; Savas Agourides, "Peter and John in the Fourth Gospel," *Studia Evangelica* IV, ed. F. L. Cross (Berlin: Akademie, 1968), 137–45; Graydon, F. Snyder, "John 3:17 and the Anti-Petrinism of the Johannine Tradition," *BR* 16 (1971): 5–15; Arthur H. Maynard, "The Role of Peter in the Fourth Gospel," *NTS* 30 (1984): 531–48; Against these views, see Raymond E. Brown, Karl P. Donfried, and John Reumann, eds. *Peter in the New Testament* (New York: Paulist, 1973).

11. Thus, the question of the meaning of *Ioudaioi*—"Jews" or "Judeans" in John can rightly be translated in both ways, depending on the context. See Steve Mason, "Jews, Judaeans, Judaizing, Judaism: Problems of Categorization in Ancient History," *JSJ* 38 (2007): 457–512.

12. This is argued by Jonathan Bernier, *Aposynagōgos and the Historical Jesus in John: Rethinking the Historicity of the Johannine Expulsion Passages*, BInS 122 (Leiden: Brill, 2013).

13. Paul N. Anderson, "Antichristic Errors—Flawed Interpretations Regarding the Johannine Antichrists;" and *idem*, "Errors of the Antichrists—Proselytizing Schism and Assimilative Teaching within the Johannine Situation," *Text and Community, Essay in Commemoration of Bruce M. Metzger*, ed. J. Harold Ellens (Sheffield: Sheffield Phoenix Press, 2007), 1:196–216; 217–40.

14. Peder Borgen, "God's Agent in the Fourth Gospel," in *The Interpretation of John*, second ed., ed. John Ashton (Edinburgh: T & T Clark, 1997), 83–95.

15. Thus, the injunction to ingest the flesh and blood of Jesus in John 6:51–58 calls for martyrological faithfulness to Christ and solidarity with his community in the face of hardship under the imperial cult and its requirements. Interestingly, Bultmann lumped John 6:60–71 in with "The Way of the Cross" rather than seeing v. 51 as part and parcel of the same thrust: Rudolf Bultmann, *The Gospel of John: A Commentary*, trans. G. R. Beasley-Murray, R. W. N. Hoare, and J. K. Riches (Philadelphia: Westminster, 1971), 443–51.

16. There is no evidence of Fortna's Signs Gospel underlying John, nor do any of Bultmann's stylistic, contextual, or theological arguments for a *Semeia* Source stack up factually.

17. I would agree with a basic two-edition approach to the composition of the Fourth Gospel: Paul N. Anderson, "On 'Seamless Robes' and 'Leftover Fragments'— A Theory of Johannine Composition," *Structure, Composition, and Authorship of John's Gospel*, in *The Origins of John's Gospel*, Vol. 2, ed. Stanley E. Porter and Hughson Ong (Leiden: Brill, 2015), 169–218.

18. See Mary L. Coloe, *Dwelling in the Household of God: Johannine Ecclesiology and Spirituality* (Collegeville, MN: Liturgical Press, 2007).

19. Chris Keith, "The Competitive Textualization of the Jesus Tradition in John 20:30–31 and 21:24–25," *CBQ* 78 (2016): 321–37.

20. Along these lines, I have applied the Social Identity Complexity Theory of Roccas and Brewer to the seven crises along these four categories: *Intersection, Dominance, Compartmentalization, Merger:* "Negotiating Complexity Within the Dialectical and Cosmopolitan Johannine Situation," *Religions* (2024; under review).

21. With de Boer, the reference to synagogue expulsions in John 16:2 seems more recent than earlier references in 9:22 and 12:42: Martin C. De Boer, "Expulsion from

the Synagogue: J.L. Martyn's History and Theology in the Fourth Gospel Revisited," *NTS* 66 (2020): 367–91.

22. Paul N. Anderson, "Anti-Semitism and Religious Violence as Flawed Interpretations of the Gospel of John," in *John and Judaism: A Contested Relationship in Context*, ed. R. Alan Culpepper and Paul N. Anderson, RBS 87 (Atlanta: SBL Press, 2017), 265–311.

23. C. K. Barrett, "Johanneisches Christentum," *Di Anfaenge des Christentums: Alte Welt und neue Hoffnung* (Stuttgart: Kohlhammer, 1987), 255–78.

24. Anderson, *"Sitz im Leben"*; idem, "Bakhtin's Dialogism."

25. The multicultural setting of the Johannine writings has been developed fully by C. H. Dodd, *The Interpretation of the Fourth Gospel* (Cambridge: Cambridge University Press, 1953); see also Charles B. Puskas and C. Michael Robbins, *The Conceptual Worlds of the Fourth Gospel: Intertextuality and Early Reception* (Eugene, OR: Cascade, 2021).

26. Domitian required his officials to refer to him as "Lord and God" (*Dominus et Deus*) in person and in written forms (Dio Cassius, *Hist. rom.* 67.4.7; 67.13.4; Suetonius, *Dom.* 13.2.

27. The parting of the ways is not actualized within the Johannine situation, as Jewish Jesus-adherents continued contacts with Jewish family and friends for decades, and even centuries, into the future. See Adam H. Becker and Annette Yoshiko Reed, eds., *The Ways that Never Parted: Jews and Christians in Antiquity and the Middle Ages* (Minneapolis: Augsburg Fortress, 2007). See also Julie Galambush, *The Reluctant Parting: How the New Testament's Jewish Writers Created a Christian Book* (New York: HarperCollins, 2005), 265–304.

28. Raimo Hakola, *Reconsidering Johannine Christianity: A Social Identity Approach* (New York: Routledge, 2015).

29. Udo Schnelle, *Antidocetic Christology in the Gospel of John: An Investigation of the Place of the Fourth Gospel in the Johannine School*, trans. Linda M. Maloney (Minneapolis: Fortress, 1992).

30. In the 1998 review of *The Christology of the Fourth Gospel* at the national SBL meetings, Kysar declared his change of mind regarding his earlier diachronic view of John's use of sources. Robert Kysar, review of *The Christology of the Fourth Gospel*: *RBL* 1 (1999): 38–43.

31. Hugo Méndez, "Did the Johannine Community Exist?," *JSNT* 42 (2020): 350–74; Paul N. Anderson, "On Biblical Forgeries and Imagined Communities—A Critical Analysis of recent Criticism," *The Bible and Interpretation* (April 2020): https://bibleinterp.arizona.edu/articles/biblical-forgeries-and-imagined-communities-critical-analysis-recent-criticism.

32. Adele Reinhartz, "Building Skyscrapers on Toothpicks: The Literary-Critical Challenge to Historical Criticism," *Anatomies of Narrative Criticism: The Past, Present, and Futures of the Fourth Gospel as Literature*, ed. Tom Thatcher and Stephen D. Moore, RBS 55 (Atlanta: SBL Press, 2008), 55–76.

33. Paul N. Anderson, "On Guessing Points and Naming Stars—The Epistemological Origins of John's Christological Tensions," in *The Gospel of St. John*

and *Christian Theology*, ed. Richard Bauckham and Carl Mosser (Grand Rapids, MI: Eerdmans, 2007), 311–45.

34. With John A. T. Robinson, "The Relation of the Prologue to the Gospel of St. John," *NTS* 9 (1962–63): 120–29.

35. The exact opposite is attested pervasively in the second century, as noted by Lightfoot, *Gospel of John*.

36. Harold W. Attridge, "The Restless Quest for the Beloved Disciple," in *Early Christian Voices: Texts, Traditions, and Symbols: Essays in Honor of François Bovon*, BInS 66 (Leiden: Brill, 2003), 70–81.

Chapter 11

Seeing with the Eyes and Hearing with the Ears

Community Hypotheses in Johannine Scholarship

Adele Reinhartz

In a scene in the fourth episode of the British sci-fi crime series *Bodies* (2023), a young police detective named Iris and a physics doctoral student named Gabriel are relaxing after dinner. As they sip their glasses of fine French wine, they discuss an age-old question: do humans have free will? Iris says yes. As an example, she describes the many choices they have each made over the course of the evening, including her own choice to open a second bottle of wine after she had sworn not to. Gabriel, however, disagrees. He insists that her choice to open that bottle was not an act of free will. Rather, it depended on:

> the millions of factors and forces that have already happened to you that you're blissfully unaware of. . . . Your prior relationship to alcohol, your parents' relationship to alcohol. Genetically, the taste buds on your tongue, the specific makeup and responsiveness that makes this wine taste just sumptuous to you, right now, in this moment. The temperature of the room, the mood you're in, the person you drink it with. My point is: Free will does not exist. It's an illusion, and a pleasant one. (Netflix, *Bodies* [2023], Episode 4, "Up the Wazoo," minutes 43:40–44:35)

Though set in the futuristic world of 2053, this scene came to mind as I gathered my thoughts on the chapters in this volume, and, more broadly, on the well-worn question of the Johannine community. The claim that the Gospel of John emerged from a group of Jewish Christ-believers that had suffered a traumatic expulsion from the synagogue has been a staple of Johannine scholarship since the initial publication of J. L. Martyn's *History and Theology in the Fourth Gospel* in 1968.[1] Since the late twentieth century, however, this claim has come under increasing scrutiny and criticism. The purpose of the present volume is to examine the state of the question and explore new approaches. As the chapters demonstrate, these new approaches may result in new or modified theories about a Johannine community, or they may point to new ways of understanding the emergence of the Gospel and letters of John without recourse to a community hypothesis.

In the first section of this response, I will attempt to place Martyn's hypothesis and the chapters in this book into the broader context of New Testament scholarship. In the second, I will outline my own engagement with the community question, past and present. My objective is not to determine which of the proposals in this book is more plausible and which approach more productive. Nor do I intend to argue that my own hypothesis is "right" or "better" than those presented. Rather, I am interested in the meta question: why have community hypotheses proven to be so durable? Throughout this discussion I am in conversation with chapter 2 of Robyn Faith Walsh's 2021 book *The Origins of Early Christian Literature: Contextualizing the New Testament within Greco-Roman Literary Culture*, titled "The Romantic 'Big Bang': German Romanticism and Inherited Methodology."[2]

FACTORS AND FORCES

J. L. Martyn described the task of the interpreter in a way that quickened the hearts and minds of many a Johannine scholar. "It is imperative," he stated,

> that we make every effort to take up temporary residence in the Johannine community. We must see with the eyes and hear with the ears of that community. We must sense at least some of the crises that helped to shape the lives of its members. And we must listen carefully to the kind of conversations in which all of its members found themselves engaged. Only in the midst of this endeavor will we be able to hear the Fourth Evangelist speak *in his own terms*, rather than in words which we moderns merely want to hear from his mouth.[3]

In order to hear the Fourth Evangelist speak in his own terms therefore meant to see with the eyes and hear with the ears of the Johannine community. To do so, Martyn argued, we must first realize that in recounting the life of Jesus, the Fourth Evangelist was also, less directly, recounting the history of

Seeing with the Eyes and Hearing with the Ears 225

a Jewish group—the Johannine community—that had been expelled from the synagogue on account of their faith in Christ as the messiah.

The starting point of Martyn's two-level reading was the Gospel's use of an unusual term: ἀποσυνάγωγος. This term appears three times in the Gospel but is not attested elsewhere in Greek literature from this era. The term means "one who is outside the synagogue" but the contexts in which it appears implies a narrower definition: someone who is removed from the synagogue for confessing Jesus as the messiah (cf. especially 9:22). Because the removal of someone from the synagogue for such a confession could not have occurred during the time of Jesus, Martyn viewed these passages as an opening, a portal, if you will, to the experience of a group or community within which and for which the Gospel was written.[4]

Martyn extrapolated a history of the Johannine community from his reading of the Fourth Gospel as a two-level drama. Recognizing the circularity of this approach, he also sought external evidence for his hypothesis, and he found it in the rabbinic references to a Jewish liturgical curse against Jewish-Christians, known as *Birkat ha-minim*. On the basis of a passage in the Babylonian Talmud, a large composite text compiled in the early sixth century CE, Martyn argued that in the late first century, an authoritative Jewish body imposed upon synagogues the requirement to institute this curse as a means to exclude Jewish Christ-confessors from the synagogue. In his view, the Gospel of John reflects the application of this new requirement to the community of Jewish Christ-confessors within which and for which the Gospel was written.

Specialists in the history of Jewish liturgy have shown conclusively that *Birkat ha-minim* was not yet in place when the Fourth Gospel was written; that there was no central authoritative body that could have imposed such a curse even had it existed; and that in any case it could not have been used to exclude Christ-confessors from the synagogue.[5] Most scholars, though not Martyn himself, accepted this analysis and removed *Birkat ha-minim* from their theories. Even with the collapse of the external evidence, however, many continued to accept Martyn's expulsion hypothesis as fact or, at least, as the most plausible and convincing explanation of the origins of the Johannine literature.[6]

Martyn generated his proposal on the basis of his own careful reading of the Gospel of John; the scholars who accepted it did so not just because they respected him and his scholarship, but because it sounded convincing on the basis of their own study of the text. And yet one cannot help but think that, even if, like Iris the detective, scholars saw themselves as exercising free will, it may well be that they are led to read the Gospel in particular ways by "millions of factors and forces" from the past of which they are blissfully unaware.

One such factor can be found in the origins of our field in European, especially German philosophy of the eighteenth and nineteenth centuries. In her 2021 book, *The Origins of Early Christian Literature: Contextualizing the New Testament within Greco-Roman Literary Culture*, Robyn Faith Walsh argues that the scholarly predisposition to view Gospels as products of specific communities rather than individual authors is a legacy of German Romantic thought. The architects of German Romanticism and Idealism, such as Schlegel, and Möhler, viewed the author as "synecdochical both of a unifying, inspirational Geist and of the community in which (usually) the author is writing."[7]

This argument is intriguing, and also persuasive, at least to me. I would add that other, more recent factors may also be at play. In the post-Holocaust era, many Christian New Testament scholars attempt to interpret the Gospel's negative statements about the Ἰουδαῖοι as something other than an antipathy to Jews. Martyn's theory can appeal to such scholars because it allows them to read those statements as an understandable response on the part of Jewish Christ-confessors to their expulsion from the synagogue. In addition, his theory's lively specificity appealed to the historical imagination; its claim to historicity, whether overt or implicit, may have compensated for the Gospel's perceived lack of usefulness for historical Jesus research. If the Gospel did not present much that was useful for reconstructing the words and deeds of the historical Jesus, at least it contributed to the historical understanding of early Christ-confessing communities.[8]

Another factor in the appeal of this hypothesis is its clarity and appeal to the imagination. Arriving as it did in the mid-twentieth century, Martyn's book was a welcome change from the turgid tomes that were the required reading in Johannine scholarship. Martyn wrote in clear and compelling language, and in doing so brought the Gospel alive in ways that the learned studies of John's source, redaction, and history-of-religions background simply could not do. We could all imagine ourselves back in the Johannine community, and experience the crushing sorrow of expulsion.

These observations suggest that the scholarly penchant for community hypotheses has indeed been shaped by inchoate factors, as Walsh has suggested. This has not, however, precluded new approaches to the issue. In his intellectual biography, Peter Brown comments on the liberating effect of community-based theories on the world of New Testament scholarship. He adds, however, that this approach "now seems overconfident, even reductionist: texts themselves are now treated as more slippery, and the social background of early Christianity itself is now seen to be more complex than we had thought."[9] Indeed it is true that since the late twentieth century our field has begun to view texts and contexts as more diverse, more complicated, and more ambiguous than in previous decades. One factor in this change is the

Seeing with the Eyes and Hearing with the Ears

openness of the field to new methods, such as literary criticism and, especially, social-scientific theories and methods.[10]

This latter move remains prominent today and is evident in several of the chapters included in this volume. In chapter 3, "The Language of John: Idiolect, Sociolect, Antilanguage, and Textual Community," David Lamb responds to some critiques of his 2014 book *Text, Context and the Johannine Community*, and reaffirms his use of a methodology based on systemic functional linguistics and multidimensional analysis. Christopher Porter's chapter, titled "Disentangling 'Mom's Spaghetti': A Socio-Cognitive Approach to the Complexity of the Johannine Community," draws on social identity theory, and specifically, a method called Structured Analysis of Group Arguments (SAGA). Laura Hunt employs three theoretical tools: Umberto Eco's semiotics; Bayes' Theorem, and J. Brian Tucker's approach to social identity analysis in her chapter, "Triangulating a Johannine Community from John 18:28–19:22."

These chapters confirm Walsh's observation that "in recent years the social sciences have added to the conversation questions about the social organization of the early Christian communities—were they egalitarian, sectarian, patriarchal, economically or socially 'stratified'?"[11] As Walsh notes, however, even in these approaches, however, "'community' has remained the starting point of analysis."[12] This point too is illustrated by the chapters in this book which, even if they do not present the "community" as their starting point, often come to conclusions with regard to the nature and composition of that community. David Lamb, for example, describes the Johannine community as a loose and embryonic textual community in which the Fourth Gospel held high status.[13] Porter begins his analysis with the Johannine epistles, and from there he argues that the Gospel was written in order to bring an implied Diaspora Jewish audience into a community that embodied a new social identity of Christ-followers. He emphasizes, however, that at the time the Gospel was written, the Johannine community remains an imagined community. Hunt suggests that the Johannine community was a network of Jewish and Roman Christ-believers in or around Ephesus that was in the process of negotiating the identity marker of law, whether Jewish or Roman.

Of course, it is not surprising that the Johannine community should take center stage in a book that is intended to "to explore the current state of the question [of the Johannine community] while shining a light on new and constructive proposals for understanding the emergence of the Johannine literature."[14] What *is* interesting is that the majority of the chapters continue to adhere to the idea of Johannine community, whether real or envisioned, even as they depart from Martyn's detailed expulsion hypothesis.

This is true not only for the essays that employ social-scientific theories but also for those that rely on rhetorical, literary, or historical modes

228   *Adele Reinhartz*

of analysis. In chapter 6, "The Johannine Community and the Johannine Community Vision: Historical Reflection, Rhetorical Construction, and Narrative Ecclesiology," Andrew Byers agrees with Martyn that the Gospel presents a multi-level drama but he believes that the horizons—the story of Jesus and the story of the community—are fused too thoroughly to be disentangled. John's Gospel, in Byers's view, is concerned to highlight the centrality of Jesus for "a social vision for how a community may be shaped around him."[15] Byers suggests that Jesus's prayer in John 17 "gives aspirational hope to a largely Jewish audience of Christ-believers who find themselves at theological and social odds with their own tradition."[16]

Chris Seglenieks's chapter, "Reading the Johannine Community in the Letters: A Method," follows Richard Bauckham in viewing the Fourth Gospel as written "for all Christians," and for that reason, he does not suggest that we can construct a specific Johannine community from the Gospel as such. The situation is different, however, for the three letters, which, in his view, are addressed to specific groups, and, furthermore, are explicit about their contexts. Seglenieks suggests that once we have determined the context of the letters, we can extrapolate from the letters to the Gospel, although this does not yield a picture of a Johannine community behind the Gospel. It is reasonable to assume, however, that the Gospel's context was a group of connected communities within the wider network of Christ-confessing groups in which Christology and ethics constituted boundary markers.

The idea that community hypotheses may be shaped by factors that are rooted in forces and factors unbeknownst to the scholars who generate them does not in itself mean that Johannine community hypotheses are wrong. It is telling, however, that the approaches used to arrive at the various community hypotheses disregard some basic premises of historical research as it is conducted with respect to other corners of the ancient world. As Walsh notes, such theories go against what is known about ancient writing practices. She states: "it is not amorphous communities but an author's network of fellow writers that is the most plausible and influential social environment for the production of literature."[17]

Walsh argues that scholars can and should break the hold of community hypotheses by viewing the evangelists not as the channels for or mediators of a community's ethos, spirit, or experiences, but as authors who engage in the literary practices that are typical of their era. She suggests that "Rather than ask what makes the gospels exceptional, we should demonstrate how they are utterly commonplace imperial writings produced by ordinary Greco-Roman writers."[18]

Two of the chapters in this volume take this approach. The chapters by Elizabeth Corsar and Hugo Méndez firmly deny the existence of a Johannine community, or, to be precise, deny the possibility of constructing such a

Seeing with the Eyes and Hearing with the Ears 229

community on the basis of the Johannine literature. Indeed, they question the very assumption that the Gospel and Letters of John relate in any way to history, that is, to a world outside the text. Rather, they view these texts explicitly as fiction and therefore not suitable for the task of historical reconstruction.

In chapter 8, "The Legacy of the Beloved Disciple: The Johannine Letters as Epistolary Fiction," Elizabeth J. B. Corsar suggests that the letters are fabrications, or more precisely, pseudo-historical letters, that were intended to bolster and continue the legacy of the Beloved Disciple. This is not to say that the Beloved Disciple himself was a historical individual, but only that subsequent audiences responded to the figure as presented in the Gospel as an authoritative figure. In her view, the letters did not all have the same author. She suggests that the author of 1 John reworked material from the Gospel, and that the author of 2 and 3 John borrowed and reworked material from both 1 John and the gospel. As fictional documents, the letters cannot be used as a basis for the reconstruction of one or more historical communities.

In chapter 7, which proposes a way for "Renewing Johannine Historical Criticism," Hugo Méndez goes one step further than Corsar by suggesting that the Gospel too is a fabricated document, with a false authorial construct. This is a point that he has developed in earlier work.[19] Nevertheless, Méndez has not given up on the historical project altogether. Rather, he argues that hypotheses about the history of the Johannine literature, including proposals for a Johannine community, should be data- rather than model-driven.

Walsh suggests that situating New Testament literature within its Greco-Roman context is a way of letting "historical research and the texts speak for themselves."[20] This brings us full circle. For all their differences in approach, Walsh and Martyn share a desire to let texts speak for themselves. Méndez may be doing the same when he insists that "Whatever alternatives to the community hypothesis emerge, they should be data-driven rather than model-driven."[21] I believe that that is what we all aspire to, but data must be interpreted, and the interpretations of data are often based on models, or, at least, assumptions that, in turn, may stem from factors and forces extraneous to the data themselves.

BREAKING THE LOOP

In pointing out how Johannine scholars, including those represented in this volume, continue to be influenced by the factors and forces, such as the community-based ideas of Christian origins from German romanticism, I am not exempting myself. I too have sought to hear the author of John's Gospel speak in his terms, and my attempts to do so have also involved some speculation about possible Johannine communities.

230   *Adele Reinhartz*

I encountered Martyn's book while I was still a doctoral student and in the early stages of working on the Gospel of John for my dissertation. My dissertation did not address Martyn's expulsion theory, nor did it engage with the possibility of a Johannine community. But, like so many others, I was captivated by Martyn's imaginative reconstruction. His reading of John sparked my imagination, as it did for so many others, and for many years post-PhD it shaped my understanding of the historical circumstances in which the Fourth Gospel was written.

In my first book on the Fourth Gospel, *The Word in the World: The Cosmological Tale in the Fourth Gospel* (1992), I expanded on Martyn's ideas by suggesting that the Gospel tells not two but three intertwined narratives.[22] The first one, evident on the text's surface, corresponds to Martyn's concept of the *einmalig* level—the story of Jesus. I referred to this level as the historical tale because it concerns the words and deeds of a person who lived at a specific time and place. The second level, corresponding to Martyn's second level reading, was what I called the ecclesiological tale, the story of a community of Jewish Christ-followers engaged in a turbulent relationship to their fellow Jews. The third level was what I termed the cosmological tale, as it focused on the relationships among God, Christ, and humankind. I argued that this cosmological tale provided the overarching narrative framework for the other two tales. Jesus's actions and words in the historical tale were meant to move the other characters within the Gospel as well as the Gospel's audiences, toward faith, that is, toward understanding his role in the cosmological tale, as God's son and agent. The community evoked in the ecclesiological tale was comprised of those who understood and believed in the role of Christ in the cosmos.

My belief in the presence of an ecclesiological, community-based, narrative within the Gospel began to waver a few short years after my first book was published.[23] Over time I had become increasingly uncomfortable with Martyn's hypothesis, for three main reasons. The first reason was the theory's homiletic utility. By reading the Fourth Gospel as a "family feud" between a Jewish Johannine community and other Jews, scholars could dismiss the Gospel's hostile statements about the Ἰουδαῖοι as a "natural" response to the traumatic experience of expulsion.[24] As a Jewish reader of the Gospel, I felt that this let both John and his interpreters off the hook far too easily. Of course, I recognized that the theory's homiletical usefulness did not mean it was wrong, but it did suggest to me that the theory itself warranted closer scrutiny.

This scrutiny led me to two other important reasons for questioning the expulsion theory. One was its limited applicability. When I endeavoured to apply Martyn's two-level reading strategy to the Gospel as a whole, I realized that it worked only for the one verse that was at the center of Martyn's

Seeing with the Eyes and Hearing with the Ears 231

analysis. This passage is John 9:22, in which the parents of a blind man whose sight had been restored by Jesus deny knowledge of his healing because, as the narrator explains, "they were afraid of the Jews; for the Jews had already agreed that anyone who confessed Jesus to be the Messiah would be put out of the synagogue." Reading the Gospel as a response to expulsion created a problem, for example, for an interpretation of John 11, in which many Jews come to comfort Mary and Martha after Lazarus's death (11:19). The Lazarus siblings were known to be followers of Jesus (e.g., 11:3, 5, 36–37). If Jews were excluding such followers from their midst, they would not have come to mourn with them. And when I tried to apply Martyn's two-level reading method to the Gospel's passages about the Samaritan woman (John 4), Mary and Martha of Bethany (John 11–12) and Mary Magdalene (John 20), no coherent picture emerged at all.[25]

The other and perhaps the most important factor is the inherent circularity of Martyn's hypothesis. Once we dismiss *Birkat ha-minim* as a tool for excluding first-century Christ-believers, we are left with a hypothesis that extrapolates a Johannine community from a small number of verses in the Gospel and then uses that extrapolation to construct a community-based backstory for the Gospel which is then used as the key to interpreting the Gospel as a whole. This circular approach is not acceptable in any realm of intellectual endeavor.[26] Why should it be acceptable in Johannine scholarship?

The problematic circularity of the community hypothesis is not lost on the contributors to this volume. Andrew Byers, for example, comments that any effort to reconstruct a Gospel community becomes entrapped in a hermeneutical circle. The absence of external evidence for a Johannine community means that "proponents of hypothetical reconstructions must live with the unavoidable vulnerability of their circular reasoning."[27]

Circular reasoning, however, is more difficult to avoid than one might think. This is evident in Laura Hunt's effort to "triangulate" a Johannine community from John 18:28–19:22. Hunt observes at the outset that most attempts to discern a community take a circular approach by constructing the community from the Gospel and then using that construction to interpret the Gospel. She proposes to avoid that circularity by beginning from the end. Rather than extrapolate a community from the sources, she postulates the existence of a group with specific traits that can plausibly be proposed as the Gospel's intended audience and context. She builds that group from the tradition that John's Gospel was composed in Ephesus, and adds to that the presence of Latinisms, and, particularly, the use of the Latin term *praetorian*, to suggest that the Johannine community was a late first-century group located in Ephesus at a time when the vernacular of the Roman Empire was transitioning from Greek to Latin. This is an intriguing approach and noble effort. Nevertheless, because Hunt draws the evidence for the Gospel's intended

232 *Adele Reinhartz*

audience and context from the Gospel (its Latinisms and the term *praetorian*) and Gospel traditions, she is still largely engaged in a circular hermeneutic.

Hunt's chapter accords with my own experience: it is extremely difficult to avoid circularity even when one is determined to do so. One can of course follow Méndez and Corsar and avoid the question of the Johannine community altogether. Yet some scholars, including myself, continue to try to imagine a plausible set of circumstances in which the Gospel may have been received, whether heard or read, and to speculate about its potential impact on its audiences. My reading of Méndez's chapter suggests to me that he may be among this group as well. He provides some guidelines that might bear fruit: to recenter authors—including fictive ones—in the study of Johannine language, by looking at the places in our sources in which authors turn to external linguistic resources. He finds an example in 3 John, which, scholars agree, breaks from typical Johannine idioms. Méndez suggests that this deviation might provide clues as to the location and ethnic or other identities of the authors, from which one might also infer the identities of the intended or implied audiences. This is an intriguing suggestion, and one hopes that Méndez or others will play it out in more detail than he was able to do in this chapter.

My own efforts in this regard are detailed in my 2018 book, *Cast Out of the Covenant*.[28] As its subtitle states, the main focus of the book is on *Jews and anti-Judaism in the Gospel of John*. My main argument, based on an analysis of the Gospel's rhetoric, is that the Gospel's rhetoric mobilizes anti-Judaism in order to persuade its audiences to come together in a new community of "children of God" centered on John's understanding of who Jesus is and what belief in Jesus as the messiah and son of God requires. Participating in this new community, however, also entails distancing oneself from those whom John refers to as the Ἰουδαῖοι. John uses Ἰουδαῖοι as a generalizing term best translated as "Jews," even though the context makes it clear that it refers to Jews who do not accept the Gospel's Christological claims. Although it is clear that Jesus and his disciples *are* Jewish, the Gospel narrator never uses the term to refer to the disciples or to Jesus. Only the Samaritan woman and Pilate—both outsiders to the group of believers within the Gospel narrative— use Ἰουδαῖος in reference to Jesus and in neither case does Jesus acknowledge the label.[29] This suggests to me that John does not view Ἰουδαῖος as an identity marker for anyone, even someone who was ethnically Jewish, who is attracted by John's rhetoric and thereby becomes part of a real or imagined community of believers in Jesus as the Christ and son of God.

To be clear, in this book I do not claim that a community of non-Ἰουδαῖοι Christ-confessors à la the Fourth Gospel existed at the time the Gospel was written, nor, in fact, at any subsequent time. The letters, and the very fact that

Seeing with the Eyes and Hearing with the Ears 233

the Gospel of John eventually became part of the Christian canon, imply that it gathered an audience that viewed it as important and meaningful. In that sense one can speak about the Gospel as creating a community, but only in the most attenuated and abstract sense of the term.

Yet circularity also has a place in my analysis. The rhetorical approach that I employ allows me to propose a hypothesis regarding the (implied) author's intentions with regard to his audience, but I do not claim that these intentions were fulfilled or actualized within any particular audience. I do, however, engage in some attempts to imagine who that audience might be, based on the Gospel itself. If I were so inclined I might refer to my attempt as hearing the Fourth Evangelist speak in his own terms (à la Martyn), letting the text speak for itself (à la Walsh), or as being data- rather than model-driven (à la Méndez). Specifically, I suggest that the Johannine passages that refer to the Greeks, and, especially, John 12:31 in which the Greeks are described as seeking to see Jesus, in contrast to the Ἰουδαῖοι who refuse to do so (12:37), may imply a pagan/polytheistic, or, in any case, non-Jewish intended audience. Underlying this speculation is the common-sense assumption that Jews are unlikely to be attracted to a text that so often uses the term Ἰουδαῖοι in vituperative ways.

I do not, however, propose this speculation as historical fact. We simply do not know who the intended audience was nor do we know whether a specifically Johannine community, whether local, or part of an embryonic network, or simply as one or more groups within a community of "all Christians" existed either before, during or after the Gospel was written. As Méndez and Corsar suggest, we might speculate but we cannot know for sure that even the letters, which seem, as Seglenieks points out, to reflect specific communities, in fact emerge from a community context.

The same is true of my suggestion that the ἀποσυνάγωγος passages, which are so easily read as references to a community's expulsion from the synagogue, may also be interpreted as an example of the ancient rhetorical device of creating fear in the readership intended to move them away from identifying as Ἰουδαῖοι. This is not to say, however, that the Gospel actually had this effect on any of its audiences, only that the expulsion passages can be read as examples of this particular rhetorical device.[30]

Despite my concerted effort to remain agnostic about any form of community hypothesis and the circularity that it inevitably entails, it is clear, as Walsh might point out, that in some sense my rhetorically based analysis is still in conversation with or even shaped by community hypotheses. Hence I must acknowledge that at least some of the factors and forces operative in the strand of Gospel scholarship that views the Gospels as products of communities remain at play in my own work, much as I might resist them. I believe

234   *Adele Reinhartz*

the same is true for the other contributions to this volume, even those that explicitly try to avoid this view.

So are scholars doomed to participate in an endless loop of community hypotheses? The final episode of *Bodies* suggests not. (Note: *Bodies* spoiler ahead!). Despite Gabriel the physicist's declaration that free will does not exist, the cycle of death depicted in the show—the endless loop in which Gabriel is murdered over and over again—is improbably broken when detectives from four different eras, including Iris from 2053, work together to break the loop. They not only solve the mystery of Gabriel's multiple deaths but also change the course of history by persuading the would-be detonator of a world-destroying nuclear bomb to exercise his free will and take his finger off the trigger.

In a less terrifying way, the idea that our hypotheses about the origins of the Johannine literature may be shaped by eighteenth- and nineteenth-century philosophical and theological currents does not condemn us to replicate them endlessly. On the contrary. Awareness of the factors external to the text that have influenced the discussion of this question frees us from the need to replicate the theories and approaches from the past, but also, if we wish, to accept those aspects that continue to make sense to us in our own efforts to see and hear the Fourth Evangelist, as we must, through our own eyes and ears.

NOTES

1. J. Louis Martyn, *History and Theology in the Fourth Gospel*, third ed. (Louisville: Westminster John Knox Press, 2003). The earlier editions were published in 1969 and 1978.

2. Robyn Faith Walsh, *The Origins of Early Christian Literature: Contextualizing the New Testament within Greco-Roman Literary Culture* (Cambridge: Cambridge University Press, 2021), 50–104.

3. Martyn, *History and Theology in the Fourth Gospel*, 29. Emphasis in the original.

4. Jonathan Bernier is one of the few who argues for the possibility of the exclusion from the synagogue as taking place in the time of Jesus. See Jonathan Bernier, *Aposynagōgos and the Historical Jesus in John: Rethinking the Historicity of the Johannine Expulsion Passages,* BInS 122 (Leiden: Brill, 2013). On the use of the term community, see Stanley K. Stowers, "The Concept of 'Community' and the History of Early Christianity," *MTSR* 23 (2011): 238–56.

5. For the evidence and arguments against viewing Birkat Ha-minim as the background to the Johannine expulsion passages, see Reuven Kimelman, "Birkat Ha-Minim and the Lack of Evidence for an Anti-Christian Jewish Prayer in Late Antiquity," in *Jewish and Christian Self-Definition, 2* (Philadelphia: Fortress, 1981), 226–44; Steven T. Katz, "Issues in the Separation of Judaism and Christianity after

70 C.E.: A Reconsideration," *JBL* 103 (1984): 43–76; Ruth Langer, *Cursing the Christians?: A History of the Birkat Haminim* (New York: Oxford University Press, 2011).

6. Among the staunch defenders of Martyn's expulsion theory are Joel Marcus and Martin de Boer. See Joel Marcus, "Birkat Ha-Minim Revisited," *NTS* 55 (2009): 523–51; Martinus C. de Boer, "The Johannine Community under Attack in Recent Scholarship," in *The Ways That Often Parted*, ed. Lori Baron, Jill Hicks-Keeton, and Matthew Thiessen, Essays in Honor of Joel Marcus (Society of Biblical Literature, 2018), 211–42; Martinus C. de Boer, "Expulsion from the Synagogue: J.L. Martyn's History and Theology in the Fourth Gospel Revisited" (SNTS, Marburg, 2019).

7. Walsh, *The Origins of Early Christian Literature*, 53.

8. For a consideration of the popularity of Martyn's book, see Adele Reinhartz, "Story and History: John, Judaism, and the Historical Imagination," in *John and Judaism: A Contested Relationship in Context.*, ed. R. Alan Culpepper and Paul N. Anderson (Atlanta: SBL Press, 2017), 113–26.

9. Peter Brown, *Journeys of the Mind: A Life in History* (Princeton: Princeton University Press, 2023), 647–48.

10. A few examples among many: R. Alan Culpepper, *Anatomy of the Fourth Gospel: A Study in Literary Design* (Philadelphia: Fortress, 1983); Michal Beth Dinkler, *Literary Theory and the New Testament*, AYBRL (New Haven: Yale University Press, 2019); Philip F. Esler, "From Ioudaioi to Children of God: The Development of a Non-Ethnic Group Identity in the Gospel of John," in *In Other Words: Essays on Social Science Methods and the New Testament in Honor of Jerome H. Neyrey*, ed. Anselm C. Hagedorn, Eric Stewart, and Zeba A. Crook (Sheffield, UK: Sheffield Phoenix Press, 2007), 106–36; Raimo Hakola, *Identity Matters: John, the Jews, and Jewishness* (Leiden: Brill, 2005).

11. Walsh, *The Origins of Early Christian Literature*, 96.

12. Walsh, 96.

13. Lamb, "Language of John," 47.

14. Skinner, "Rise, Demise," 3.

15. Byers, "Johannine Community Vision," 123.

16. Byers, "Johannine Community Vision," 130.

17. Walsh, *The Origins of Early Christian Literature*, 55.

18. Walsh, 99.

19. Hugo Méndez, "Did the Johannine Community Exist?" *JSNT* 42 (2020): 350–74.

20. Walsh, *The Origins of Early Christian Literature*, 99.

21. Mendez p. 7

22. Adele Reinhartz, *The Word in the World: The Cosmological Tale in the Fourth Gospel* (Atlanta: Scholars Press, 1992).

23. For a detailed argument, see Adele Reinhartz, "The Johannine Community and Its Jewish Neighbors: A Reappraisal," in *What Is John? Literary and Social Readings of the Fourth Gospel.*, vol. 2 (Atlanta: Scholars Press, 1998), 111–38.

24. Robert Dean Kysar, "The Promises and Perils of Preaching on the Gospel of John," *Dialog* 19 (1980): 214–20. Kysar at this stage accepted this view though he later changed his mind. See Robert Kysar, "The Expulsion from the Synagogue: The

Tale of a Theory," in *Voyages with John Charting the Fourth Gospel* (Waco: Baylor University Press, 2006), 237–45.

25. Adele Reinhartz, "Women in the Johannine Community: An Exercise in Historical Imagination," in *A Feminist Companion to John*, ed. Amy-Jill Levine and Marianne Blickenstaff, vol. 2 (London; New York: Sheffield Academic Press, 2003), 14–33.

26. Circular reasoning has been criticized from the time of Aristotle. See Aristotle, *Posterior Analytics*, Book 1. "Now demonstration must be based on premisses prior to and better known than the conclusion; and the same things cannot simultaneously be both prior and posterior to one another: so circular demonstration is clearly not possible in the unqualified sense of 'demonstration,' but only possible if 'demonstration' be extended to include that other method of argument which rests on a distinction between truths prior to us and truths without qualification prior, i.e., the method by which induction produces knowledge." https://classics.mit.edu/Aristotle/posterior .1.i.html. Translation by G. R. G. Mure.

27. Byers, "Johannine Community Vision," 119.

28. Adele Reinhartz, *Cast out of the Covenant: Jews and Anti-Judaism in the Gospel of John* (Lanham, MD: Lexington Books/Fortress Academic, 2018).

29. Reinhartz, 84–86.

30. Here it seems to me that my "propulsion theory" may have been overinterpreted by Byers and Hunt, who both refer to it.

Bibliography

Abrams, Dominic, and Michael A. Hogg. "Metatheory: Lessons from Social Identity Research." *Personality and Social Psychology Review* 8.2 (2004): 98–106.

Agourides, Savas. "Peter and John in the Fourth Gospel," *Studia Evangelica* IV. Ed. F. L. Cross. Berlin: Akademie, 1968, 137–45.

Aitken, James K., and James Carleton Paget, eds. *The Jewish-Greek Tradition in Antiquity and the Byzantine Empire*, first edition. New York: Cambridge University Press, 2014.

Ajayi, Temitope Michael. "Anti-language, Slang and Cyber Scam Subculture among Urban Youth in Southwestern Nigeria." *International Journal of Cyber Criminology* 13 (July–December 2019): 511–33.

Anderson, Benedict. *Imagined Communities: Reflections on the Origin and Spread of Nationalism*. Revised edition. London and New York: Verso, 1991.

Anderson, Paul N. "Antichristic Errors—Flawed Interpretations Regarding the Johannine Antichrists," and idem, "Errors of the Antichrists—Proselytizing Schism and Assimilative Teaching within the Johannine Situation." Pages 196–216 and 217–40 in *Text and Community, Essay in Commemoration of Bruce M. Metzger*, Vol. 1. Edited by J. Harold Ellens. Sheffield: Sheffield Phoenix Press, 2007.

———. "Anti-Semitism and Religious Violence as Flawed Interpretations of the Gospel of John." Pages 265–311 in *John and Judaism: A Contested Relationship in Context*. Edited by R. Alan Culpepper and Paul N. Anderson. Resources for Biblical Study 87. Atlanta: SBL Press, 2017.

———. "Aspects of Historicity in John: Implications for Archaeological and Jesus Studies." Pages 587–618 in *Jesus and Archaeology*. Edited by James H. Charlesworth. Grand Rapids: Eerdmans, 2006.

———. "Bakhtin's Dialogism and the Corrective Rhetoric of the Johannine Misunderstanding Dialogue: Exposing Seven Crises in the Johannine Situation." Pages 133–59 in *Bakhtin and Genre Theory in Biblical Studies*; Semeia Studies 63. Edited by Roland Boer. Atlanta: Society of Biblical Literature, 2007.

———. "Identity and Congruence—The Ethics of Integrity in the Johannine Epistles." Pages 331–51 in *Biblical Ethics and Application: Purview, Validity, and Relevance of Biblical Texts in Ethical Discourse*. Kontexte und Normen neutestamentlicher Ethik (Contexts and Norms of New Testament Ethics) 9. Edited Ruben

Zimmermann and Stephan Joubert. Wissenschaftliche Untersuchungen zum Neuen Testament 1.384. Tübingen: Mohr Siebeck, 2017.

———. "Jesus, the Eschatological Prophet in the Fourth Gospel: A Case Study in John's Dialectical Tensions." Pages 271–99 in *Reading the Gospel of John's Christology as Jewish Messianism: Royal, Prophetic, and Divine Messiahs*. Edited by Ben Reynolds and Gabriele Boccaccini. Ancient Judaism and Early Christianity 106. Leiden: Brill, 2018.

———. "Mark and John—The Bi-Optic Gospels." Pages 175–88 in *Jesus in Johannine Tradition*. Edited by Robert T. Fortna and Tom Thatcher. Louisville: Westminster John Knox, 2001.

———. "Mark, John, and Answerability: Interfluentiality and Dialectic between the Second and Fourth Gospels." *Liber Annuus* 63 (2013): 197–245.

———. "Negotiating Complexity Within the Dialectical and Cosmopolitan Johannine Situation." *Religions* (2024; under review).

———. "On Guessing Points and Naming Stars—The Epistemological Origins of John's Christological Tensions." Pages 311–45 in *The Gospel of St. John and Christian Theology*. Edited by Richard Bauckham and Carl Mosser. Grand Rapids: Eerdmans, 2007.

———. "On 'Seamless Robes' and 'Leftover Fragments'—A Theory of Johannine Composition." Pages 169–218 in *The Origins of John's Gospel*. Edited by Stanley E. Porter and Hughson T. Ong. Leiden: Brill, 2016.

———. "On Biblical Forgeries and Imagined Communities—A Critical Analysis of recent Criticism." *The Bible and Interpretation* (April 2020): https://bibleinterp .arizona.edu/articles/biblical-forgeries-and-imagined-communities-critical -analysis-recent-criticism.

———. "Petrine Ministry and Christocracy: A Response to Ut Unum Sint." *One in Christ* 40:1 (2005): 3–39.

———. "Raymond Brown's *Community of the Beloved Disciple*—A New Introduction by Paul N. Anderson." New York: Paulist, 2024.

———. "Revelation 17:1–14." *Interpretation* 63.1 (2009): 60–61.

———. "Revelation and Rhetoric in John 9:1–10:21—Two Dialogical Modes Operative within the Johannine Narrative." Pages 441–70 in *The Gospels and Ancient Literary Criticism: Continuing the Debate on Gospel Genre(s)*. Edited by David P. Moessner, Matthew Calhoun, and Tobias Nicklas. Wissenschaftliche Untersuchungen zum Neuen Testament 1.451. Tübingen: Mohr Siebeck, 2020.

———. *The Christology of the Fourth Gospel: Its Unity and Disunity in the Light of John 6*, third edition. Eugene: Cascade Books, 2010.

———. "The Cognitive Origins of John's Christological Unity and Disunity." *Horizons in Biblical Theology; An International Dialogue* 17 (1995): 1–24.

———. "The Community that Raymond Brown Left Behind: Reflections on the Johannine Dialectical Situation." Pages 47–93 in *Communities in Dispute: Current Scholarship on the Johannine Epistles*. Edited by R. Alan Culpepper and Paul N. Anderson. Early Christianity and Its Literature 13. Atlanta: Society of Biblical Literature, 2014.

Bibliography

———. *The Fourth Gospel and the Quest for Jesus: Modern Foundations Reconsidered.* Library of New Testament Studies 321. London: T&T Clark, 2006.

———. "The Johannine Logos-Hymn: A Cross-Cultural Celebration of God's Creative-Redemptive Work." Pages 219–42 in *Creation Stories in Dialogue: The Bible, Science, and Folk Traditions* (Radboud Prestige Lecture Series by Alan Culpepper). Edited by R. Alan Culpepper and Jan van der Watt. Biblical Interpretation Series 139. Leiden: Brill, 2016.

———. "The Having-Sent-Me Father—Aspects of Agency, Encounter, and Irony in the Johannine Father-Son Relationship." *Semeia* 85 (1999): 33–57.

———. "The Origin and Development of the Johannine *Egō Eimi* Sayings in Cognitive-Critical Perspective." *Journal for the Study of the Historical Jesus* 9 (2011): 139–206.

———. *The Riddles of the Fourth Gospel: An Introduction to the Gospel of John.* Minneapolis: Fortress, 2011.

———. "The *Sitz im Leben* of the Johannine Bread of Life Discourse and its Evolving Context." Pages 1–59 in *Critical Readings of John 6.* Edited by R. Alan Culpepper. Biblical Interpretation Series 22. Leiden: E.J. Brill, 1997.

———. "The Son of Zebedee and the Fourth Gospel: Some Clues on John's Authorship and the State of the Johannine Question." Pages 17–82 and 241–49 in *El Evangelio de Juan. Origen, Contenido, Perspectivas—The Gospel of John. Origin, Content, Perspectives. Colección Teología Hoy* 80. Edited by Bernardo Estrada and Luis Guillermo Sarasa. Bogota: Editorial Pontificia Universidad Javeriana / Studiorum Novi Testamenti Societas, 2018.

———. "'You Have the Words of Eternal Life!' Is Peter Presented as Returning the Keys of the Kingdom to Jesus in John 6:68?" *Neotestamentica* 41:1 (2007): 6–41.

Anderson, Paul N., with Felix Just, S.J., and Tom Thatcher, eds. *John, Jesus, and History, Volume 1: Critical Appraisals of Critical Views.* Symposium Series 44. Atlanta / Leiden: SBL Press / E.J. Brill, 2007.

———. *John, Jesus, and History, Volume 2: Aspects of Historicity in the Fourth Gospel.* Early Christianity and Its Literature 2. Atlanta / Leiden: SBL Press / E. J. Brill, 2009.

———. *John, Jesus, and History, Volume 3: Glimpses of Jesus Through the Johannine Lens.* Early Christianity and its Literature 18. Atlanta: SBL Press, 2016.

Aristotle. *Posterior Analytics.* Translated by G. R. G. Mure. CreateSpace Independent Publishing Platform, 2016.

Ashton, John. *Understanding the Fourth Gospel.* Oxford: Oxford University Press, 2009.

Atkins, J. D. *The Doubt of the Apostles and the Resurrection Faith of the Early Church.* Wissenschaftliche Untersuchungen zum Neuen Testament 2.495. Tübingen: Mohr Siebeck, 2019.

Attridge, Harold W. *Essays on John and Hebrews.* Wissenschaftliche Untersuchungen zum Neuen Testament 1.264. Tübingen: Mohr Siebeck, 2010.

———. *History, Theology, and Narrative Rhetoric in the Fourth Gospel.* The Pére Marquette Lecture in Theology. Milwaukee: Marquette University Press, 2019.

———. "Johannine Christianity." Pages 125–43 in *The Cambridge History of Christianity: Origins to Constantine*. Edited by Margaret M. Mitchell, Frances M. Young, and K. Scott Bowie. Cambridge: Cambridge University Press, 2006.

———. Review of *Text, Context and the Johannine Community: A Sociolinguistic Analysis of the Johannine Writings*, by David A. Lamb. *Catholic Biblical Quarterly* 78.3 (2016): 556–57.

———. "The Restless Quest for the Beloved Disciple." Pages 71–80 in *Early Christian Voices: In Texts, Traditions, and Symbols: Essays in Honor of François Bovon*. Edited by David H. Warren, Ann Graham Brock and David W. Pao. Biblical Interpretation Series 66. Leiden: Brill, 2003.

Auer, Peter and Frans Hinskens. "The Role of Interpersonal Accommodation in a Theory of Language Change." Pages 335–57 in *Dialect Change: The Convergence and Divergence of Dialects in Contemporary Societies*. Edited by Peter Auer, Frans Hinskens, and Paul Kerswill. Cambridge: Cambridge University Press, 2005.

Augustine, *Confessions*. Edited and translated by C. J. B. Hammond. Loeb Classical Library 26–27. Cambridge: MA; Harvard University Press, 2016.

Augoustinos, Martha. "History as a Rhetorical Source: Using Historical Narratives to Argue and Explain." Pages 135–45 in *How to Analyze Talk in Institutional Settings: A Casebook of Methods*. Edited by Alec W. McHoul and Mark Rapley. London: Continuum, 2001.

Aune, David E. Review of *The Gospel of John in Christian History: Essays for Interpreters*, by J. Louis Martyn, *Catholic Biblical Quarterly* 43.1 (1981): 137–39.

Baker, Paul. *Fabulosa! The Story of Polari, Britain's Secret Gay Language*. London: Reaktion Books, 2019.

Banks, Robert J. *Paul's Idea of Community: Spirit and Culture in House Churches*. Grand Rapids: Baker, 2020.

Barash, Jeffrey Andrew. "Qu'est-ce que la mémoire collective? Réflexions sur l'interprétation de la mémoire chez Paul Ricoeur." *Revue de Métaphysique et de Morale* 2 (2006): 85–95.

Barclay, John M. G. "Ἰουδαῖος: Ethnicity and Translation." Pages 46–58 in *Ethnicity, Race, Religion: Identities and Ideologies in Early Jewish and Christian Texts, and in Modern Biblical Interpretation*. Edited by Katherine M. Hockey and David G. Horrell. London: T & T Clark, 2018.

———. "Mirror-Reading a Polemical Letter: Galatians as a Test Case." *Journal for the Study of the New Testament* 31.1 (1987): 79–93.

———. "Universalism and Particularism: Twin Components of Both Judaism and Early Christianity." Pages 207–24 in *A Vision for the Church: Studies in Early Christian Ecclesiology in Honour of J. P. M. Sweet*. Edited by Marcus Bockmuehl and Michael B. Thompson. Edinburgh: T & T Clark, 1997.

Barker, James W. *John's Use of Matthew*. Minneapolis: Fortress, 2015.

Barlow, Michael. "Individual differences and usage-based grammar." *International Journal of Corpus Linguistics* 18.4 (2013): 443–78.

Barrett, C. K. *Essays on John*. London: SPCK, 1982.

Bibliography 241

———. "Johanneisches Christentum." Pages 255–78 in *Die Anfänge des Christentums: Alte Welt und neue Hoffnung*. Ed. Jürgen Becker. Stuttgart: W. Kohlhammer, 1987.

———. *The Gospel According to St. John: An Introduction with Commentary and Notes on the Greek Text*, second edition. Philadelphia: Westminster, 1978.

Barton, Stephen C. "Can We Identify the Gospel Audiences?" Pages 173–94 in *The Gospel for All Christians: Rethinking the Gospel Audiences*. Edited by Richard Bauckham. Grand Rapids: Eerdmans, 1998.

Basden, Andrew. *Foundations and Practice of Research: Adventures with Dooyeweerd's Philosophy*. Routledge Advances in Research Methods. Abingdon: Routledge, 2020.

Bauckham, Richard. "For Whom Were Gospels Written?" Pages 26–44 in *The Gospel for all Christians: Rethinking the Gospel Audiences*. Edited by Richard Bauckham. Grand Rapids: Eerdmans, 1998.

———. "For Whom Were Gospels Written?" *HTS Teologiese Studies/Theological Studies* 55.4 (1999): 865–82.

———. "John for Readers of Mark." Pages 147–71 in *The Gospel for All Christians: Rethinking the Gospel Audiences*. Ed. Richard Bauckham. Grand Rapids: Eerdmans, 1998.

———. *The Gospels for All Christians: Rethinking the Gospel Audiences*. Grand Rapids: Eerdmans, 1998.

———. *The Testimony of the Beloved Disciple: Narrative, History, and Theology in the Gospel of John*. Grand Rapids: Baker Academic, 2007.

Bauer, Walter. *Orthodoxy and Heresy in Earliest Christianity*. Edited by Robert A. Kraft, Gerhard Krodel. Translated by David Steinmetz. Philadelphia: Fortress Press, 1971.

Baumgarten-Crusius. Ludwig F. O. *Theologische Auslegung der Johanneischen Schriften*, 2 volumes. Jena: Fredrich Luden, 1843.

Baur, Ferdinand Christian. *The Church History of the First Three Centuries*. Translated by Allan Menzies. 2 volumes, thirdedition. London: Williams and Norgate, 1878.

Beal, Timothy. "Reception History and Beyond: Toward the Cultural History of Scriptures." *Biblical Interpretation* 19.4–5 (2011): 357–72.

Becker, Adam H. and Annette Yoshiko Reed, eds. *The Ways that Never Parted: Jews and Christians in Antiquity and the Middle Ages*. Minneapolis: Augsburg Fortress, 2007.

Becker, Eve-Marie, Helen K. Bond, and Catrin H. Williams. *John's Transformation of Mark*. London: Bloomsbury T&T Clark, 2021.

Bennema, Cornelis. "The Historical Reliability of the Gospel of John." *Foundations* 67 (2014): 4–25.

Bérenger-Badel, Agnès. "Formation et compétences des gouverneurs de province dans l'empire romain." *Dialogues d'histoire ancienne* 30.2 (2004): 35–56.

Berger, Peter L. and Thomas Luckmann. *The Social Construction of Reality: A Treatise in the Sociology of Knowledge*. New York: Anchor, 1967.

Bergs, Alexander. "The Uniformitarian Principle and the Risk of Anachronisms in Language and Social History." Pages 80–98 in *The Handbook of Historical*

242 Bibliography

Sociolinguistics. Edited by J. M Hernández-Campoy and J. C. Conde-Silvestre. John Wiley & Sons, 2012.

Bernier, Jonathan. *Aposynagōgos and the Historical Jesus in John: Rethinking the Historicity of the Johannine Expulsion Passages.* Biblical Interpretation Series 122. Leiden: Brill, 2013.

Biber, Douglas and Susan Conrad. *Register, Genre, and Style.* Cambridge Textbooks in Linguistics. Cambridge: Cambridge University Press, 2009.

Bickermann, E. "*Utilitas Crucis*: Observations sur les récits du procès de Jésus dans les évangiles canoniques." *Revue de l'Histoire des Religions* 112 (1935): 169–241.

Blomberg, Craig L. "The Gospels for Specific Communities and All Christians." Pages 111–33 in *The Audience of the Gospels: The Origin and Function of the Gospels in Early Christianity.* Edited by Edward W. Klink III. Library of New Testament Studies 353. London: T & T Clark, 2010.

―――. *The Historical Reliability of John's Gospel.* Downers Grove, IL: InterVarsity Press, 2001.

Bockmuehl, Markus. *Simon Peter in Scripture and Memory: The New Testament Apostle in the Early Church.* Grand Rapids: Baker Academic, 2012.

Bolinger, Dwight. *Aspects of Language*, second edition. New York: Harcourt, Brace, Jovanovich, 1975.

Bond, Helen K. "Barabbas Remembered." Pages 59–71 in *Jesus and Paul: Global Perspectives in Honor of James D. G. Dunn for His 70th Birthday.* Edited by B. J. Oropeza, C. K. Robertson, and Douglas C. Mohrmann, Library of New Testament Studies 414. London: T & T Clark, 2009.

Boomershine, Thomas E. "The Medium and Message of John: Audience Address and Audience Identity in the Fourth Gospel." Pages 92–120 in *The Fourth Gospel in First-Century Media Culture.* Edited by Anthony Le Donne and Tom Thatcher. London: T & T Clark, 2013.

Borgen, Peder. *Bread from Heaven: An Exegetical Study of the Concept of Manna in the Gospel of John and the Writings of Philo.* Novum Testamentum Supplements 10. Leiden: E.J. Brill, 1965.

―――. "God's Agent in the Fourth Gospel." Pages 83–95 in *The Interpretation of John*, 2nd ed. Edited by John Ashton. Edinburgh: T & T Clark, 1997.

Botha, Pieter. *Orality and Literacy in Early Christianity.* Biblical Performance Criticism 5. Eugene, OR: Cascade, 2012.

―――. "The Historical Domitian—Illustrating Some of the Problems of Historicity." *Neotestamentica* 23 (1989): 45–59.

Bourdieu, Pierre. *Distinction: A Social Critique of the Judgement of Taste.* Translated by Richard Nice. Cambridge, MA: Harvard University Press, 1979.

Brakke, David. "Parables and Plain Speech in the Fourth Gospel and the Apocryphon of James." *Journal of Early Christian Studies* 7.2 (Summer 1999): 187–218.

Brant, Jo-Ann A. *Dialogue and Drama: Elements of Greek Tragedy in the Fourth Gospel.* Peabody, MA: Hendrickson, 2004.

―――. *John.* Paideia Commentaries on the New Testament. Grand Rapids: Baker Academic, 2011.

Brewer, Marilynn B. "Social Identity Complexity and Acceptance of Diversity." Pages 9–33 in *The Psychology of Social and Cultural Diversity*. Edited by Richard J. Crisp. Oxford: Wiley-Blackwell, 2010.

Brooke, Alan E. *A Critical and Exegetical Commentary on the Johannine Epistles*. London: Bloomsbury, 2014.

Brown, Peter. *Journeys of the Mind: A Life in History*. Princeton: Princeton University Press, 2023.

Brown, Raymond E. "Johannine Ecclesiology: The Community's Origins." *Interpretation* 31.4 (1977): 379–93.

———. "Not Jewish Christianity and Gentile Christianity but Types of Jewish/ Gentile Christianity," *Catholic Biblical Quaterly* 45 (1983): 74–79.

———. Review of J. Louis Martyn, *History and Theology in the Fourth Gospel* in *Union Seminary Quarterly Review* 23 (1968): 392–94.

———. *The Churches the Apostles Left Behind*. New York: Paulist Press, 1984.

———. *The Community of the Beloved Disciple*. New York: Paulist, 1979.

———. *The Epistles of John*. Anchor Bible 30. New York: Doubleday, 1983.

———. *The Gospel According to John*. 2 volumes. Anchor Bible 29-29A. New York: Doubleday, 1966–70.

Brown, Raymond E. and John P. Meier. *Antioch and Rome: New Testament Cradles of Catholic Christianity*. Mahwah, NJ: Paulist, 1983.

Brown, Raymond E., Karl P. Donfried, and John Reumann, eds. *Peter in the New Testament*. Minneapolis / New York: Augsburg /Paulist, 1973.

Brown, Sherri. "What Is Truth? Jesus, Pilate, and the Staging of the Dialogue of the Cross in John 18:28–19:16a." *Catholic Biblical Quarterly* 77.1 (2015): 69–86.

Brunt, P. A. "*Laus imperii*." Pages 288–323 In *Roman Imperial Themes*. Oxford: Clarendon, 1990.

———. *Roman Imperial Themes*. Oxford: Clarendon, 1990.

Bultmann, Rudolf K. *The Gospel of John: A Commentary*. Translated by G. R. Beasley-Murray, R. W. N. Hoare, and J. K. Riches. Philadelphia: John Knox, 1971.

———. *The Johannine Epistles: A Commentary on the Johannine Epistles*. Hermeneia. Translated by R. Philip O'Hara, Lane C. McGaughy, and Robert W. Funk. Edited by Robert W. Funk. Philadelphia: Fortress Press, 1973.

Burkill, T. Alec. Review of J. Louis Martyn, *History and Theology in the Fourth Gospel* in *Journal of Biblical Literature* 87.4 (1968): 439–42.

Burridge, Richard. "About People, by People, for People: Gospel Genre and Audiences." Pages 113–45 in *The Gospels for All Christians*. Edited by Richard Bauckham. Grand Rapids: Eerdmans, 1998.

———. *What Are the Gospels? A Comparison with Graeco-Romans Biography*, third edition. Baylor: Baylor University Press, 2018.

Byers, Andrew J. *Ecclesiology and Theosis in the Gospel of John*. Society for the Study of the New Testament Monograph Series, 166. Cambridge: Cambridge University Press, 2017.

———. "Is the Johannine Community Hypothesis Still Viable?" *Didaktikos* 6.3 (2023): 33–36.

244 *Bibliography*

———. *John and Others: Jewish Relations, Christian Origins, and the Sectarian Hermeneutic.* Waco, TX: Baylor University Press, 2021.

———. "One Flock, One Shepherd, One God: The Oneness Motif of John's Gospel." Pages 195–215 in *One God, One People: Unity and Oneness in Early Christianity.* Edited by Stephen C. Barton and Andrew J. Byers. Resources for Biblical Studies 104. Atlanta: SBL Press, 2023.

Carson, D. A. *The Gospel According to John.* Pillar New Testament Commentary. Grand Rapids: Eerdmans, 1991.

Carter, Warren. *John and Empire: Initial Explorations.* New York: T & T Clark, 2008.

———. "Social Identities, Subgroups, and John's Gospel: Jesus the Prototype and Pontius Pilate (John 18.28–19.16)." Pages 235–51 in *T&T Clark Handbook to Social Identity in the New Testament.* Edited by J. Brian Tucker and Coleman A. Baker. London: Bloomsbury, 2014.

Cassidy, Richard J. *John's Gospel in New Perspective: Christology and the Realities of Roman Power.* Edited by Paul N. Anderson. Johannine Monograph Series 3. Eugene, OR: Wipf & Stock, 2015.

Castelli, Elizabeth A. *Martyrdom and Memory: Early Christian Culture Making.* Gender, Theory, and Religion. New York: Columbia University Press, 2004.

Chanikuzhy, Jacob. *Jesus, the Eschatological Temple: An Exegetical Study of Jn 2,13-22 in the Light of the Pre-70 C.E. Eschatological Temple Hopes and the Synoptic Temple Action.* Contributions to Biblical Exegesis and Theology 57. Leuven: Peeters, 2012.

Chapman, David W. *Ancient Jewish and Christian Perceptions of Crucifixion.* Grand Rapids: Baker Academic, 2010.

Charlesworth, James H. *The Beloved Disciple: Whose Witness Validates the Gospel of John?* Valley Forge, PA: Trinity Press International, 1995.

Choi, Jin Young. "John's Writings and Empire: Views of Empire Studies and Postcolonial Criticism." Pages 162–89 in *The Oxford Handbook of Postcolonial Biblical Criticism.* Edited by R. S. Sugirtharajah. Oxford: Oxford University Press, 2018.

Cinnirella, Marco. "Exploring Temporal Aspects of Social Identity: The Concept of Possible Social Identities." *European Journal of Social Psychology* 28.2 (1998): 227–48.

Cirafesi, Wally V. *John Within Judaism: Religion, Ethnicity, and the Shaping of Jesus-Oriented Jewishness in the Fourth Gospel.* Ancient Judaism and Early Christianity 112. Leiden: Brill, 2021.

———. "Rethinking John and 'the Synagogue' in Light of Expulsion from Public Assemblies in Antiquity." *Journal of Biblical Literature* 142 (2023): 677–97.

———. "The Johannine Community Hypothesis (1968–Present): Past and Present Approaches and a New Way Forward." *Currents in Biblical Research* 12.2 (2014): 17–93.

———. "The 'Johannine Community' in (More) Current Research: A Critical Appraisal of Recent Methods and Models." *Neotestamentica* 48.2 (2014): 341–64.

Clarke, Susanna. *Jonathan Strange & Mr. Norrell.* London: Bloomsbury, 2004.

Bibliography

Cohen, Shaye J. D. "'Those Who Say They Are Jews and Are Not': How Do You Know a Jew in Antiquity When You See One?" Pages 1–45 in *Diasporas in Antiquity*. Edited by Shaye J. D. Cohen and Ernest S. Frerichs. Atlanta: Scholars Press, 1993.

Collingwood, R. G. *The Idea of History*. Oxford: Oxford University Press, 1956.

Collins, Raymond F. "Speaking of the Jews: 'Jews' in the Discourse Material of the Fourth Gospel." Pages 158–75 in *Anti-Judaism and the Fourth Gospel: Papers of the Leuven Colloquium, 2000*. Jewish and Christian Heritage Series 1. Edited by Reimund Bieringer, Didier Pollefeyt, and Frederique Vandecasteele-Vanneuville.

Coloe, Mary. *Dwelling in the Household of God: Johannine Ecclesiology and Spirituality*. Collegeville, MN: Liturgical Press, 2007.

———. *God Dwells with Us: Temple Symbolism in the Fourth Gospel*. Collegeville, MN: Liturgical Press, 2001.

Conway, Colleen M. "New Historicism and the Historical Jesus in John: Friends or Foes?" Pages 199–216 in *John, Jesus, and History, Vol 1: Critical Appraisals of Critical Views*. Edited by Paul Anderson, Felix Just, and Tom Thatcher. Atlanta: Society of Biblical Literature, 2007.

Coser, Lewis A. *The Functions of Social Conflict*. Reprint. London: Routledge, 1998.

Cruise, Colin G. *The Letters of John*. Pillar New Testament Commentary. Grand Rapids: Eerdmans, 2000.

Crystal, David. *A Dictionary of Linguistics and Phonetics,* sixth edition. Oxford: Blackwell, 2008.

Cullmann, Oscar. *The Johannine Circle: Its Place Among the Disciples of Jesus and in Early Christianity. A Study in the Origin of the Gospel of John.* Translated by J. Bowden. New Testament Library. London: SCM, 1976.

Culpepper, R. Alan. *Anatomy of the Fourth Gospel: A Study in Literary Design.* Foundations and Facets. Philadelphia: Fortress, 1987.

———. Review of J. Louis Martyn, *History and Theology in the Fourth Gospel* in *Review and Expositor* 76.4 (1979): 573–75.

———. *The Johannine School: An Evaluation of the Johannine-School Hypothesis Based on an Investigation of the Nature of Ancient Schools.* SBL Dissertation Series 26. Missoula, MT: Scholars, 1975.

Culpepper, R. Alan and Paul N. Anderson, eds. *John and Judaism: A Contested Relationship in Context*. Resources for Biblical Study 87. Atlanta: SBL Press, 2017.

Culpepper, R. Alan and Paul N. Anderson, eds. *Communities in Dispute: Current Scholarship on the Johannine Epistles*. Early Christianity and its Literature 13. Atlanta: SBL, 2014.

Dawson, Zachary K. Review of David A. Lamb, *Text, Context and the Johannine Community: A Sociolinguistic Analysis of the Johannine Writings, Dialogismos* 1.1 (2016): 1–4.

De Boer, Martinus C. "*Birkat Ha-Minim* Revisited." *New Testament Studies* 55.4 (2009): 523–51.

———. "Expulsion from the Synagogue: J.L. Martyn's History and Theology in the Fourth Gospel Revisited." *New Testament Studies* 66.3 (2020): 367–91.

246   *Bibliography*

————. "Narrative Criticism, Historical Criticism, and the Gospel of John." *Journal for the Study of the New Testament* 47 (1992): 35–48.

————. "The Johannine Community Under Attack in Recent Scholarship." Pages 211–41 in *The Ways That Often Parted: Essays in Honor of Joel Marcus*. Edited by Lori Baron, Jill Hicks-Keeton, and Matthew Thiessen. Early Christianity and Its Literature 24. Atlanta: SBL Press, 2018.

————. "The Nazoreans: Living at the Boundary of Judaism and Christianity." Pages 239–62 in *Tolerance and Intolerance in Early Judaism and Christianity*. Edited by Graham N. Stanton and Guy G. Stroumsa. Cambridge: Cambridge University, 1998.

————. "The Story of the Johannine Community and its Literature." Pages 63–82 in *The Oxford Handbook of Johannine Studies*. Edited by Judith M. Lieu and Martinus C. de Boer. Oxford: Oxford University Press, 2018.

Decker, Rodney J. "Markan Idiolect in the Study of the Greek of the New Testament." Pages 43–66 in *The Language of the New Testament: Context, History, and Development*. Edited by Stanley E. Porter and Andrew Pitts. Linguistic Biblical Studies 6. Leiden: Brill, 2013.

Demetrius, *On Style*. Edited and translated by W. H. Fyfe, S. Halliwell, D. C. Innes, and W. Rhys Roberts. Loeb Classical Library 199. Cambridge; MA; Harvard University Press, 1995.

Dench, Emma. *Romulus' Asylum: Roman Identities from the Age of Alexander to the Age of Hadrian*. Oxford: Oxford University Press, 2005.

den Hollander, William. *Josephus, the Emperors, and the City of Rome: From Hostage to Historian*. Ancient Judaism and Early Christianity 86. Leiden: Brill, 2014.

Despotis, Athanasios. Review of David A. Lamb, *Text, Context and the Johannine Community: A Sociolinguistic Analysis of the Johannine Writings*. *Religious Studies Review* 42.1 (2016): 44.

Dinkler, Michal Beth. *Literary Theory and the New Testament*. Anchor Yale Bible Reference Library. New Haven: Yale University Press, 2019.

Do, Toan. "The Epistles of John." Pages 444–58 in *The State of New Testament Studies: A Survey of Recent Research*. Edited by Scot McKnight and Nijay K. Gupta. Grand Rapids: Baker Academic, 2019.

Dodd, C. H. *Historical Tradition in the Fourth Gospel*. Cambridge: Cambridge University Press, 1963.

————. *The Interpretation of the Fourth Gospel*. Cambridge: Cambridge University Press, 1953.

————. *The Johannine Epistles*. Hodder & Stoughton: London, 1946.

Doole, J. Andrew. "To Be 'An Out-of-the Synagoguer.'" *Journal for the Study of the New Testament* 43.3 (2021): 389–410.

Donfried, Karl P. "Ecclesiastical Authority in 2-3 John." Pages 325–33 in *L'Evanglie de Jean*. Edited by Marinus de Jonge. Bibliotheca Ephemeridum Theologicarum Lovaniensium 44. Leuven: Leuven University Press, 1977.

Dovidio, John F., Samuel L. Gaertner, and Tamar Saguy. "Another View of 'We': Majority and Minority Group Perspectives on a Common Ingroup Identity." *European Review of Social Psychology* 18.1 (2007): 296–330.

Bibliography

Dray, William H. *The Historical Imagination: R. G. Collingwood's Idea of History.* Oxford: Oxford University Press, 2011.

Droge, Arthur J. "The Status of Peter in the Fourth Gospel: A Note on John 18:10–11." *Journal of Biblical Literature* 109 (1990): 307–11.

Dube, Musa W. "John 18:2–19: A Postcolonial Trickster Reading of the Arrest and Trial of Jesus." *Tubinger Theologische Quartalschrift* 2 (2022): 54–73.

Dube, Musa W. and Jeffrey L. Staley, eds. *John and Postcolonialism: Travel, Space, and Power, Bible and Postcolonialism.* Sheffield: Sheffield Academic, 2002.

Duke, Paul D. *Irony in the Fourth Gospel.* Atlanta: John Knox Press, 1985.

Dunderberg, Ismo. "The Beloved Disciple in John: Ideal Figure in an Early Christian Controversy." Pages 243–69 in *Fair Play: Diversity and Conflicts in Early Christianity: Essays in Honour of Heikki Räisänen.* Edited by Ismo Dunderberg, Christopher Tuckett, and Kari Syreeni. Novum Testamentum Supplements 103; Leiden: Brill, 2002.

Dunn, James D.G. "John's Gospel and the Oral Gospel Tradition." Pages 157–85 in *The Fourth Gospel in First-Century Media Culture.* Edited by Anthony Le Donne and Tom Thatcher. London: T & T Clark, 2013.

———. *The Partings of the Ways: Between Christianity and Judaism and Their Significance for the Character of Christianity,* second edition. London: SCM, 2006.

Eco, Umberto. *A Theory of Semiotics.* Bloomington: Indiana University Press, 1976.

Edwards, Ruth B. *The Johannine Epistles.* Sheffield: Sheffield Academic, 1996.

Ehrlich, Uri and Ruth Langer, "The Earliest Texts of the *Birkat Haminim.*" *Hebrew Union College Annual* 76 (2005): 63–112.

Ehrman, Bart D. *Forgery and Counterforgery: The Use of Literary Deceit in Early Christian Polemics.* Oxford: Oxford University Press, 2012.

———. *The New Testament: A Historical Introduction to the Early Christian Writings,* seventh edition. Oxford: Oxford University Press, 2019.

Ellis, Nicholas J. "Biblical Exegesis and Linguistics: *A Prodigal History.*" Pages 227–45 in *Linguistics and New Testament Greek: Key Issues in the Current Debate.* Edited by David Alan Black and Benjamin L. Merkle. Grand Rapids: Baker Academic, 2020.

Ellis, Peter F. *The Genius of John: A Composition-Critical Commentary on the Fourth Gospel.* Collegeville, MN: Liturgical, 1984.

Elowsky, Joel C., *Commentary on the Gospel of John: Theodore of Mopsuestia.* Translated by Marco Conti. Edited by Thomas C. Oden and Gerald L. Bray. Ancient Christian Texts. Downers Grove, IL: IVP Academic, 2010.

Esler, Philp F. "Community and Gospel in Early Christianity: A Response to Richard Bauckham's *Gospels for All Christians.*" *Scottish Journal of Theology* 51 (1998): 235–48.

———. "From Ioudaioi to Children of God: The Development of a Non-Ethnic Group Identity in the Gospel of John." Pages 106–36 in *In Other Words: Essays on Social Science Methods and the New Testament in Honor of Jerome H. Neyrey.* Edited by Anselm C. Hagedorn, Eric Stewart, and Zeba A. Crook. Sheffield: Sheffield Phoenix Press, 2007.

248 *Bibliography*

————. "Social-Scientific Readings of the Gospel and Letters of John." Pages 237–58 in *The Oxford Handbook of Johannine Studies*. Edited by Judith M. Lieu and Martinus C. de Boer. Oxford: Oxford University Press, 2018.

Esler, Philip F. and Ronald A. Piper. *Lazarus, Mary and Martha: Social-Scientific Approaches to the Gospel of John*. Minneapolis: Fortress, 2006.

Estes, Douglas. *The Temporal Mechanics of the Fourth Gospel*. Biblical Interpretation Series 92. Leiden: Brill, 2008.

Estrada, Rodolfo Galvan, III. *A Pneumatology of Race in the Gospel of John: An Ethnocritical Study*. Eugene, OR: Pickwick, 2019.

Ford, David F. *The Gospel of John: A Theological Commentary*. Grand Rapids: Baker Academic, 2021.

Forger, Deborah L. "Divine Embodiment in Jewish Antiquity: Rediscovering the Jewishness of John's Incarnate Christ." PhD dissertation. University of Michigan, 2017.

————. "Jesus as God's Word(s): Aurality, Epistemology and Embodiment in the Gospel of John." *Journal for the Study of the New Testament* 42 (2020): 274–302.

Fournier, Julien. *Entre tutelle romaine et autonomie civique: L'administration judiciaire dans les provinces hellénophones de l'empire romain, 129 av. J.C.–235 ap. J.C.* Athènes: Ecole française d'Athènes, 2010.

Frey, Jörg. *Die johanneische Eschatologie*. 3 volumes. Wissenschaftliche Untersuchungen zum Neuen Testament 1.96, 1.110, 1.117. Tübingen: Mohr Siebeck, 1997–2000.

————. *The Glory of the Crucified One: Christology and Theology in the Gospel of John*. Translated by Wayne Coppins and Christoph Heilig. Baylor-Mohr Siebeck Studies in Early Christianity. Waco, TX/Tübingen: Baylor/Mohr Siebeck, 2018.

————. *Theology and History in the Gospel of John: Tradition and Narration*. Waco, TX: Baylor University Press, 2018.

Fuglseth, Kåre. *Johannine Sectarianism in Perspective: A Sociological, Historical, and Comparative Analysis of Temple and Social Relationships in the Gospel of John, Philo, and Qumran*. Novum Testamentum Supplements 119. Leiden: Brill, 2005.

Fuhrmann, Christopher J. *Policing the Roman Empire: Soldiers, Administration, and Public Order*. Oxford: Oxford University Press, 2012.

Furlong, Dean. *The Identity of John the Evangelist: Revision and Reinterpretation in Early Christian Sources*. Lanham, MD: Lexington/Fortress Academic, 2020.

Gadamer, Hans-Georg. *Truth and Method*. Revised edition. Translated by Joel Weinsheimer and Donald G. Marshall. London: Bloomsbury Academic, 2021.

Galambush. Julie. *The Reluctant Parting: How the New Testament's Jewish Writers Created a Christian Book*. (New York: HarperCollins, 2005), 265–304.

Gaventa, Beverly Roberts. "The Archive of Excess: John 21 and the Problem of Narrative Closure." Pages 240–52 in *Exploring the Gospel of John: In Honor of D. Moody Smith*. Edited by R. Alan Culpepper and C. Clifton Black. Louisville: Westminster John Knox, 1996.

Genuyt, François. "La comparution de Jésus devant Pilate: Analyse sémiotique de Jean 18,28–19,16." *Religious Studies Review* 73.1 (1985): 133–46.

Bibliography

Glancy, Jennifer. "Torture: Flesh, Truth, and the Fourth Gospel." *Biblical Interpretation* 13.2 (2005): 107–36.

Goodman, Martin. "Nerva, the *Fiscus Judaicus* and Jewish Identity." *Journal of Roman Studies* 79.1 (1989): 40–44.

Gorman, Michael J. "John's Implicit Ethic of Enemy-Love." Pages 135–158 in *Johannine Ethics: The Moral World of the Gospel and Epistles of John.* Edited by Sherri Brown and Christopher W. Skinner. Minneapolis: Fortress, 2017.

Gray, Bethany and Jesse Egbert. "Editorial: Register and Register Variation." *Register Studies* 1.1 (2019): 1–9.

Grayston, Kenneth. "Jesus and the Church in St. John's Gospel." *London Quarterly and Holborn Review* 35 (1967): 106–15.

Grenfell, Bernard P. and Arthur S. Hunt (eds.). *The Oxyrhynchus Papyri: Part II.* (London: Egypt Exploration Fund, 1899), 296.

Griffith, Terry. "A Non-Polemical Reading of 1 John: Sin, Christology and the Limits of Johannine Christianity." *Tyndale Bulletin* 49.2 (1998): 253–76.

———. *Keep Yourselves from Idols: A New Look at 1 John.* Journal for the Study of the New Testament Supplement Series 233. London: Sheffield Academic, 2002.

Hägerland, Tobias. "John's Gospel: A Two-Level Drama?" *Journal for the Study of the New Testament* 25 (2003): 309–22.

Hahn, Ferdinand. "Sehen und Glauben im Johannesevangelium." Pages 521–37 in *Studien zum Neuen Testament 1.* Edited by Jörg Frey and Juliane Schlegel. Wissenschaftliche Untersuchungen zum Neuen Testament 1.191. Tübingen: Mohr Siebeck, 2006.

Haines-Eitzen, Kim. "Textual Communities in Late Antiquity." Pages 246–57 in *A Companion to Late Antiquity.* Edited by Philip Rousseau, with the assistance of Jutta Raithal. Oxford: Wiley-Blackwell, 2009.

Hakola, Raimo. *Identity Matters: John, the Jews, and Jewishness.* Leiden: Brill, 2005.

———. *Reconsidering Johannine Christianity: A Social Identity Approach.* New York: Routledge, 2015.

Hakola, Raimo, and Adele Reinhartz. "John's Pharisees." Pages 131–48 in *In Quest of the Historical Pharisees.* Edited by Jacob Neusner and Bruce Chilton. Waco, TX: Baylor University Press, 2007.

Hallbäck, Geert. "The Gospel of John as Literature: Literary Readings of the Fourth Gospel." Pages 31–46 in *New Readings in John: Literary and Theological Perspectives: Essays from the Scandinavian Conference on the Fourth Gospel, Arhus, 1997.* Edited by Johannes Nissen and Sigfred Pedersen. Journal for the Study of the New Testament Supplement Series 182. Sheffield: Sheffield Academic, 1999.

Halliday, Michael A. K. "Anti-languages." *American Anthropologist* 78.3 (1976): 570–84.

———. *Language and Society: Volume 10 of the Collected Works of M. A. K. Halliday.* Edited by Jonathan J. Webster. London: Continuum, 2007.

———. *Language as Social Semiotic: The Social Interpretation of Meaning.* London: Arnold, 1978.

Hanink, Johanna. "The *Life* of the Author in the Letters of 'Euripides.'" *Greek, Roman, and Byzantine Studies* 50.4 (2010): 537–64.

Haslam, S. Alexander. *Psychology in Organizations: The Social Identity Approach.* New York: SAGE, 2004.

Haslam, S. Alexander, Stephen D. Reicher, and Michael J. Platow. *The New Psychology of Leadership: Identity, Influence and Power.* Hove, UK: Psychology Press, 2011.

Hayes, Christine. *What's Divine About Divine Law? Early Perspectives.* Princeton: Princeton University Press, 2015.

Heath, Jane. "'Textual Communities': Brian Stock's Concept and Recent Scholarship on Antiquity." Pages 5–35 in *Scriptural Interpretation at the Interface between Education and Religion: In Memory of Hans Conzelmann.* Edited by Florian Wilk. Themes in Biblical Narrative 22. Leiden, Brill, 2018.

Hedrick, Charles W. "Authorial Presence and Narrator in John: Commentary and Story." Pages 74–93 in *Gospel Origins and Christian Beginnings: In Honor of James M. Robinson.* Edited by James E. Goehring, Charles W. Hedrick, Jack T. Sanders, and Hans Dieter Betz. Sonoma, CA: Polebridge Press, 1990.

Heilig, Christoph. "The New Perspective (on Paul) on Peter: Cornelius's Conversion, the Antioch Incident, and Peter's Stance Towards Gentiles in the Light of the Philosophy of Historiography." Pages 459–96 in *Christian Origins and the Establishment of the Early Jesus Movement.* Edited by Stanley E. Porter and Andrew W. Pitts, Texts and Editions for New Testament Study 12. Leiden: Brill, 2018.

Hengel, Martin. *The Johannine Question.* Translated by John Bowden. London: SCM, 1989.

Hicks-Keeton, Jill. *Arguing with Aseneth: Gentile Access to Israel's "Living God" in Jewish Antiquity.* Oxford: Oxford University Press, 2018.

Hill, Charles E. *The Johannine Corpus in the Early Church.* Oxford: Oxford University Press, 2004.

Hingley, Richard. *Globalizing Roman Culture: Unity, Diversity and Empire.* London: Routledge, 2005.

Hollington, Andrea and Nico Nassenstein. "From the Hood to Public Discourse: The Social Spread of African Youth Languages." *Anthropological Linguistics* 59.4 (Winter 2017): 390–413.

Holloway, Paul A. *Philippians: A Commentary, Hermeneia* (Minneapolis, MN: Fortress, 2017), 21n166.

Horrell, David G. *Ethnicity and Inclusion: Religion, Race, and Whiteness in Constructions of Jewish and Christian Identities.* Grand Rapids: Eerdmans, 2020.

Horsfall, Nicholas M. "Virgil, History and the Roman Tradition." *Prudentia* 8 (1976): 73–89.

Horsley, Richard, and Tom Thatcher. *John, Jesus, and the Renewal of Israel.* Grand Rapids: Eerdmans, 2013.

Hudson, Richard Anthony. *Sociolinguistics,* second edition. Cambridge: Cambridge University Press, 1996.

Bibliography

Hunt, Laura J. "Alien and Degenerate Milk: Embodiment, Structure and Viewpoint in Four Nursing Metaphors." *Journal for Interdisciplinary Biblical Studies* 4.1 (2022): 119–56.

———. "Alternatives to Mirror Reading." In *Socio-Scientific Approaches to Religious Enmity*. Edited by Christopher Porter. Routledge Interdisciplinary Perspectives on Biblical Criticism. London: Routledge, (forthcoming).

———. "Jesus Caesar: A Roman Reading of John 18:28–19:22." PhD dissertation; University of Wales Trinity Saint David, 2017.

———. *Jesus Caesar: A Roman Reading of the Johannine Trial Narrative*. Wissenschaftliche Untersuchungen zum Neuen Testament 2.506. Tübingen: Mohr Siebeck, 2019.

———. *John: A Social Identity Commentary*. T&T Clark Social Identity Commentaries on the New Testament. London: T&T Clark, forthcoming.

———. "Samaritan Israelites and Jews under the Shadow of Rome: Reading John 4:1–45 in Ephesus." In *Religions: Exploring the Complexity of Identities and Boundaries within the New Testament World* (under review).

Jackson Claire Rachel and Soldo Janja. "Introductions: Fictions of Genre." Pages 1–20 in *›Res vera, Res ficta‹: Fictionality in Ancient Epistolography*. Trends in Classics: Supplementary Series 149. Edited by Claire Rachel Jackson and Janja Soldo. Berlin: De Gruyter, 2023.

Jobes, Karen H. *1, 2, & 3 John*. Zondervan Exegetical Commentary on the New Testament. Grand Rapids: Zondervan, 2014.

Johnstone, Barbara. *The Linguistic Individual: Self-Expression in Language and Linguistics*. Oxford: Oxford University Press, 1996.

Josephus. *The Jewish War*, Volume III. Translated by Henry St. J. Thackeray. Loeb Classical Library 210. Cambridge, MA: Harvard University Press, 1928.

Kahl, Brigitte. *Galatians Re-Imagined: Reading with the Eyes of the Vanquished*. Minneapolis: Fortress Press, 2010.

Kanagaraj, J. J. "The Implied Ethics of the Fourth Gospel: A Reinterpretation of the Decalogue." *Tyndale Bulletin* 52.1 (2001): 33–60.

Käsemann, Ernst. *The Testament of Jesus*. Translated by Gerhard Krodel (1968). Johannine Monograph Series 6. Edited by Paul N. Anderson. Eugene: Wipf & Stock, 2017.

Katz, Steven T. "Issues in the Separation of Judaism and Christianity after 70 C.E.: A Reconsideration." *Journal of Biblical Literature* 103.1 (1984): 43–76,

Keener, Craig S. *The Gospel of John: A Commentary.* 2 volumes. Peabody, MA: Hendrickson, 2003).

Keith, Chris. "The Competitive Textualization of the Jesus Tradition in John 20:30–31 and 21:24–25." *Catholic Biblical Quarterly* 78.2 (2016): 321–37.

Kennedy, George A. *Progymnasmata: Greek Textbooks and Prose Composition*. Atlanta: Society of Biblical Literature, 2003.

Kerr, Alan. *The Temple of Jesus' Body: The Temple Theme in the Gospel of John*. Journal for the Study of the New Testament Supplements Series 220. London: Sheffield Academic Press, 2002.

252 Bibliography

Kierdorf, Wilhelm. *Mos maiorum*. Brill's New Pauly. Edited by Hubert Cancik and Helmuth Schneider. Leiden: Brill, 2006.

Kierspel, Lars. *The Jews and the World in the Fourth Gospel: Parallelism, Function, and Context*. Wissenschaftliche Untersuchungen Zum Neuen Testament 2.220. Tübingen: Mohr Siebeck, 2006.

Kimelman, Reuven. "*Birkat Ha-Minim* and the Lack of Evidence for an Anti-Christian Jewish Prayer in Late Antiquity." Pages 226–44 in *Jewish and Christian Self-Definition*. Volume 2. Edited by Ben F. Meyer and E. P. Sanders. Philadelphia: Fortress, 1981.

King, Karen L. *What Is Gnosticism?* Cambridge, MA: Harvard University Press, 2003.

Klink, Edward W. III. "Expulsion from the Synagogue?: Rethinking a Johannine Anachronism." *Tyndale Bulletin* 59.1 (2008): 99–118.

———. "Gospel Audience and Origin: The Current Debate." Pages 1–26 in *The Audience of the Gospels: The Origin and Function of the Gospels in Early Christianity*. Edited by Edward W. Klink III. Library of New Testament Studies 353. London: T & T Clark, 2010.

———. "The Gospel Community Debate: State of the Question." *Currents in Biblical Research* 3.1 (2004): 60–85.

———. *The Sheep of the Fold: The Audience and Origin of the Gospel of John*. Society for New Testament Studies Monograph Series 141; Cambridge: Cambridge University Press, 2007.

Kloppenborg, John S. *Christ's Associations: Connecting and Belonging in the Ancient City*. New Haven: Yale University Press, 2019.

———. "Disaffiliation in Associations and the ἀποσυνάγωγος of John." *HTS Theological Studies* 67 (2011): Art. #962, 16 pages, doi: 10.4102/hts.v67i1.962.

Knoppers, Gary N. *Jews and Samaritans: The Origins and History of Their Early Relations*. Oxford: Oxford University Press, 2013.

Kobel, Esther, *Dining with John: Communal Meals and Identity Formation in the Fourth Gospel and its Historical and Cultural Context*. Biblical Interpretation Series 109. Leiden: Brill, 2011.

Koester, Craig R. "Why Was the Messiah Crucified? A Study of God, Jesus, Satan, and Human Agency in Johannine Theology." Pages 163–80 in *The Death of Jesus in the Fourth Gospel*. Edited by Gilbert Van Belle. Leuven: Peeters, 2007.

Korner, Ralph J. "συναγωγή and Semi-Public Associations." Pages 224–46 in *Greco-Roman Associations, Deities, and Early Christianity*. Edited by Bruce W. Longenecker. Waco, TX: Baylor University Press, 2022.

Kotrosits, Maia. *The Lives of Objects: Material Culture, Experience, and the Real in the History of Early Christianity*. New Studies in Religion. Chicago: University of Chicago Press, 2020.

Kratz, Reinhard G. "Die Rezeption Von Jeremia 10 Und 29 Im Pseudepigraphen Brief Des Jeremia." *Journal for the Study of Judaism in the Persian, Hellenistic, and Roman Period* 26.1 (1995): 2–31.

Kruse, Colin G. *The Letters of John*. Pillar New Testament Commentary. Grand Rapids: Eerdmans, 2000.

Kuang, R. F. *Babel: An Arcane History*. London: HarperVoyager, 2022.

Bibliography

Kuecker, Aaron. "Ethnicity and Social Identity." Pages 59–77 in *T&T Clark Handbook to Social Identity in the New Testament*. Edited by J. Brian Tucker and Coleman A. Baker. London: Bloomsbury, 2014.

———. "Filial Piety and Violence in Luke-Acts and the Aeneid: A Comparative Analysis of Two Trans-Ethnic Identities." Pages 211–33 in *T&T Clark Handbook to Social Identity in the New Testament*. Edited by J. Brian Tucker and Coleman A. Baker. London: Bloomsbury, 2014.

Kügler. Joachim. *Der Jünger, den Jesus liebte: Literarische, theologische und historische Untersuchungen zu einer Schlüsselgestalt johanneischer Theologie und Geschichte*. Stuttgarter biblische Beiträge 16; Stuttgart: Verlag Katholisches Bibelwerk, 1988.

Kuhl, Joseph W. "The Idiolect, Chaos, and Language Custom far from Equilibrium: Conversations in Morocco." Unpublished PhD dissertation; University of Georgia, 2003.

Kysar, Robert. "Community and Gospel: Vectors in Fourth Gospel Criticism." *Interpretation* 31.4 (1977): 355–66.

———. "The Promises and Perils of Preaching on the Gospel of John." *Dialog* 19.3 (1980): 214–20.

———. "The Whence and Whither of the Johannine Community." Pages 65–81 in *Life in Abundance: Studies of John's Gospel in Tribute to Raymond E. Brown, S.S.* Edited by John R. Donahue. Collegeville, MN: Liturgical Press, 2005.

———. *Voyages with John: Charting the Fourth Gospel*. Waco, TX: Baylor, 2005.

Kysar, Robert, Sandra M. Schneiders, R. Alan Culpepper, Graham Stanton, Alan G. Padgett, and Paul N. Anderson. Review of *The Christology of the Fourth Gospel*: *Review of Biblical Literature* 1 (1999): 38–72.

Labahn, Michael. *Jesus als Lebensspender: Untersuchungen zu einer Geschichte der johanneischen Tradition anhand ihrer Wundergeschichten*. Beihefte zur Zeitschrift für die neutestamentliche Wissenschaft 98. Berlin: DeGruyter, 1999.

———. "Literary Sources of the Gospel and the Letters of John." Pages 23–43 in *The Oxford Handbook of Johannine Studies*. Edited by Judith M. Lieu and Martinus de Boer. Oxford: Oxford University Press, 2018.

Labov. William. *Sociolinguistic Patterns*. Philadelphia: University of Pennsylvania Press, 1972.

Lamb, David A. *Text, Context and the Johannine Community: A Sociolinguistic Analysis of the Johannine Writings*. Library of New Testament Studies 477. London: Bloomsbury T & T Clark, 2014.

Lamb, David A. and Thora Tenbrink. "Evaluating Jesus and other 'Heroes': An Application of Appraisal Analysis to Hellenistic Greek Texts in the 'Lives' Genre." *Language, Context and Text* 4.2 (2022): 227–58.

Langer, Ruth. *Cursing the Christians? A History of the Birkat Haminim*. New York: Oxford University Press, 2011.

Larsen, Kasper Bro. *Recognizing the Stranger: Recognition Scenes in the Gospel of John*. Biblical Interpretation Series 93. Leiden: Brill, 2008.

Le Donne, Anthony. "Memory, Commemoration and History in John 2.19-22: A Critique and Application of Social Memory." Pages 186–204 in *The Fourth Gospel in First-Century Media Culture*. Edited by Anthony Le Donne and Tom Thatcher. London: T&T Clark, 2013.

Lefkowitz, Natalie and John S. Hedgcock. "Anti-language: Linguistic innovation, identity construction, and group affiliation among emerging speech communities." Pages 347–76 in *Multiple Perspectives in Language Play*. Edited by Nancy Bell. Language Play and Creativity 1. Berlin: De Gruyter, 2017.

Leroy, Herbert. *Rätsel und Missverständnis: ein Beitrag zur Formgeschichte des Johannesevangeliums*. Bonner biblische Beiträge 30; Bonn: Peter Hanstein, 1968.

Levine, A. J. "Matthew and Anti-Judaism." *Currents in Theology and Mission* 34.6 (2007): 409–16.

Lieb, Hans-Heinrich. *Linguistic Variables: Towards a Unified Theory of Linguistic Variation*. Amsterdam: John Benjamins, 1993.

Lieu, Judith M. *I, II, & III John: A Commentary*. New Testament Library. Louisville: Westminster John Knox, 2008.

———. *Christian Identity in the Jewish and Graeco-Roman World*. Oxford: Oxford University Press, 2004.

———. "The Audience of the Johannine Epistles." Pages 123–45 in *Communities in Dispute: Current Scholarship on the Johannine Epistles*. Edited by R. Alan Culpepper and Paul N. Anderson. Early Christianity and Its Literature 13; Atlanta: SBL Press, 2014.

———. "Us or You? Persuasion and Identity in 1 John." *Journal of Biblical Literature* 127.4 (2008): 805–19.

Liew, Tat-Siong Benny. "Ambiguous Admittance: Consent and Descent in John's Community of 'Upward' Mobility." Pages 193–242 in *John and Postcolonialism: Travel, Space, and Power*. Edited by Musa W. Dube and Jeffrey L. Staley. London: Bloomsbury, 2002.

Lim, Sung Uk. *Otherness and Identity in the Gospel of John*. Cham: Palgrave Macmillan, 2021.

Lincoln, Andrew T. *The Gospel according to St. John*. Black's New Testament Commentary. London: Continuum, 2006.

———. *Truth on Trial: The Lawsuit Motif in the Fourth Gospel*. Peabody, MA: Hendrickson, 2000.

Lindars, Barnabas. *The Gospel of John*. New Century Bible Commentary. Grand Rapids: Eerdmans, 1987.

Litwa, David. "Literary Eyewitnesses: The Appeal to an Eyewitness in John and Contemporaneous Literature." *New Testament Studies* 64 (2018): 343–61.

Loader, William R. G. *The Johannine Epistles*. Epworth Commentaries. London: Epworth, 1992.

Logan, Alistair H. B. "The Johannine Literature and the Gnostics." Pages 171–85 in *The Oxford Handbook of Johannine Studies*. Edited by Judith M. Lieu and Martinus C. de Boer. Oxford: Oxford University Press, 2018.

Longenecker, Bruce W. *Greco-Roman Associations, Deities, and Early Christianity*. Waco, TX: Baylor University Press, 2022.

Louwerse, Max M. "Semantic Variation in Idiolect and Sociolect: Corpus Linguistic Evidence from Literary Texts." *Computers and the Humanities* 38 (2004): 207–21.

Bibliography

Malherbe, Abraham J. *Social Aspects of Early Christianity.* Baton Rouge: Louisiana State University Press, 1977.

Malina, Bruce J. "John's: The Maverick Christian Group: The Evidence of Sociolinguistics," *Biblical Theology Bulletin* 24.4 (1994): 167–82.

———. *The Gospel of John in Sociolinguistic Perspective.* 48th Colloquy of the Center for Hermeneutical Studies. Berkley: Center for Hermeneutical Studies, 1985.

Malina, Bruce J. and Richard L. Rohrbaugh. *Social-Science Commentary on the Gospel of John.* Minneapolis: Fortress, 1998.

Manetho. *History of Egypt and Other Works.* Translated by W. G. Waddell. Loeb Classical Library 350. Cambridge, MA: Harvard University Press, 1940.

Marcus, Joel. "Birkat Ha-Minim Revisited." *New Testament Studies* 55.4 (2009): 523–51.

———."Idolatry in the New Testament." *Interpretation* 60.2 (2006): 152–64.

Markschies, Christoph. *Christian Theology and its Institutions: Prolegomena to a History of Early Christian Theology.* Translated by Wayne Coppins. Baylor Mohr Siebeck Studies in Early Christianity. Waco, TX: Baylor University Press, 2015.

Marquis, Émeline. "Introduction: Epistolary Fiction vs Spurious Letters." Pages 1–22 in *Epistolary Fiction in Ancient Greek Literature.* Philologus 19. Edited by Émeline Marquis. Berlin: De Gruyter, 2023.

Marshall, I. Howard. *The Epistles of John.* New International Commentary on the New Testament. Grand Rapids: Eerdmans, 1978.

Martínez, Javier. "Pseudepigraphy." Pages 401–16 in *A Companion to Late Antique Literature.* Edited by Scott McGill and Edward J. Watts. New York: Wiley, 2018.

Marty, Jacques. "Contribution à l'étude des problèmes johanniques: Les petites épîtres 'II et III Jean.'" *Revue de l'histoire des religions* 91 (1925): 200–11.

Martyn, J. Louis. "A Law-Observant Mission to Gentiles: The Background of Galatians." *Scottish Journal of Theology.* 38.3 (1985): 307–24.

———. *History and Theology in the Fourth Gospel,* third edition. Louisville, KY: Westminster John Knox, 2003.

———. *The Gospel of John in Christian History: Seven Glimpses into the Johannine Community.* Edited by Paul N. Anderson. Johannine Monograph Series 8. Eugene: Wipf & Stock, 2019.

Mason, Steve. "Jews, Judaeans, Judaizing, Judaism: Problems of Categorization in Ancient History," *Journal for the Study of Judaism* 38 (2007): 457–512.

Mathison, Sandra. "Why Triangulate?" *Educational Researcher* 17.2 (1988): 13–17.

Matthiessen, Christian M. I. M. "Register in Systemic Functional Linguistics." *Register Studies* 1.1 (2019), 10–41.

Maxwell, Kathy Reiko. *Hearing Between the Line: The Audience as Fellow-Worker in Luke-Acts and Its Literary Milieu.* Library of New Testament Studies 425. London: T & T Clark, 2010.

Maynard, Arthur H. "The Role of Peter in the Fourth Gospel." *New Testament Studies* 30 (1984): 531–48.

Meeks, Wayne A. "The Man from Heaven in Johannine Sectarianism." *Journal of Biblical Literature* 91.1 (1972): 44–72.

———. *The Prophet-King: Moses Traditions and the Johannine Christology.* Novum Testamentum Supplements 14. Leiden: Brill, 1967.

Méndez, Hugo. "Did the Johannine Community Exist?" *Journal for the Study of the New Testament* 42.3 (2020): 350–74.

Milroy, James. "Internal vs. External Motivations for Linguistic Change." *Multilingua* 16 (1997): 311–23.

Mitchell, Margaret M. "Patristic Counter-Evidence to the Claim that 'The Gospels Were Written for All Christians.'" *New Testament Studies* 51 (2005): 36–79.

Moloney, Francis J. *Belief in the Word: Reading John 1–4.* Minneapolis: Fortress, 1993.

———. "From Cana to Cana (Jn. 2:1–4:54) and the Fourth Evangelist's Concept of Correct (and Incorrect) Faith." *Salesianum* 40 (1978): 817–43.

———. *Glory Not Dishonor: Reading John 13–21.* Minneapolis: Fortress, 1998.

———. *Signs and Shadows: Reading John 5–12.* Minneapolis: Fortress, 1996.

Moore, Alison Rotha. "Register Analysis in Systemic Functional Linguistics." Pages 418–37 in *The Routledge Handbook of Systemic Functional Linguistics.* Edited by Tom Bartlett and Gerard O'Grady. Abingdon: Routledge, 2017.

Moore, Stephen D. *Empire and Apocalypse: Postcolonialism and the New Testament.* The Bible in the Modern World 12. Sheffield: Sheffield Phoenix Press, 2006.

Morgan, Teresa J. *Literate Education in the Hellenistic and Roman Worlds.* Cambridge: Cambridge University Press, 1998.

———. *Roman Faith and Christian Faith: Pistis and Fides in the Early Roman Empire and Early Churches.* Oxford: Oxford University Press, 2015.

Motyer, Stephen. "The Fourth Gospel and the Salvation of Israel: An Appeal for a New Start." Pages 84–87 in *Anti-Judaism and the Fourth Gospel: Papers of the Leuven Colloquium, 2000.* Jewish and Christian Heritage Series 1. Edited by Reimund Bieringer, Didier Pollefeyt, and Frederique Vandecasteele-Vanneuville.

———. *Your Father the Devil? A New Approach to John and 'the Jews.'* Carlisle, Cumbria: Paternoster, 1997.

Mufwene, Salikoko S. *The Ecology of Language Evolution.* Cambridge: Cambridge University Press, 2001.

Myers, Alicia D. "Jesus's Ongoing Ministry in 1 John: Priestly Purification and Intercession in 1 John 1:5–2:2." *Perspectives in Religious Studies* 48 (2021): 243–55.

———. "Just Opponents?: Ambiguity, Empathy, and the Jews in the Gospel of John." Pages 159–76 in *Johannine Ethics: The Moral World of the Gospel and Epistles of John.* Edited by Sherri Brown and Christopher W. Skinner. Minneapolis: Fortress, 2017.

———. *Reading John and 1, 2, 3 John: A Literary and Theological Commentary.* Reading the New Testament: Second Series. Macon, GA: Smyth & Helwys, 2019.

———. "The Gospel of John." Pages 334–49 in *The State of New Testament Studies: A Survey of Recent Research.* Edited by Scot McKnight and Nijay K. Gupta. Grand Rapids: Baker Academic, 2019.

———. "Us and Them: Lessons from 1 John's Antichrist Polemic." *Word and World* 41.1 (2021): 42–50.

Bibliography

―――. "We Speak the Truth: Rhetoric, Epistemology, and Audience Participation in John 3:1–21." *Interpretation* 77 (2023): 325–35.

Neyrey, Jerome. *An Ideology of Revolt: John's Christology in Social-Science Perspective.* Philadelphia: Fortress, 1988.

Nongbri, Brent. "The Use and Abuse of P52: Papyrological Pitfalls in the Dating of the Fourth Gospel." *Harvard Theological Review* 98.1 (2005): 23–48.

North, Wendy E. S. *A Journey Round John: Tradition, Interpretation and Context in the Fourth Gospel.* Library of New Testament Studies 534, London: Bloomsbury T & T Clark, 2015.

―――. Review of David A. Lamb, *Text, Context and the Johannine Community: A Sociolinguistic Analysis of the Johannine Writings, Review of Biblical Literature* 07/2015. https://www.sblcentral.org/API/Reviews/9873_10917.pdf.

Novenson, Matthew. "Paul's Former Occupation in *Ioudaismos.*" Pages 24–39 in *Galatians and Christian Theology.* Edited by Mark Elliott, Scott Hafemann, N. T. Wright, and John Frederick. Grand Rapids: Baker Academic, 2014.

O'Donnell, Matthew Brook. *Corpus Linguistics and the Greek of the New Testament.* New Testament Monographs 6. Sheffield: Sheffield Phoenix Press, 2005.

Olsson, Birger. *Structure and Meaning in the Fourth Gospel: A Text Linguistic Analysis of John 2:1–11 and 4:1–42.* Coniectanea Biblica 6. Stockholm: Almqvist, 1974.

Ong, Hughson T. *The Multilingual Jesus and the Sociolinguistic World of the New Testament.* Linguistic Biblical Studies 12. Leiden: Brill, 2016.

Onuki, Takashi. *Gemeinde und Welt im Johannesevangelium: Ein Beitrag zur Frage nach der theologischen und pragmatischen Funktion des johanneischen 'Dualismus.'* Wissenschaftliche Monographien zum Alten und Neuen Testament 6. Neukirchen-Vluyn: Neukirchener, 1984.

Overman, J. Andrew. "The Destruction of the Temple and the Confirmation of Judaism and Christianity." Pages 253–77 in *Jews and Christians in the First and Second Centuries: The Interbellum 70–132 CE.* Edited by Joshua J. Schwartz and Peter J. Tomson. Brill, 2017.

Painter, John. *1, 2, and 3 John.* Sacra Pagina 18. Collegeville, MN: Liturgical Press, 2008.

―――. "The 'Opponents" in 1 John." *New Testament Studies* 32.1 (1986): 48–71.

Pancaro, Severino. *The Law in the Fourth Gospel: The Torah and the Gospel, Moses and Jesus, Judaism and Christianity According to John.* Novum Testamentum Supplements 42. Leiden: Brill, 1975.

Parsenios, George L. *First, Second, and Third John.* Paideia. Grand Rapids: Baker Academic, 2014.

Peirano, Irene. *The Rhetoric of the Roman Fake: Latin Pseudepigrapha in Context.* Cambridge: Cambridge University Press, 2012.

Petersen, Norman R. *The Gospel of John and the Sociology of Light: Language and Characterization in the Fourth Gospel.* Valley Forge, PA: Trinity Press International, 1993.

Portela, Orlando. "The Letters of Euripides." Pages 153–65 in *Epistolary Narratives in Ancient Greek Literature.* Edited by Owen Hodkinson, Patricia Rosenmeyer, and Evelien Bracke. Leiden: Brill, 2013.

Bibliography

Porter, Christopher. A. "'Hic Sunt Dracones' Mapping the Rebellious Social Dynamics of Bel and the Snake from the Daniel and Joseph Competitive Court-Tales." *Biblical Theology Bulletin* 51.2 (2021): 78–87.

———. *Johannine Social Identity Formation after the Fall of the Jerusalem Temple: Negotiating Identity in Crisis.* Biblical Interpretation Series 194. Leiden: Brill, 2022.

———. "Which Paul? Whose Judaism? - A Socio-Cognitive Approach to Paul within Judaism." Pages 91–106 in *Paul Within Judaism.* Edited by Michael F Bird, Ruben Buhner, Jörg Frey, and Brian S. Rosner. Wissenschaftliche Untersuchungen zum Neuen Testament 2.507. Tubingen: Mohr/Siebeck, 2023.

———. "Will the Real Οἱ Ἰουδαῖοι Please Stand Up?" Pages 62–80 in *The Enduring Impact of the Gospel of John.* Edited by Dorothy Lee, Robert Derrenbacker, and Muriel Porter. Interdisciplinary Studies. Eugene, OR: Wipf & Stock, 2022.

Porter, Christopher A., and Brian S. Rosner. "'All Things to All People': 1 Corinthians, Ethnic Flexibility, and Social Identity Theory." *Currents in Biblical Research.* 19.3 (2021): 286–307.

Powell, Mark Allan. "Narrative Criticism: The Emergence of a Prominent Reading Strategy." Pages 19–43 in *Mark as Story: Retrospect and Prospect.* Edited by Kelly R. Iverson and Christopher W. Skinner. Resources for Biblical Study 65. Atlanta: Society of Biblical Literature, 2011.

Poynton, Cate. *Language and Gender: Making the Difference,* second edition. Oxford: Oxford University Press, 1989.

Puskas, Charles B. and C. Michael Robbins. *The Conceptual Worlds of the Fourth Gospel: Intertextuality and Early Reception.* Eugene: Cascade, 2021.

Quintilian, *The Orator's Education.* 5 volumes. Edited and translated by D. A. Russell. Loeb Classical Library 127. Cambridge; MA; Harvard University Press, 2002.

Radford, Gary P. *On Eco.* Wadsworth Philosophers Series. Australia: Thomson, 2003.

Rapley, Mark, and Martha Augoustinos. "'National Identity' as a Rhetorical Resource." Pages 194–210 in *Language, Interaction and National Identity - Studies in the Social Organisation of National Identity.* Cardiff Papers in Qualitative Research. Edited by Stephen Hester and William Housley. Farnham, UK: Ashgate, 2002.

Reeves, Rodney. *Spirituality According to John: Abiding in Christ in the Johannine Writings.* Downers Grove, IL: IVP Academic, 2021.

Reicher, Stephen, Nick Hopkins, and Susan Condor. "Stereotype Construction as a Strategy of Influence." Pages 94–118 in *The Social Psychology of Stereotyping and Group Life.* Edited by Russell Spears, Penelope J. Oakes, Naomi Ellemers, and S. Alexander Haslam. Malden: Blackwell Publishing, 1997.

Reicher, Stephen, and Fabio Sani. "Introducing SAGA: Structural Analysis of Group Arguments." *Group Dynamics: Theory, Research, and Practice* 2.4 (1998): 267–84.

Reinhartz Adele. "Building Skyscrapers on Toothpicks: The Literary-Critical Challenge to Historical Criticism." Pages 55–76 in *Anatomies of Narrative Criticism: The Past, Present, and Future of the Fourth Gospel as Literature.* Edited by Tom Thatcher and Stephen D. Moore. Resources for Biblical Study 55. Atlanta: Society of Biblical Literature, 2008.

Bibliography

———. *Cast Out of the Covenant: Jews and Anti-Judaism in the Gospel of John.* Lanham, MD: Lexington/Fortress Academic, 2018.

———. "'Children of the Devil': John 8:44 and Its Early Reception." Pages 43–54 in *Confronting Antisemitism from the Perspectives of Christianity, Islam, and Judaism*. An End To Anti-Semitism Volume 2. Edited by Armin Lange, Kerstin Mayerhofer, Dina Porat and Lawrence H. Schiffman. Berlin: De Gruyter, 2020.

———. "'Common Judaism,' 'The Parting of the Ways,' and 'The Johannine Community.'" Pages 69–87 in *Orthodoxy, Liberalism, and Adaptation: Essays on Ways of Worldmaking in Times of Change from Biblical, Historical and Systematic Perspectives*. Studies in Religion and Theology 15. Edited by Bob E. J. H. Becking. Leiden: Brill, 2011.

———. "Forging a New Identity: Johannine Rhetoric and the Audience of the Fourth Gospel." Pages 123–134 in *Paul, John, and Apocalyptic Eschatology: Studies in Honour of Martinus C. de Boer*. Edited by J. Krans, L. J. L. Peerbolte, P.-B. Smit, and A. W. Zwiep. Novum Testamentum Supplements 149. Leiden: Brill, 2013.

———. "Incarnation and Covenant: The Fourth Gospel through the Lens of Trauma Theory." *Interpretation* 69 (2015): 35–48.

———. "'Jews' and Jews in the Fourth Gospel." Pages 341–56 in *Anti-Judaism and the Fourth Gospel: Papers of the Leuven Colloquium, 2000*. Jewish and Christian Heritage Series 1. Edited by Reimund Bieringer, Didier Pollefeyt, and Frederique Vandecasteele-Vanneuville. Leiden: Brill, 2001.

———. "Judaism in the Gospel of John." *Interpretation* 63 (2009): 382–93.

———. "Story and History: John, Jesus, and the Historical Imagination." Pages 113–26 in *John and Judaism: A Contested Relationship in Context*. Edited by Tom Thatcher and Paul N. Anderson. Atlanta: SBL Press, 2017.

———. "The Jews in the Fourth Gospel." Pages 121–37 in *The Oxford Handbook of Johannine Studies*. Edited by Judith M. Lieu and Martinus C. de Boer. Oxford: Oxford University Press, 2018.

———. "The Johannine Community and its Jewish Neighbors: A Reappraisal." Pages 111–138 in *What Is John? Volume II: Literary and Social Readings of the Fourth Gospel*. Symposium Studies 7. Edited by F. F. Segovia. Atlanta: Scholars Press, 1998.

———. *The Word in the World: The Cosmological Tale in the Fourth Gospel.* Society of Biblical Literature Monograph Series 45. Atlanta: Society of Biblical Literature, 1992.

———. "Women in the Johannine Community: An Exercise in Historical Imagination." Pages 14–33 in *A Feminist Companion to John*. Volume 2. Edited by Amy-Jill Levine and Marianne Blickenstaff. London: Sheffield Academic Press, 2003.

Reis, David M. "Jesus' Farewell Discourse, 'Otherness,' and the Construction of a Johannine Identity." *Studies in Religion/Sciences Religieuses* 32 (2003): 39–58.

Rensberger, David. *Johannine Faith and Liberating Community*. Philadelphia: Westminster Press, 1988.

———. *Overcoming the World: Politics and Community in the Gospel of John.* London: SPCK, 1989.

Revell, Louise. *Roman Imperialism and Local Identities*. Cambridge: Cambridge University Press, 2009.

Reynolds, Benjamin E. *John Among the Apocalypses: Jewish Apocalyptic Traditions and the "Apocalyptic" Gospel*. Oxford: Oxford University Press, 2020.

Rhoads, David and Donald Michie. *Mark as Story: An Introduction to the Narrative of a Gospel*. Minneapolis: Fortress, 1982.

Richey, Lance Byron. *Roman Imperial Ideology and the Gospel of John*. Catholic Biblical Quarterly Monograph Series 43. Washington, DC: Catholic Biblical Association of America, 2007.

Robinson, John A. T. "The Relation of the Prologue to the Gospel of St. John," *New Testament Studies* 9 (1962–1963): 120–29.

Robson, David. "The Secret 'Anti-Languages' You're Not Supposed to Know." *BBC Future*. Published February 12, 2016, https://www.bbc.com/future/article/20160211-the-secret-anti-languages-youre-not-supposed-to-know.

Rochette, Bruno. *Le latin dans le monde grec: Recherches sur la diffusion de la langue et des lettres latines dans les provinces hellénophones de l'empire romain*. Brussels: Latomus, 1997.

Roitto, Rikard. "Identity in 1 John: Sinless Sinners Who Remain in Him." Pages 493–510 in *T&T Clark Handbook to Social Identity in the New Testament*. Edited by J. Brian Tucker and Coleman A. Baker. London: Bloomsbury, 2014.

———. "The Johannine Information War: A Social Network Analysis of the Information Flow between Johannine Assemblies as Witnessed by 1-3 John." Pages 69–84 in *Drawing and Transcending Boundaries in the New Testament and Early Christianity*. Edited by Jacobus Kock, Martin Webber and Jermo van Nes. Beiträge zum Verstehen der Bibel 38. Zürich: LIT, 2019.

Rollens, Sarah E. "Does 'Q' Have Any Representative Potential." *Method and Theory in the Study of Religion* 23.1 (2011): 64–78.

———. "The Anachronism of 'Early Christian Communities.'" Pages 307–24 in *Theorizing 'Religion' in Antiquity*. Edited by N. P. Roubekas. London: Equinox, 2018.

———. "The Kingdom of God is Among You: Prospects for a Q Community." Pages 224–41 in *Christian Origins and the Establishment of the Early Jesus Movement*. Edited by by Stanley E. Porter and Andrew W. Pitts. Early Christianity in its Hellenistic Environment 4; Leiden: Brill, 2018.

Rosenmeyer, Patricia A. *Ancient Epistolary Fictions: The Letter in Greek Literature*. Cambridge: Cambridge University Press, 2001.

———. *Ancient Greek Literary Letters: Selections in Translation*. New York: Routledge, 2017.

Runesson, Anders. *The Origins of the Synagogue: A Socio-Historical Study*, Coniectanea Biblica, New Testament 37. Stockholm: Almqvist & Wiksell, 2001.

Russell, A. Sue. "A Genealogy of Social Identity Theory." Pages 1–24 in *T&T Clark Social Identity Commentary on the New Testament*. Edited by J. Brian Tucker and Coleman A. Baker. London: T & T Clark, 2020.

Sani, Fabio. "When Subgroups Secede: Extending and Refining the Social Psychological Model of Schism in Groups." *Personality and Social Psychology Review* 31.8 (2005): 1074–86.

Bibliography

Schechter, Solomon. "Genizah Specimens." *Jewish Quarterly Review* 10 (1898): 197–206.

Schmid, H. "How to Read the First Epistle of John Non-Polemically." *Biblica* 85.1 (2004): 24–41.

Schnackenburg, Rudolf. *The Gospel According to St. John.* Translated by Kevin Smyth. 3 volumes. London: Burns & Oates, 1968, 1980, 1982.

———. *The Johannine Epistles.* New York: Crossroad, 1992.

Seglenieks, Christopher. "Desertion or Exclusion: Relationships with the Outgroup in the Johannine Writings." In *Figuring the Enemy: Socio-Scientific Approaches to Religious Enmity.* Edited by Christopher A. Porter. Routledge Interdisciplinary Perspectives on Biblical Criticism (forthcoming).

———. Review of David A. Lamb, *Text, Context and the Johannine Community: A Sociolinguistic Analysis of the Johannine Writings. Colloquium* 50.1 (2018): 110.

Schenke, H.-M. "The Function and Background of the Beloved Disciple in the Gospel of John." Pages 111–25 in *Nag Hammadi, Gnosticism, and Early Christianity.* Edited by Charles W. Hedrick and R. Hodgson Jr. Peabody, MA: Hendrickson, 1986.

Schneiders, Sandra M. "The Raising of the New Temple: John 20:19–23 and Johannine Ecclesiology." *New Testament Studies* 52 (2006): 337–55.

Schnelle, Udo. *Antidocetic Christology in the Gospel of John: An Investigation of the Place of the Fourth Gospel in the Johannine School.* Translated by Linda M. Maloney. Minneapolis: Fortress Press, 1992.

Sellew, Melissa (Phillip). "Thomas Christianity": Scholars in Search of a Community." Pages 11–35 in *The Apocryphal Acts of Thomas.* Edited by Jan B. Bremmer. Leuven, Peeters, 2001.

Sheridan, Ruth. "Johannine Sectarianism: A Category Now Defunct?" Pages 142–66 in *The Origins of John's Gospel.* Edited by Stanley E. Porter and Hughson T. Ong, Johannine Studies 2. Leiden: Brill, 2016.

———. "John's Prologue as Exegetical Narrative." Pages 171–90 in *The Gospel of John as Genre Mosaic.* Edited by Kasper Bro Larsen. Studia Aarhusiana Neotestamentica 3. Göttingen: Vandenhoeck & Ruprecht, 2015.

Sim, David C. "The Gospels for All Christians? A Response to Richard Bauckham." *Journal for the Study of the New Testament* 24.2 (2001): 3–27.

Skinner, Christopher W. *Mark.* New Word Biblical Themes. Grand Rapids: Zondervan Academic, forthcoming 2026.

———. "Narrative Readings of the Religious Authorities in John: A Response to Urban C. von Wahlde." *Catholic Biblical Quarterly* 82 (2020): 424–36.

———. *Reading John.* Cascade Companions. Eugene, OR: Cascade, 2015.

Smith, Anthony D. *The Ethnic Origins of Nations.* Oxford: Blackwell, 1986.

Smith, D. Moody. *Johannine Christianity: Essays on its Setting, Sources, and Theology.* Columbia, SC: University of South Carolina Press, 1984.

———. *The Composition and Order of the Fourth Gospel.* Johannine Monograph Series 2, Eugene: Wipf & Stock, 2015.

Smith, Justin Marc. *Why Βίος? On the Relationship between Gospel Genre and Implied Audience.* Library of New Testament Studies 518. London: Bloomsbury T & T Clark, 2015.

Smith, Mark S. *Where the Gods Are: Spatial Dimensions of Anthropomorphism in the Biblical World*. Anchor Yale Bible Reference Library. New Haven: Yale University Press, 2016.

Smith, Tyler. *The Fourth Gospel and the Manufacture of Minds in Ancient Historiography, Biography, Romance, and Drama*. Biblical Interpretation Series 173. Leiden: Brill, 2019.

Snyder, Graydon, F. "John 3:17 and the Anti-Petrinism of the Johannine Tradition." *Biblical Research* 16 (1971): 5–15.

Sommer, Benjamin D. *The Bodies of God and the World of Ancient Israel*. Cambridge: Cambridge University Press, 2009.

Sproston, Wendy E. "Witnesses to What Was ἀπ' ἀρχῆς: 1 John's Contribution to Our Knowledge of Tradition in the Fourth Gospel." Pages 138–60 in *The Johannine Writings*. Edited by Stanley E. Porter and Craig A. Evans. Sheffield: Sheffield Academic, 1995.

Staples, Jason A. *The Idea of Israel in Second Temple Judaism: A New Theory of People, Exile, and Israelite Identity*. Cambridge: Cambridge University Press, 2021.

Starr, Raymond J. "The Circulation of Literary Texts in the Roman World." *Classical Quarterly* 37 (1987): 213–23.

Stibbe, Mark W. G. *John as Storyteller: Narrative Criticism and the Fourth Gospel*. Society for New Testament Studies Monograph Series 73. Cambridge: Cambridge University Press, 1992.

Stock, Brian. *The Implications of Literacy: Written Language and Models of Interpretation in the Eleventh and Twelfth Centuries*. Princeton: Princeton University Press, 1983.

Stock, Brian. *Listening for the Text: On the Uses of the Past*. Philadelphia: University of Pennsylvania Press, 1990.

Stowers, Stanley. "The Concept of 'Community' and the History of Early Christianity." *Method and Theory in the Study of Religion* 23.3–4 (2011): 238–56.

Strecker, G. *The Johannine Letters: A Commentary on 1, 2, and 3 John*. Edited by Harold W. Attridge. Translated by L. M. Maloney. Hermeneia: A Critical and Historical Commentary on the Bible. Minneapolis: Fortress, 1996.

Streett, Daniel R. *They Went Out from Us: The Identity of the Opponents in First John*. Beihefte zur Zeitschrift für die neutestamentliche Wissenschaft 177. Berlin: De Gruyter, 2011.

Syreeni, Kari. *Becoming John: The Making of a Passion Gospel*. Library of New Testament Studies 590. London: Bloomsbury/T&T Clark, 2020.

Tajfel, Henri. *Differentiation between Social Groups: Studies in the Social Psychology of Intergroup Relations*. European Monographs in Social Psychology 14. London: Academic Press, 1978.

Tajfel, Henri, M. G. Billig, R. P. Bundy, and Claude Flament. "Social Categorization and Intergroup Behaviour." *European Journal of Social Psychology.* 1.2 (1971): 149–78.

Tan, Yak-Hwee. "The Johannine Community: Power and Identity as a New Lens of Interpretation." Pages 83–95 in *Soundings in Cultural Criticism: Perspectives and*

Methods in Culture, Power, and Identity in the New Testament. Edited by Francisco Lozada Jr. and Greg Carey. Minneapolis: Fortress, 2013.

Tchaikovsky, Adrian. "Adrian Tchaikovsky Interview: Writing Mind-Blowing Worlds," on Wizards, Warriors, and Words: A Fantasy Writing Advice Podcast, Episode 1.19. Online: https://youtu.be/UWR7GxexhFw.

Tolkien, J. R. R. *The Silmarillion.* Edited by Christopher Tolkien. London: HarperCollins, 2013.

Thatcher, Tom. "Cain the Jew the AntiChrist: Collective Memory and the Johannine Ethic of Loving and Hating." Pages 350–73 in *Rethinking the Ethics of John: 'Implicit Ethics' in the Johannine Writings.* Edited Jan G. van der Watt and Ruben Zimmermann. Wissenschaftliche Untersuchungen zum Neuen Testament 291. Tübingen: Mohr Siebeck, 2012.

———. *Greater than Caesar: Christology and Empire in the Fourth Gospel.* Minneapolis: Fortress, 2009.

———. "'I Have Conquered the World': The Death of Jesus and the End of Empire in the Gospel of John." Pages 140–63 in *Empire in the New Testament.* Edited by Stanley E. Porter and Cynthia Long Westfall. Mcmaster Divinity College Press New Testament Study Series. Eugene, OR: Pickwick, 2011.

———. "John's Memory Theater: A Study of Composition in Performance." Pages 73–91 in *The Fourth Gospel in First-Century Media Culture.* Edited by Anthony Le Donne and Tom Thatcher. London: T & T Clark, 2013.

———. *Memory and Identity in Ancient Judaism and Early Christianity: A Conversation with Barry Schwartz.* SBL Semeia Studies 78. Atlanta: SBL Press, 2014.

Thiselton, Anthony C. *New Horizons in Hermeneutics: The Theory and Practice of Transforming Biblical Reading.* Grand Rapids: Zondervan, 1992.

Thompson, Marianne Meye. *John: A Commentary.* New Testament Library. Louisville: Westminster John Knox, 2015.

Tolmie, D. Francois. "Pontius Pilate: Failing in More Ways Than One." Pages 578–97 in *Character Studies in the Fourth Gospel: Narrative Approaches to Seventy Figures in John.* Edited by Steven A. Hunt, D. Francois Tolmie, and Ruben Zimmermann. Wissenschaftliche Untersuchungen zum Neuen Testament 1.314. Tübingen: Mohr Siebeck, 2013.

Trebilco, Paul. *Outsider Designations and Boundary Construction in the New Testament.* Cambridge: Cambridge University Press, 2017.

———. *The Early Christians in Ephesus from Paul to Ignatius.* Grand Rapids: Eerdmans, 2007.

Tucker, J. Brian. *Remain in Your Calling: Paul and the Continuation of Social Identities in 1 Corinthians.* Eugene, OR: Pickwick, 2011.

Van Belle, Gilbert. *The Signs Source in the Fourth Gospel. Historical Survey and Critical Evaluation of the Semeia Hypothesis.* Bibliotheca Ephemeridum Theologicarum Lovaniensium 116. Leuven: Peeters, 1994.

van den Heever, Gerhard. "Space, Social Space, and the Construction of Early Christian Identity in First Century Asia Minor." *Religion and Theology* 17.3–4 (2010): 205–243.

van der Watt, J. and R. Zimmermann eds. *Rethinking the Ethics of John: 'Implicit Ethics' in the Gospel of John*. Kontexte und Normen neutestamentlicher Ethik / Contexts and Norms of New Testament Ethics 3. Tübingen: Mohr Siebeck, 2012.

van Tilborg, Sjef. *Reading John in Ephesus*. Novum Testamentum Supplements 83. Leiden: Brill, 1996.

Vincent, Benet and Jim Clarke. "The Language of A Clockwork Orange: A Corpus Stylistic approach to Nadsat." *Language and Literature* 26.3 (2017): 247–64.

Von Harnack, Adolf. "Uber den dritten Johannesbrief." Pages 3–27 in *Texte und Untersuchungen zur Geschichte der altchristlichen Literatur* 15:3. Leipzig, 1887.

von Wahlde, Urban C. *Gnosticism, Docetism, and the Judaisms of the First Century: The Search for the Wider Context of the Johannine Literature and Why it Matters*. Library of New Testament Studies 517. New York: Bloomsbury/T & T Clark, 2015.

―――. "Johannine Literature and Gnosticism," Pages 221–54 in *From Judaism to Christianity: Tradition and Transition. A Festschrift for Thomas H. Tobin, S.J., on the Occasion of His Sixty-fifth Birthday*. Novum Testament Supplements 136. Leiden: Brill, 2011.

―――. "Narrative Criticism of the Religious Authorities as a Group Character in the Gospel of John: Some Problems." *New Testament Studies* 63 (2017): 222–45.

―――. *The Earliest Version of John's Gospel: Recovering the Gospel of Signs*. Good News Studies. Collegeville, MN: Michael Glazier, 1989.

―――. *The Gospel and Letters of John*, 3 vols. Eerdmans Critical Commentary. Grand Rapids: Eerdmans, 2010.

―――. *The Johannine Commandments: 1 John and the Struggle for the Johannine Tradition*. Theological Inquiries. Mahwah, NJ: Paulist, 1990.

Walsh, Robyn Faith. *The Origins of Early Christian Literature: Contextualizing the New Testament within Greco-Roman Literary Culture*. Cambridge: Cambridge University Press, 2021.

Watson, David F. "Amplification Techniques in 1 John: The Interaction of Rhetorical Style and Invention." *Journal for the Study of the New Testament* 51.1 (1993): 99–123.

―――. "1 John 2.12-14 as Distributio, Conduplicatio, and Expolitio: A Rhetorical Understanding." *Journal for the Study of the New Testament* 35.1 (1989): 97–110.

Watson, Francis. *Gospel Writing: A Canonical Perspective*. Grand Rapids: Eerdmans, 2013.

―――. "Toward a Literal Reading of the Gospels." Pages 195–217 in *The Gospels for All Christians: Rethinking the Gospel Audiences*. Edited by Richard Bauckham. Grand Rapids: Eerdmans, 1998.

Wead, David W. *The Literary Devices in John's Gospel*. Revised edition. Edited by Paul N. Anderson and R. Alan Culpepper. Eugene, OR: Wipf & Stock, 2018.

Wendland, Ernst. "The Rhetoric of Reassurance in First John: 'Dear Children' versus the 'Antichrists.'" *Neotestamentica* 41.1 (2007): 173–219.

White, Benjamin L. "Reclaiming Paul? Reconfiguration as Reclamation in 3 Corinthians." *Journal of Early Christian Studies* 17.4 (2009): 497–523.

Bibliography

Whitenton, Michael R. *Configuring Nicodemus: An Interdisciplinary Approach to Complex Characterization*. Library of New Testament Studies 549. London: Bloomsbury/T & T Clark, 2019.

Williams, Catrin H. "(Not) Seeing God in the Prologue and Body of John's Gospel." Pages 79–98 in *The Prologue of the Gospel of John*. Edited by Jan G. van der Watt, R. Alan Culpepper, and Udo Schnelle. Wissenschaftliche Untersuchungen zum Neuen Testament 1.359. Tübingen: Mohr Siebeck, 2016.

———. "Patriarchs and Prophets Remembered: Framing Israel's Past in the Gospel of John." Pages 187–212 in *Abiding Words: The Use of Scripture in the Gospel of John*. Edited by Alicia D. Myers and Bruce G. Schuchard, Resources for Biblical Study 81. Atlanta: SBL Press, 2015.

Williams, Catrin H. and Christopher Rowland. *John's Gospel and Intimations of Apocalyptic*. London: Bloomsbury, 2014.

Williams, Logan. "Was All Early Gospel Writing Competitive? Situating the Gospel of John within Greek Literary Culture." University of Nottingham Biblical Studies Seminar. March 2022.

Williams, Michael Allen. *Rethinking "Gnosticism": An Argument for Dismantling a Dubious Category*. Princeton: Princeton University Press, 1996.

Wilson, Brittany E. "Seeing Jesus, Seeing God: Theophany and Divine Visibility in the Gospel of John." Pages 59–62 in *Early High Christology: John among the New Testament Writers*. Edited by Chris Blumhofer, Diane Chen, and Joel B. Green. Minneapolis: Fortress Press, forthcoming.

———. *The Embodied God: Seeing the Divine in Luke-Acts and the Early Church*. Oxford: Oxford University Press, 2021.

Wisse, Frederik. "Historical Method and the Johannine Community." *ARC: The Journal of the Faculty of Religious Studies, McGill University* 20.1 (1992): 35–42.

Woll, David. *Johannine Christianity in Conflict: Authority, Rank, and Succession in the First Farewell Discourse*. Society of Biblical Literature Dissertation Series 60. Chico, CA: Scholars Press, 1981.

Woolf, Greg. "Becoming Roman, Staying Greek: Culture, Identity and the Civilizing Process in the Roman East." *The Cambridge Classical Journal* 40 (1994): 116–43.

———. "Inventing Empire in Ancient Rome." Pages 311–22 in *Empires: Perspectives from Archaeology and History*. Edited by Susan E. Alcock, Terence N. D'Altroy, Kathleen D. Morrison, and Carla M. Sinopoli. Cambridge: Cambridge University Press, 2001.

Wright, Arthur M. *The Governor and the King: Irony, Hidden Transcripts, and Negotiating Empire in the Fourth Gospel*. Eugene, OR: Pickwick, 2019.

Zhakevich, Mark. *Follow Me: The Benefits of Discipleship in the Gospel of John*. Interpreting Johannine Literature. Lanham, MD: Lexington/Fortress, 2021.

Index

Abrams, Dominic, 84
Agourides, Savas, 220
Aitken, James K., 87
Ajayi, Temitope Michael, 64
Alcock, Susan E., 110
Anderson, Benedict, 137
Anderson, Paul N., 4, 14, 19, 20, 38, 40, 59, 60, 66, 77, 78, 85, 86, 152, 171, 190, 197, 219, 220, 221, 222, 235, 267
Ashton, John, 80, 87, 220
Atkins, J. D., 43
Attridge, Harold W., 60, 149, 153, 154, 156, 162, 171, 179, 191, 216, 222
Auer, Peter, 155, 156
Augoustinos, Martha, 70, 84
Aune, David E., 135

Baker, Coleman A., 41, 85
Baker, Paul, 64
Barash, Jeffrey Andrew, 112
Barclay, John M. G., 28, 41, 43, 133, 138
Barker, James W., 39
Barlow, Michael, 62
Baron, Lori, 134, 152, 235
Barrett, C. K., 40, 41, 42, 113, 206, 221
Bartlett, Tom, 61
Barton, Stephen C., 108, 138

Basden, Andrew, 53, 60, 64
Bauckham, Richard, 9, 10, 17, 18, 24, 26, 28, 39, 79, 86, 93, 108, 135, 152, 162, 171, 204, 222, 228
Bauer, Walter, 27, 40, 137
Baumgarten-Crusius, Ludwig F. O., 169
Baur, Ferdinand Christian, 137
Beal, Timothy, 155
Beasley-Murray, George R., 83, 220
Becker, Adam H., 221
Becker, Eve-Marie, 39
Becking, Bob E. J. H., 20, 83
Bennema, Cornelis, 19
Bérenger-Badel, Agnès, 113
Berger, Peter L., 69, 83
Bergs, Alexander, 61
Bernier, Jonathan, 15, 38, 86, 137, 220, 234
Betz, Hans Dieter, 61
Biber, Douglas, 46, 47, 50, 60
Bickermann, E., 113
Bieringer, Reimund, 15, 18, 112
Bird, Michael F., 87
Black, C. Clifton, 137
Black, David Alan, 61
Blomberg, Craig, 18, 136
Blumhofer, Chris, 193
Bockmuehl, Markus, 137, 138
Bolinger, Dwight, 156

267

Bond, Helen K., 39, 113
Boomershine, Thomas E., 86
Borgen, Peder, 15, 204, 220
Botha, Pieter, 40
Bourdieu, Pierre, 68, 83, 87
Bowden, John, 16, 63, 135
Bracke, Evelien, 170
Brakke, David, 65
Brant, Jo-Ann A., 64
Bray, Gerald L., 113
Bremmer, Jan B., 40, 154
Brewer, Marilynn B., 109, 221
Brock, Ann Graham, 153, 171
Brown, Peter, 226, 235
Brown, Raymond E., 3, 6, 7, 8, 10, 14, 15, 16, 23, 38, 39, 40, 41, 42, 43, 45, 46, 59, 60, 65, 66, 67, 68, 118, 119, 122, 133, 135, 140, 144, 152, 153, 154, 155, 157, 162, 169, 171, 176, 177, 183, 190, 197, 198, 199, 200, 201, 202, 204, 206, 210, 211, 212, 213, 215, 218, 219, 220, 238
Brown, Sherri, 19, 111
Buhner, Ruben, 87
Bultmann, Rudolf, 6, 15, 68, 83, 153, 163, 171, 204, 220
Burkill, T. A., 6, 16
Burridge, Richard, 39, 62, 171
Byers, Andrew J., 4, 13, 81, 87, 115, 135, 136, 137, 138, 177, 208, 217, 228, 231, 235, 236

Carey, Greg, 136
Carson, D. A., 136
Cassidy, Richard J., 219
Castelli, Elizabeth A., 114
Chanikuzhy, Jacob, 84
Chapman, David W., 112
Charlesworth, James H., 153
Chen, Diane, 193
Chilton, Bruce, 86
Choi, Jin Young, 136
Cinnirella, Marco, 84, 88
Cirafesi, Wally V., 15, 43, 60, 61, 107, 138, 183, 184, 193, 194

Clarke, Jim, 64
Clarke, Susannah, 115, 134
Cohen, Shaye J. D., 109
Collingwood, R. G., 134
Collins, Raymond F., 112
Coloe, Mary L., 84, 221
Conde-Silvestre, J. Camilo, 61
Condor, Susan, 85
Conway, Colleen M., 190
Coppins, Wayne, 136, 137
Corsar, Elizabeth J. B., 4, 13, 157, 177, 178, 188, 214, 215, 216, 218, 228, 229, 232, 233, 267
Coser, Lewis A., 80, 87
Crisp, Richard J., 109
Crook, Zeba A., 235
Cross, F. L., 220
Crystal, David, 51, 62
Cullman, Oscar, 16, 40, 135
Culpepper, R. Alan, 6, 16, 17, 19, 40, 46, 60, 68, 86, 137, 152, 162, 171, 193, 219, 221, 235

D'Altroy, Terence N., 110
Dawson, Zachary, 61
deBoer, Martinus, 9, 15, 18, 19, 38, 41, 56, 63, 65, 134, 135, 152, 154, 171, 221, 235
Decker, Rodney J., 63
Dench, Emma, 109
den Hollander, William, 193
Despotis, Athanasios, 61
Do, Toan, 134
Dodd, C. H., 15, 39, 171, 221
Donahue, John R., 15, 135, 152
Donfried, Karl P., 220
Doole, J. Andrew, 64
Dooyeweerd, Herman, 48, 60
Dovidio, John F., 110
Dray, William H., 134
Dube, Musa W., 114, 136, 194
Duke, Paul D., 111, 113
Dunderberg, Ismo, 153
Dunn, James D. G., 73, 85, 110, 113

Index

Eco, Umberto, 91, 92
Edwards, Ruth, 153, 158, 169
Egbert, Jesse, 61
Ehrlich, Uri, 18
Elliott, Mark, 87
Ellis, Nicholas J., 48, 61
Ellis, Peter F., 16
Elowsky, Joel C., 113
Esler, Philip F., 18, 48, 52, 53, 58, 63, 84, 111, 235
Estes, Douglas, 39
Estrada, Rodolfo Galvan, 92, 107, 114
Evans, Craig A., 42

Flexsenhar III, Michael, 95, 108
Ford, David, 52, 60, 64
Forger, Deborah, 183, 192, 193
Fournier, Julien, 113
Frederick, John, 87
Frerichs, Ernest S., 109
Frey, Jörg, 24, 39, 87, 121, 122, 125, 131, 135, 136, 137, 155, 208
Fuhrmann, Christopher J., 193
Furlong, Dean, 59

Gadamer, Hans-Georg, 119, 123, 135, 136, 137
Gaertner, Samuel L., 111
Galambush, Julie, 221
Gathercole, Simon, 137
Gaventa, Beverly Roberts, 137
Genuyt, François, 112, 114
Glancy, Jennifer, 113
Goehring, James E., 61
Goodman, Martin, 110
Gorman, Michael J., 43
Gray, Bethany, 61
Green, Joel B., 193
Grenfell, Bernard P., 62
Griffith, Terry, 42, 43
Gupta, Nijay K., 134, 152
Gusfield, Joseph, 59

Hafemann, Scott, 87
Hagedorn, Anselm C., 235

Hägerland, Tobias, 18
Haines-Eitzen, Kim, 65
Hakola, Raimo, 83, 85, 86, 88, 120, 128, 129, 130, 136, 137, 142, 152, 153, 155, 162, 171, 205, 208, 221, 235
Hallbäck, Geert, 102, 112
Halliday, Michael A. K., 46, 48, 51, 52, 53, 60, 61, 63
Hammond, C. J. B., 170
Hanink, Johanna, 170
Haslam, S. Alexander, 84, 85
Hayes, Christine, 110
Heath, Jane, 56, 58, 65
Hedgcock, John S., 53, 64
Hedrick, Charles W., 61, 153
Heilig, Christoph, 108, 136
Hengel, Martin, 51, 63
Hernández-Campoy, Juan M., 61
Hicks-Keeton, Jill, 87, 134, 152, 235
Hill, Charles E., 57, 66
Hingley, Richard, 109, 110
Hinskens, Frans, 155, 156
Hoare, R. W. N., 15, 220
Hockey, Katherine M., 138
Hodgson Jr., R., 153
Hodkinson, Owen, 170
Hogg, Michael A., 84
Hollington, Andrea, 64
Holloway, Paul A., 108
Hopkins, Nick, 85
Horrell, David G., 107, 109, 138
Horsfall, N. M., 110
Horsley, Richard, 85
Hudson, Richard Anthony, 156
Hunt, Arthur S., 62
Hunt, Laura J., 4, 12, 13, 89, 178, 181, 206, 227, 231, 267
Hunt, Steven A., 113

Iverson, Kelly R., 17

Jackson, Claire Rachel, 159, 169, 170
Jobes, Karen H., 41, 42
Johnstone, Barbara, 155

Just, Felix, 171, 190

Kanagaraj, Jey J., 44
Katz, Steven T., 234
Keener, Craig S., 62, 74, 85
Keith, Chris, 77, 78, 86, 205, 221
Kennedy, George A., 170
Kerr, Alan, 84
Kierdorf, Wilhelm, 110
Kierspel, Lars, 75, 85
Kimelman, Reuven, 18, 86, 234
King, Karen L., 154
Klink III, Edward W., 10, 15, 18, 19, 45, 46, 59, 60, 79, 86, 136, 152
Kloppenborg, John S., 41, 42, 193
Knoppers, Gary N., 109
Kobel, Esther, 55, 65
Koester, Craig R., 113
Kok, Jacobus, 66, 155
Korner, Ralph J., 193
Kotrosits, Maia, 180, 181, 182, 185, 191, 192, 194
Kraft, Robert A., 137
Krans, Jan, 19, 38
Kratz, Reinhard G., 170
Krodel, Gerhard, 137
Kruse, Colin G., 43, 171
Kuecker, Aaron, 107, 109, 110
Kügler, Joachim, 153
Kuhl, Joseph W., 155
Kysar, Robert D., 15, 118, 135, 139, 140, 143, 151, 152, 155, 210, 211, 221, 235

Labahn, Michael, 155, 162, 171
Labov, William, 148, 155
Lake, Kirsopp, 154
Lamb, David A., 4, 11, 19, 24, 39, 42, 45, 60, 61, 62, 63, 64, 66, 92, 107, 155, 176, 177, 191, 203, 204, 217, 227, 235
Langer, Ruth, 18, 234
Le Donne, Anthony, 85
Lefkowitz, Natalie, 53, 64
Leroy, Herbert, 146, 155

Lieb, Hans-Heinrich, 155
Lieu, Judith M., 15, 38, 55, 63, 65, 135, 150, 151, 152, 154, 171
Liew, Tat-siong Benny, 114, 136
Lim, Sung Uk, 194
Lincoln, Andrew T., 17, 92, 107, 108, 113, 114, 162, 171
Lindars, Barnabas, 153, 162, 171, 219
Litwa, David, 153
Loader, William R. G., 188, 194
Logan, Alistair H. B., 154
Longenecker, Bruce W., 193
Louwerse, Max M., 62
Lozada Jr., Francisco, 136
Luckmann, Thomas, 69, 83

Malherbe, Abraham, 26, 40
Malina, Bruce, 51, 52, 53, 63, 64, 113, 155
Maloney, Linda M., 18, 221
Marcus, Joel, 134, 152, 235
Markschies, Christoph, 137
Marquis, Émeline, 170
Marshall, I. Howard, 43
Martínez, Javier, 160, 170
Marty, Jacques, 153
Martyn, J. Louis, 1, 3, 5, 6, 7, 8, 10, 14, 15, 16, 18, 23, 24, 38, 40, 46, 60, 67, 68, 79, 86, 90, 107, 116, 117, 118, 119, 120, 121, 122, 123, 124, 125, 129, 130, 133, 134, 135, 136, 137, 140, 157, 169, 176, 177, 183, 190, 197, 198, 199, 201, 206, 208, 210, 213, 218, 219, 221, 224, 225, 226, 227, 228, 229, 230, 231, 233, 234, 235
Mason, Hugh J., 108
Mason, Steve, 15, 84, 220
Mathison, Sandra, 106
Matthiessen, Christian M. I. M., 61
Maxwell, Kathy Reiko, 179, 191, 194
Maynard, Arthur H., 220
McHoul, Alec W., 84
McKnight, Scot, 134, 152

Meeks, Wayne A., 6, 8, 16, 55, 60, 67, 69, 83, 85, 112, 146, 155
Méndez, Hugo, 4, 13, 19, 41, 46, 65, 88, 122, 136, 139, 153, 154, 157, 162, 169, 171, 177, 178, 186, 191, 210, 211, 212, 213, 215, 218, 221, 228, 229, 232, 233, 235
Merkle, Benjamin L., 61
Meyer, Ben F., 86
Michie, Donald, 17
Milroy, James, 155
Mitchell, Margaret M., 18, 154
Mohrmann, Douglas C., 113
Moloney, Francis J., 17, 84
Moore, Alison Rotha, 61
Moore, Stephen D., 17, 111, 135, 222
Morgan, Teresa, 160, 170
Morrison, Kathleen D., 110
Motyer, Stephen, 18, 37, 43, 80, 81, 87
Mufwene, Salikoko S., 155
Myers, Alicia D., 4, 14, 19, 152, 175, 190, 191, 194, 195

Nassenstein, Nico, 64
Neusner, Jacob, 86
Neyrey, Jerome, 16, 235
Nice, Richard, 83
Nissen, Johannes, 112
Nongbri, Brent, 109
Novenson, Matthew, 87

Oden, Thomas C., 113
O'Donnell, Matthew Brook, 49, 62
O'Grady, Gerard, 61
Olsson, Birger, 16
Ong, Hughson T., 38, 61, 220
Onuki, Takashi, 137
Oropeza, B. J., 113
Oulton, J. E. L., 153
Overman, J. Andrew, 84

Paget, James Carleton, 87
Painter, John, 41, 43
Pancaro, Severino, 16, 101, 112
Pao, David W., 153, 171

Parsenios, George L., 152, 171, 188, 195
Pedersen, Sigfred, 112
Peerbolte, L. J. Lietaert, 19, 38
Peirano, Irene, 159, 170
Pierce, Madison N., 137
Pitts, Andrew, 63, 108, 152
Platow, Michael J., 85
Pollefeyt, Didier, 15, 18, 112
Portela, Orlando, 170
Porter, Christopher, 4, 12, 19, 24, 39, 67, 84, 87, 88, 109, 178, 185, 205, 206, 217, 227
Porter, Stanley E., 38, 42, 63, 108, 112, 152, 220
Powell, Mark Allan, 17
Poynton, Cate, 47, 60
Puskas, Charles B., 221

Radford, Gary P., 108
Raithal, Jutta, 65
Rapley, Mark, 70, 84
Reed, Annette Yoshiko, 221
Reeves, Rodney, 14
Reicher, Stephen D., 70, 80, 84, 85, 87
Reinhartz, Adele, 4, 14, 15, 17, 18, 19, 20, 24, 28, 38, 39, 43, 55, 65, 81, 82, 83, 86, 87, 88, 91, 106, 107, 108, 116, 120, 122, 128, 129, 130, 134, 135, 141, 152, 176, 177, 180, 190, 191, 208, 211, 222, 223, 235, 236
Reis, David M., 194
Rensberger, David, 16, 111
Reumann, John, 220
Revell, Louise, 109, 110
Reynolds, Benjamin E., 192
Rhoads, David, 17
Riches, John K., 15, 220
Richey, Lance Byron, 112, 114
Robbins, C. Michael, 221
Robertson, C. K., 113
Robinson, John A. T., 222
Robson, David, 53, 64
Rochette, Bruno, 97, 110

Rohrbaugh, Richard, 52, 63, 64, 113, 155
Roitto, Rikard, 41, 59, 66
Rollens, Sarah, 24, 25, 26, 27, 28, 40, 152
Rosenmeyer, Patricia, 158, 159, 169
Rosner, Brian S., 84, 87
Rousseau, Philip, 65
Rowland, Christopher, 192
Runesson, Anders, 193
Russell, A. Sue, 107
Russell, D. A., 170

Saguy, Tamar, 111
Sanders, E. P., 18, 83, 86
Sanders, Jack T., 61
Sani, Fabio, 70, 80, 84, 87
Schechter, Solomon, 5, 16
Schenke, Hans-Martin, 153
Schlegel, Juliane, 136, 226
Schmidt, Hansjörg, 42
Schnackenburg, Rudolf, 43, 56, 62, 65
Schnelle, Udo, 18, 193, 221
Schuchard, Bruce G., 191
Schwartz, Barry, 180, 191
Schwartz, Joshua J., 84
Seglenieks, Christopher, 1, 4, 11, 23, 38, 41, 42, 43, 48, 61, 83, 88, 177, 190, 201, 217, 228, 233
Segovia, Fernando F., 18, 39, 152
Sellew, Melissa (Phillip), 40, 154
Sheridan, Ruth, 39, 55, 63, 65
Sim, David C., 17, 39
Sinopoli, Carla M., 110
Skinner, Christopher W., 1, 3, 17, 19, 44, 152, 176, 197, 235
Smit, Peter-Ben, 19
Smith, Anthony D., 107
Smith, D. Moody, 204
Smith, Eliot R., 109
Smith, Justin Marc, 62
Smith, Mark S., 192
Smith, Tyler, 191
Smyth, Kevin, 62
Snyder, Graydon F., 220

Soldo, Janja, 159, 169, 170
Sommer, Benjamin D., 192
Sproston, Wendy E., 42
Staley, Jeffrey L., 114, 136, 194
Standhartinger, Angela, 95, 108
Stanton, Graham N., 18
Staples, Jason A., 87
Steinmetz, David, 137
Stewart, Eric, 235
Stibbe, Mark W. G., 111
Stock, Brian, 12, 19, 47, 54, 55, 56, 57, 58, 59, 60, 64, 65, 66, 203
Stowers, Stanley, 24, 25, 26, 27, 28, 38, 40, 141, 149, 152, 153, 156, 234
Strecker, Georg, 43
Streett, Daniel R., 42
Stroumsa, Guy G., 18
Sugirtharajah, R. S., 136
Syreeni, Kari, 17, 153

Tajfel, Henri, 69, 70, 84, 90, 106
Tan, Yak-Hwee, 136
Tenbrink, Thora, 62
Thatcher, Tom, 17, 20, 85, 86, 102, 112, 135, 171, 190, 191, 194, 220, 222
Thiessen, Matthew, 134, 152, 235
Thiselton, Anthony C., 109
Thompson, Marianne Meye, 108, 109, 110, 111, 114
Thompson, Michael B., 138
Tolkien, J. R. R., 115, 134
Tolmie, D. Francois, 113
Tomson, Peter J., 84
Trebilco, Paul, 38, 39, 41, 42, 43
Tucker, J. Brian, 41, 85, 89, 98, 99, 101, 107, 109, 111, 112, 227
Tuckett, Christopher, 153

Van Belle, Gilbert, 113
Vandecasteele-Vanneuville, Frederique, 15, 18, 112
van den Heever, Gerhard, 111
van der Watt, Jan, 43, 193, 194
van Nes, Jermo, 66
van Tilborg, Sjef, 112

Index

Vincent, Benet, 64
von Harnack, Adolf, 220
von Wahlde, Urban C., 16, 17, 68, 83, 137, 154

Walsh, Robyn Faith, 19, 40, 90, 107, 224, 226, 227, 228, 229, 233, 234, 235
Warren, David H., 153, 171
Watson, Duane F., 41
Watson, Francis, 77, 86, 135
Webber, Martin, 66
Wendland, Ernst, 51
Westfall, Cynthia Long, 112
White, Benjamin L., 170
Whitenton, Michael R., 191

Williams, Catrin H., 39, 180, 183, 191, 192, 193
Williams, Logan, 78, 86
Williams, Michael Allen, 154
Wilson, Brittany, 183, 192, 193
Wisse, Frederik, 90, 91
Woll, David, 16
Woolf, Greg, 109, 110
Wright, Arthur M., 113
Wright, N. T., 87

Zarate, Michael A., 109
Zhakevich, Mark, 136
Zimmermann, Ruben, 43, 113, 194
Zwiep, Arie W., 19, 38

About the Contributors

Paul Anderson serves as professor of Biblical and Quaker Studies at George Fox University in Newberg, Oregon and as Extraordinary Professor of Religion at the North-West University of Potchefstroom, South Africa. Author or editor of some thirty books and over 250 published essays, his Johannine books include *The Christology of the Fourth Gospel*, *The Fourth Gospel and the Quest for Jesus*, and *Riddles of the Fourth Gospel*. His contextual introduction to the New Testament is *From Crisis to Christ*. A founding member of the John, Jesus, and History Project, he has edited or co-edited six of its books and is editing four more, for a total of thirteen.

Andrew Byers teaches at Ridley Hall, Cambridge as lecturer in New Testament and serves as affiliated lecturer in the Faculty of Divinity at the University of Cambridge. He is the author of two monographs on the Johannine Literature: *Ecclesiology and Theosis in the Gospel of John* (CUP, 2017) and *John and the Others* (Baylor, 2021). He has also served as a co-editor for *Gospel Reading and Reception in Early Christian Literature* (CUP, 2022), *One God, One People: Oneness and Unity in Early Christianity* (SBL Press, 2023), and *Theology, Religion, and Stranger Things* (Lexington/Fortress, forthcoming 2025).

Elizabeth J B Corsar teaches at St. Padarn's Institute Cardiff. Her first book is *John's Reworking of Mark: A Study in Light of Compositional Practice* (WUNT II, forthcoming).

Laura J. Hunt is honorary fellow of the University of Wales, Trinity Saint David. Her doctoral thesis, *Jesus Caesar: A Roman Reading of the Johannine Trial Narrative*, was published in 2019 in the WUNT 2 series of Mohr Siebeck. Besides Bayes Theorem, she is interested in semiotics, cognitive metaphor theory, social identity theory, and multilingualism. She has published articles on breastfeeding metaphors in *JIBS* (2022), and on Samaritan

276 *About the Contributors*

Israelite, Jewish, and Roman identities in *Religions* (2023). Her social identity analysis of 1 Peter appeared in the *T&T Clark Commentary on Social Identity in the NT* in 2020.

David A. Lamb is honorary research fellow in Religions and Theology at the University of Manchester, England. He has also been a visting scholar in Linguistics at Bangor University, Wales. He was co-chair of the British New Testament Conference Johannine Literature Seminar Group for four years. He is author of *Text, Context and the Johannine Community: A Sociolinguistic Analysis of the Johannine Writings* (T & T Clark).

Hugo Méndez is assistant professor of Religious Studies at the University of North Carolina at Chapel Hill, where he teaches New Testament and Early Christianity. He is the author of *The Cult of Stephen in Jerusalem* (Oxford University Press, 2022) and co-author of *The New Testament*, eighth ed. (Oxford University Press, 2024).

Alicia D. Myers is associate professor of New Testament and Greek at Campbell University Divinity School (USA) and research fellow at the University of the Free State in Bloemfontein, South Africa. She writes primarily on the Gospel and Letters of John, including numerous articles and essays as well as a 2019 commentary *Reading John and 1, 2, 3 John* (Smyth & Helwys). She also authored an *Introduction to the Gospels and Acts* (Oxford, 2022) and explored ancient understandings of conception, childbirth, and nursing in *Blessed Among Women? Mothers and Motherhood in the New Testament* (Oxford, 2017).

Christopher A Porter is post-doctoral research fellow at Trinity College Theological School in Melbourne, Australia; part of the University of Divinity. He approaches the Fourth Gospel through the lens of socio-cognitive methodologies and discursive approaches. Building upon the Social Identity approach framework he has previously looked at the nature of identity formation and schism within the Johannine texts in *Johannine Social Identity Formation after the Fall of the Jerusalem Temple: Negotiating Identity in Crisis* in the Brill Biblical Interpretation Series.

Adele Reinhartz is distinguished university professor at the University of Ottawa, where she is also professor in the Department of Classics and Religious Studies. Her main research contributions have been in the study of ancient Jewish/Christian relations, as well as religion and film. Adele served as the general editor of the *Journal of Biblical Literature* from 2012–2019 and as the president of the Society of Biblical Literature in 2020. Adele was inducted into the Royal Society of Canada in 2005, and into the American Academy for Jewish Research in 2014. Her most recent books are *Cast Out of the Covenant: Jews and Anti-Judaism in the Gospel of John* (2018) and *The Bible and Cinema: An Introduction* (2nd edition, 2022).

Christopher Seglenieks works at the Bible College of South Australia, an affiliated college of the Australian College of Theology. His work has primarily focused on the Johannine literature and the theme of faith, but with a concern for the purpose and effect of texts with regard to their audience. In addition to several articles, he has written *Johannine Belief and Graeco-Roman Devotion* (Mohr Siebeck, 2020).

Christopher W. Skinner is professor of New Testament and Early Christianity and Graduate Program Director in the Theology Department at Loyola University Chicago. He has written or edited eleven books and published nearly three dozen articles, essays, and book chapters. His primary areas of interest are the Johannine Literature, the Synoptic Gospels, and the Gospel of Thomas. He is currently completing a book on the Christology of Mark's Gospel (Baker Academic) and beginning work on the Anchor Yale commentary on the Gospel of Thomas (Yale University Press).